MW00364409

THE DRIVE ON MOSCOW

Pg 174 Logistic shortcoming STOPS
German OB AGC oct 2
Pgs 262-263
Russian Reinf Schedule
DAY BY DAY pgs 280-283
75 OB Red Army west
Front 15 NOV

THE DRIVE ON MOSCOW 1941

OPERATION TAIFUN AND GERMANY'S FIRST CRISIS OF WORLD WAR II

BY **NIKLAS ZETTERLING &**
ANDERS FRANKSON

CASEMATE
Philadelphia & Oxford

Published in the United States of America and Great Britain in 2012 by
CASEMATE PUBLISHERS
908 Darby Road, Havertown, PA 19083
and
10 Hythe Bridge Street, Oxford, OX1 2EW

Copyright 2012 © Niklas Zetterling and Anders Frankson

ISBN 978-1-61200-120-3
Digital Edition: ISBN 978-1-61200-133-3

Cataloging-in-publication data is available from the Library of Congress and
the British Library.

10 9 8 7 6 5 4 3 2 1

Printed and bound in the United States of America.

For a complete list of Casemate titles please contact:

CASEMATE PUBLISHERS (US)
Telephone (610) 853-9131, Fax (610) 853-9146
E-mail: casemate@casematepublishing.com

CASEMATE PUBLISHERS (UK)
Telephone (01865) 241249, Fax (01865) 794449
E-mail: casemate-uk@casematepublishing.co.uk

All photos courtesy of Krigsarkivet, Stockholm (The Military Archives of Sweden)

CONTENTS

The German advance east during Operation *Taifun* went initially very good, but there were three factors that could slow them down: the weather, supply problems, and of course the Red Army. When the Germans began Operation *Taifun*, they knew they were in a race against the clock, but they did not know when their time would run out.

PREFACE

Many battles have been described as turning points in World War II, particularly El Alamein and Stalingrad. However, compared to many battles of the war, El Alamein was a small affair. The decisive effects of it are disputed, and in any case, it took place in an area of less than major strategic importance. Operations conducted in the Middle East in autumn 1942 may have been significant to British decision-makers, but involved only a very small share of the German armed forces and no US or Soviet formations.

Stalingrad is a better candidate, as far larger forces were engaged and from September 1942 to February 1943, the fighting in the city on the Volga attracted much attention from both Adolf Hitler and Josef Stalin. It can also be argued that prior to Stalingrad the Red Army seldom possessed the initiative, but afterward Soviet forces rarely allowed the Germans to dictate the course of events. Despite these compelling arguments, and the library of words written about this costly, well-known battle, the claims may have been exaggerated. We would argue that by the time fighting began at Stalingrad, the Germans had already lost the war. Admittedly, Hitler had launched a major summer campaign in eastern Ukraine in June 1942, but it was not large enough to knock the Soviet Union out of the conflict. Hence, the real turning point must be found earlier.

Launched in June 1941, Operation *Barbarossa* was a gamble. Hitler intended to subjugate the Soviet Union in six months. War planning, including long-term plans for the economy, was based on the assumption that the enemy in the east would be defeated. However, Hitler had seriously underestimated the Soviet capacity to wage war, and so German forces in the east were still battling against the Red Army in September 1941. The Germans felt they had to end the campaign before the winter came, preferably by a decisive victory at Moscow.

They made their final bid in late September/early October, when Operation *Taifun* (*Typhoon*) was launched. This was the long-awaited attack on Moscow, and the Germans initially recorded tremendeous success. However, after little more than a week, they were stuck in mud and the prize of Moscow slipped out of their grasp.

This was Hitler's first major defeat. Admittedly the Luftwaffe had failed to bring Britain to her knees in 1940, but Hitler was already devoting most of his energy to planning the attack on the Soviet Union while air battles raged over southern England. The invasion of the Soviet Union was his main project, and the failure at the gates of Moscow meant that his plans had been irrevocably thwarted.

The argument that Germany lacked the capacity to defeat the Soviet Union is plausible; however, Hitler and his entourage seem not to have held that opinion, and neither did many outside the Soviet Union. The German failure at Moscow made clear to many observers that Germany might not emerge victorious from the colossal struggle in the east.

The sheer scope of the battle of Moscow was exceptional. Both sides committed more than a million men to the battle; the Red Army also lost nearly a million men, but still the German forces were halted. This indicates the resources, and the importance, assigned to the battle by the two dictators. We hope the reader will enjoy our description and analysis of this important chapter in the history.

PROLOGUE

I n the evening of September 26, 1941 it dawned upon German army
surgeon Hermann Türk that the day had been remarkable. He had not
heard a single shot fired in anger, nor a single bursting shell or bomb.
While he had of course experienced many such days previously in his life,
they had been all too rare since June 22, when the 3rd Panzer Division had
crossed the border between Germany and the Soviet Union.[1]

As an army surgeon, Türk was not expected to participate in combat,
but he was assigned to one of the division's four motorized infantry battalions. This meant that he was seldom far from the action and quite often
found himself in the front line assisting with the evacuation of wounded
soldiers. During the past three months, the division had suffered 4,375
casualties, of which around three-quarters were wounded. The vast majority of these casualties had been incurred by the four infantry battalions
and Türk had had to patch up many soldiers so they could be evacuated
west to medical facilities.[2]

As the 3rd Panzer Division had been one of the spearheads in Panzer
Group 2, which was commanded by Colonel General Heinz Guderian,
Türk had travelled many kilometers on Soviet roads. After crossing the
border south of Brest-Litovsk, the division had dashed east. Bobruisk had
fallen to the 3rd Panzer Division on June 28, after an advance of more
than 400km. The fluid German operations continued and the 3rd Panzer
Division crossed the Dnepr after hard fighting. Later, Türk and his comrades participated in the large encirclement operation near Kiev. This time,
Türk's division was one of the spearheads of the northern pincer.

The Kiev battle resulted in the encirclement of a huge Soviet force in

September and eventually more than 600,000 Soviet soldiers marched into German captivity. However, with every passing day, the autumn drew nearer. The encirclement operation was hardly over when the 3rd Panzer Division began to regroup in a northeasterly direction. On September 25, Türk reached the area where the division would rest and refit. He was assigned suitable quarters in a village but he had to evacuate them after a few hours, as partisans were believed to be active there. Under cover of darkness, his unit moved to another village and spent most of September 26 on maintenance. To the great delight of many soldiers, a mailbag arrived from Germany and letters from parents, fiancées, and other relatives were sources of joy for the soldiers.

Hopes for a long period of rest contrasted with rumors of an imminent major offensive. Türk was well aware that the vehicles were already badly worn and many of the replacement soldiers were not as well-trained and experienced as those they replaced. The division badly needed a period of rest, maintenance, and training. So far, no order had yet indicated an offensive. Türk had only heard rumors.[3]

On September 26, Türk was finally informed: an offensive was indeed imminent. Few details were revealed, but he believed that the attack would be launched on October 1 and the objective would be Tula. He did not know how far away Tula was, but he hoped that the offensive would be over in two weeks. However, there were ominous signs. On the night of September 26–27, the thermometer showed -3°C. Nevertheless, preparations continued according to plan. Türk thought that as the Germans had been enormously successful thus far, another victory could be expected.[4]

Türk's unit remained stationed at the same location through September 28, enabling the chaplain to conduct a field service before regrouping on the following day. The vehicles had hardly begun to move when rain started to fall. After three months travelling on Russian roads, Türk knew full well how quickly rain could render them impassable, but the late season did not allow the Germans any further delays. They had to attack now or not at all.[5]

■ ■ ■

In late September 1941, the German units on the Eastern Front were mainly composed of veterans who had fought since the launch of Operation *Barbarossa* on June 22. In stark contrast, most of the Red Army soldiers in the western military districts were either dead or in German captivity. However, this did not mean that the Soviet commanders lacked soldiers; the vast reserves that were moved forward during the summer and autumn sufficed to replace the destroyed units.[6]

It was not just the rank and file that had suffered exceptionally high losses; many senior commanders had also been lost. The rapidly created new armies needed commanders, and the commanders needed competent staff and specialists to assist them. On August 21, a young NKVD officer, Major Shabulin, arrived in Moscow where he was soon assigned to the recently formed Fiftieth Army. He immediately set out to equip himself for the task, but he was delayed by the belated arrival of fuel and tyres for his car. By the evening of August 25 his car was finally ready and Shabulin set out for Tula.[7]

In some ways, the NKVD (*Narodnyy Komissariat Vnutrennikh Del*, People's Commissariat for Internal Affairs) can be regarded as Stalin's equivalent to Hitler's SS (Schutzstaffel, Protection Squadron), but the Soviet organization had a longer history under other names. The NKVD was commanded by Lavrenti Beria, who like Stalin originated from Georgia. The NKVD was the security service, but Beria's realm also included armed forces, for example the border troops. Furthermore, NKVD officers were posted with every Red Army unit. The organization also ran the Gulag, the Soviet forced labor camp system.

Shabulin slept in his car that night, the first of many spent sleeping in uncomfortable positions, even after he arrived at Vyshkovitshi, a village near Bryansk, where Fiftieth Army would be committed during the following weeks. His appointment did not require him to regularly take part in combat, but fighting was never distant.[8]

In September 1941, the Luftwaffe dominated the skies above the Soviet formations. Just a few days after arriving, on August 28, Shabulin witnessed Soviet antiaircraft defenses trying to shoot down German fighters, a taste of what was to come. Shabulin's position required him to travel frequently by car, visiting the combat units attached to Fiftieth Army. His trips occasionally brought him to Bryansk, where several blocks had been damaged or destroyed by German air attacks.[9]

On some occasions, Shabulin found time for leisure. When he visited the front on September 5, he availed himself of the opportunity to bathe in the river Desna. However, the tranquillity was disturbed by the sight of

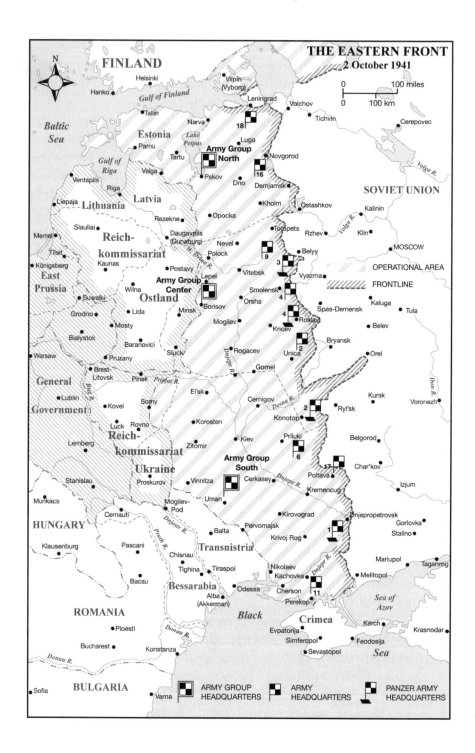

a German aircraft attacking a target in the distance. This was followed by a heavy Luftwaffe attack on the forward Soviet defenses that lasted for two hours. As far as Shabulin could see, all German aircraft departed undamaged after unloading their deadly cargo.[10]

The Fiftieth Army managed to hold most of its positions during September and Shabulin continued his frequent visits to combat units. He gradually formed an impression of the situation and the attitudes of the soldiers. On September 30, he wrote an extensive summary in his diary, from a briefing he had had with the Fiftieth Army commander, Major General Mikhail Petrov, at his command post the day before. Shabulin noted that the manpower situation was difficult, as most of the soldiers in the Fiftieth Army had been recruited from areas now occupied by the Germans. According to Shabulin, they wanted to go home rather than continue fighting. The inactivity at the front and the monotonous existence in the foxholes was taxing their morale. Sometimes soldiers did not return from reconnaissance missions. Also, there were many cases of drunkenness among the commanders.[11]

On his return from the meeting with the army commander, Shabulin noted as he passed a kolkhoz (collective farm) that large quantities of grain and hay remained on the fields. Most of it would be lost, as there was no-one left to harvest the produce, but the soldiers used the hay to feed their horses and searched for potatoes and firewood. Shabulin had already seen the grave shortages in the army and was not surprised that the soldiers searched for anything valuable in the fields and farms. Many of them were from farming families and knew where to search.[12]

■ ■ ■

On the last day of September, Shabulin described a gloomy atmosphere in his diary. Like Türk, he was better informed than the average "Ivan" or "Fritz." However, the Fiftieth Army was but one of 15 Soviet armies entrusted with the defense of the capital, and Shabulin had heard only rumors from the other armies.

Only the most senior commanders in the respective countries had a fairly comprehensive understanding of the situation. At the top were Stalin and Hitler, but despite their power, the scale of the campaigning on the Eastern Front, and the size of the armed forces involved prevented them from micromanagement of operations, even if they had wished to do so.

To some extent this came about as the war developed its own logic rather than proceeding according to the wishes of the dictators. The war had raged for three months and had caused the Red Army immense casualties. Debacles had been followed by disasters, and Stalin's hopes to launch a counteroffensive soon after the German assault had been utterly thwarted. The Wehrmacht had also suffered significant casualties, but on a far smaller scale than those experienced by Stalin's armed forces. Despite the enormous German victories, the expected Soviet collapse had not occurred; but Hitler could look back at the past three months with more satisfaction than Stalin.

One of the reasons that the war was unpredictable was that it was a struggle between two opposing wills, both trying to anticipate and negate the other's actions. The immense dimensions of the conflict also played their part, as it was impossible for one man to control everything, particularly during fast-moving fluid operations. Consequently, Hitler and Stalin had to depend—perhaps to a far greater extent than they would have preferred—on an elaborate chain of command.

There was a significant difference between the German and Soviet chains of command on the Eastern Front. Both dictators communicated directly with their staffs, Stalin with the Stavka (General Headquarters for the Armed Forces), and Hitler with the Oberkommando der Wehrmacht (OKW, Supreme Command of the Armed Forces). But while the Soviet army groups, which were called fronts, were directly subordinated to the Stavka, the German command structure included an additional level between the army group and the OKW. Between the German army groups and the OKW was placed the Oberkommando der Heeres (OKH), which was the supreme command of the army. The origin of this command structure was the transformation of the department of war into the armed forces supreme command (OKW) in 1938, when the secretary of war, Field Marshal Werner von Blomberg, was forced to resign. Hitler himself assumed the newly created position of commander in chief of the armed forces and Gen Wilhelm Keitel was appointed head of the OKW. With hindsight, it can be concluded that Keitel's influence remained less decisive than his lofty position might lead on to assume. During World War I, the OKH had been in charge of the military operations and still had jurisdiction on the Eastern Front in 1941–45.[13]

The two most prominent men in the OKH were Field Marshal

Walther Brauchitsch, commander in chief of the army, and Col. General
Franz Halder, chief of staff of the OKH. Hitler's relations with von Brauchitsch and Halder were strained, especially with von Brauchitsch who he
had himself appointed. Unable to stand up to Hitler in a discussion, von
Brauchitsch often remained silent when the German dictator was present.
When von Brauchitsch had to speak, he argued with a surly voice that Hitler disliked.[14]

Both von Brauchitsch and Halder advocated Moscow as the primary
objective when the planning for Operation *Barbarossa* began, and they did
not depart from that standpoint. However, it was not the geographical
object that mattered most to them. They rather argued that the defense
of Moscow would attract the bulk of the Soviet armed forces which they
considered the real target. By destroying the Red Army, the war would be
brought to a successful conclusion. Hitler on the other hand was more interested in economic assets and wanted to strangle the influx of resources
to the Soviet military and use them for his own purposes. These conflicting
views had already clashed during the planning for the invasion of the
Soviet Union during the summer of 1940, and they had not been recon-
ciled at the end of summer 1941.[15]

The very successful encirclement operation in the Kiev area, which
was concluded in September, opened the routes to the eastern parts of
Ukraine. Finally the OKH was given a free hand to begin the offensive on
Moscow that it had always advocated. It was given the code name *Taifun*
(*Typhoon*). Army Group Center, commanded by Field Marshal Fedor von
Bock, was given responsibility for the attack, and several of the panzer
units that had been diverted from the army group were now sent back
from the neighboring northern and southern groups. Von Bock also
received additional reinforcements from Germany.

Stalin and the Stavka, including the chief of staff Marshal Boris Shaposhnikov and his deputy, Aleksandr Vasilevsky, had always regarded
Moscow as the Germans' main objective. They therefore found the direction of the German advance completely incomprehensible at times. They
could not know about the rift between Hitler and the German army high
command. Of course there were differences of opinion among the Soviet
leaders too, but they were mainly between the Stavka and the front commanders and did not permeate the overall strategy.[16]

Shaposhnikov and Vasilevsky had both attended the military school

at Lefortovo near Moscow. A former colonel of the tsar's army, Shaposhnikov was 58 years old at the time of the battle of Moscow. Vasilevsky
was 13 years younger and had left the tsar's army with the rank of captain
in 1917. Stalin had considerable confidence in these two experienced officers, and they were two of his most trusted advisors.

These echelons of the command structure were responsible for the
overall decision-making. They formulated goals, directed reinforcements,
replacements, and new equipment, and decided upon priorities, for example concerning the allocation of ammunition, fuel and other items vital to
a fighting army. They also had detailed knowledge of what had transpired
during the previous months of operations.

The Soviet commanders were concerned, and for good reason. Their
aircraft had been attacked on their airfields when the Germans launched
their surprise attack on June 22. On the ground, Soviet divisions had been
shattered by German panzer formations dashing east. Most of the Soviet
frontier formations were destroyed, and the swift German spearheads
soon engaged the second Soviet echelon. Efforts to halt the Germans
along the Dnepr failed, and Smolensk fell to the invaders in mid-July. This
meant that the Germans had covered two-thirds of the distance from the
border to Moscow in under a month. It is hard to conceive a sequence of
events more ominous to Stalin and his commanders.

Surprisingly, the German advance on the central sector came to a halt
in the second half of July. The threat to Moscow would not grow any
greater over the next two months. Focus was shifted to the northern and
southern sectors of the main front. The German advance to Leningrad,
the second largest city in the Soviet Union, was also very rapid. In mid-
July, the Germans had established bridgeheads on the northeast bank of
the Luga River, approximately 130 kilometers (80 miles) from the great
city on the Neva River. Leningrad was almost within their grasp, but there
the German advance halted, as extended supply lines caused problems.
Nevertheless, in September they enveloped Leningrad, intending to starve
the city into submission. At this time, Stalin and the Soviet commanders
could not have known that this was the German plan for Leningrad.

In the south, the Germans pushed east in the Ukraine, where Col.
General Mikhail Kirponos' Southwest Front offered more effective resistance than the Soviet forces further north. Even so, Kirponos only managed to slow the German advance, and the price paid in blood was very

high, although no worse than it was in the central sector of the front. In mid-July, the Germans were not far from Kiev, but Kirponos' units had managed to avoid major encirclements. However in August, the first cauldron in Ukraine was created by the Germans near Uman, where more than 100,000 Soviet soldiers were captured. Compared to some of the encirclements on the central sector this was not impressive, but at the end of August, the German 2nd Panzer Group was directed south from Army Group Center. It entered Ukraine from the north and the ensuing operation in which it linked up with the 1st Panzer Group, driving up from the south, resulted in the largest encirclement thus far on the Eastern Front. More than 600,000 prisoners were taken and Kirponos was killed in the battle.

■ ■ ■

The disaster at Kiev resulted mainly from decisions made by the two dictators. Hitler had pressed his army commanders to halt Army Group Center and divert panzer formations to the flanks, while Stalin had insisted on holding Kiev until it was too late to withdraw, despite the grave situation. General Georgiy Zhukov, at that time acting as chief of general staff, wanted to evacuate Kiev. His efforts were in vain and he was reshuffled to command the Reserve Front. Shaposhnikov was reinstated as chief of staff. Stalin's decision doomed the defenders at Kiev. Although the German advance rate was considerably slower than in previous major encirclement operations, they had managed to bag a huge Soviet force, but probably only because the Soviet forces had not been ordered to retreat in time.[17]

The Kiev operation was concluded in the latter part of September. But even before that, the Germans had to decide what their next objective would be. At the end of September, the front ran from the southern tip of Lake Ladoga almost straight south to the Black Sea, just east of the Perekop isthmus, where the Crimea joined the mainland. There were several alternatives, but one thing was clear: the Germans would make the next move.

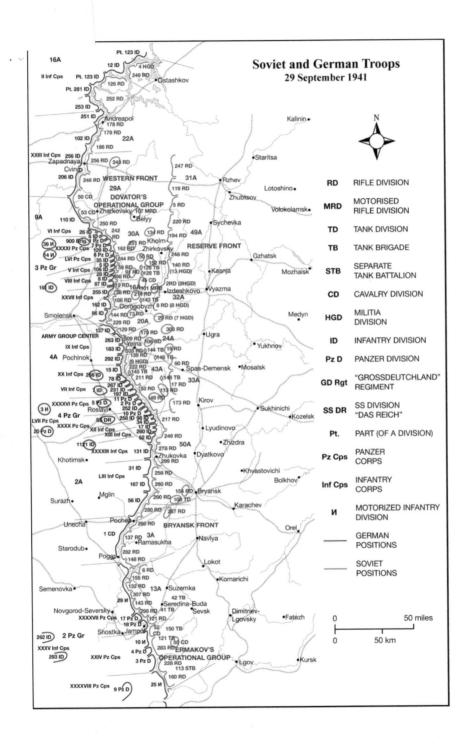

Soviet and German Troops
29 September 1941

N

RD	RIFLE DIVISION
MRD	MOTORISED RIFLE DIVISION
TD	TANK DIVISION
TB	TANK BRIGADE
STB	SEPARATE TANK BATTALION
CD	CAVALRY DIVISION
HGD	MILITIA DIVISION
ID	INFANTRY DIVISION
Pz D	PANZER DIVISION
GD Rgt	"GROSSDEUTCHLAND" REGIMENT
SS DR	SS DIVISION "DAS REICH"
Pt.	PART (OF A DIVISION)
Pz Cps	PANZER CORPS
Inf Cps	INFANTRY CORPS
И	MOTORIZED INFANTRY DIVISION
——	GERMAN POSITIONS
——	SOVIET POSITIONS

0   50 miles

0   50 km

ONE

THE SOVIET DEFENSE OF MOSCOW

T he disaster at Kiev clearly showed that the Germans held the initiative. Soviet commanders now had to focus on defense. The huge losses at Kiev left them with few means to halt the Germans in the Ukraine, at least in the immediate future. In the Leningrad area, the Germans had apparently halted. The situation was less serious than it had been, but remained precarious.

Strong Soviet forces were positioned west of Moscow. In all, they amounted to about 1.25 million men, approximately 1,050 tanks and over 10,000 guns and mortars, positioned between Ostashkov in the north and Vorosba in the south. Three front commands had to share these resources and 15 armies were subordinated to the fronts.[1]

The three front commands responsible for the defense of Moscow were, from south to north, Bryansk Front, Reserve Front and West Front. The Bryansk Front was commanded by 48-year-old General Andrei Eremenko. He had been serving in the Far East when the Germans attacked. Soon he was ordered to Europe and the central sector, where the Germans advanced astonishingly fast at the end of June. Eremenko served as commander of West Front during three brief periods, in place of Marshal Semen Timoshenko. In August, Eremenko was summoned to a meeting with Stalin and on August 16 he was appointed commander of the recently created Bryansk Front. At the end of September, Eremenko had three armies plus an "operational group" directly subordinated to him. His divisions were evenly distributed along his front sector, except for three divisions held in reserve near Bryansk. His plans called for the reserve to counterattack in either a northwesterly or southwesterly direction as necessary. It is clear that a German attack in the general direction of Bryansk was expected and the reserve had been positioned accordingly.[2]

Eremenko had one more reserve, located farther south. The 42nd Tank Brigade was located south of Suzemka, ready to attack toward Yampol and Gluchov. Eremenko's three other tank brigades were also located in the vicinity. Despite the tank brigades, this sector was one of Eremenko's weakest. He would be hard-put to halt a determined German attack from the southwest. Except for the reserve at Bryansk, his defenses had little depth. The distance from the front to the reserve was more than 150 kilometers (93 miles), which meant that bringing the reserves into action against a German attack would take time.[3]

Of the three fronts defending the approaches to Moscow, Eremenko's was the weakest. He had little more than 1,700 guns and mortars and only 259 tanks. His front sector was rather wide, so slightly fewer than 250,000 men were spread along a front of 300 kilometers (186 miles). On the other hand, the distance from the front to the capital was much greater than at the other two fronts.[4]

■ ■ ■

The Reserve Front was positioned north of Eremenko's Bryansk Front and its armies were disposed in a peculiar way. It was commanded by Marshal Semen Budjonny (anglicized spelling: Budenny), who had allotted the front sector between Kirov and Yelnya to his two strongest armies. Most of his other formations were placed in a belt behind the West Front. The latter defended the front from Yelnya to the Ostashkov area, where two divisions from the Reserve Front were responsible for the defense of the front line. The sector further north was defended by the forces of the Northwest Front. Combined, the two armies Budjonny had placed between Kirov and Yelnya comprised approximately 200,000 men. Also, he had positioned an additional army behind them as reserve, bringing the strength on this sector to 260,000 men. Budjonny thus had more personnel defending his front than Eremenko had along his much long front.[5]

At the age of 58, Budjonny was one of the true veterans of the Red Army. He had known Stalin since the Civil War, when they had served in the same formation. This was probably one of the main reasons why Budjonny was one of only two marshals to survive the purges of 1937–38. He subsequently received command of an army during the Winter War with Finland, 1939–40, but did not achieve any success. Nevertheless, he was given overall command of the operations in Ukraine in July 1941, a position which meant that he had to coordinate the efforts of Southwest Front and South Front. Again Budjonny failed to shine and Stalin decided to replace him with Timoshenko in September. The aged marshal was not left without any share, as he received command of the Reserve Front when Zhukov departed to organize the defense of Leningrad, which was in more imminent danger. [6]

■ ■ ■

The third and final front on the central sector was the West Front, commanded by Col. General Ivan Konev. He was originally a political officer, but he commanded the Nineteenth Army on June 22, 1941. It became embroiled in heavy fighting in the Vitebsk–Smolensk area. On September 12, he replaced Marshal Timoshenko as commander of the West Front and thus had to shoulder most of the responsibility for defending the capital. For this task, Konev had six armies.[7]

Konev's armies were deployed from Yelnya northwards. He had placed all armies in the front and none in reserve, as large parts of the Reserve Front were deployed behind him. He decided to position his strongest formations on both sides of the main road from Smolensk to Moscow. Three armies were detailed to this sector, which was less than one-third of the front line he was responsible for.[8]

The defense plan created by Konev and his staff, dated September 20, 1941, discussed six possible main directions from which the Germans might attack. According to a report from September 28, two of them were identified as particularly important. One of them was along the main road, where Konev had already placed a significant part of his resources. The second possible German attack direction was towards Rzhev, further north. Countermeasures were discussed in the report, but it was concluded that the reserves were already positioned to deal with the two threats that were regarded as most serious. One of the reserves was located just north of Dorogobush, near the highway, while the second was deployed in the Belyy area. The first consisted of four divisions and four brigades and the second comprised four divisions, two of them cavalry. These reserve groupings included the majority of Konev's 486 tanks.[9]

The armies subordinated to the front also created defense plans and sent them to the staff of the higher command echelon for approval. Lt. General Konstantin Rokossovsky, who led the Sixteenth Army, stated in his memoirs that his staff worked on a detailed defense plan during the second half of September. It included plans for a scenario in which the enemy broke through, which described how a withdrawal and delaying actions would be conducted. Rokossovsky argued that the enemy's superior mobility and possession of the initiative would make such an operation complicated. The front commander, Konev, deleted this part of the Sixteenth Army's defense plan.[10]

There were a number of weaknesses in the defenses along the three fronts. No notable forces were located at the important junctions of Orel, Rzhev and Vyazma. The division of responsibility between the West Front and the Reserve Front was a potential problem as it could result in delays when reserves had to be committed. The coordination of airpower was another weak point. The Soviet armed forces had not yet introduced the practise of coordinating ground and air forces when allocating an air army to a front, as would be common later during the war. For example, all air units in the Reserve Front were subordinated to the two frontline armies, while Eremenko had placed most of his air assets under the Thirteenth Army. The West Front had chosen to use its air units as a central resource. In addition to the airpower attached to the three fronts, there were considerable air formations that belonged to the strategic air force and the air defense of Moscow. No less than about 60% of all the Soviet aircraft that could fight in the area west of Moscow belonged to these latter two categories. There was no unified command and control system for the airpower.[11]

The Soviet supply service had received its new command organization at front and army level in August 1941. It had not yet been honed into a smoothly working structure. Many commanders and other officers had recently received their appointments, like Nicolai Antipenko, who served as chief of the supply service at the Forty-Ninth Army staff.

Prior to the change in August, supply was either managed by the operations section of the staff, or someone was temporarily appointed to ensure that supply arrived at the combat units. Little thought had been devoted to the problem before the war broke out, as the supply services seemed to work fine during exercises. The strains of war proved much more severe, however, and the coordination was often insufficient.

Soon after the German invasion, Antipenko was recalled to Moscow from Lwow and the battles in the south. He was assigned the task of ensuring that the recently formed Thirtieth Army was properly supplied. He received a map showing the location of the army staff before leaving Moscow in mid-July. When he arrived in the Belyy area he could not find the staff in the location marked on the map. He continued along the road and met a group of soldiers running towards him. He halted his car and asked the men if they knew where he could find the staff. One of them answered, panting: "I don't know where the staff is, but on the other side of the small hill there are fascists." Antipenko did not hesitate. He promptly turned his car around.

■ ■ ■

Before the creation of the position of chief of the supply service, the war council of the Thirtieth Army suggested that Antipenko assume responsibility for the supply service of the army, as he already worked extensively with such issues. Antipenko set out to the front headquarters to report, but upon arrival he met Major General Vasiley Vinogradov, who was already on his way to the Thirtieth Army to become chief of the supply service. Antipenko was ordered to go back to Moscow. There he found an order telling him to go to Tbilisi in the Caucasus and become chief of staff of the border troops. As he did not want to leave the front, Antipenko managed to get the post of head of supply service at the Forty-Ninth Army. This army belonged to the Reserve Front and was positioned right behind the Thirtieth Army, which belonged to the West Front.[12]

Planning a defensive operation can often be more challenging than planning an offensive operation. The attacker usually dictates the course of events and enjoys certain important advantages (advantages that probably contributed to the decision to attack in the first place). The defender has the difficult task of anticipating the enemy's moves, and he often has to cope with other disadvantages. At the end of September, the Soviet defenders did not suffer from numerical inferiority, but there were other weaknesses to consider, the most fundamental of which was the lower combat power of the Soviet units, which resulted from inferior tactics, training and junior leadership.[13]

At the time, the condition of Soviet combat units varied considerably. Some units were fresh, but had received little training. Other formations were seriously depleted after costly battles. It is worthwhile examining the particular difficulties faced by a few units to see the variety and scale of the problems facing the Red Army.

The rifle divisions formed the backbone of the Soviet army. A very large portion of Soviet manpower was allotted to the rifle divisions; there were a great number of them, and at the beginning of the war their combined personnel strength was considerable. The 242nd Rifle Division was one of 82 divisions detailed for the defense of Moscow. It was located on the West Front sector, attached to the Thirtieth Army. The 242nd Rifle Division had begun to form in the Kalinin area on June 27, less than a week after the initial German onslaught. Just two weeks later, the 242nd Division became attached to the Thirtieth Army as a reserve division, which demonstrates the gravity of the situation. One of the measures used to replace the Red Army's catastrophic casualties was to use personnel from the NKVD's border troops to form rifle divisions. Approximately 1,500 officers and men from the NKVD were placed in fifteen rifle divisions created soon after the German attack.[14]

Captain David Dragunsky was appointed chief of staff of the 242nd Rifle Division just before the Germans launched their attack on Moscow. When war broke out, he was a tank officer attending a course at the Frunze Academy in Moscow, but on June 22 itself, he happened to be near Bialystok in Byelorussia on a field exercise. Dragunsky and his comrades were ordered to return to Moscow as soon as possible. They left Bialystok burning behind them and travelled through Minsk and Smolensk to Moscow.[15]

Many of the course attendees, including Dragunsky, were eager to be sent to the front, but they had to wait. Instead they could study a map at the large entrance hall of the Frunze Academy, where the front line was indicated. Red flags represented Soviet units and blue marked hostile forces. The daily changes indicated alarming enemy progress and Dragunsky had to force himself to concentrate on the course, instead of being distracted by the ominous developments at the front.[16]

Dragunsky could not avoid noting that the training he was undergoing emphasized offensive action. This was in line with the Red Army field manual, but he began to observe an increasing focus on defense.[17]

Finally Dragunsky's name was on the list of officers being dispatched to the front. He and the three other tank officers listed were instructed to go to Rzhev, where a new tank division, the 110th, was forming. The departure proved more complicated than expected, as the bureaucracy did not loosen its grip despite the war. Dragunsky and the other officers first had to get twenty signatures before they could report to the commander of the academy and start preparing for their voyage.[18]

When the four officers arrived at the Rzhev area, they looked for a place to rest in a pine forest, where the 110th Tank Division staff was located. They were received by Colonel Chernov, the division commander, who informed them that the division was organizing an independent tank battalion to be sent to the front. Dragunsky's comrade, Major Grigoriev, who had been preliminarily appointed to command a regiment, was asked to suggest a commander for the battalion that was being created. Grigoriev recommended Lieutenant Dragunsky, as he already had some combat experience. He had fought with light T-26 tanks in the Far East.

The battalion Dragunsky was to command had a plethora of tank models, including old T-26s and BT-5s, but also brand new KVs and T-34s. It was ordered to march to Belyy and from there proceed to the 242nd Rifle Division. Upon arrival, the battalion was enthusiastically welcomed by Major General Kovalenko of the 242nd Rifle Division, who was extremely happy to receive tanks as reinforcement. To his great joy, Dragunsky was pleased to find that he knew the chief of staff of the division, Lt. Coonell Viktor Glebov, whom he had met at the Frunze Academy.

There was no time to rest for Dragunsky. His battalion was to immediately attack, together with a rifle battalion. Inadequate radio communications forced Dragunsky to rely on liaison officers bringing him attack orders. Time dragged as he and his battalion waited in their positions, ready to launch the attack. Artillery fire and bursting bombs could be heard on both sides of their attack sector as they waited for the liaison officer to show up. Finally a dented armored car arrived and the liaison officer handed over the attack order. During Napoleon's invasion of Russia in 1812, the officer would have been riding a horse, but little else had changed, which says something about the shortcomings of Soviet military communications at this early stage of the war. After receiving the order to attack, Dragunsky's battalion set out for its baptism of fire, but the results were disappointing. Ten tanks were knocked out and more than 20 soldiers were killed or wounded.[19]

Dragunsky's tank battalion remained attached to the 242nd Rifle Division as it participated in battles in the Smolensk area during August. Eventually all the battalion's tanks were lost. Surviving crews fought as infantry after their tanks had been knocked out, until early September when the remnants of the battalion were ordered to the Urals. The 242nd Rifle Division also suffered heavy losses, including the commander Kovalenko, who was badly wounded. The chief of staff, Lieutenant Colonel Glebov, replaced him.[20]

When the tank battalion was about to depart, Dragunsky was informed that he had been promoted to captain and appointed to chief of staff of the 242nd Rifle Division. He was as surprised as he was disappointed and his men were of the same opinion. Dragunsky described the moment:

> Glebov approached me and said with a low voice: "I can't change the order of a senior commander. And besides, you don't have to pride yourself on being a tanker. To me, rifle soldier, aviator, and gunner sound equally glorious, provided they bravely defeat the enemy."[21]

Dragunsky had to accept his new task and the division began to prepare to defend Moscow. Glebov did not miss an opportunity to humorously point out that Dragunsky was a born infantryman. Dragunsky replied that he would sooner or later return to an armored unit.

The new appointment meant that Dragunsky had to learn about the rifle division from the bottom up. The term rifle division originated from the days of the tsar, when the best infantry except the guards was called "rifle." In October 1918, it was decided that all Red Army infantry divisions would be called rifle divisions. At the beginning of the war, the Table of Organization & Equipment (TO&E) detailed that a rifle division at full strength would number 14,500 officers and men, 78 artillery pieces, 66 mortars (not counting light mortars), 12 antiaircraft guns (AA), and 54 antitank guns (AT). However the 242nd Rifle Division was organized according to a new TO&E issued on July 29. The new lists prescribed 10,800 men, 36 artillery pieces, 24 mortars (not counting light mortars), 10 AA guns, and 18 AT guns.[22] The 242nd Rifle Division actually possessed a complete antitank battalion, making it slightly stronger than the prescribed organization.[23]

The German prewar infantry division had, at full strength, approximately 17,000 officers and men, 74 artillery pieces, 54 mortars (not counting light mortars), 75 AT guns and no AA guns.[24] A German infantry regiment numbered slightly more than 3,000 men. Thus the three infantry regiments possessed 53% of the division's personnel. This share was significantly lower than in a Soviet rifle division, where the rifle regiments accounted for almost 75% of the manpower of the division.[25]

Generally, the Soviet rifle divisions had lighter artillery pieces than their German counterparts. The artillery consisted of 76.2mm regimental howitzers, 76.2mm guns and 122mm howitzers, while the German infantry divisions had 7.5cm and 15cm infantry howitzers and 10.5cm and 15cm howitzers. One reason for the Soviet choice of lighter calibers was the poor roads in the Soviet Union. Lighter weapons meant lower axle pressure, lighter towing vehicles or fewer horses. A Soviet 122mm howitzer weighed 2.5 tons, significantly less than a German 15cm howitzer, which weighed in at 5.4 tons. The two weapons had similar range, but the Soviet fired lighter shells.[26]

Dragunsky's division had to defend a front sector spanning more than 20 kilometers (12 miles). This was considerably more than most divisions of the Sixteenth Army, which had sectors ranging from four to 13 kilometers to defend. Dragunsky pointed out that the division was unable to create a second echelon. All its resources had to be deployed in the forward defenses. Being an armored officer, Dragunsky emphasized the lack of tanks on several occasions.[27]

The lull east of Smolensk in September gave the division breathing space. The soldiers used the opportunity to dig deeper into the ground. Day and night, they improved their defenses. It remained unclear whether they would be tested before the onset of the winter.[28]

SOVIET STRENGTH DURING OPERATION TAIFUN, OCTOBER 1, 1941[29]				
	NUMBER OF SOLDIERS (APPROX.)	GUNS AND MORTARS	TANKS	RIFLE DIVISIONS
BRYANSK FRONT	240,000	1,743	259	24
RESERV FRONT	470,000	4,752	301	28
WEST FRONT	540,000	4,029	486	30
TOTAL	1,250,000	10,524	1,046	82

Differences between the two opponents were not confined to the organization of the units. There were several other interesting differences between the Red Army and the German forces, including the ages of the senior commanders. When the forces assembled in September 1941, Stalin was 62 years old, while Hitler was a decade younger. However, while the Soviet dictator was notably older than the German, the opposite could be said of their senior officers. Marshal Semen Budjonny, the hero from the Civil War, was in his 59th year and was the elder of the Red Army. He was however something of an exception. The average age of the Soviet army and front commanders was 44. At 52, Major General Vasily Dolmatov, commander of the Thirty-First Army, was the next oldest after Budjonny. Brigade Commissar Dmitry Onuprienko, of the Thirty-Third Army, was

The road network in the Soviet Union was less dense than in Western Europe. Thus, fewer alternative roads existed and the distances were larger. According to a German staff officer, Moscow would have lost its best protection against a modern conqueror had the roads in the country been better. The condition of the roads was quite frequently discussed, and was a problem that would grow into monumental proportions.

the youngest at just 34. Colonel Generals Konev and Eremenko were 43 and 48 respectively.[30] In fact, all the Soviet front commanders during the war were younger than Stalin. His comrades from the Civil War, marshals Voroshilov and Budjonny, were closest to him in age. Then came Col. General Maks Reiter, who was eight years younger than Stalin. All the other commanders were at least 10 years younger than the dictator. It might seem plausible to blame the 1937–38 purges, but in fact we have to look elsewhere for the reason behind this gap. The prominent officers who lost their lives in the purges were at least ten years younger than Stalin. Rather, the reason for the comparative youth of the senior Soviet commanders can be attributed to the fact that the Red Army was a recent creation.

The army had effectively been dissolved at the end of the last tsar's reign, and the Bolsheviks had had to create a completely new army, although many former tsarist officers would be included in its ranks. Consequently, most of the Red Army's officers were young for the rank they had achieved.

These commanders had also passed through the career system quite rapidly in order to reach the senior levels of command at such a young age. Of the 15 army commanders on the approaches to Moscow in late September, only three had commanded an army on June 22, 1941. Six of them had been appointed to an army command in August and most of them had commanded divisions or corps when the Germans attacked. Five of them had been transferred from the NKVD to become army commanders during the summer.[31] The disasters at the beginning of the war had caused Stalin to turn to the NKVD and transferred personnel in order to promote stability and steadfastness, but the results were inconsistent.

The future Marshal Zhukov met one of these NKVD generals, Major General Konstantin Rakutin, in August when he assumed command of the Reserve Front, which included Rakutin's Twenty-Fourth Army. Zhukov wrote:

> I had never before met Rakutin. His situation report impressed me favorably, but it was apparent that his training in tactics and operations was inadequate. He of course suffered from the same disadvantages common to officers and generals from the NKVD border troops; they had not had any chance to develop their knowledge of operational art.[32]

Zhukov's observation can of course be regarded as an isolated anecdote, but his statement is hardly surprising. After all, a man like Rakutin did not possess the experience of a regular army officer and had not received as much relevant training. Training and experience would prove highly necessary when the defenders of Moscow faced probably one of the best trained and most experienced armies ever.

The oldest of the German generals on the front west of Moscow in 1941 was Hermann Metz, aged 63, and the youngest was Walther Model, 50. The commander of Army Group Center, Field Marshal Fedor von Bock, was 60 years old. One of his army commanders, Col. General Adolf Strauss who led the Ninth Army, was actually two years older. Their age meant that all German senior commanders had commanded formations during World War I as junior officers. The average age of the German army commanders on the Eastern Front was 58, while the age of the 22 corps commanders averaged 55. Thus, most of them were older than Hitler, who was 52. In contrast to Stalin, who was senior, older and more experienced than his offiers, Hitler was younger than almost all his senior commanders.[33]

Model, the youngest of the German generals on the Moscow sector, had been a lieutenant at the beginning of World War I. The German officers knew from personal experience the chaos of war and its effect on orders and effective command. The German mission-oriented tactics provided a way to cope with chaos, confusion and ambiguity. German officers knew the value of grasping the initiative and they also had experience from their two recent and very successful campaigns: Poland 1939, and in the west in 1940. Some of them had also participated in the Balkans campaign during the spring of 1941. They were very confident, and trusted in their soldiers.[34]

The Red Army, which had displayed serious shortcomings in the Winter War against Finland (November 30, 1939–March 13, 1940), was widely regarded as a clay colossus, but few realized the enormity of the resources possessed by Stalin. Finland had been saved by Red Army overconfidence and the Soviet commanders' gross underestimate of the Finnish resolve and skills.

Late in the summer, the German generals began to realize that the campaign in the east was not proceeding as expected. The war was not only raging at the front, but also in rear areas, where partisan activity was ceaseless. Furthermore, the Red Army was not broken, despite suffering immense casualties and losses of equipment. New Soviet units were constantly arriving at the front. The 1940 campaign in the west had lasted only six weeks and had led to the defeat of what many observers considered to be the strongest army in Europe. By now, the German forces had fought constantly for three months, with all the attendant losses and wear and tear. There was no time for rest and recuperation when battles were fought day after day, week after week, and month after month.

The Red Army units on the gates to Moscow were given some breathing space when Army Group Center dispatched forces north and south to assist operations in the Leningrad area and Ukraine, but at the end of September these operations were concluded. Henceforth, the Germans would focus on Moscow.

MAPS ARE WEAPONS

Both sides had to work hard to secure reliable maps in sufficient numbers during the campaigns on the Eastern Front. Sometimes the maps lacked detail and in other cases they simply did not correspond to reality. Since much planning was based on information from maps, the implications were serious. The importance of detailed and accurate maps can hardly be exaggerated.

Most of the problems encountered by the Red Army stemmed from the deep German advance. On June 22, the general staff had issued maps for the area west of the line Petrozavodsk–Vitebsk–Kiev–Odessa, as the enemy was not expected to advance further than that. However, this line was breached by the Germans on July 10. In great haste, new maps had to be produced in large numbers, as the Red Army had few or no suitable maps covering the area where operations were now taking place. According to Sergei Shtemenko at the Soviet General Staff, maps covering more than one and a half million square kilometers, in many different scales, had to be produced in the second half of 1941.[35]

The Germans experienced more serious problems, as they lacked up-to-date information. Many of their maps were based on information dating back to World War I or even earlier. General Gotthars Heinrici wrote in his diary on October 18:

> It was particularly troublesome to find that our maps were not good enough. The so-called old Russian maps were wholly outdated and virtually useless. Areas showed as forests could turn out to be open fields. Roads were found in other places than indicated on the maps and half the villages could not be found on the maps. Sometimes captured maps are available and they are much more accurate than the German 1:100000, clear, precise and modern. However, at the moment we have none and are sitting here half blind.[36]

The work in the map sections was difficult. For examle, the map section in Panzer Group 3 asked OKH in vain for printing equipment for maps. After prompting them many times, some equipment actually arrived on June 7, two weeks before Operation *Barbarossa* was to be launched. However, the panzer group still had to find vehicles for the equipment. Altogether, 532,000 map sheets were issued to Panzer Group 3 before June 22. Thereafter, Panzer Group 3 established map depots in Vilnius, Vitebsk, Smolensk and finally Demidov, in order to avoid having to drive all way to Königsberg and Insterburg, where the central depots were located. All in all, Panzer Group 3 had 690 pallets of maps, with a combined weight of more than 30 tons. Soon the Germans realized that the Soviet 1:100,000 maps were better and initiated a major effort to copy them. The troops soon learnt how to read Soviet maps in cyrillic script.[37]

Ocassionally, one finds comments from Soviet veterans that the Germans had better maps, but this probably refers to the printing quality rather than the accuracy of the information. No fewer than 107 million map sheets were distributed from central Soviet map depots to fronts and armies. Both paper quality and printing were often poor and the maps quickly wore out. Occasionally the haste was so great that maps were printed using only one color.[38]

As the German tank guns—and the antitank guns— were marginally effective against the Soviet medium tank T-34 at best, the Germans had to rely on Luftwaffes 8.8cm anti-aircraft guns to knock them out. These guns fired shells at such high muzzle-velocity that they could destroy the T-34 even at long range.

■ *TWO*

OPERATION TAIFUN—*THE GERMAN PLANS*

O n September 6, Hitler issued directive No. 35. Operations at Leningrad and in the Ukraine were in full swing when the directive was
being drafted, but the German senior commanders felt confident
that current operations were proceeding satisfactorily and so focused on
the next stage after their conclusion. For this reason, Hitler's directive did
not bother with current operations, only with the future. As soon as the
encirclement and destruction of Soviet forces in the Ukraine had been completed, the Soviet armies west of Moscow would be thoroughly defeated.[1]

Hitler's directive contained no major surprises. Army Group North
would, in cooperation with the Finns, establish a solid ring around
Leningrad and not later than September 15 would send air units and mechanized army formations south. They would reinforce Army Group Center,
which would attack and defeat the Soviet fronts west of Moscow. Hitler
estimated that the attack could be launched at the end of September.[2]

According to the directive, the Soviet combat units were the main targets during the initial phase of the operation. Once the Soviet armies had
been destroyed, the advance towards the Soviet capital would begin. The
sequence was in many ways reasonable, but there were problems to consider. As the autumn rains could be expected soon, there was little time
available for both phases. The decision when to initiate the second phase—
the advance on Moscow—could thus be critical. To anticipate the proper
moment would require careful consideration. On the other hand, the
Germans had few other options. As they lacked numerical superiority, they
could hardly advance on Moscow before the Soviet armies in front of it
had been destroyed.

The German army officers were relieved when they learned that the offensive towards Moscow would be resumed. To them, this was the key direction, as they believed the Red Army would dispatch most of its forces to defend the capital. An advance towards Moscow would offer the Germans the chance to defeat the bulk of the Soviet forces, thus paving the way for the occupation of the vast country.

■ ■ ■

Hitler's directive meant that the direction of attack long preferred by the army officers would finally receive priority. However, before the offensive could be launched, preparations had to be made. Reinforcements would be transferred from other armies to Army Group Center and the supply of fuel, ammunition and provisions had to arranged. On September 11, the chief of army general staff, Col. General Franz Halder, met the quartermaster general, Eduard Wagner, who provided a description of the supply situation on the Eastern Front.[3]

The railroads were the pillars on which the German supply system rested. The distance from Germany to the front deep in the Soviet Union was so great that no other means of transport was suitable (at least until the last few miles to the combat units). Army Group Center had hardly advanced east at all since mid-July. This had permitted the repair and conversion work on the railroads to catch up. During the first nine days of September an average of 29 trains arrived daily at Army Group Center, which sufficed to supply the units and stockpile supplies for the planned offensive. However, the number of trains was not enough to provide any surplus capacity. It was sufficient, but only barely.[4]

The German build-up was not without its share of problems. Several motorized units would travel long distances, which meant that they consumed considerable quantities of gasoline and diesel. Consumption would increase further when the offensive began. Fuel supply was problematic not only because it was difficult to transport the necessary quantities to the front but also because Germany was short of gasoline and other petroleum products. Halder and Wagner concluded that they had to persuade Hitler to reduce the allotment to the civilian sector. Unless this happened, they feared that the attacking units might suffer from fuel shortages when the offensive had been launched.[5]

▪ ▪ ▪

Preparations, decisions and planning for a major offensive of the kind envisaged by the Germans took place at many levels in the military command structure. Halder's and Wagner's discussions were part of the decision making at the highest level as they were responsible for the influx of reinforcements and supplies, two crucial components of the offensive.

As commander of Army Group Center, Field Marshal Fedor von Bock was responsible for operational planning. He had to make decisions about the directions in which his armies would attack, their initial aims and related issues. However, von Bock's situation was complicated as, while German military tradition granted considerable latitude to field commanders, Operation *Taifun* was by far and away the most important military undertaking at the time, meaning that it was almost inevitable that men further up in the hierarchy would feel tempted to interfere. Many discussions thus preceded decisions, including operational decisions, but von Bock managed to grant much freedom to his subordinates.

There was an additional circumstance which complicated planning and preparation. Major military operations are often prepared from a relatively static position, which means that the situation changes marginally while planning is conducted. Field Marshal von Bock did not have this luxury. Admittedly the activity was low on his front sector, but that was not the case to the north and south of his army group, which is where many of the reinforcements would come from. This meant that the precise time units would arrive remained uncertain, as was the condition they would arrive in.

Most seriously, many of the panzer formations were engaged in battles elsewhere. Guderian's panzer group was deeply committed to the encirclement operation in Ukraine. This important force would not become available until that operation was concluded and the combat units would be exhausted. Col. General Hermann Hoth's Panzer Group 3 had also been dispatched from Army Group Center. Part of it had been sent to the Leningrad area and part to the Toropets area. These two panzer groups were destined to play key roles in the forthcoming attack on Moscow. Furthermore, Panzer Group 4, under command of Col. General Erich Hoepner, would be dispatched from Army Group North, to which it had been attached since the beginning of Operation *Barbarossa*.

In fact, the situation was even more complicated because the divisions that had hitherto been part of a certain panzer group would not necessarily fight within the same panzer group during Operation *Taifun*. This was particularly true for Panzer Groups 3 and 4. Hoth's Panzer Group 3 had had four panzer divisions but only one of them would remain under his command. On the other hand, he had received two panzer divisions from Panzer Group 4. The latter had handed over all of its three original panzer divisions and instead received five other divisions.

The fact that the panzer groups would be allotted panzer divisions other than those with which they had previously operated was not particularly alarming. Far worse was the fact that it remained uncertain when the divisions would arrive and be ready for the offensive. This all resulted from the tight schedule von Bock had to follow. On September 15 he wrote in his diary that the winter would begin soon and the offensive would have to produce a decisive success before the weather deteriorated. Any delay, even waiting for further combat units, could have disastrous consequences.[6]

■ ■ ■

From the very beginning, the Germans assumed that the Soviet forces facing Army Group Center would have to be thoroughly defeated. To achieve this goal quickly, most of the enemy would have to be encircled and captured. The Germans had by this time amassed considerable relevant experience. Senior German commanders appear to have unanimously supported the idea that significant Soviet forces should be surrounded, but there were disagreements how this should be accomplished. Most importantly, there was the question of how deep the pincers should meet. The OKH advocated Vyazma as a suitable point where the spearheads of panzer groups 3 and 4 would meet. Field Marshal von Bock disagreed. He preferred the Gzhatsk area, farther east than Vyazma, as the meeting point for panzer groups 3 and 4. As his proposals did not provoke any comments from OKH, he called Halder on September 13. They finally agreed that the inner pincers would meet at Vyazma and the outer ones further east, according to von Bock's wishes. Questions of this kind bounced back and forth between the senior commanders and gradually the plan for the forthcoming operation solidified. On September 19 it was given the code name *Taifun*.[7]

Army Group Center was reinforced before the operation toward Moscow, with one additional Panzer Group command and five panzer divisions. Among these five were 11th Panzer Division from Army Group South.

The town of Vyazma, despite frequently cropping up in discussions between senior German officers at this time, was not particularly significant. Founded in the 11th century, it was home to about 30,000 people, most of whom were occupied in professions related to agriculture, such as tanning or making flax. Hence, Vyazma would have had little military significance had it not been situated on one of the main approaches to Moscow: when the German generals glanced at their maps, they saw a communications junction on which two advancing forces could converge.[8]

The German planning for Operation *Taifun* may appear superficial, as the senior commanders did not produce any detailed directives. This was not solely due to the limited time available. The German armed forces had amassed considerable experience of similar operations, and the officers and staff further down the chain of command were well trained for the task that lay ahead. This meant that the senior commanders could focus on the aims and objectives of the operations, while the conduct of it was taken care of by the subordinate commanders and their personnel.

Three armies and three panzer groups were to take part in the operation. Most of them had fought with Army Group Center since July. The major exception was Panzer Group 4, which had belonged to Army Group North since June, but now had to move several hundred kilometers south. Colonel General Hoepner and his staff would be allotted several divisions they were unfamiliar with. On top of it, Panzer Group 4 would be given one of the key tasks.

Arriving from the north, Panzer Group 4 would be inserted in the central sector of Army Group Central, for which the Fourth Army was responsible. Several of the Fourth Army infantry divisions were attached to Panzer Group 4 for the initial attack, but aside from them, Hoepner had many new panzer divisions to acquaint himself with. He had previously had three panzer divisions, the 1st, 6th and 8th. The former two were transferred to Panzer Group 3, while the 8th Panzer Division remained with Army Group North. Instead, Hoepner received five new panzer divisions. The 10th had previously been part of Panzer Group 2. The 2nd and 5th panzer divisions were fresh units that were transferred to the Eastern Front for Operation *Taifun*. The 11th Panzer Division was moved from Panzer Group 1 in the Ukraine. Finally, the 20th Panzer Division had been transferred from Panzer Group 3. In fact there was an additional panzer division to consider, the 19th, which was in army group reserve, but might be put at Hoepner's disposal later.[9]

Together with Guderian, Hoepner had the most difficult deployment process before Operation *Taifun*. On September 12, while battles still raged in the Leningrad area, Lt. Colonel Joachim von Schön-Angerer, with some of his colleagues at the Panzer Group 4 staff, flew to Borisov to discuss the forthcoming operation. The following day, they took part in a meeting where they learned which units would soon be attached to Panzer Group 4; the day after, they met officers from XL Panzer Corps, which would be assigned a key role in the attack. On September 15 the staff officers from Panzer Group 4 met colleagues from the staff of Army Group Center, before flying back to report to Hoepner on September 16.[10]

When he had discussed the information with Hoepner and received the latter's opinions, von Schön-Angerer returned to Army Group Center on September 17. He met von Bock and explained Hoepner's views. One of the issues von Schön-Angerer had discussed with the representatives of the XL Panzer Corps was the dimensions of the projected encirclement at Vyazma. This issue was, as we have seen, very important to von Bock. On the same day he met von Schön-Angerer, von Bock wrote a letter to Halder, urging for a more extensive encirclement.[11]

At this time, the fighting at Leningrad had abated to such an extent that Hoepner could fly to Army Group Center on September 18 and meet von Bock. From then, Hoepner took over responsibility for the planning of the part Panzer Group 4 would play in the offensive. On September 19 he reconnoitred the terrain where his soldiers would attack and analyzed deployment plans. Hoepner also met General Georg Stumme, commander of XL Panzer Corps, to discuss the offensive. Stumme had already given much thought to the attack and presented his ideas at the meeting. By that evening a preliminary plan had been drafted, which Hoepner presented at Army Group Center the following day.[12]

Only two weeks remained before the offensive would be launched, but the plans were still open to change, not least because of deployment delays, as units failed to arrive as expected. However, this did not induce von Bock to postpone the offensive. He would rather attack without some of his units than delay the attack. Field Marshal Walther von Brauchitsch, chief of the German Army, concurred.[13]

The infantry also found it problematic to move into the staging areas. Major General Lothar Rendulic, who commanded the 52nd Infantry Division, commented that his division was stretched out over 35 kilometers (20 miles) while on march and required an entire day to cross a river if there was only one crossing available. A motorized formation of similar size occupied more road space, but as it moved much faster, a bridge crossing did not take as long as it did the infantry division. Also, there were many bridges that could not carry the weight of the 15cm howitzer, which one of the battalions in the artillery regiment was equipped with. As a result, the artillery could be forced to take lengthy detours. These could be avoided if railroad bridges were found nearby, as the latter were strong enough to take the howitzers.[14]

Although the main characteristics of the plan had been settled, unfolding events forced Hoepner to change details. Initially, the XL and LVII Panzer Corps had been assigned to conduct the initial attack, while XLVI Panzer Corps was held in reserve. However, on September 21 this was changed, with the LVII and XLVI Panzer Corps exchanging roles. Also, the condition of certain panzer divisions proved alarming, particularly the 19th and 20th, which would be attached to LVII Panzer Corps. These divisions had fought almost incessantly since the opening of the campaign on June 22.[15] Of course the German units were all suffering wear and tear from campaigning, but not to such an extent that their combat power was significantly diminished. In many cases the condition of the vehicles caused the gravest concern. This was the case with the 20th Panzer Division, which used predominantly captured and confiscated French vehicles. It was estimated that the division would need a period of at least eight days to repair vehicles and perform maintenance. The 19th Panzer Division suffered from similar problems.[16]

While battleworn units required attention and time, there was nothing that could be done when units did not arrive at the staging area as expected. With less than five days to go before the launch of the offensive, less than half of Hoepner's GHQ units had arrived. The poor condition of the roads did not help, and Hoepner eventually suggested that the 19th Panzer Division not be moved to the area where the rest of Panzer Group 4 was assembled. Instead it would be brought forward along the highway between Roslavl and Smolensk after the start of the operation.[17]

The gathering of forces for the attack was naturally of paramount importance, but there were many other elements to resolve such as the establishment of robust communications. The German combat units were comparatively well equipped with radios, but wireless communications could not cope with the expected demands. Furthermore, secrecy usually demanded that radio silence had to be observed. Codes might be compromised if the enemy monitored radio traffic, and it was also often possible to glean valuable information from the radio traffic even if it was successfully encrypted. Telephone lines could be tapped, but overall the risks were much smaller than with radio; but to depend on telephones meant that wires had to be laid. To facilitate the employment of Panzer Group 4, the signals regiment of Fourth Army was ordered to build the network for the group's staff. This also meant that Hoepner's staff would be connected to Luftwaffe units.[18]

Air to ground cooperation required further preparations. Many discussions took place between representatives from Panzer Group 4 and Luftflotte 2, which commanded the air units in the sector corresponding to Army Group Center. At this time of the year, dawn arrived too late to allow close air support before the ground units started the offensive. Field Marshal Albert Kesselring, who commanded Luftflotte 2, suggested that air attacks should be launched despite the limited visibility. By directing them at targets at a safe distance from the front line, air attacks could lower Soviet morale and boost German morale, without risking fratricide.[19]

Although the Luftwaffe could hardly exert a substantial influence on the outcome of initial attacks on the ground, there were many other important tasks for them to undertake. German intelligence had identified a Soviet reserve in the Spas-Demenskoye area. It would be attacked by the Luftwaffe to prevent it from counterattacking Panzer Group 4. Also, the Germans believed there was a Soviet reserve at Vyazma, which the Luftwaffe could target. Furthermore, the Germans assumed Soviet reinforcements would be brought forward from the Moscow area, which Luftflotte 2 would attack.[20]

Like their ground brethren, the Luftwaffe units participating in Operation *Taifun* had little time to prepare. One of the most important units was the VIII Air Corps, commanded by General Wolfram von Richthofen, cousin to the Red Baron of World War I fame. This corps had developed into what could be described as the Luftwaffe's ground support specialists. At this time, many of its units were badly in need of maintenance, and this prevented them from exerting their full effectiveness during *Taifun*.[21]

The VIII Air Corps had been supporting operations in the Army Group North area and the short pause between these operations and *Taifun* allowed little time for planning and preparations. On September 24, von Bock was reminded about the tight schedule. The day began with a Soviet air attack on his staff early in the morning. Later, von Brauchitsch arrived to discuss the forthcoming offensive. One of the topics was the VIII Air Corps and how, according to von Bock, Army Group North protracted its transfer to Army Group Center. He also argued that the Ninth Army's attack needed air support and emphasized that it was necessary for the VIII Air Corps to arrive very soon. In the evening he learnt that Hitler had also delayed the 36th Motorized Division.[22]

∎ ∎ ∎

The difficulties encountered by Panzer Group 4 and the supporting Luftwaffe units were possibly somewhat greater than experienced by other German units, but not much. Panzer Group 2, which had participated in the Kiev encirclement, had to hasten north to get into position for Operation *Taifun*. The three infantry armies and Panzer Group 3 were already on the Army Group Center front sector, but as their units were battleworn, or were arriving from other areas, their situation was far from ideal.

The German difficulties should of course be compared with those experienced by their opponent, and the Red Army certainly had its share of problems. The battles fought during the summer had given the Germans good reason to expect success. They were confident that their string of victories would be extended when the Soviet capital at last was designated as the goal.

Altogether, Army Group Center mustered about 1.2 million men.[23] The German attacking force thus lacked numerical superiority, but that was something the Germans were used to. Except during the campaigns in Poland in 1939 and the Balkans in 1941, the German army units had at best enjoyed local numerical superiority, where they chose to make their main effort. Of course Army Group Center would concentrate forces at certain sectors of the front during Operation *Taifun*. In particular, the sectors where the panzer groups would attack were given high priority. In the planned encirclement around Vyazma, Panzer Group 3 would constitute the left prong and Panzer Group 4 the right. Panzer Group 2 was located at the southern end of Army Group Center's front. This was mainly a result of its commitment to the Kiev operation. Guderian's forces were thus positioned furthest from Moscow. On the other hand, Panzer Group 2 would start two days ahead of the other units of Army Group Center.

The fact that one panzer group would start two days ahead risked alerting the Red Army, but the Germans did not regard this as a serious risk. As Panzer Group 2 was starting far to the south, from a staging area near Gluchov, it would not evident from its initial movements that Moscow was the aim. Rather, its move could be interpreted as part of an offensive into east Ukraine. The Germans concluded that the Red Army officers would not understand the German intentions when Guderian attacked, and the fact that his forces would have to cover 500 kilometers (300 miles) to reach Moscow during their northeasterly advance justified the early start.

The first goal for Guderian would be Orel and the encirclement of Soviet forces in the Bryansk area. However, the opportunities for an encirclement were not as favorable as in the Vyazma area. Panzer Group 2 would constitute the right prong, but there was no strong left prong available, as the Germans only had three panzer groups. Guderian's efforts might be in vain if Soviet forces were able to sneak out to the northeast. It was a potential weakness, but the Second Army, commanded by Col. General Maximilian von Weichs, was to attack from the area west and northwest of Bryansk. This formation lacked panzer or motorized units, but it was hoped that it could capitalize on Hoepner's breakthrough and it did not have to advance very far.

■   ■   ■

The *Taifun* plan was quite typical for German operational thinking. In this respect it was unremarkable. On the other hand, to conceive a plan as ambitious as this without any superiority of forces was indeed remarkable. Also, a very swift advance was expected, as the autumn rains were due to turn the roads into impassable canals of clay, virtually useless for movement except for tracked vehicles. The Germans were nevertheless highly optimistic.

ANGLO-SOVIET COOPERATION

Great Britain and the United States decided to support the Soviet Union soon after the launch of Operation *Barbarossa*. Russia and Britain formed an alliance on July 12, agreeing to assist and support each other in the war against Germany; and sixteen days later, Harry Hopkins, President Roosevelt's envoy, arrived in Moscow. The trade agreement between the Soviet Union and the United States was extended for another year on August 2.[24]

Soviet newspapers gave great coverage to Harry Hopkins' visit and the US–Soviet agreement was used extensively in Soviet propaganda targeting German soldiers. During World War I, US participation in the war had tipped the scales and ensured Germany's defeat, and this was something Soviet propagandists assumed was vivid in German soldiers' memories. Soviet leaflets dropped over German lines included the sentence: "Thus, America has also joined the struggle on the Eastern Front against Hitlerite Germany."[25]

US–Soviet rapprochement traced its origins to the prewar years. President Franklin D. Roosevelt had showed a positive attitude towards the Soviet Union and had pushed for the establishment of diplomatic relations with Stalin. Together with the Soviet foreign secretary Maksim Litvinov, Roosevelt signed an agreement on diplomatic relations on November 16, 1933.[26] Roosevelt also released Soviet assets in American banks, which had been locked as a consequence of the Winter War, on June 24, 1941. Some of it was used to purchase 50 fighter aircraft, including a number of Curtis P-40 Tomahawks. Attempts to buy heavy Boeing B-17 bombers met with no success, but five B-25 Mitchell medium bombers were purchased.[27]

An important conference was held in Moscow September 29–October 1. Lord Beaverbrook represented Britain and Averell Harriman the United States, while Stalin himself presented the Soviet view. Negotiations resulted in a lend-lease agreement, with Great Britain and the United States, providing the Soviet Union with weapons, equipment and materials needed for the struggle against Germany.[28]

The agreement would soon have tangible results, with Britain sending 361 tanks and 330 light armored vehicles to the Soviet Union in 1941. American combat vehicles began to arrive in January 1942, but by then the United States had entered the war as a belligerent.[29]

American fighters arrived earlier, and pilots from the Soviet 126th Fighter

Regiment engaged in combat in their Curtis P-40 Tomahawks outside Moscow on October 12. Before the end of 1941, 230 P-40 Tomahawks, 15 P-40 Kittyhawks, one P-39 Airacobra and five B-25 Mitchells were delivered to the Soviet forces. Britain shipped 484 Hawker Hurricanes in 1941.[30]

At first, the only route used for lend-lease was over Archangelsk and Murmansk, in Arctic Convoys, but from 1942 the Western powers also sent equipment through the Persian Corridor, which ran through Iran to the southern part of the Soviet Union. From September 1942, a third route was opened, the Pacific Route, over Alaska and to eastern Siberia.

The cooperation was not free from friction. One stumbling block was the future borders in Europe. Stalin wanted to retain the borders from 1941, while his new Western allies advocated the reinstatement of the 1939 borders.[31]

The German light tank Panzer II, armed with a 20mm gun, was still used in large numbers by the German armored forces. The only tank that was present in larger numbers was the Panzer III.

■ *THREE*

GUDERIAN ATTACKS

ain fell on September 29, making the roads soft. Guderian's soldiers had worked hard to get into position for the attack, as delays could not be accepted. But parts of his panzer group, mainly the XLVIII Panzer Corps, were still engaged in combat. But despite all difficulties, Guderian's units were ready in time. The general offensive towards Moscow had still not been proclaimed in the early hours of September 30, though of course Guderian, his staff and senior commanders were all informed about the purpose of the operation.[1]

Corporal Paul-Heinz Flemming served in the 11th Company, 3rd Infantry Regiment of 3rd Panzer Division. He remembered a cold journey by motorcycle on September 29, arriving at a village that evening. It began to rain as he was shown the path to a school where he was to have his quarters. Flemming was lucky not to arrive any later as many soldiers were delayed by the rain and muddy roads and those who walked ended up with wet boots. Flemming ran out of luck though, as his hopes to spend the night comfortably came to nothing. Instead, he had to content himself with a straw-covered dugout.[2]

The night was very cold and Flemming was woken very early. His regiment would launch its attack at 4:45 a.m. Flemming watched the German soldiers' advance, which was met by something he called an "aria" from the Soviet light artillery. Soviet rocket artillery also joined the battle, although Flemming did not see it cause any casualties. Despite enemy fire, the German formation made good progress and soon the first prisoners were marched to the rear area.[3]

As corporal in a rifle regiment, Flemming's knowledge of what tran-

49

spired was limited to the area around him, but on this day his experience coincided with the general pattern at XXIV Panzer Corps, which was commanded by General Leo Geyr von Schweppenburg. The German troops made swift progress even without close air support, as low clouds prevented the aircraft from attacking enemy combat units. Instead, Luftflotte 2 directed attacks against Soviet road movements far behind the front.[4]

Of Guderian's units, the 4th Panzer Division would play the key role. It broke through the Soviet defenses early in the morning, even though the planned air support did not materialize. As so many times before, Kampfgruppe Eberbach in the 4th Panzer Division was in the lead. Its composition illustrates the flexibility of the German battle groups. On September 29, Colonel Heinrich Eberbach was given control of several different units, either from the 4th Panzer Division or temporarily attached units. The panzer regiment of the 4th Panzer Division was the core, but Eberbach also possessed antiaircraft units, antitank units, recon units, artillery, engineers and infantry. He thus had a versatile formation. This mode of operations was typical for the German army.[5]

Early on September 30, less than an hour before the German artillery opened fire, Eberbach headed a briefing. When his subordinate commanders had been instructed they waited half an hour while the artillery fired upon targets ahead of the German positions. The fire was not remarkably heavy. The purpose was to disrupt rather than destroy Soviet defenses. Five minutes after the guns went silent, Eberbach's tanks moved forward along the main road from Gluchov to Sevsk. The gunners shifted their sights onto targets on the flanks, to allow the battle group to advance swiftly.[6]

The intelligence report compiled by Panzer Group 2 on September 29 had concluded that the Soviet defenses were weak. A quick breakthrough was expected, although resistance might be strong locally. The veracity of this intelligence is borne out by the success Eberbach's men enjoyed on September 30. Here and there, minor battles were hard fought, but overall the troops surged forward very swiftly. Late in the day they were also assisted by Luftwaffe reconnaissance aircraft, which reported on the situation ahead of the advancing tanks. In the evening, they had reached Kruglaya Polyana, about 25 kilometers (15 miles) into the Soviet defenses.[7]

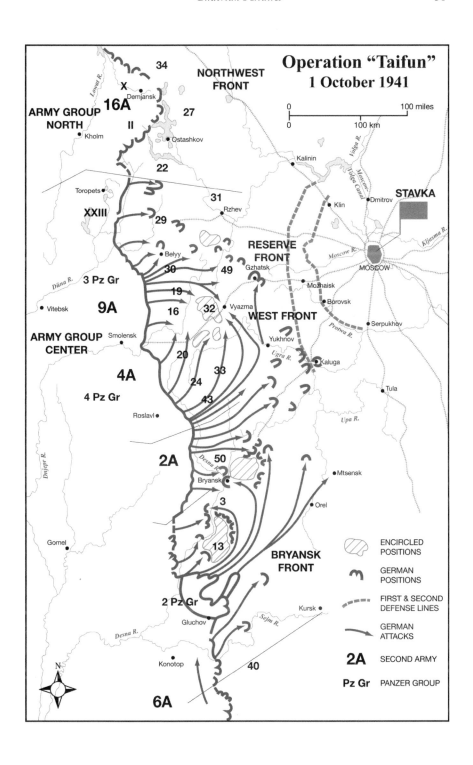

Operation "Taifun"
1 October 1941

Eberbach's deep thrust was the most important success achieved by Guderian's units, but the famous panzer general had more to be pleased with. The fact that bad flying weather had prevented air support for most of the day did not matter much, as the ground units completed their tasks anyway. The 3rd Panzer Division, which was also part of XXIV Panzer Corps, also broke through the Soviet defenses, slightly to the south of 4th Panzer Division.[8]

General Joachim Lemelsen's XLVII Panzer Corps was deployed to the north of XXIV Panzer Corps and met stronger resistance. This prevented it from advancing more than half the distance covered by von Schweppenburg's corps. Lemelsen's men continued to advance after dusk and hoped to attain greater success the following day.[9]

If his telephone conversation with Stalin at 2:30 a.m. on October 1 is any indication, Eremenko was not unduly concerned. He hoped that counterattacks, using three tank brigades, infantry and the cavalry group, would push the enemy back. In response to Stalin's inquiry about the air units, Eremenko replied that overall there were enough aircraft, but he had too few Ilyushin ground-attack planes. Stalin promised that the Stavka would provide more air support.[10]

The head of the operations section on the Bryansk Front staff, Col. Leonid Sandalov, wrote in his memoirs that they had expected the main German attack to be directed towards Bryansk. There was a strong enemy grouping in the Roslavl area (actually Panzer Group 4), which seemed to pose a threat to Bryansk. Eremenko and his staff concluded that Guderian's attack on September 30 was not the main German attack and decided to keep the main reserve, which included the 108th Tank Division, near Bryansk.[11]

Despite this situation assessment, the Stavka was very concerned about Guderian's success, and sent an order to the Forty-Ninth Army, which was commanded by Maj Gen Ivan Zakharkin. His formation was instructed to depart from the Reserve Front, where it was located in the Sychevka area between Vyazma and Rzhev, and move to Kursk, behind the southern flank of the Bryansk Front. Its divisions would entrain on October 2–4.[12]

The order to transfer the Forty-Ninth Army south surprised Antipenko. He considered the divisions attached to the army on the Reserve Front to be strong and their defenses well prepared. He believed that the enemy might break through the Thirtieth Army, but would then be halted by the Forty-Ninth Army. During the movement, trains carrying men and equipment of the Forty-Ninth Army were attacked by the Luftwaffe.[13]

Soviet reactions to Guderian's initial attack were slow and fumbling. This is hardly surprising, as it was often difficult to quickly recognise what the enemy was up to; and there were usually several possible scenarios to be considered. Reports from subordinate units could be exaggerated, but with so little time available, it was not possible to double-check everything. It appears the Germans were correct in assuming that Guderian's early start would not jeopardize Operation *Taifun*.

■ ■ ■

In the early morning on October 1, Guderian's staff received reports from the corps. The two most important, XXIV and XLVII, reported that the night had passed without any notable occurrences. The situation was more worrying at XLVIII Panzer Corps on the southern wing. It had warded off several enemy attacks in the night. However, despite the troubles in the south, the situation was very favorable. In particular, the 4th Panzer Division's success seemed to promise further triumphs in the future.[14]

At 7:00 a.m., Kampfgruppe Eberbach resumed its attack. The fact that it was part of 4th Panzer Division did not prevent it from cooperating with other units. For example, the battle group soon detached two battalions to cooperate with a battalion from 3rd Panzer Division to clear a wooded area just south of the main road Eberbach was advancing along. This is a good example of the flexibility of the German battle groups and their capacity to rapidly adapt to changes in circumstances.[15]

Kampfgruppe Eberbach continued in its role as spearhead and advanced very fast. During the first day of the offensive, air support had been almost non-existent, with the only contribution from the Luftwaffe being some reconnaissance missions. During the second day weather improved slightly and Stuka aircraft supported Eberbach at Sevsk, which was captured together with the important bridges just to the north of the town.[16]

Guderian arrived at Eberbach's command post soon after the capture of Sevsk. On being informed about the situation he was delighted. When Guderian asked Eberbach if it was possible to continue to Dmitrovsk-

Orlovsky, the answer was a prompt yes. Guderian moved to the forward line, despite a Soviet air attack. He met one of the battalion commanders in Panzer Regiment 35, Major Ernst von Jungenfeldt, and expressed his gratitude to the soldiers and their performance.[17]

Eberbach created a force about the size of a battalion and ordered it to take the lead in the attack towards Dmitrovsk-Orlovsky. It set out almost immediately and thereby avoided a friendly fire incident, when a German aircraft bombed those parts of Kampfgruppe Eberbach still in Sevsk, wounding and killing several soldiers. The hastily formed advance unit reached Dmitrovsk-Orlovsky at 9:45 p.m. and established defense positions for the night.[18]

By capturing Dmitrovsk-Orlovsky, the Germans had penetrated deeply into the Soviet defenses. Within two days, the 4th Panzer Division's advance had covered 120 kilometers (75 miles) as the crow flies. It was a very impressive achievement, completed without significant losses.[19]

Of all Guderian's units, the 4th Panzer Division advanced fastest, but overall the XXIV and XLVII Panzer Corps made very good progress. The Germans had torn a big hole in the Soviet defenses and had exploited it faster than most Soviet units could retreat. A disaster for the defenders loomed imminent and Guderian did not take his foot off the accelerator. He ordered the advance to continue to Orel on the following day.

Better weather on October 1 had allowed Luftflotte 2 to contribute more effectively. Direct air support to the combat units was not prominent and the Stuka attack at Sevsk was more of an exception than the norm. German aircraft did, however, attack many targets well ahead of the advancing ground units, in particular troop concentrations and vehicles moving on the roads, not least on the flanks of the advancing units. Also, several attacks were directed at the Soviet rail network. These did not have an immediate impact on the battle, but could prove important in the following days by preventing Soviet reserves from moving up to the front fast enough.[20]

At 5:00 a.m. on October 2, Stalin spoke with the chief of staff of the Bryank Front, Major General Georgiy Zakharov. Zakharov did not know that the Germans had already captured Dmitrovsk-Orlovsky, but he did inform Stalin that German units were advancing towards the town. Stalin did not appear overly worried. Optimistically he told Zakharov that two rifle divisions and two tank brigades would arrive via Orel on October 3–4. Zakharov replied that a staff officer would be sent to meet the reinforcements.[21]

Reinforcements were of course welcome, but Eremenko's situation had only just begun to deteriorate. It would soon become even worse, but this time, the disasters would not be confined to his sector.

When Operation *Barbarossa* began there existed few units with armored halftracks. Such vehicles were very desirable, but German industry could not keep up with demand. Most of the Panzer divisions' infantry had at most one company equipped with such vehicles—thus the German infantry rode on the tanks or in lorries, as did the Red Army.

■ *FOUR*

THE MAIN GERMAN ATTACK BEGINS

D uring the night of October 1–2, the German officers read their men Hitler's order of the day. Not all of them heard it, as some were on sentry duty, or manning forward combat positions or observation posts, but many could listen. The order read:

Soldiers!

Today the final, main and decisive battle of this year begins. It will result in the defeat of the enemy in front of us, as well as the instigator of this war—England. By neutralizing the enemy in the east, we will eliminate England's last ally on the continent and a terrible threat to the German Reich and all of Europe, a threat of a kind not seen since the days of the Huns and the Mongols. The thoughts of the German people will be with you in the following weeks, even to a greater extent than before.

We already owe you so much, for all you and our allies have achieved. All Germans will be with you, for you will afford the Fatherland, with God's help, not only victory, but also the most important prerequisite for peace.

Adolf Hitler.

Such proclamations may have impressed many, but the experienced staff officers of Panzer Group 3 probably paid more attention to the reports from other units on the Eastern Front. News from Guderian's panzer group was particularly interesting and augured success for Hoth's attack. Guderian's swift breakthrough indicated that the Soviet defense was weak, and the German success in the south would probably attract enemy reinforcements, pulling them far away from Hoth's forces on the northern wing.

Nothing notable happened during the night of October 1–2. The combat units had reached their intended positions under cover of darkness, and at 1:00 a.m. the corps reported that they were ready to attack. Occasional artillery fire could be heard in the night, but that did not worry Hoth and his staff. They waited calmly for the German artillery to open fire at 6:00 a.m.[1]

Panzer Group 3 made a good start. Some German radio operators had tuned their sets on frequencies used by Soviet transmitters and they could hear unencrypted desperate messages, for example: "Reinforcements can't be sent, river crossings must be held." Another message read: "I have assumed command, the commander has been killed in action." Perhaps most telling of all was: "Can't hold positions any longer, will destroy radio set." The German commanders of course interpreted such reports as indicating that the Soviet defenders could not resist the German attack.[2]

The Soviet artillery posed no serious threat to Panzer Group 3 this morning. The German officers had at least two explanations. The first was the German artillery barrage at the beginning of the offensive, which may have caused significant damage to batteries, communications and fire directors. The other was the Luftwaffe, whose presence above the Soviet artillery may have caused the gunners to remain under cover. The beautiful weather suited Luftflotte 2 well and many of its missions on October 2 were directed at targets ahead of Panzer Group 3. The aircraft attacked vehicles, artillery positions, fieldworks and troop concentrations behind the Soviet defense line. Altogether, 259 bomber sorties and 58 dive-bomber sorties were directed at the area into which Panzer Group 3 would attack.[3]

Overall the attack developed according to plan for Panzer Group 3, but there were some problems. The XLI Panzer Corps was comparatively weak, consisting of one panzer and one motorized division. They had been transferred from Army Group North and some elements had not yet arrived. Nevertheless, they jumped off successfully in the morning, but at about 11:00 a.m. they ran into trouble. A marsh could only be crossed on a causeway, but the causeway had been blown up by the Soviet defenders before the Germans arrived.[4] The engineer units were very important in situations like this, creating new roads or improving existing ones, allowing vehicles involved in an attack to continue moving forward. During the first day, the engineers made important contributions to the success of the German advance, not only at the marsh causeway.[5]

Three panzer divisions were attached to Hoth's panzer group, among them the 7th Panzer Division, commanded by Major General Hans von Funck, which had belonged to the Panzer Group since June 1941. It would distinguish itself again while leading Hoth's offensive. Funck's division set out at 6:15 a.m., when the artillery fire at the forward enemy positions ceased, and rapidly surged forward. It met only intermittent artillery fire until it reached a river. The engineers immediately began to build a bridge, but later in the evening a reconnaissance troop found one that was intact. A strong bridgehead was created, from which the advance could continue.[6]

In addition to the 7th Panzer Division the LVI Panzer Corps also had the 6th Panzer Division. As both these divisions were worn from months of campaigning, the number of serviceable tanks was reduced. Therefore, the 7th Panzer Division's tanks were transferred to the 6th Panzer Division to form a strong tank brigade. It advanced rapidly and in the afternoon, Hoth and his staff were informed by reconnaissance aircraft about the tank brigade's success. The brigade continued east and captured a bridgehead across the river Vop, from where it battled on further east. During the first day of the offensive, it advanced approximately 30 kilometers (18 miles).[7]

Hermann Hoth had enjoyed a good start to the offensive, particularly for LVI Panzer Corps, and especially the temporarily formed tank brigade. The northern prong of the German attack on Vyazma had already penetrated deep into the Soviet position. The apparently weak Soviet defenses bewildered Hoth and his staff, leading to much speculation.[8]

During the first day, LVI Panzer Corps were alarmed to discover that the Soviet defenders had already prepared their positions for the winter. They had installed iron stoves and heaters and created good cover against the expected harsh weather. They had also brought forward winter clothing. The Germans considered these ominous signs, particularly as the autumn rains would come before the winter.[9]

■ ■ ■

Erich Hoepner's Panzer Group 4 was the southern prong of the attack towards Vyazma. Its staging area was in the central sector of Army Group Center. Hoepner's men would be forced to cross the river Desna in order to punch a hole in the Soviet defense line. The center of gravity was placed at the sectors where XL and XLVI Panzer Corps would attack.[10]

Some of the supporting artillery had still not arrived by the evening of October 1. This was partly attributable to the shortage of towing vehicles, which in turn was a consequence of the prolonged fighting. However, the soldiers were confident. They had listened to Hitler's order of the day and Hoepner also wrote an order of the day in which he reminded the soldiers that October 2 would have been the birthday of Field Marshal Paul von Hindenburg, who had defeated Russian forces at Tannenberg in 1914. To what extent the soldiers were impressed and affected by such texts is unclear, but it seems unlikely they were wholly ineffective. Perhaps the soldiers were more encouraged by the hope that this would be the last major offensive, deciding the campaign in the east. If so, then once it was crowned by victory, they would be able to go on leave.[11]

■ ■ ■

Hoepner's artillery opened fire at 5:30 a.m., according to plan. The barrage was fierce rather than long. Stuka aircraft attacked targets on the eastern side of Desna. As the Germans would have to cross a river, the panzer units were initially held back. The infantry would attack first, establish bridgeheads and allow the engineers to create bridges. Then the tanks would take the lead.[12]

Occasionally luck accompanied the Germans. The 252nd Infantry Division captured an intact Soviet 12-ton war bridge. In other sectors, the infantry successfully captured bridgeheads, but harassing Soviet artillery fire made the engineers' work hazardous. Despite such difficulties, the 2nd Panzer Division began to cross the Desna at 9:30 a.m., and two hours later the 10th Panzer Division also moved onto the eastern bank of the river. From then on the German offensive picked up steam.[13]

The 10th Panzer Division advanced faster than all the other units of Panzer Group 4. Its breakthrough is an interesting example of command in the German army. East of the Desna, the tributary Snopot flowed through a valley. The Germans captured an intact railroad bridge, which was used by the wheeled vehicles, while the tanks forded the river. As the men of one of the tank battalions were waiting on the eastern bank of the Snopot for an attack order, they suddenly came under Soviet artillery fire. The battalion had not been informed about any air support, but soon the tankers saw Stukas diving down on the Soviet artillery. Major Georg von Grundherr, who commanded the panzer battalion, immediately gave attack orders, despite the fact that he had not received any such instructions.[14] The attack met with great success. His tanks punched a hole in the Soviet defenses and immediately penetrated deeply. The other battalion in the panzer regiment also seized the opportunity. That evening, the German tanks reached Beresovka, but they did not halt. During the night they continued in an east-northeasterly direction. They advanced 40 kilometers (25 miles) in the first 24 hours of the German offensive.[15]

No German unit advanced deeper into the Soviet defenses on October 2 than the 10th Panzer Division; in fact it penetrated so far that on the first day of the offensive, the Soviet defenders were already being put in a very awkward position, one from which they would struggle to extricate themselves. Other German units were also successful; the 11th Panzer Division, as well as the 2nd and 5th, also made very good progress. Panzer Group 4 concluded in the evening that a breakthrough had already been achieved and the following days would be devoted to exploiting it as rapidly as possible.[16]

Budjonny and his staff did not yet realize how serious the situation was. In the evening, orders to counterattack were issued. For example, three rifle divisions from the Thirty-Second Army were ordered to move from the Izdeshkova area to the area where Hoepner had broken through. The Reserve Front estimated that the divisions would need two and a half days to reach the area of Hoepner's breakthrough, provided they moved in daylight. It was a very unrealistic order. In two to three days, Hoepner's tanks could cover very long distances in the bright autumn weather. Also, the three divisions were former militia units that had recently been incorporated into the Red Army. Now they were being instructed to counterattack a well-trained and experienced German panzer group, which was already advancing at breakneck speed.[17]

The German panzer divisions had—as expected—played the main role in the attack, but the efforts of other units were also important. The majority of the divisions were infantry, and although they were not given as important missions as the panzers, they were committed to attacks. One example is the 34th Infantry Division, which fought to the south of 10th

Panzer Division, on the right wing of Panzer Group 4.[18]

Lieutenant Georg Hoffmann had arrived at the 34th Infantry Division early in August, one of the many replacements for killed or wounded officers and men. He was immediately given command of the antitank company in the 80th Infantry Regiment, a position he still held at the beginning of October, when fierce artillery fire heralded the start of the German offensive. According to Hoffmann, the ground shuddered from the violent explosions, when shells from gun barrels and rockets from Nebelwerfers found their targets, and he considered how terrifying, and deadly, the artillery attack must be for the enemy. At the same time, the sight of the shells raining down on the enemy raised the morale of the German soldiers waiting in their foxholes. Hoffmann was pleased with the preparatory fire and felt certain that the day would end well.[19]

Hoffmann's company stormed across the Desna. A bridge had been set ablaze by Soviet defenders, but it had not been completely destroyed and Hoffmann's soldiers made use of it. Fire from Soviet mortars and antitank guns landed unpleasantly close, but did not cause any injuries. Despite successfully crossing the river, Hoffmann was ordered to stay with his company at the small bridgehead due to a planned Stuka attack. Hoffmann did not like waiting in a confined area at which the enemy could easily direct fire, but there was no other option. Furthermore, Hoffmann thought the Soviet defenders were pulling out and a golden opportunity was being wasted. Nevertheless, Hoffmann welcomed the prospect of air support, which was in stark contrast to previous battles when he and his men had felt deserted.[20]

Mishaps are frequent in war and Hoffmann witnessed one on October 2. His men had laid mines and clearly marked the field. Despite the precautions, a vehicle drove into the minefield and detonated one of the mines. The driver escaped unhurt, but there were three other men in the vehicle. One of them was the regiment commander, who was lightly wounded. The second was the adjutant, Sergeant Wies, who was badly wounded. The third was Hoffmann's old friend, Lieutenant Müller-Hoisen, who was killed. The vehicle was destroyed. Major Brüll, commander of III Battalion, temporarily assumed command of the regiment.[21]

The 34th Infantry Division advanced east during the day and had reached halfway to Kirov by the evening. It was an impressive performance for an infantry division. The soldiers were told to find suitable places to sleep that night before continuing the following day. Hoffmann was fortunate to find a deserted Soviet bunker and slept well in the relative safety created by the soldiers who had built it.[22]

■ ■ ■

Virtually everything had proceeded as smoothly as the Germans had hoped. Field Marshal von Bock did not have to make many decisions. When the planning and preparations were completed and the offensive began, he confined himself to monitoring the course of events. The army group commander drove to the Panzer Group 4's command post, from which he had a good overview of the Desna valley. According to von Bock, it took longer than necessary to construct bridges in the XLVI Panzer Corps sector, but he appears not to have been particularly concerned when he proceeded to the Fourth Army.[23]

Field Marshal von Bock only made brief entries in his diary to describe the events on October 2, but they were illuminating, particularly the first two sentences: "The attack went according to plan. We advanced so easily that we began to suspect the enemy was giving up his positions." Undeniably, the German offensive had started very well.[24]

The Luftwaffe had made a concerted effort on October 2. Their main task was to support Army Group Center, and for this purpose, 977 bombing and ground-attack sorties had been undertaken, as well as 376 fighter and 34 reconnaissance sorties. A large share of the sorties were directed at the areas into which Panzer Group 3 and 4 would advance, Guderian's soldiers had to manage virtually without air support. In addition to attacking ground units, road convoys, fieldworks, staffs and artillery positions, Luftwaffe 2 also launched many attacks against the railroads connecting the Soviet front with Moscow. The purpose was of course to strangle movement of reinforcements and supplies. Given the extent of the German air operations, losses must be regarded as quite small. Altogether, 11 German aircraft were lost on the Eastern Front on October 2. The Germans claimed to have destroyed 42 Soviet aircraft, 37 of them in air-to-air engagements.[25]

It is difficult to assess the effects of the German air strikes, as they seldom caused substantial losses in the Soviet ground combat units. The most important effect was the confusion and the delays they caused. However, according to the Stavka, more fighter cover was needed for the transports. Accordingly, fighter regiments from the Air Defense (*Protivo-Vozdushnaya Obor,* PVO) were ordered to operate from airfields near Rzhev, Vyazma and Kirov, and their mission was to protect railroad lines from Rzhev to Zanozhaya and from Moscow to Tula.[26]

■ ■ ■

When an offensive was launched, the defender could usually not immediately see what was going on. Unreliable communications meant information was delayed, or never arrived. This was most likely to happen in sectors where the worst setbacks occurred due to the enemy cutting communications, or because the units that were supposed to report were simply destroyed in their entirety. Even if the information eventually reached the person it was intended for, it would pass through many command echelons before reaching senior commanders or commanders on adjacent front sectors. All this made it very difficult for the Soviet commanders to recognize the magnitude of the looming disaster.

But if the senior commanders were not yet seeing the full picture, men farther down the hierarchy had hardly a glimpse. Major Shabulin and the Fiftieth Army were located about halfway between Panzer Group 2 and Panzer Group 4, which meant that the German attacks initially appeared to be happening at a safe distance. On October 2, Shabulin was being offered breakfast—tea, bread, cheese and juice—when he finally heard that the neighboring Thirteenth Army, on their left flank, had been attacked. Despite his position as head of the special NKVD section in the Fiftieth Army, he was only informed about Guderian's offensive two days after it had begun.[27]

Soon afterwards, Shabulin heard the thunder of artillery. Enemy aircraft passed above him and the Soviet antiaircraft units opened fire. However, he saw no other signs of fighting on October 2. He had no idea what had caused the artillery fire; only rumors and guesses were available to explain what was going on. The Fiftieth Army was located between two German main attack directions and was thus not immediately engaged. At the end of the day it was finally clear that the Germans had attacked on many sectors of the front. Shabulin was told they had crossed the Desna farther north. The artillery could still be heard in the evening.[28]

■ ■ ■

Konev realized in the evening that the German offensive had created a dangerous situation. As Hoepner's forces had attacked the sector defended by Budjonny, Konev focused on the threat posed by Hoth's panzer group. He decided to commit his most important reserve, the Boldin Group, to halt the German LVI Panzer Corps. Boldin's forces consisted of the 101st Motorized Rifle Division, the 152nd Rifle Division and the 126th and 128th Tank Brigades. Altogether he had almost 200 tanks, but only 21 were T-34s or KV-1s. Lieutenant General Ivan Boldin was already something of a legend. He had been encircled in Byelorussia during the summer, but he—and 1,644 soldiers—managed to sneak back to the Soviet lines in August. He and his men had marched almost 600 kilometers (370 miles) over 39 days, and had managed to do so without being seen by the Germans. Now Konev gave him the mission to push the German panzers back.[29]

Boldin's group would attack in three columns. Boldin himself joined the 101st Division and the 128th Tank Brigade which were directed towards Kholm-Zhirkovsky, east of the river Solya. On the western side of the river, the 152nd Division advanced on Darovatka and the 126th Tank Brigade with 61 tanks was directed towards Igoryevskaya.[30]

The next few days would show if Boldin could succeed. If he couldn't, the situation would be very serious.

The Waffen-SS and the regular army have often been described as rivals. This may have been true to some extent, but it seems that the rivalry mainly took place at the top command level. Soldiers on the battlefield often cooperated. The Waffen-SS soldiers here are manning a 3.7cm anti-aircraft gun.

FIVE

THE OFFENSIVE CONTINUES

Guderian's panzer group had started two days ahead of the main German offensive, and had continued to attack on October 2. Kampfgruppe Eberbach was still in the lead and attacked towards Kromy, southwest of Orel. It is quite possible that Eberbach's men were hampered more by lack of fuel than the Soviet defenders. Supply difficulties had been expected; in fact they were almost unavoidable during such a swift advance, but Eberbach's resupply had been aided by the fact that the roads had dried after the rains of September 29/30.[1]

Fuel did not reach Kampfgruppe Eberbach until noon on October 2, but when refueling was completed, the Germans resumed their rapid advance. Soviet airpower tried to halt the enemy, but despite directing no fewer than 37 air attacks on Kampfgruppe Eberbach, the Germans were not significantly delayed. They reached the large concrete road bridge south of Kromy, where they encountered a resting Soviet vehicle column. The German tanks, with guns blazing, drove past the enemy vehicles and continued into Kromy, which was illuminated by moonlight. They came across a local bus, still following the ordinary timetable, which they halted as they had consumed almost all their fuel. A German interpreter tried a ruse. He called the post office at Orel and reported that no trace of any Germans had been seen in the Kromy area. It is unclear what effect his trick had, but it is clear that Guderian's lead units were less than 40 kilometers (25 miles) from Orel. Such a distance could be covered in a few hours once their vehicles had been refueled. Nothing suggested that the important city of Orel had seen preparations for defense against the dangerous enemy just hours away.[2]

The 3rd Panzer Division, also part of XXIV Panzer Corps, made very good progress too. However, Hermann Türk recorded a very unpleasant experience in his diary. The 394th Motorized Infantry Regiment which he belonged to resumed the attack at 5:00 a.m. on October 2. Dense fog at first limited visibility, but the sun soon evaporated the mist, revealing a beautiful day. Türk was about ten kilometers from Sevsk when Soviet aircraft attacked his unit. Instead of bombs, the aircraft dropped canisters, which after hitting the ground split and released spherical objects the size of Edam cheeses. At the same time the aircraft poured out phosphorus oil. Soon there were two thunderous explosions. Türk came running when he heard another explosion about a minute later. Evidently the aircraft had also dropped ordnance with some kind of time-delay fuses. A large splinter fell close to Türk and splattered him with mud. About 50 meters forward, he saw fire and thick smoke. The round "cheeses" continued to explode. First, smoke belched and then a huge flame shot out, followed by even more smoke. The smell of the smoke reminded Türk of garlic. A lorry caught fire but it was possible to extinguish the flames before it was too late. A soldier grabbed one of the spheres and threw it into a nearby well. Türk felt this was a brave, well-intentioned action, but thought it unwise to ruin a valuable source of water. Three men had been seriously wounded by the burning phosphorus. One man's entire face was swollen. Several other soldiers had less serious wounds, received when the phosphorus burned holes in their uniforms.[3]

Corporal Paul-Heinz Flemming had spent a good night, sleeping well in a warm Russian house. The following day, October 2, he saw little fighting, but he heard rumors that the 4th Panzer Division had reached Orel. It is not unusual for soldiers in combat units to see very little action some days, even when a major offensive is unfolding, especially when the advance is swift. Flemming did however see many vehicles heading northeast. The rather weak road network was under the utmost strain. In the evening, Flemming once again found a house where he could spend the night.[4]

Although their information was far from complete, it was clear to the Stavka that the events of October 2 necessitated new plans. In the morning of October 3, a directive signed by Shaposhnikov was sent to the Forty-Ninth Army, which had been ordered to Kursk. Instead of Kursk, the Forty-Ninth Army staff would move to less distant Sukhinichi and take

The railways were the pillars on which German supply rested. Army Group Center had hardly advanced in an easterly direction since mid-July, and this had permitted the repair and conversion work on the railroads to catch up.

command of rifle divisions in the Karachev and Belev areas, in order to protect Eremenko's flank against Guderian's advance.[5]

Heinrich Eberbach intended to give new orders to his units on the morning of October 3. However, several of his subordinate commanders had already thought ahead. Lieutenant Colonel Wilhelm Hochbaum had been in the lead before and now advocated the immediate resumption of the offensive towards Orel, as he believed the situation was very favorable. Eberbach concurred and the battle group soon set out.[6]

Soviet airpower was again very active as Kampfgruppe Eberbach advanced on Orel. German fighters did not appear until the evening, but despite the fact that the enemy had local air superiority, Kampfgruppe Eberbach advanced swiftly. Ground battles were also fought, for example when the Germans reached something that appeared to be a military training camp.[7]

The Soviet opposition, in the air and on the ground, did not halt the German onslaught. Eberbach's lead units reached Orel in the afternoon. The city and its more than 100,000 inhabitants appeared wholly unaware of the presence of enemy forces. The trams were still running when German tanks entered the streets, but the tank guns ended all Soviet efforts to follow their timetables. Industrial plants were being dismantled for evacuation east, but this process was interrupted by the deep German thrust.[8]

Eberbach's tanks did not only surprise the civilian authorities and the local population: the commander of the Orel military district, Lt. General A.A. Churin, was quietly working in his office when an orderly dashed into the room. The orderly excitedly informed Churin that there were German tanks in the city. Very hastily, Churin and his staff had to escape to Mtsensk.[9]

The German capture of Orel was important in many ways. Not only did many roads and railroads intersect at Orel, but many vital telephone lines also passed through the city. The latter was particularly true for the Bryansk Front. Communications with the general staff, neighboring fronts and Eremenko's units in the south were cut when 4th Panzer Division captured Orel. In order to lead his units effectively, Eremenko had to move his staff to Belov.[10]

Eberbach's men continued through Orel and captured ground to the northeast. They had covered, on average, over 50 kilometers (30 miles) a day since the offensive began. The success was won without paying a heavy price in blood. Between September 30 to October 3, the battle group recorded 34 killed and 121 wounded. Six tanks had been knocked out. This was a low price for their spectacular success, and the 4th Panzer Division had captured almost 1,600 prisoners, most of them taken by Eberbach's units.[11]

The 4th Panzer Division had given Guderian his most important success, but the reports from other sectors were also very promising. The panzer regiment of the 3rd Panzer Division cut the important Bryansk–Kharkov railroad. The XLVII Panzer Corps widened the breach in the Soviet defenses and exploited it deeply. It could thus be directed in a northerly direction towards Bryansk.[12]

■ ■ ■

Guderian's attack in the south was spectacular, but it took place far from

Moscow. This made it less serious than the attacks launched by Panzer Groups 3 and 4, which both continued on October 3. The 10th Panzer Division's panzer regiment had torn a huge hole in Budjonny's defense and penetrated deeply on the first day. This effort had consumed most of the regiment's fuel and therefore it could not continue in the lead on October 3. It had, however, opened the way for other parts of the division. The motorized infantry took the lead, together with some tanks that had been refuelled.[13]

As Panzer Group 4 had already achieved a breakthrough, the decision was how this should be exploited. Discussions before the offensive had resulted in three main options for Panzer Group 4. The first was to turn north, advance rather close to the original Soviet defense line, and converge with Panzer Group 3. The second was to follow a more easterly route and meet Hoth's tanks at a point closer to Moscow. The third alternative was to advance northeast, towards Moscow. As the 10th Panzer Division had made such a clean breakthrough at this very early stage, Panzer Group 4 could simultaneously pursue two or more objectives.

Although these were the three alternatives considered by the German generals, there were further options, or at least there were further German options considered by the Soviet commanders. In particular, the Bryansk Front believed Panzer Group 4 might turn south and, together with Panzer Group 2, encircle most of the Bryansk Front. This was of course regarded as particularly serious by the Bryansk Front staff. The chief of staff, Zakharov, described it as:

> The enemy hastens to grab our front with a pincer-like operation, exactly as he did against the Southwest Front [the Kiev pocket].[14]

To continue the offensive without losing momentum, Panzer Group 4 prioritized the repair of the large road bridge over the Desna, on the highway between Roslavl and Moscow. The LVII Panzer Corps had been kept in reserve and it could not be successfully employed until the bridge was repaired. Meanwhile, the XL Panzer Corps advanced in a northeasterly direction, while the XLVI Panzer Corps turned north and advanced in such a way that it could complete "the small pocket." The XL Panzer Corps received instructions to do the same in the evening. It should cross the Ugra River and thereafter be ready to advance on Vyazma. Later in the evening, Field Marshal Günther von Kluge, commander of Fourth Army, demanded that the XL Panzer Corps should reach Vyazma as soon as possible, as aerial reconnaissance had reported Soviet units retreating towards Moscow on the road from Yartzevo.[15]

Hoth had made a good start and expectations ran high during the night. In particular, much was expected from the ad hoc panzer brigade on October 3. It received its mission for the forthcoming day on the radio soon after midnight, as did other parts of 6th Panzer Division. It was ordered to cross the Dnepr at Kholm-Zhirkovsky and then continue towards Vyazma.[16]

The panzer brigade set out in the lead at 6:00 a.m. The 25th Panzer Regiment, which had been transferred from the 7th Panzer Division, attacked on the left wing and the 11th Panzer Regiment on the right. The former met weak resistance and managed to establish a bridgehead across the Dnepr at about 5:00 p.m., while the 11th Panzer Regiment encountered stronger enemy forces.[17]

German air reconnaissance disclosed Soviet troop movements, including tanks, on the roads south of Kholm-Zhirkovsky. The Germans could not know it, but they had spotted elements of the Boldin group, including the 128th Tank Brigade, which possessed seven KV tanks, one T-34 and 53 tanks of other types. The 6th Panzer Division was duly informed, but it did not alter its plans. It continued east during the day and established a bridgehead across the Dnepr; in total it had covered approximately 60 kilometers (37 mies) since the start of the offensive.[18]

Of all Hoth's units, the LVI Panzer Corps enjoyed the greatest success, but the XLI Panzer Corps also performed well. However difficult terrain and vehicle columns crossing each other prevented the corps from advancing faster. During the night of October 3–4, the XLI Panzer Corps, in particular the 1st Panzer Division, was subjected to many Soviet air attacks.[19]

In the evening, Hoth could look back on a successful day, which had mostly gone according to plan. The bridgehead across the Dnepr would allow 6th and 7th Panzer Divisions to turn south and approach Vyazma, thereby sealing the encirclement together with Panzer Group 4. It still remained unclear, though, what the Red Army was about to do.

Hitler seems to have expected weak resistance from the Red Army. On October 3, he made a speech to the German people. He described the events during the past years and focused on the war, which according to him had been instigated by the Freemasons and the Jews. After a brief description of the war up to June 1941, he began to talk about the most relevant campaign at the current time: Operation *Barbarossa*. He claimed that the Germans had not lost the initiative for one moment. He emphasized the accuracy and effectiveness of the planning, the combat power and bravery of the German soldiers, and the quality of their weapons. Hitler did however admit that one estimate had been wrong. The German assessment of the Soviet preparations had been far too conservative. He had not been able to imagine the gigantic war preparations made by the enemy in the east. Hitler argued that the German attack had just barely saved not only Germany but also Europe from ruin. He had not been able to tell the German people about this before, but on this day he chose to do so and the reason was that the enemy in the east had finally been slain and would not rise again.

Obviously the speech was propaganda, but there were more than a few grains of truth in it. Most importantly, Hitler confessed that German planners had vastly underestimated the Soviet war potential. Hitler glossed over this failure, but the meaning was clear. He also pictured a German war machine that worked efficiently and accomplished its tasks. In many ways, this was a fair judgement. Had the Soviet forces, including reserves, been of the size estimated by German intelligence, then there is little doubt that Operation *Barbarossa* would have succeeded, perhaps even before the beginning of October. However, at this stage of the war, Hitler was probably still convinced that Soviet resistance would soon collapse. He would be very disappointed, though, because German underestimation of the Soviet capacity for waging war was to become a recurring theme over the coming weeks.[20]

■ ■ ■

Early on October 2, German fire withered the positions of the 242nd Rifle Division. As part of Thirtieth Army, it was located on the axis of advance that Hoth's panzer group would follow, and Panzer Group 3 hit the Soviet division hard. It broke straight through and Konev's fierce counterattacks did not restore the situation. A major from the general staff arrived amid chaos and handed over an order instructing the 242nd Rifle Division to retreat to the Belyy area, where the Thirtieth Army would organize a new defense line. The division's commander, Glebov, was also informed that the Germans had broken through further south, severing communications between Thirtieth and Nineteenth armies. He and his chief of staff, Dragunsky, did all in their power to gather the remnants of the division and retreat towards Belyy. Enemy forces had already captured Baturino, the division's main supply base, meaning that no more ammunition, food and medicine could be obtained. At dawn on October 4, about 3,000 men from the division set out together to try and escape the encirclement.[21]

■ ■ ■

Little information on the German offensive had reached Shabulin on October 2. That night he slept in an earthen hovel, not waking until 7:30 a.m. Upon being told that a comrade, Kolyesnikov, had arrived at the staff, Shabulin hurried to exchange information and views. They both felt it disgraceful that the Germans had acheived yet another victory in breaking through the Thirteenth Army to the south. It was also said that the enemy had already captured Kromy and was thus threatening to cut off the Fiftieth Army.[22]

Shabulin and Kolyesnikov set out to visit the 258th Rifle Division at noon and remained there for two hours. They got the impression that the Soviet artillery fire was strong and the infantry prepared for attack. An order to recapture lost positions had been given. Later in the evening Shabulin noted in his diary that the situation remained unclear. According to him, the signals units did a poor job and the staff did not perform their duties either. Shabulin went further and denounced the men in the rear areas as cowards, who he claimed had already prepared themselves for headlong flight.[23]

Some of Shabulin's diary entries are colorful. On this day he also wrote:

> My God, aren't there too many fawners here. K. says that the NKVD has already deserted Orel. But we are presently 150 kilometers west of Orel. Such confusion! Such clumsiness! A firm hand would be needed here. A well-conceived onrush and the Germans would run, without looking back. Their forces are, compared to our army, visibly exhausted and the Germans are surprised that we retreat.

Shabulin seems to have at least partly based his image of the enemy on a few German defectors, hardly representative of the German army. The rumors of the NKVD deserting Orel were more than true, as the Germans had captured the city. Shabulin's analysis of the relative strength of the opposing forces appears worse than naïve, but like most others engulfed in these events, he had just small fragments of information upon which to form an impression of the overall situation. There was far more he didn't know than he knew, but such a limitation seldom discourages people from forming a firm opinion.

■ ■ ■

Field Marshal Kesselring, who commanded Luftflotte 2, emphasized to German army officers that the air force could not prevent Soviet forces from escaping eastwards through Vyazma. He thus stressed the need for the panzers to reach Vyazma on October 4. The Germans interpreted the weak Soviet resistance as a sign that the enemy was withdrawing, which meant that they might escape encirclement. As the Germans did not want to just push the enemy back, but inflict a crushing defeat, this was serious.[24] In fact the Germans had exaggerated the Soviet inclination for withdrawal, and actually the panzer divisions had advanced too fast for most of the Soviet units to keep up with the pace. Panzer Group 3 now had to ensure that the LVI Panzer Corps in particular could continue to advance at speed. The panzer brigade remained in the lead. During the night before 4 October, the starry sky was so bright that visibility was surprisingly good. The Germans regarded this as a sign of good fortune for the day that would soon dawn.[25]

Good weather was not only exploited by the German air force. At 6:45 a.m., Soviet aircraft bombed the 6th Panzer Division's forward command post, and 15 minutes later the division commander reported that the southern bridgehead was under attack from Soviet ground units, including tanks. This would turn out to be the prelude to large-scale tank battles.[26]

During the afternoon, the Germans decided to dissolve the panzer brigade. The 7th Panzer Division became responsible for the northern bridgehead across the Dnepr, including the elements of the division that had been temporarily attached to the 6th Panzer Division. The latter became embroiled in hard fighting to secure the communications up to the bridgehead. Freiherr von Funck's 7th Panzer Division would take the lead, but lack of fuel prevented it from dashing forward until October 5.[27]

On October 4, the 11th Panzer Regiment, part of 6th Panzer Division, fought a battle with a Soviet tank brigade. Fifteen German tanks were put out of action, while the Germans claimed to have knocked out 28 Soviet tanks. The exact Soviet losses cannot be established, as few records have survived. However, the brigade was deleted from the Soviet order of battle after the clash.[28]

Soviet partisan units were soon formed behind German lines, which forced the Germans to deploy units for anti-partisan warfare. A directive signed by Stalin and Molotov on 29 June provided instructions for the initiation of partisan operations in occupied territory. In many cases, the partisan units were formed from soldiers that had been surrounded or cut off from their parent units.

The Soviet units that counterattacked the LVI Panzer Corps at the bridgehead claimed to have destroyed many German tanks, but this is a gross exaggeration as neither the 6th nor the 7th Panzer Division suffered heavy losses during these days. The Soviet losses were, however, significant. The 126th Tank Brigade reported 60% losses up to October 7, while the main group, commanded by Boldin, reported up to 70% casualties. Incessant enemy air attacks were blamed for the losses. Whatever the reason, Konev's main reserve was now a spent force and had failed to halt the LVI Panzer Corps, at best managing to delay the German advance.[29]

Field Marshal Kesselring's wishes for October 4 were not fulfilled, but that does not mean the German army did not realise the importance of quickly bringing the pincers together. In fact, the war diary of Panzer Group 3 contains an entry stating that Kesselring's request was unnecessary. The slow progress on October 4 cannot be attributed to lack of insight, but to lack of fuel and Soviet opposition.[30]

■ ■ ■

Like Panzer Group 3, Hoepner's panzer group aimed for the alluring main road leading from Smolensk to Moscow. They advanced apace on October 4, but there was some confusion among the senior commanders as to where the units should be directed. When Panzer Group 4 began the operation, it had attacked along a line almost parallel to the main road from Smolensk to Moscow. It would have to turn north to complete the encirclement, but as the panzer group consisted of several corps, it was not evident which of them that should turn first and when the turn would be initiated.[31]

Major General Wolfgang Fischer's 10th Panzer Division remained in the lead. On October 4 it reached Mosalsk, about 120 kilometers (75 miles) from where it began its advance on October 2. Such speed was remarkable and the division had reached a point far east of Vyazma. Luftwaffe reconnaissance reports suggested that Soviet units were retreating, but the 10th Panzer Division had penetrated deeply enough to render a Soviet withdrawal very difficult.[32]

Three other panzer divisions—the 2nd, 5th, and 11th—attacked on the left flank of the 10th Panzer Division. They had not managed to keep up with Fischer's pace and were now instructed to turn north, towards Vyazma. Hoepner's units still had about 75 kilometers (47 miles) remaining, while Hoth's lead elements had to cover 50 kilometers (30 miles) to reach Vyazma. The gap between the German pincers was thus still quite wide, but could be closed within two days by the panzers. Considering that most of the Soviet formations would have to move at least 100 kilometers (60 miles) to reach relative safety—and they had comparatively few motor vehicles—it would prove very difficult to avoid encirclement. In fact they would have found it difficult to escape even had they had been ordered to withdraw immediately after the Germans had struck.[33]

Guderian's advance on the army group's southern wing was redirected after the capture of Orel. The XXIV Panzer Corps did believe that it was possible, or desirable, to continue northeast to Tula, as that would require other units to cover their flanks and the delivery of more fuel to Orel. These conditions were not easy to fulfil and the 4th Panzer Division made very little progress on October 4.[34]

The other divisions of Panzer Group 2 continued attacking. Of particular importance were the attacks towards Karachev, which was located on the railroad between Bryansk and Orel. Should Guderian's attacks result in the encirclement of substantial Soviet units, he had to advance swiftly to the north and establish contact with lead units from the Second Army. In the evening, the spearhead of the 18th Panzer Division was located about 20 kilometers (12 miles) south of Karachev.[35]

SIX

ENCIRCLEMENT

*T*he situation late on October 4 spelled disaster for the Soviet forces west of Moscow, as many of the units were in grave danger of becoming cut off within a few days. Panzer Groups 2 and 4 had cut huge holes in the defense line and their lead units had already reached far to the east of the original Soviet defenses where they were able to ravage the enemy rear area. They had, however, outrun their supplies and the fuel situation in particular was hampering German efforts to exploit their success. The Germans were also considering what they would do once the Soviet forces had been encircled. By and large, the first phase—the breakthrough—could be regarded as completed. The second phase, the destruction of the Soviet units, would soon begin. The third phase, exploiting their success by advancing eastwards, would follow, but the chances of success in this phase depended on the right choices being made before the second phase began.

Field Marshal von Bock was responsible for the decisions concerning the second and third phases, but Halder and Brauchitsch also had a say and none of the three men could be certain that Hitler would not interfere. Most importantly, it was necessary to decide which units would complete the defeat of the Soviet units on the frontline and which would instead focus on advancing deeply and so creating favorable conditions for the third phase.

It was difficult to make decisions as events on the ground continued to unfold, and commanders were formulating plans based on information that was incomplete, or that would soon become out-of-date. This could lead to misunderstanding, vacillation, and confusion, as demonstrated by

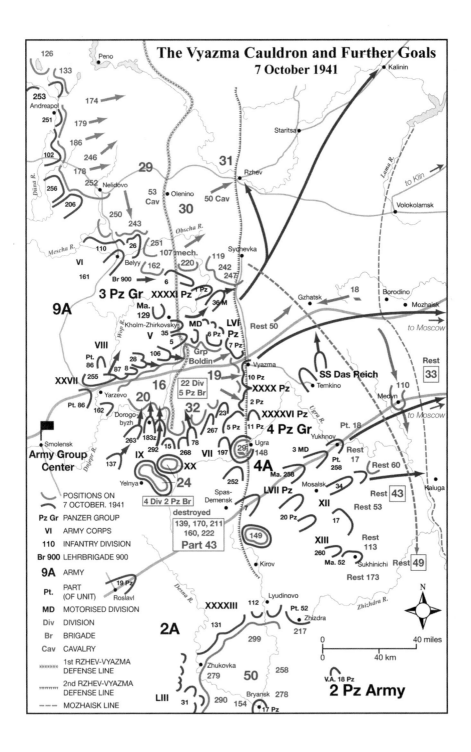

The Vyazma Cauldron and Further Goals
7 October 1941

the tasks given to Guderian's panzer group after the capture of Orel. Two main plans were discussed. The first was to continue along the main road to the city of Tula, located halfway between Orel and Moscow. The second alternative was to focus on the capture of Bryansk and the encirclement of Soviet units in that area. Guderian first received a directive from the OKH instructing him to remain on the western side of the Oka River and not advance on Tula. But hardly had Guderian been informed about this by von Bock, when Halder contacted the panzer general directly and gave him other instructions.[1]

Supply was of paramount importance for the operations. Guderian's dash to Orel had left him more than 200 kilometers (124 miles) from his jump-off position. Advancing towards Tula would stretch the lines of supply even further. Supplies usually had to be moved by rail over longer distances, but relatively few railroads followed the German axis of advance. The most important railroad to Orel passed through Bryansk. This was a strong argument for temporarily suspending the advance on Tula and shifting attention to Bryansk. Also, an important railroad ran from Bryansk to Kaluga and then to Moscow.[2]

Stalin and the Stavka did not immediately realize the gravity of the situation around Vyazma. This was in no small part due to the poor communications, which had not improved much since World War I. Telephone lines conveyed most of the information and could seldom be replaced by radio when they were cut. The speed of the German operations caused many Soviet commanders to lose control of their units. These problems affected every layer in the command structure, including the Stavka, which found it hard to obtain a timely and accurate picture of the situation.

To assist the commanders and the staffs of the West and Reserve fronts, the GKO (*Gosudarstvennyj komitet oborony*, State Defense Committee) sent its representatives Voroshilov and Molotov to the Gzhatsk–Moshaisk area. The deputy chief of staff of the Stavka, Aleksandr Vasilevsky, accompanied them. They arrived on October 5.[3]

On October 5, the GKO ordered that ten reserve armies should form along the line that ran from Vytegra through Rybinsk, Gorki, Saratov, and Stalingrad to Astrakhan. Even before the Germans launched Operation *Taifun*, several new rifle divisions had begun forming in the Moscow and Orel military districts. Despite the crisis at the front, these units continued to train.[4]

■ ■ ■

By the morning on October 5, it was abundantly clear that Panzer Group 2—which was renamed Second Panzer Army on this day—as well as Panzer Group 4 had made clean breakthroughs. It was less clear that Panzer Group 3 had met with similar success, as it had hardly made any progress on October 4. However, if the LVI Panzer Corps made good progress on October 5, any lingering doubts would be dispelled.

The 7th Panzer Division had regained control over all its units, but the fuel situation remained precarious. The division spent the morning on October 5 at its bridgehead on the eastern bank of the Dnepr, waiting for fuel. The Luftwaffe contributed by transporting fuel by air. Approximately 55 cubic meters (12,100 gallons) was dropped in the area held by 7th Panzer Division, of which 20 cubic meters (4,400 gallons) had been ear-marked for the 25th Panzer Regiment. The division did not being its attack until 2:00 p.m. The objective was Kamenets, and in their path lay partly fortified Soviet defenses.[5]

At 2:30 p.m., with tanks as the vanguard and supported by infantry from the 6th Motorized Infantry Regiment and virtually all the division's artillery, the 7th Panzer Division attacked. The Soviet defense proved stub-born, supported by strong artillery. The defenders also used Molotov cock-tails in their attempts to knock out German tanks. Despite hard fighting, the German tanks battled their way forward and at 5:30 p.m. they captured Kamenets. The 7th Panzer Division had covered about ten kilometers (6 miles) in three hours. It was not yet clear whether a decisive success had been won, but it soon would be.[6]

The 6th Panzer Division, which attacked on the right wing, had a harder day. Soviet attacks, including heavy tanks, hit the 6th Panzer as well as the 129th Infantry Division. Both German divisions intended to attack, but unclear information about promised air support as well as the Soviet assaults, prevented them from launching their attacks. In the evening the division commander, Lt. General Franz Landgraf, was informed about the success of his northern neighbor. He suggested that the 6th Panzer Divi-sion be pulled out and inserted behind the 7th Panzer Division. The 6th Panzer Division's bridgehead across the Dnepr would be used by infantry divisions, which had now reached the river. Landgraf was ordered to attack from the bridgehead, but one of his motorized infantry regiments, the 4th, would be transferred to the 7th Panzer Division.[7]

■ ■ ■

Gradually Soviet countermeasures began to materialize, but it was very difficult to do anything effective against such a swiftly acting enemy. Late in the afternoon on October 5, Shaposhnikov sent an order to the Fifty-Second Army in the Leningrad area. Two rifle divisions that had recently arrived from Central Asia should be transferred to the Moscow sector. The 312th Division was directed to the railroad station at Narofominsk, while the 316th Division was to move to Volokolamsk. Both divisions were organized according to the old tables of organization, which meant that they had approximately 14,000 men each.[8]

Lack of information on his own front sector and on adjacent sectors was irritating Lt. General Rokossovsky. He was finding it difficult to keep up with the fighting on his front, or the condition of his units. Suddenly he received an order on October 5, from the West Front headquarters, instructing him to go to Vyazma with his staff and organize a counterattack in the direction of Yukhnov. Five rifle divisions with supporting elements waited in Vyazma. His present front sector would be handed over to Lt. General Philipp Ershakov, commander of the Twentieth Army. Rokossovsky's chief of staff, Mikhail Malinin, exclaimed: "Leave the troops in this moment! It is absolutely incomprehensible!" On Malinin's advice, Rokossovsky asked for a written confirmation of the order, which arrived by air in the night. The order was signed by Konev and the political officer Bulganin. The Twentieth Army took over almost immediately, enabling Rokossovsky and his staff to travel to Vyazma.[9]

In the evening, the Stavka decided to transfer command of the Reserve Front's two armies on the right wing, the Thirty-First and Thirty-Second, to West Front. It was hoped coordination would improve. Budjonny thus retained command over three armies (Twenty-Fourth, Thirty-Third, and Forty-Third) as he had already lost the Forty-Ninth Army.[10]

The remnants of 242nd Rifle Division approached Belyy, according to the order dated October 3. On the outskirts of the town, the men of the division were met by fire and they concluded that Belyy had already been captured by the enemy. The commander Glebov and the chief of staff Dragunsky could not get into contact with the Thirtieth Army staff and Glebov decided to march east of Belyy. In the morning on October 5, Zhuralyev, deputy commander of Thirtieth Army, appeared at 242nd Division. Finally Glebov and Dragunsky received some information. Zhuralyev, travelling on a KV tank, headed for the 107th Motorized Rifle Division to arrange a counterthrust in the direction of Belyy and Dukhovshchin. He ordered the 242nd Rifle Division to march on Vassilyevo-Shanicha, southwest of Sychevka and the purpose was to cover Zhuralyev's flank in the Sychevka-direction during the counterthrust.

The division reached the intended area, but Zhuralyev's attack met with no success. Gradually, the 242nd Division's position became more dangerous, particularly when its supplies of food were exhausted. Reports came in that the enemy was pushing forward on all sectors. An improvised staff meeting was held at the 242nd Division in the morning of October 7 to discuss a retreat. Communications with the army staff had been severed. Glebov suggested that the unit should move east, past Sychevka and further north to the wooded area north of Gzhatsk in the hope of finding the army again. Dragunsky advocated a more northerly march, toward Rzhev, where he hoped to link up with either Twenty-Second or Twenty-Ninth Army. The division commissar Khrapunov exclaimed: "But we are attached to the Thirtieth Army. Why should we march to another army?"

Dragunsky pointed out that it did not matter much which army they fought with, and a northerly route was less risky. Khrapunov was not swayed, but Glebov asked the gathered officers and they supported Dragunsky. Glebov pondered the decision for about an hour, before settling for the northern route.[11]

■ ■ ■

Early on October 5, Panzer Group 2 received a weather forecast from Luftflotte 2. Very favorable conditions were predicted for that day on all sectors, but the forecast was less optimistic about following days. The weather was of course of paramount importance. Autumn rains were expected soon, which could render the roads impassable.[12] Of course both sides could exploit the good weather; Soviet airborne troops landed between Orel and Mtsensk. When the Germans realized, they directed Stuka aircraft to attack the air-landed units, which could obstruct German forces advancing on Mtsensk. A detachment from the 4th Panzer Division was sent on an outflanking move and managed to capture important bridges on the way to Mtsensk. Soviet ground-attack aircraft failed to halt the Germans, who captured Ivanovka and crossed the river. The German detachment reached a point approximately 20 kilometers (12 miles) northeast of Orel before halting to take up positions for the night. They could observe Soviet tanks ahead.[13]

On October 5, Soviet commanders made further efforts to halt or at least delay the advancing German forces. Group Ermakov, positioned at the front on September 29, had been forced into a headlong retreat. As the group had been on the southern part of Guderian's attack sector, it retreated straight east. At best, it could defend Kursk from the west, but since Guderian's tanks had already captured Kromy and Orel, Kursk was also threatened from the north. Colonel A.S. Gryaznov and his 7th Guards Rifle Division were heading south when a countermanding order reached him and instructed him to march towards Kursk. In the evening on October 5, a cavalry division and a motorcycle regiment were attached to Gryaznov. Shaposhnikov ordered Gryaznov to defend the area between Lgov and Fatezh, which meant that he should cover Kursk from the north. Shaposhnikov added that Gryaznov was henceforth directly subordinated to the Stavka and he was expected to report in the morning as well as in the evening.[14]

■ ■ ■

The German force advancing between Orel and Mtsensk was small, not least because the fuel supply did not permit large forces to be moved. Should the XXIV Panzer Corps attack with all its strength, 500 cubic meters (110,000 gallons) of fuel had to be transported by air to Orel within 24 hours. This was unrealistic, as to transport such an amount in one day would require an immense armada of transport aircraft.[15]

The following days would show that Guderian attached little importance to the thrust to Mtsensk. The other panzer division in the XXIV Panzer Corps, the 3rd Panzer Division, would cross the supply routes of the 4th Panzer Division and attack north from the Orel area towards Belev. The 10th Motorized Division, which was also part of the XXIV Panzer Corps, was busy mopping up pockets of resistance in the area behind the two panzer divisions. After completing this mission, it would be deployed to cover the corps' southeastern flank.[16]

All three divisions of the XLVII Panzer Corps were also attacking northwards. Guderian's immediate concern was to establish connection with the Second Army. This would allow him to bring supplies forward and also cut off sizeable Soviet forces, including the Fiftieth Army where

Shabulin served. It appears Shabulin was yet unaware of the danger threatening him and many others, but it was clear to him that they were in a very unfavorable situation.[17]

Shabulin had met the army commander, General Petrov, in a small forest in the evening of October 4. They discussed the situation and Petrov asked Shabulin how many people he had ordered shot. After a while Petrov ordered a bottle of vodka. The two men continued to discuss the situation, which was anything but rosy, not only in the Fiftieth Army sector but right along the front from the Gulf of Finland to the Black Sea. Shabulin noted in his diary that the Germans had driven a wedge into the Soviet front. According to Shabulin, the Red Army had as always lost its head and become incapable of action.[18]

Shabulin did not wake up until 8:00 a.m. on October 5. Three hours later he set out for the 260th Rifle Division, where he spent some time with the chief of staff. After a nap, wash and shave in the afternoon, Shabulin had an excellent supper with the commander of the special section, General Kleyman. The conversation mostly dealt with the 260th Rifle Division, which had not been pushed back during the preceding days. It was rumored that some German soldiers were fighting in little more than a field blouse, trousers and boots, and men were scavenging coats from fallen Soviet soldiers.[19]

The Thirteenth and Fiftieth armies were in grave danger of being surrounded by the Germans, particularly the Thirteenth Army. On October 6, the Soviet situation deteriorated further. The German XLVII Panzer Corps had been advancing north for a few days, behind the Soviet Fiftieth Army. The 18th Panzer Division advanced on the right wing, heading for Karachev, while the 17th Panzer Division on the left wing closed in on Bryansk.[20]

The Bryansk Front organized a task force commanded by Lieutenant General Maks Reiter to defend Karachev. Reiter was born in Ventspils, Latvia, and had joined the Red Army in 1919. At 55, he was one of the oldest officers. His force comprised the 108th Tank Division and the 194th Rifle Division. This Soviet countermeasure came too late, as Major General Walther Nehring's 18th Panzer Division approached Karachev rapidly. Major Ernst von Zeschau led tanks from the III Panzer Battalion of 18th Panzer Regiment, supported by panzer grenadiers, into Karachev, capturing it without much difficulty on October 5. His attack proceeded so

Major General Aleksandr Vasilevsky was one of Stalin's most important military advisors. He was promoted to Lieutenant General on 28 October 1941.

smoothly that it resembled a peacetime exercise. The only notable obstacle was a heavy KV tank, probably from the 108th Tank Division, which was encountered in the evening. By advancing rapidly, the Germans had fore-stalled the Soviet defensive measures. It only remained for the Bryansk Front to try to salvage as much as possible, as the loss of Bryansk itself could become a reality in a matter of days, or hours.[21]

The city of Bryansk dated from the 12th century and was mainly located on the western bank of the Desna. Recently, the part on the eastern side of the river had expanded significantly through the creation of many industrial plants; and the establishment of a major railroad station. At the outbreak of war, Bryank was home to approximately 80,000 inhabitants. Though Bryansk was not a major city, it was an important objective for the Germans, as vital roads and railroads converged there. Without this communication hub, it would be difficult to supply Guderian's units, should they continue to advance in a northeasterly direction.[22]

Tanks of the 39th Panzer Regiment and infantry from the 63rd Motorized Infantry Regiment led the 17th Panzer Division's attack on Bryansk. Under a beautiful autumn sky, the German force advanced on fairly good roads on October 5. It only met scattered resistance initially, but a wooden bridge proved too weak for the heavy vehicles and partially collapsed. Very cautiously, the German vehicles crossed one by one.[23]

In the afternoon, the rifle soldiers suddenly heard Soviet artillery fire. Soon afterwards the leading German tanks opened fire. A glance at the map revealed that the German force had reached a long tank ditch. The obstacle, located about 13 kilometers southwest of Karachev, did not appear insurmountable. The regimental commander followed the lead elements and quickly gave new instructions. An infantry battalion, supported by tanks and artillery, initiated an outflanking move.[24]

Fire from Soviet machine guns and 76.2mm guns reverberated as the German force set out on its outflanking move. The Germans pushed forward for a while, but eventually they realized that the attempt would not succeed without suffering heavy casualties. They promptly abandoned the plan. At that moment Lt. General Hans-Jürgen von Arnim, the division commander, arrived. He gave new instructions. The enemy forces ahead would be nailed to their positions while elements of 17th Panzer Division advanced behind some hills. The effort led to the capture of the village of Akulova, but as the sun set, fighting petered out.[25]

There was little rest for the soldiers during the night of October 5–6. Firefights broke out at irregular intervals. Although not heavy and costly, such skirmishes kept the soldiers awake. In the morning the Germans struck. They quickly broke through the Soviet defenses, but a destroyed bridge caused delay. Nevertheless, the lead German motorized infantry battalion and its attached tanks drove on towards Bryansk. They approached the city from the east and their most important goal was the Desna bridges.[26]

The German force passed forests and marshes before they saw the first buildings of Bryansk. Rash attacks into built-up areas were dangerous. Well concealed defenders could cause havoc when the attackers advanced along streets that offered little cover against bullets and exploding shells. Caution was usually vital, but this time the Germans gambled. They were pursuing a very important object and they believed that the Soviet defenses were disorganized. Risks were thus acceptable and the German force drove into Bryansk. Perhaps the soldiers recalled how Orel had been captured a few days before.[27]

Suddenly shells exploded around the Germans. They realized that the fire was direct and a few moments later they saw two heavy Soviet tanks. They drove straight towards the German column, in which a few vehicles were hit and caught fire. One of the Soviet tanks drove into a German vehicle and crushed it. Fortunately for the German infantry soldiers, friendly tanks appeared on the scene. One of the Soviet tanks was immobilized by a track hit and the other turned and disappeared.[28]

Meanwhile, another part of the German force had slipped around the Soviets and driven quickly towards the Desna bridges. The regiment commander was unaware of this group's mission, but he was soon informed on the radio that the bridges had been captured intact. The coup had thus succeeded. The important junction, with its bridges, roads and railroads was in German hands. This would bring many advantages for the Germans, as the success would enable them to improve their supply situation and also opened the way to continue north and cut off other Bryansk Front formations.[29]

Lieutenant Erich Bunke served in the antitank battalion, 31st Infantry Division, which was sent to clear the city. In his memoirs he described an incident which resembles events of far more recent wars. During a search of eastern Bryansk, Bunke's unit found a party assembly place. As at many other places in the Soviet Union, a statue of Lenin stood in the middle. The German soldiers decided to topple this statue, as they had many others before. A towing wire was attached to the neck of the figure and connected to a Krupp-Protze truck. The driver accelerated and brought the statue crashing down from its plinth. A few Russian women witnessed the act; Bunke thought they looked terrified.[30]

Major Shabulin was informed about the fall of Bryansk. He did not believe that the commanders were panic stricken, but clearly many of them were nervous. An attempt to retake Bryansk was prepared, but no report of success ever reached Shabulin. He realized that encirclement was imminent and he thought the front command had lost its head. He believed it would be better to let the individual armies act on their own.[31]

Of all the German armies and panzer groups, Hoepner's Panzer Group 4 was arguably in the best position. On October 5, the 10th Panzer

Division continued towards Vyazma. The division set out in a northerly direction from the Mosalsk area, led by motorized infantry and tanks. The division covered almost 30 kilometers (18 miles) during the day, which was a significant success and it was achieved despite fuel supply problems and broken bridges.[32]

The 10th Panzer Division's lead elements made even swifter progress on October 6, during which they gradually turned northwest. They continued after dusk and reached Vyazma before dawn on October 7. The main road from Smolensk to Moscow had been cut.[33]

For the Germans, the capture of Vyazma was a major victory, but it was not enough. They wanted to encircle the Soviet forces west of Vyazma, and in order to do that the spearheads of Panzer Group 3 and 4 needed to meet. Panzer Group 4 had to advance from the northwest, but by the evening of October 5, Hoth's most advanced unit was the 7th Panzer Division, which still had about 40 kilometers (25 miles) to cover before reaching Vyazma.[34]

The fuel situation improved sufficiently to allow the 7th Panzer Division to attack at dawn on October 6. The panzer regiment and reconnaissance battalion took the lead. The previous afternoon it seemed that a breakthrough had been achieved, and this was confirmed on October 6. The 7th Panzer Division rapidly approached Vyazma. It attacked so swiftly that it reached the city's main highway at 5:00 p.m. The 6th Panzer Division met stiffer resistance, but also made good headway as it attacked in a southeasterly direction. The success of the LVI Panzer Corps allowed the German to close the gap at Vyazma. Panzer Groups 3 and 4 could establish contact during the night of October 6–7.[35]

Hundreds of thousands of Soviet soldiers were trapped in the encirclement. Rokossovsky and his staff did manage to escape, but only just. They had arrived at Vyazma on October 6 to assume command over the troops that would counterattack in the Yukhnov area. The most senior commander at Vyazma was General Nikitin. As far as he knew, there were no regular units at Vyazma, only some militia formations. Nikitin and Rokossovsky went to the cathedral where the local party leadership had gathered. The situation deteriorated in the afternoon on October 6. Lestev, the commander of the political section of the West Front, was present and he was surprised to hear that no troops were available. He exclaimed: "How can this be possible? I have just arrived from the headquarters, which is moving to a new location. I was ensured that there would be at least five divisions waiting here, ready to be attached to the Sixteenth Army." They did not have any time to discuss the matter further as the alarm was raised: German tanks were in the city. Rokossovsky, Lestev and a few other officers went up the bell tower to look over the city. Glimpsing German vehicles they realized they had to leave Vyazma immediately as there were no units to defend the town. They barely managed to escape.[36]

The most important weapon for the German rifle squad was the machine gun MG-34. In the light machine gun role, it could be equipped with a bipod and 50-round drum-shaped magazine. The barrel was designed to be easily replaced to avoid overheating during sustained fire.

THEY WERE HANGED OUTSIDE THE WINDOW

After the German invasion, Soviet partisan units were soon formed behind German lines. A directive signed by Stalin and Molotov on June 29 set out the program for partisan operations in occupied territory. In many cases, partisan units were formed from soldiers who had been surrounded or cut off from their parent units. Partisan units were quite often commanded by NKVD officers, for example from the border troops. Partisan activity showed that there was still a Soviet presence, and even some limited control, in occupied areas.[37]

Before the invasion, the Germans had allocated units to maintain control over occupied enemy territory behind the German advance. Also, the German High Command assigned specific units to "cleanse" areas of Jews, although security and police units were also involved in this dirty business. Many Germans believed that Jews and Bolsheviks were almost the same kind of people, which led to the conclusion that if all Jews were shot, it would solve some of the Germans' other problems as well. Major General Baron von Bechtolsheim, commander of the 707th Infantry Division, captured the sentiment succinctly: "a Jew is a partisan, a partisan is a Jew." So eliminating Jews would mean that areas were also free of partisans. Units under von Bechtolsheim's command, whose staff was located in Minsk, killed 19,000 people during 1941.[38]

The Germans introduced public executions in occupied areas, believing such measures would frighten the population into submission. According to German authorities, partisans were bandits and terrorists, and their crimes justified capital punishment. Capital punishment became normal treatment for irregular forces captured by the Germans. General Gotthard Heinrici, commander of XLIII Corps, wrote in his diary on November 7:

> I told Beutelsbacher not to hang partisans within 100 meters from my window. It is not a pretty sight in the morning. Moy replied that Goethe had lived next to the gallows for three weeks in Jena.[39]

Lieutenant Beutelsbacher was an interpreter at the corps staff. He originated from Odessa and his family had suffered badly at the hands of the Bolsheviks. Together with the field police, he was constantly looking for partisans. Johannes Moy was an author and he served as interpreter on the staff.

The few railroads served as arteries for Army Group Center during Operation *Taifun* and they had to be protected against sabotage. Field Marshal von Kluge ordered his Fourth Army to place signs at all stations, crossroads etc, stating that the railroad was a prohibited area to anybody without valid documents:

> Anybody, who despite prohibition signs, appears illicitly at railroad areas will be executed. This should be pursued ruthlessly in every case.[40]

Execution was not confined to such cases. Prisoners of war could be shot when they no longer had the strength to march to camps, their only "crime" being exhaustion. The news of such killings spread like wildfire among the population, as noted by the propaganda department at Army Group Center. General Alfred Jodl at the OKW suggested that new phrases be used, such as: "prisoners stopped not because they lacked strength, but because they did not want to march." Apparently the solution was not better treatment, but better propaganda.[41]

The German propaganda offered liberation from the so-called Jewish-Bolshevik yoke, but public executions sent another message: a new yoke would replace the old one.

One popular German move was the reopening of many churches. The Orthodox Church had been very important in Russia before the Bolshevik assumption of power. Major General Lothar Rendulic, commander of the 52nd Infantry Division described his impression of Kaluga:

> There were a number of prominent buildings and multi-story buildings in Kaluga from the tsar's days, when Kaluga was a regional administrative center. However much of the city and the suburbs was built of wood. Among the surprisingly many churches, there were a few whose architectural beauty left a deep impression.

> When Rendulic began to think about the unfortunate people who had managed to create such edifices despite their poverty, he regarded the churches as an illuminating example of misuse of the people. However, such misuse was in the spirit of the times.[42]

A fundamental problem for defenders on the Eastern Front was the sheer size of the theatre. Inevitably, the length of front to defend would be great, making it difficult to concentrate defensive artillery fire, as the guns were spread out thinly. The attacker, who held the initiative, could more easily concentrate assets to the critical sectors.

SEVEN

CUT OFF

The German art of war recommended encirclement operations. They had figured prominently in Poland and Western Europe, and would figure even more prominently during Operation *Barbarossa*. On many occasions, the Germans cut off and captured very large enemy forces. During the very first weeks of Operation *Barbarossa*, huge Soviet forces were encircled in the Bialystok area and about 300,000 prisoners were captured. Major encirclements also took place at the battles at Smolensk and Uman, where enormous numbers of Soviet soldiers became prisoners. The largest encirclement operation had taken place in the Kiev area during September.

Encircling the enemy meant that his supply lines were cut, he couldn't escape by retreating, and so he was forced to fight at a disadvantage. This enabled the Germans to inflict severe losses without suffering more than modest casualties themselves. The encirclement scenario would now be repeated, on a grand scale. Not only were Soviet units about to be cut off at Vyazma, Guderian's Panzer Army had maneuvered itself into a position from where it could encircle further Soviet forces north and west of Bryansk. It is impossible to tell exactly how many Soviet soldiers were in danger of being encircled, but 750,000 seems to be a realistic estimate.

To command such a large force in this very perilous situation was a challenging task indeed. Ammunition depots and other vital stores had to be protected from roaming German panzers. Soviet officers commanding those units encircled had to adapt to the new situation immediately and they had to take into consideration the effect of encirclement on their men's morale.

Soviet commanders outside the German pincers also faced difficult decisions. While they could try to relieve the encircled units, this was hardly a realistic option. No such attempt had succeeded before and the resources available between the German spearheads and Moscow were insufficient. It was more realistic to try to slow the German attempts to advance on Moscow, an aim which would be furthered if the encircled armies tied up German units for as long as possible.

Efforts to rebuild defenses west of Moscow were initiated. On October 6, a Stavka directive ordered the creation of the Mozhaisk Defense Line. Units were ordered to take up positions along the line, but the line was not entirely new. Back on July 18, Lt. General Pavel Artemev, commander of the Moscow Military District, had received an order from Zhukov, then chief of staff at the Stavka, to prepare the Mozhaisk line with three reserve armies. This preparation continued until the end of July, when the Germans appeared to halt in the Smolensk area and fighting raged in the Yartzevo-Elnya-Roslavl-Mogilev area instead.[1]

Four towns were pivotal to the new defense line west of Moscow: Volokolamsk, Mozhaisk, Maloyaroslavets, and Kaluga, located along a 230-kilometer (143-mile) long line. Tula anchored the southern end of the line. Almost every military resource that could be found in the Moscow area was sent to the new line. Reinforcements included a hastily cobbled-together regiment of students from the Supreme Soviet RSFSR Military School, which was sent to Volokolamsk. Students from the Moscow Military-Political School were sent to Mozhaisk and students from two military schools in Podolsk were transported to Maloyaroslavets.[2]

On October 10 Vasiljevsky was travelling back to Moscow after visiting the front. He used the opportunity to direct units that had successfully disengaged, instructing them to move to certain parts of the defense line. He was assisted by the artillery commander of the Reserve Front, Major General Leonid Govorov, who possessed two truck columns.[3]

Many Soviet reinforcements were rushed forward, and one example was a force sent in the direction of Orel. It would soon fight a small battle near Mtsensk, which has become fairly well known, but unfortunately, misunderstood almost as often as it has been described. The story began on September 30, when Maj. General Dmitri Lelyushenko was working at his desk at the main office of the tank troops. He received an order to appear at the Stavka after midnight. He was puzzled, as he had just submitted his report on the formation of new tank brigades. During the past month, he had worked hard to provide the new brigades with men and equipment. The order, however, did not leave him with any choice. Lelyushenko departed and went through a dark and desolate Moscow to meet Stalin.

The Soviet dictator did not keep Lelyushenko waiting. He remembered that comrade Dmitri had asked for a command at the front and now he would have his chance. Stalin entrusted him with the 1st Guards Rifle Corps and gave Lelyushenko the task of halting Guderian's advance in the Orel area. It was a brief meeting, and Stalin then sent Lelyushenko to Shaposhnikov, who would take care of all necessary details.[4]

Shaposhnikov quickly briefed Lelyushenko. He would have four to five days to form a corps comprising two guards rifle divisions, two tank brigades, and supporting units. He also received command over the 6th Reserve Aviation Group with its four aviation regiments. He immediately began to gather a staff by calling colleagues and friends. Major General Aleksey Kurkin from the tank troops became Lelyushenko's deputy.

Lelyushenko was summoned to appear at the Stavka again late on October 1. As well as Stalin, he met Voroshilov, Mikoyan and Shaposhnikov. The deteriorating situation had motivated the hastily summoned meeting. Lelyushenko was told that he had to assemble his units in two days rather than five. He was ordered to fly to Orel with Pavel Zhigarev, who commanded the air force, to investigate the situation in the Orel area personally. Lelyushenko objected to this as there were no units available in the area. He preferred to assume command of the 36th Motorcycle Regiment in Moscow and travel by road to Tula, where he could attach units from the artillery school before proceeding to Orel. Stalin endorsed the plan. Lelyushenko immediately phoned the commander of the motorcycle regiment and ordered him to have his unit ready within two hours.[5]

When Lelyushenko arrived at Tula on October 2, the artillery pieces, including 152mm howitzers, 76.2mm guns and 45mm antitank guns, were assembled at the exercise field, but no prime movers were immediately available. Lelyushenko requisitioned buses from the city to tow the guns. His headquarters arrived at Mtsensk the following morning. Mtsensk was a small town about 50 kilometers (30 miles) northeast of Orel, with canning plants for meat and fruit. According to the original plan, Lelyushenko and his staff would have arrived on October 4, gathered the units on October 5 and advanced southwest on October 6.

Everything did not go according to plan, but on October 4 Lelyushen-ko reconnoitred. He soon met four motorcycles, one of which was ridden by Lt. Colonel I.I. Piyashev, commander of the 34th NKVD Regiment. Piyashev told Lelyushenko that he had been ordered to go to Orel, but Lelyushenko instead ordered him and his regiment to become part of the 1st Guards Rifle Corps and to take up defensive positions across the Orel–Mtsensk road and await the arrival of further units from the corps.

At the same time, Colonel Mikhail Katukov's 4th Tank Brigade began to arrive at Mtsensk railroad station. Katukov and Lelyushenko met in the afternoon and agreed that further reconnaissance was needed as they had no idea where Guderian's tanks were. Later that afternoon, Lelyushenko was informed that one more tank brigade was on its way. However, the ink on the order had hardly dried before it was countermanded: the brigade would be directed to Yukhnov instead. The 4th Tank Brigade remained attached to Lelyushenko and it took up defensive positions along the river Optukha, next to the NKVD units, on the night of October 4–5.[6]

Early on October 5, Katukov got a foretaste of something that would soon have a profound influence on operations. Rain turned the roads that his motorcycles would reconnoitre into a morass. The motorcyclists tried to procure horses in nearby villages, in the hope of restoring some of the unit's mobility. On the same day, further reinforcements, in the form of the 6th Guards Rifle Division and the 11th Tank Brigade, arrived at the Mtsensk railroad station. To Lelyushenko's disappointment, the 5th Guards Rifle Division was redirected—to Medyn—just like the tank brigade he had almost received. Stavka regarded the German advance further north, in the Yukhnov area, as very threatening. The units that actually arrived at Mtsensk were directed to the Perviy Voin area, where they took up positions on hills and ridges, from which they could observe most of the area in front of them.[7]

On October 6, Katukov received an unexpected visitor. An orderly came to the staff and reported that a Captain Chumak wanted to speak with him. Katukov did not recognize the visitor's name, but was informed that he had arrived on orders from Lelyushenko. Chumak presented himself as the commander of a rocket artillery battalion and his orders were to support Katukov. The tank brigade commander had never heard or seen the weapon in action but had heard about its great effect. There were rumors that it provoked dread in the enemy. Katukov and a few staff officers came out to take a look at the strange weapon, but the sight of it did not impress them. Katukov wrote: "In front of us we saw an ordinary truck with protruding steel rails." Chumak realized that the officers were sceptical and said. "Just wait! When the organ plays for the first time, you will change your opinion." Later, after seeing the battalion in action, Katukov admitted that he had been deeply impressed.[8]

The 1st Guards Rifle Corps was not the only major formation sent to halt Guderian. It was also joined by the 5th Airborne Corps. Two of its brigades, the 10th and 201st, were ready. Colonel S. S. Guryev, who commanded the corps, was ordered to air transport his units from Kolomna and Tula to the airfield at Orel on October 3 and defend the city. However, when the first soldiers landed, they were met by enemy fire, as Guderian's tanks had already captured Orel. Only parts of the 201st Airborne Brigade actually landed at Orel airfield. The other parts of the corps were redirected to the field at Optukha, northeast of Orel along the Orel–Mtsensk road. Almost 5,000 soldiers arrived by air transport and they would subsequently fight with Lelyushenko's corps.[9]

The 4th Panzer Division had been unable to maintain the speed of its advance after capturing Orel, due to the difficulties caused by its long supply lines. Also, troops had to be diverted to other tasks, reducing the strength of the attacking force. Nevertheless, a small battle group did advance on Mtsensk on October 5. In the evening it formed a hedgehog defense approximately two to three kilometers north of a small river, Legoshcha. At midnight the battle group received orders to advance towards Mtsensk at dawn.[10]

No major German attack on Mtsensk could be launched at this time: the battle group only consisted of one motorcycle battalion, one panzer battalion, an additional panzer company, and supporting artillery and antiaircraft guns. Although the bulk of the 4th Panzer Division was committed elsewhere, the battle group set out at 9:00 a.m. on October 6.[11]

A bridge spanning a ravine had been blown up, but the Germans were able to cross it regardless. The small German force rapidly continued towards the small river Lisitsa, where they captured a bridge before it was blown up. Beyond the river, elevated ground afforded the Soviet defenders a dominating position and they opened fire from tanks and antitank guns. Despite unfavorable circumstances, the Germans managed to neutralize the defenders.[12]

When they continued their attack, the Germans were met by fire from heavy Soviet tanks, which knocked out one German tank, although the crew managed to bail out. The Soviet tanks fired at a range of about 1,500 meters, which exceeded the effective range of the weak German tank guns. However, the German force brought better weapons—one 10cm gun and two 8.8cm antiaircraft guns—which were deadly even at long range.[13]

The fighting flowed back and forth. The large German guns proved very effective against the Soviet tanks, but they were also very vulnerable. Both 8.8cm guns were knocked out by Soviet tank fire, but the Germans managed to push back the Soviet tanks that attacked from the hills. The price of this success was nine German tanks damaged or destroyed, but casualties were low. Unfortunately, no reliable information on Soviet losses has been found.[14]

After the battle, the Germans retreated across the river they had crossed earlier, but the Soviet tanks also pulled back. At nightfall, a blizzard concealed movements. When it cleared in the morning, German reconnaissance indicated that there were no enemy forces ahead. The Germans again moved to the eastern side of the Lisitsa river, but soon a Panzer III was hit, which persuaded the Germans to stop the advance and take up defensive positions.[15]

The action fought between Orel and Mtsensk has resulted in a number of myths. It has been claimed that most of the 4th Panzer Division's tanks were lost, but actually only six were irrevocably lost. It has been argued that the German division suffered a major defeat southeast of Mtsensk, but as the bulk of the division was not even there, such a claim is untenable.[16]

It has also been argued that Soviet counterattacks, of the kind conducted by Katukov's 4th Tank Brigade, halted Operation *Taifun*.[17] This appears to be a gross exaggeration. The battle at Mtsensk was very small compared to the gigantic battle fought west of Moscow. Furthermore, nothing in the war diaries of the German panzer groups suggest that battles of this kind were more than pinpricks.[18]

If anything, the German commanders were more worried about attacks from the surrounded forces. Panzer Group 4, as well as Field Marshal von Bock, were anxious to capitalize on the enemy's weakness in the area between Hoepner's panzer group and Moscow. They did not expect any problems with Soviet counterattacks. Rather, they wanted to strike while the iron was hot.[19]

On October 7, Guderian received orders to advance on Tula, but the snow that had fallen during the night made the roads very soft and muddy. The consequences were serious. It would take much longer to bring necessary supplies to the Orel area, and the shifting of forces to the area southwest of Mtsensk would also be hampered. The small battle group in the area was far to weak too capture Tula on its own. Furthermore, Guderian also had to close the ring around the Soviet forces not yet fully encircled in the Bryansk area. This would tie up resources, so attacks on Tula would have to wait for the time being.[20]

Contemporary German sources, such as unit war diaries and personal diaries, show that the Germans did not notice any particular pressure from Soviet units east of the pincers. The encircled Soviet forces did cause the Germans some worries, as mopping up the cauldrons would take some time. The condition of the roads was quite frequently discussed, as this was a problem that would grow to monumental proportions. The problems of weather and the encircled troops combined to make the German advance east difficult.[21]

■ ■ ■

By encircling Bryansk, the Germans had improved their chances of encircling Eremenko's northern wing. Guderian, however, had causes for concern. Snow and rain on October 6 had made the roads wet and the bad weather continued on October 7. The roads deteriorated rapidly. It was noted in the Second Panzer Army war diary that the roads were very muddy and in many places completely impassable.[22]

The change in the weather heralded the coming of winter. No winter clothing had yet been issued to the German soldiers, and the Second Panzer Army had not received lubricants for vehicles or artillery that was usable for low temperatures. The Second Panzer Army sent two clear messages about the recent blizzards and the lack of winter equipment to the quartermaster general and to the central army quartermaster office, asking in plain language where winter uniforms and antifreeze could be found.[23]

However winter was still a relatively remote problem, completely overshadowed by the boggy autumn roads. Guderian's units were spread over a large area and he still had to seal off the encirclement north and west of Bryansk. A gap between Second Army and Second Panzer Army remained. The mud made shifting units and closing the gap much more demanding.

As if these problems were not enough, Guderian also received an order instructing him to capture Kursk, a mission given to the XLVIII Panzer Corps. It had operated along the Kursk axis since September 30. The task was thus not entirely new, but it nevertheless confirmed that Guderian's resources were scattered.[24]

The shape of the front line allowed the Germans to create two smaller pockets, one south of Bryansk and one to the north. The Second Army closed in on Bryansk from the west. As the 17th Panzer Division had already captured Bryansk, the Soviet Thirteenth Army could be bagged and the important railroad from Roslavl to Bryansk could also be brought under German control. Further Soviet forces could be encircled north of the railroad.[25]

■ ■ ■

Major Shabulin was by now well aware of the looming danger of encirclement. He was informed quite early on the morning of October 7 that it had been decided to move the staff from the location where it had been for quite some time. Although he had no choice, Shabulin found it slightly sad to abandon the earth hut in the grove where he had spent so much of the past month. Shabulin noted in his diary that all three armies of the Bryansk Front, close to 240,000 men, might be encircled and destroyed.[26]

It was said that an order from Moscow had been issued, instructing all armies to pull back. Shabulin believed this would cause all soldiers to flee in panic. Not one single Soviet aircraft had been seen in the preceding days, and cities were abandoned without a fight. The fortifications, created with so much effort, would now be abandoned. Temporary command over the Bryansk Front forces north of Guderian's breakthrough was given to General Petrov, the commander of Fiftieth Army. Shabulin met him and an eerie conversation took place:

"I will soon be shot," Petrov said.

"Why?" Shabulin asked.

"Well, I have been appointed temporary commander of the front."

"If you have been designated as commander, you will have to take control and do everything for victory."

"Oh yes, but you know how serious the situation is. We don't even know where the Third and Thirteenth armies are."[27]

Shabulin knew all too well how bad the situation was, and it would yet deteriorate further. The retreat continued. An artillery ammunition dump was blown up. Shabulin saw the enormous glow of fire when the ammunition detonated. Some areas on the other hand showed no sign of fighting when Shabulin arrived. In one hamlet, all the villagers had stayed and were busy harvesting potatoes. None of them appeared to know anything about the fighting at the front, but then even Shabulin did not have much information. As Red Army communications heavily relied on telephone lines, timely information was much harder to obtain once units began to move.[28]

While Shabulin and hundreds of thousands of Soviet soldiers tried to escape encirclement, the Germans made strong efforts to close the pockets. The cauldron at Vyazma was sealed off even tighter, and two pockets were formed north and southwest of Bryansk. A German bulletin announced that a second pocket had been created near Bryansk. This infuriated von Bock and he phoned Halder to emphasize that he had never deliberately spoken about a pocket at Bryansk, as the cordon was thinly manned. He pointed out that two Soviet attempts to break out had been repelled only with great difficulty.[29]

It wasn't only bulletins interfering with von Bock's work; at about 3:00 p.m. on October 10 he received an order from Hitler. It told him to send the 19th Panzer Division and the Grossdeutschland Regiment to Guderian immediately. The purpose was to prevent Soviet forces encircled south of Bryansk from breaking out.[30]

Exasperated, von Bock sent a reply in which he explained that the 19th Panzer Division was at the moment fighting in the Yukhnov area. Should it be turned south, it would cross roads badly needed for supply purposes. Furthermore, the supply situation in the area Hitler wanted to send the 19th Panzer Division was very bad. The vehicles might well arrive low on fuel and be unable to find any fuel to top up. Von Bock demanded a decision concerning the roads: should priority be given to moving units or supplies?[31]

Von Bock's objections produced the desired result. The 19th Panzer Division would not be sent south. Rather, it would continue to attack in a northeasterly direction. He did not manage to keep the Grossdeutschland Regiment where he wanted though. It was directed south, albeit not as far south as von Bock had feared. One pocket had been formed south of Bryansk and one north of Bryansk. The Grossdeutschland Regiment would be engaged at the latter.[32]

The problems von Bock encountered cannot overshadow the fact that the German offensive had thus far been an overwhelming success. Most of the Soviet forces covering the approaches to Moscow had been encircled. Considering the even force ratio at the beginning of the operation, this had been accomplished remarkably quickly, and at low cost to the Germans. As the pockets were rather shallow, the infantry could very soon take an active part in the mopping up. This would free panzer and motorized divisions for the continued offensive eastward. The weather remained the major German concern, as mud could quickly immobilize lorries and horse-drawn vehicles.

At least 700,000 Soviet soldiers were caught in the cauldrons, and already in the second week of October many of them began to surrender. There were other Soviet units that would not give up easily, such as the 242nd Rifle Division. Many German units were also moving in the area it retreated through, but the Germans were headed for Kalinin and Moscow. Marching north, the remnants of 242nd Division reached the main road between Sychevka and Rzhev near Ossuga on October 9. There they were attacked by German ground and air units. Under cover of darkness, the Soviet soldiers managed to escape and march about 20 kilometers north. A patrol reported on October 11 that approximately 25 to 30 kilometers remained to the front line. The sergeant commanding the patrol pointed at the map and said that it was incorrect. He showed where a hamlet, a small bridge leading to it and a railroad were located but not indicated on the map. Also, there were 15 sealed railroad cars on the tracks. With the patrol leading the way, Captain Dragunsky set off with a battalion to the area the sergeant had indicated. They hoped to find weapons and ammunition in the cars, but instead they found food, household equipment and iron products. The soldiers took as much flour, grain and coffee as they could carry and brought it to the field kitchens. At last the men had plenty to eat. The experience showed them they could not always trust the maps and they had to scout the terrain ahead.

By using the bridge found by the patrol, Dragunsky reached the hamlet. He and an orderly knocked on the door of one of the houses. A woman opened the door. Dragunsky thought that her sad face did not encourage conversation. For some reason, Dragunsky commented on this and asked her why she was so negative. That was a mistake: "What did you expect? That we would be dancing with joy?" Her reply was given with a stern voice and she went on to say that everything was lost and ruined. Dragunsky tried put new heart into the woman and said that it was not altogether bad. The woman did not relent and burst out:

> You always retreat, always pulling back, leaving us to the mercy of the enemy. But we expect you to protect us. I presume you are here to ask how you find your way back? Soldiers appear all the time, but they only have one thought, how to get to Rzhev. So far, not one of them has asked about the way to the west.

Dragunsky calmed the woman and they left each other as friends. Dragunsky promised to return and he kept his promise, as he came to see the woman in 1945 when he travelled from Moscow to participate in the Berlin operation.[33]

▪ ▪ ▪

Stalin gradually became convinced he needed a new commander to handle the crisis at Vyazma. The present set of commanders appeared not to be up to the task, but there were not many other suitable candidates. One alternative was to recall Marshal Timoshenko from the Ukraine, but Stalin was not convinced he was the man for the job.

The best remaining alternative was the 45-year-old General Georgiy Zhukov, who commanded the Leningrad Front at the beginning of October. He had held that appointment for a month and been responsible for the defense of the second largest city in the Soviet Union. The former Stavka representative, Marshal Voroshilov, was seen to have done more harm than service when he was responsible for the defense of Leningrad. This had prompted Stalin to send Zhukov to organize the defense of the great city on the Neva River. Zhukov's task was simple and clear: prevent the Germans from capturing Leningrad. On October 5, Zhukov received a telegram, informing him that Stalin wanted to talk to him. Stalin told Zhukov to fly to Moscow, to discuss the grave situation. Zhukov answered that he could fly the next morning. However, delays prevented him from departing and he did not take off until October 7.[34]

Zhukov possessed many of the characteristics Stalin needed for the dangerous situation west of Moscow. He was hard, tough and fearless. He did not wait to get a clear picture. Instead, he tried to solve the problem immediately—often by resorting to attack—a procedure that was often costly. Zhukov believed a certain amount of competition between his subordinate commanders was sound, as he thought it spurred them to make greater efforts. The tough general also possessed something resembling a gambler's mentality. The losses of the past days were history and he did not go around fretting over them. He looked forward and tried to handle the situation as it was and come out victorious next time.

When Zhukov arrived on October 7, he quickly realized that the situation was chaotic. First he visited Konev and the West Front. Then he proceeded to the Reserve Front to speak with Budjonny. Unfortunately, no one could tell him the exact location of the headquarters. It was supposed to be somewhere near Maloyaroslavets, a small town that had had about 10,000 inhabitants before the war. At the Obninskoe railroad station, Zhukov found soldiers laying telephone wire, suggesting a staff might be nearby. He was right, the front headquarters had arrived at its new location two hours earlier. Zhukov met the army commissar, L.Z. Mekhlis, and the chief of staff, A.F. Anisov. He asked where Budjonny was, but none of the officers could tell him. They knew Budjonny had gone to visit the Forty-Third Army the previous day, but they did not know what had happened to him since.

Zhukov decided to go to the Yukhnov area to investigate. He travelled past the village Strelkovka, where he had grown up. It turned out that the new Reserve Front headquarters was located about ten kilometers from his childhood home. Zhukov used the opportunity to ensure that his mother and sister, with her children, were evacuated. When he arrived at Maloyaroslavets, Zhukov at first got the impression that the town was completely deserted, but soon he found two cars parked next to the local party headquarters at the center. They turned out to belong to Budjonny. Zhukov entered the building and found Budjonny leaning over a map. They shook hands and Budjonny asked: "Where do you come from?" "From Konev," Zhukov replied. Budjonny continued: "How is the situation over there? We haven't had any contact with the West Front for the past two days. Yesterday, when I visited Forty-Third Army, the front headquarters moved and I don't know where it is."

Zhukov replied that he had found the headquarters and told Budjonny its location. The two high-ranking officers parted, and on October 8 Zhukov assumed command of the Reserve Front. Two days later the West and Reserve fronts were combined under Zhukov.[35]

Zhukov's new role was not the only change in the Soviet chain of command west of Moscow. Lieutenant General Artemev was again made responsible for the defense of the Mozhaisk area when the Moscow Reserve Front was created under his command on October 9. A few days later, on October 12, a new order placed the Moscow Reserve Front units under Zhukov.[36]

• • •

Zhukov sent an order to all his subordinate units on October 13. It clearly outlined what units commanded by him could expect, including the warning that those who deserted their positions without permission would be executed on the spot. The order concluded with the phrase: "Not one step back! Forward for the Motherland!"[37]

While Zhukov was trying to impose himself on the West Front, his old friend and fellow cavalry commander, Lieutenant General Rokossovsky was trying to find his way back to the Soviet lines with his staff after their precipitate escape from Vyazma. The group tried to escape in a northeasterly direction, towards Gzhatsk. They soon met an NKVD cavalry squadron, which attached itself to the group of officers. The squadron proved very useful for scouting and patrolling.

Skirmishes with German recon units occasionally erupted. When the Soviet force reached a small village, they paused to eat some food. Rokossovsky took cover in a house together with Malinin and a few other officers. While a young solider was reporting to Rokossovsky after patrolling, a voice from a dark corner of the house interrupted: "What will you do now, comrade commander?"

Rokossovsky turned around and found an old, grey-bearded man lying in the bed. The man's eyes were fixed on Rokossovsky and with distressed voice he uttered: "Comrade commander, go on and leave us here in the lurch. Have we not given everything we have to the Red Army?"

Rokossovsky felt stung by the old man's words. The old man went on to say that he was a former soldier who had fought against the Germans. They had not allowed enemies to enter Russia, but what had happened now? Rokossovsky and his fellow officers tried to convince the man that the setbacks were only temporary and that they would soon be back. Their words did not appear to convince the old man, who ended the conversation by saying that he was ailing, otherwise he would himself have taken part in the defense of Russia.[38]

The march towards Gzhatsk was resumed, and after a while the group finally joined the 18th Rifle Division, a militia division of the Thirty-Third Army that was retreating eastward. On October 9, safety was finally reached.

Upon his return, Rokossovsky received an order that he should report to the front headquarters. His chief of staff Malinin had a feeling that there was something in the wind and recommended that Rokossovsky should bring the written order he had received before he left his army. As Malinin had anticipated, Rokossovsky was tried by a tribunal for insubordination, but was acquitted thanks to the written order.

The Vyazma-Bryansk disaster was the worst calamity suffered yet by Russia in World War II. The Kiev operation had been a huge disaster for the Red Army, but Vyazma-Bryansk was turning into the greatest encirclement battle in history, with the number of prisoners exceeding those taken in previous battles.

AWE-INSPIRING WEAPONS

Both sides used rocket artillery on the Eastern Front. The main advantage of such weapons was their ability to release a large number of warheads in quick succession at a target area. However, accuracy was poor and the projectiles would consequently be spread over a larger area than conventional artillery. In the German army, the rocket artillery was called "Nebelwerfer" which means "fog launcher." There was already an older weapons system with that name, which was used to project artificial fog on the battlefield. Two different kinds of mortars had been developed for this purpose, the Nebelwerfer 35 and the 10cm Nebelwerfer 40. To disguise the new weapon, it was given the same name as the system already in use. This was probably not intended to be any more than temporary, but the name would linger. Not until 1944 did the more accurate term "Raketenwerfer" (rocket launcher) come in use. The Red Army also used cover names. All rocket artillery units received the designation "Guards Mortar Units," which has caused confusion in published books on the Eastern Front.

The Red Army had no combat-ready rocket artillery units on June 22, 1941, but development proceeded swiftly. Combat trials with 82mm rockets launched from aircraft had been made when fighting the Japanese in Mongolia in 1939. The Red Army began by forming units with two different rockets, M-8 82mm and M-13 132mm, with launchers fitted to vehicles, primarily lorries. The former rocket had a range of 5 kilometers, while the latter could hit targets at a distance of 8.5 kilometers. The weapons were nicknamed Katyusha by the Soviet troops, while the Germans called them "Stalin organs," because of their howling sound.

On July 5, 1941, Red Army Captain Ivan Flyorov's battery opened fire with its 132mm launchers, which were fitted to heavy trucks. This attack on units of German Army Group Center was the combat debut for Soviet rocket artillery. (See Appendix 20 for the expansion of Soviet rocket artillery units.)[39]

Unlike the Red Army, the Germans decided to mount their 15cm rocket launchers on carriages, which required a vehicle to tow them. In addition to these systems, both armies had heavier rockets. The launchers for these were simply placed on the ground. They required more time to prepare for fire, but the larger calibers were more lethal. Initially, the Red Army used 200mm rockets, but later introduced a 300mm version. The Germans had 28cm and 32cm versions. There were two different kinds of payloads available: conventional high-explosive and a kind of incendiary variant based on diesel oil.

When launching Operation *Barbarossa*, the Germans had five rocket artillery regiments, each with three battalions. Each battalion had 18 launchers of the type Nebelwerfer 15cm/41. It had six barrels and could fire rockets with a range of up to seven kilometers. A battalion could release a salvo of 108 rockets against its target. The model had been in production since 1940 and it would be manufactured until the end of the war. In addition, some engineer units had launchers designed for placement on the ground. Also, the Germans had developed a special system for the engineer units in panzer divisions. A company with armored half-tracks could have rocket launchers fitted to the sides of the vehicle. This was first used in fighting at the river Lama west of Moscow in November 1941.[40]

German research in rocket-propelled weapons dated back to the 1920s, when the German armed forces still clandestinely conducted research together with the Soviet Union. Germany needed training and testing facilities for weapons prohibited by the Versailles Treaty, while the Red Army got insight into new technology of which it only had limited or no experience, such as tanks and submarines. However, the clauses of the Versailles Treaty did not mention rocket artillery so the Germans could do their research, development and testing at home, while the Red Army worked alone.[41]

Neither side appears to have been aware of the other's development of rocket artillery, and the very fact that the Soviet work was shrouded in great secrecy suggests a lack of awareness that the Germans already had such weapons. The Germans were equally unaware of Soviet development of rocket artillery. The first report submitted to OKH on Soviet rocket artillery was dated August 7, 1941, when Katyushas were used in the Elnya battle.[42]

EIGHT

STRATEGIC DECISIONS

With most of the defenders west of Moscow in the bag, the Germans had many options. Obviously they would have to defeat and capture the encircled enemy forces, but the senior commanders had to think a few steps beyond that task. In fact, the situation outside Moscow was intimately linked to the entire German war effort. Many decisions taken before Operation *Barbarossa* would have dire consequences unless Operation *Taifun* produced the intended success.

When Hitler decided to attack the Soviet Union, industrial production and raw material issues were also considered. The war in the west dragged on and the Germans believed that, sooner or later, the United States would join Britain. Indeed, some influential German decision-makers already regarded the United States as a clandestine British ally. By spring 1941, no rapid conclusion to the war in the west could be envisaged. To the contrary, everything suggested the struggle would be protracted. In 1941, the situation was still favorable to the Germans, who did not see an immediate threat in the west. Thus there was a window of opportunity, which the Germans could use to defeat the Soviet Union.[1]

A war with the Soviet Union would first and foremost be a task for the army, while the navy and air force would play the lead role in the war against the western powers. This meant that production of army weapons and equipment received high priority during 1940 and the first half of 1941. Very soon after German forces crossed the Soviet border, the focus of production shifted to equipment needed by the air force and navy. The assumptions on which these decisions were based also resulted in the lack of winter equipment for Army Group Center.[2]

As it took months or even years to prepare for new production, it was impossible to change priorities on short notice. The consequences of decisions could thus linger long and this was exactly the danger facing the Germans in October 1941. Armaments production had already begun to give lower priority to army weapons and munitions, so prolonged fighting in Russia could turn out to be very problematic. Furthermore, the invasion of the Soviet Union had been expected to result in new supplies of important raw materials, particularly crude oil, which was badly needed for the German war effort.[3]

The Germans had, effectively, already mortgaged the expected victory over the Soviet Union. If Stalin's empire did not fall, the Germans would have many problems in addition to continued fighting on the Eastern Front. They risked shortages of weapons and ammunition for the army units fighting in the east, which instead of being reduced in number would probably have to be reinforced. Furthermore, the war in the west continued to require vast amounts of fuel oil and aviation gasoline, and the Germans were counting on using the oil fields in the Caucasus to supplement their limited resources. All this meant that anything short of a decisive victory at Moscow could have serious repercussions on the entire German war effort. A heavy responsibility rested on von Bock's shoulders, and as he would discover, he would not be allowed to make decisions without interference from above.[4]

Field Marshal von Bock had feared adverse weather even before Operation *Taifun* was launched. The second week of October confirmed his worst fears. As the roads became ever muddier, von Bock's offensive ground to a halt. The consequences of the delay were so terrible that they were almost unbearable to consider. The overall strategic situation almost forced the Germans to stake everything to achieve a decisive success. However, such gambling might be very dangerous to Army Group Center. As the entire German grand strategy was a gamble, there were few alternatives available and it would eventually become clear that Army Group Center was the forfeit placed on the table.

However, in mid-October, Army Group Center was not in a dangerous position. The first phase had been a resounding success, and the encircled Soviet units could be defeated without much difficulty. On October 10, von Bock visited the 87th Infantry Division, where he was given an optimistic description of the situation. The division was engaged in the

As the partisans grew stronger, Luftwaffe personal were deployed for anti-partisan warfare. The Luftwaffe soldiers here are armed with MP-34 (ö) submachine guns, originally produced for the Austrian police forces.

efforts to reduce the pocket west of Vyazma. It had actually lost contact with the enemy, suggesting that only weak opposition remained. The division commander estimated that over 200,000 prisoners had already been captured by the German forces that had sealed off the cauldron.[5]

Hence, von Bock was not unduly concerned about the encircled Soviet troops in the immediate future. On the morning of October 11, the army high command asked him how he wanted to conduct future operations. He sat down to draft a written proposal, but had not completed this when an explicit directive from the army high command ordered him to capture Kalinin. This was puzzling, as a thrust towards Kalinin—as the city of Tver was called 1931–90—would mean a deviation from the general objective of Moscow. Admittedly, the city had previously rivalled Moscow for commercial trade on the upper Volga, but in the 20th century, Kalinin was no longer a rival to the great city further south. About 250,000 people lived in Kalinin, which was an important inland port. There were also many industries in the suburbs. The central parts of Kalinin had been rebuilt according to a uniform plan after being ravaged by fire in the 18th century. In October 1941, the city was poorly prepared to withstand a German assault.[6]

The reasoning behind the shocking directive was that decision-makers in Berlin had seen an opportunity for army groups Center and North to clinch the area northwest of Kalinin, allowing them to cut the railroad between Moscow and Leningrad. However, it is debatable whether that railroad was of much importance to the Red Army in its current critical situation.

For the moment, Panzer Group 3 was the only German force that could attack towards Kalinin, but it could only send part of its forces, as it was plagued by supply problems. Nevertheless, the army high command's decision left von Bock with only Panzer Group 4 and Fourth Army to attack towards Moscow.[7]

Field Marshal von Bock was pleased to hear that the encircled Soviet soldiers were rapidly surrendering. On October 12 he noted that the number of prisoners had grown dramatically. His staff monitored the situation, and two days later they assessed the Soviet defenses west of Moscow as being very weak.[8] The weakness of the enemy suggested that no imminent danger loomed, at least for the foreseeable future. Army Group Center could continue planning and von Bock reluctantly included the capture of Kalinin in his plans. That evening, von Bock discussed the plan with von Brauchitsch and the latter endorsed it. Early on October 13, von Bock met Colonel Adolf Heusinger, head of OKH's operations section. Heusinger said that Hitler had decided that Moscow would be surrounded and that the inner ring around the city would not be tighter than the circular railroad around the outskirts of the capital.[9]

Hitler's directive left little room for interpretation. As Moscow was to be surrounded, the offensive should continue. There was also another important implication. The Soviet capital would not be captured as soon as possible, but surrounded. This was not a sudden impulse from Hitler. Rather, it was the logical conclusion of a train of thought that had begun several months earlier.

Many influential persons in Germany feared serious food shortages. Germany had periodically experienced starvation during World War I, which may have contributed to her defeat. When war broke out in 1939, German authorities were very concerned about food for the German people. This concern was made even more important as fertilizers could not be imported due to the British sea blockade.

The swift German conquest of Poland, the Netherlands, Denmark and France brought important agricultural areas under German control, but the food supply remained problematic. Agricultural output diminished in wartime. Horses and vehicles had been requisitioned and the Germans continued this practice in the conquered areas. Fertilizers remained scarce. Much of the labor force had been allocated to the armaments industry, leaving fewer people to do farming work.[10]

When the Germans planned Operation *Barbarossa*, food supply was an important consideration. Hitler had demanded "living space" in the east at least since he wrote *Mein Kampf* (Vol. 1, 1925, Vol. 2, 1926) and one of the reasons was to secure food. However, Soviet farming did not produce any surplus, except in Ukraine. In fact, food was in short supply in the Soviet Union. This did, however, not bother Hitler and his entourage. The German army in the east would mainly live off the land and thereby free up food for the German population.[11]

The scheme left an important question unanswered: how would the Soviet population be fed? The answer was simple and brutal: with whatever was left after the Germans had satisfied their needs. Considering that the area to be occupied was vast, while resources available to control it would be scarce, it would be impossible for the Germans to impose strict control. Even if the Germans had intended to completely cut off food supply to the Soviet population, they lacked the means to accomplish such a devious aim. Furthermore, as the Germans wanted to maintain and preferably improve farming, they needed the rural population to some extent.

The large cities were another matter. The inhabitants depended on food being transported from surrounding agricultural areas. When planning *Barbarossa*, far-reaching decisions and plans were made for the future occupation of the vast expanses in the east. The citizens in the Soviet cities would not receive food, unless they were needed to work in certain industries. Undoubtedly, this would leave millions starving.

It would not be possible for the German to completely cut off food supply to the cities, as the black market would most likely ensure that some food trickled through. Also, some would undoubtedly flee German-occupied cities, but this should not detract from the very real hardships endured by many in the Soviet cities under German occupation and the fact that the number of victims would eventually be very high. Leningrad would be particularly hard hit. It had a large population, and when the Germans reached Schlüsselburg on the shore of Lake Ladoga on September 8, all communications on land were cut off. Food could no longer be transported into the city along land routes, and the Germans prevented the citizens from leaving the area.

Leningrad had only been cut off for a few weeks when the Germans launched Operation *Taifun*. Its citizens had not yet endured the hardships of the cold winter, when food stores ran low. To many, it was clear that the future would be grim unless the German blockade was lifted. Hitler had similar plans for Moscow, but on an even larger scale. Not only would the capital be surrounded, but German units would also be forbidden from accepting its capitulation. Attempts to flee the city were met by fire, except in specially denoted gaps, through which citizens could flee to the east. German soldiers were forbidden to give food to Moscow's citizens or even to assist them in fighting fires.[12]

Neither the citizens of Moscow, nor the Soviet leadership, knew of the plans drafted in Berlin. However, the Soviet leadership at least knew that the capital was in grave danger. It took some more days before the man in the street knew that the enemy had shattered the defenses west of Moscow. On October 10, the news agency TASS announced that the male population of Moscow, except those employed in armaments production and similar work, had been summoned to construct fieldworks. This was a clear indication that events had taken an unfavorable direction.[13]

Calling for the civilian population to dig trenches, construct strongpoints and create various other kinds of field works was nothing new. It had happened many times before, including earlier in 1941, but the effects of such measures should not be exaggerated. After much shovelling a tank ditch could be created, but unless it was defended by strong regular units, it was an obstacle the enemy could easily overcome. To bring reinforcements forward remained the most important task.

Zhukov continued to work hard to create the Mozhaisk Line and halt enemy forces heading east. At the moment, he had four armies in the line: the Sixteenth in the Volokolamsk area, the Fifth in the vicinity of Mozhaisk, the Forty-Third around Maloyaroslavets, and finally the Forty-Ninth in the Kaluga area. Hard fighting had already raged around Kaluga and the Germans had captured the city. The Forty-Ninth Army's staff was located at Ferzikovo, east of Kaluga. Further north, in the vicinity of Naro-Fominsk, the Thirty-Third Army reorganized. Zhukov managed to cobble together something resembling a defense line centered around four towns west of Moscow, while the defenses at Tula protected his left flank.[14]

Rokossovsky arrived at Volokolamsk on October 14, after his recent escape from Vyazma. He had brought his staff, which was not only fortunate for him, but also useful when the work to reorganize the defenses began. Staff officers were sent to visit existing units and to bring retreating ones under control. The full-strength 316th Rifle Division was already in position and Rokossovsky noted that he had not seen such a well-equipped formation in a long time. When he met the commander, Major General Ivan Panfilov, Rokossovsky felt he would get along well with him, and he would eventually come to appreciate Panfilov's taciturn humor.

To improve antitank defenses, Rokossovsky decided to bring antiaircraft guns to the front line. The number of guns in the 316th Rifle Division sector increased dramatically when four independent antitank gun regiments were sent to positions within its sector. Riflemen were posted to protect the antitank guns against German motorized infantry. The 3rd Cavalry Corps, commanded by Major General Lev Dovator, was among the first units that arrived after escaping encirclement. Its two cavalry divisions were depleted, but Rokossovsky found their mobility useful. They could be employed in counterattacks, but support would be needed as the cavalry could not hold its own against German tanks.[15]

Many efforts were made to halt scattered soldiers retreating east. For example, the Forty-Ninth Army created an assembly point at Serpukhov, to which officers and men who had escaped encirclement were directed to receive provisions and care. Antipenko, responsible for supply matters in the army, emphasized how important it was that the stragglers felt they received attention. It was particularly important to halt any motor vehicles driving east, especially as they could be towing guns or transporting other important equipment.[16]

■ ■ ■

Stalin and his generals clearly realized the immense danger to Moscow. The mood in the capital was uneasy, but not yet given to panic. Stalin was kept continuously informed about the situation. Staff Officer Sergey Shtemenko, who served at the general staff for the greater part of the war, described the hard work that went into keeping him informed. The officers at the operations section, which Shtemenko belonged to, had to submit situation reports to Stalin, usually three times per day. The least demanding was the morning telephone briefing at about 10:00–11:00 a.m. when Stalin was updated on what had transpired during the late night and early morning. At about 4:00 p.m., Stalin received a new report about what had taken place during the day. The last and most comprehensive report was presented to Stalin in person. Usually the headquarters was informed by phone at about 11:00 p.m. that it was time to present the comprehensive report on the day's activities.

This was presented to Stalin and a number of senior officers, such as Nikolai Voronov, the Red Army artillery commander, and Yakov Fedorenko, the Red Army armored forces commander. Members of the Politburo were often present at the meeting, which frequently lasted until 3:00 or 4:00 a.m. Sometimes the sessions ended earlier, and then Stalin often liked to watch a movie with the other participants, commonly films showing accounts from the front. However, some of the officers found it hard to enjoy the movies. Shtemenko wrote: "Our brains were working on completely different problems. We knew that vast work awaited us, but none dared to leave. It was as if I sat on hot needles and held on to my suitcase with maps."[17]

Every senior officer at the general staff had a prescribed rest period when he was supposed to sleep, a scheme instigated by Stalin. Vasilyevsky's rest period was between 4:00 and 10:00 a.m. during the battle of Moscow. When Shtemenko was appointed head of the operations section, in May 1943, he was also given a specific rest period, in his case between 2:00 and 7:00 p.m. The work load was extremely heavy and no one could keep up. Shtemenko wrote:

Some of my comrades later suffered from nervous exhaustion or heart problems. After the war, many of them had to be transferred to the reserve, before they had reached the prescribed retirement age.

In reality, they were burnt out. The late meetings with Stalin and the massive workload mean that Vasilyevsky stayed up after 4:00 a.m. and worked, despite the fact that this was his specificed rest period. Stalin did not like such "cheating." Occasionally he phoned Vasilyevsky between 4:00 and 10:00 a.m. but Vasilyevsky had instructed his adjutant, Lieutenant Grinenki, to answer and say that he was asleep. Stalin usually answered: "Very good." Lying to the powerful dictator must have been nerve-racking for Lieutenant Grinenki.[18]

The memoirs of those who served under Stalin describe a man who wanted clear and precise reports and who strongly disliked receiving information that later turned out to be incorrect. Shtemenko described how the general staff checked the reports from the formations at the front. Sometimes they adjusted the reports so instead of reporting that town X was liberated, the reports were changed to say "We are fighting for town X." A sudden German counterattack could change the situation and it was better to err on the side of caution. Stalin did not accept flattering descriptions or even tiny lies. He could react harshly when discovering such behavior. He possessed strong willpower, but was also impulsive. Usually he remained calm and composed, but sometimes he lost his patience and his objectivity.[19]

An example from late November is illuminating. An irritated Stalin phoned Zhukov about a village not far from Moscow: "Do you know that Dedovsk has been captured by the enemy?" Zhukov replied that he was unaware of this and received a scolding for not having a clear picture of what had transpired on his front. Stalin ordered Zhukov to personally organize a counterattack and liberate Dedovsk. Zhukov called Rokossovsky, who commanded the forces in the sector where Dedovsk was located. He told Zhukov that the Germans had not captured Dedovsk, but the small village of Dedovo. Zhukov called Stalin, but the dictator refused to budge. He demanded that Zhukov should retake the village at all costs. Furthermore, he should bring the commander of Fifth Army, General Govorov: "He is an artillery man and let him assist Rokossovsky directing the artillery fire in his sector."

Zhukov realized that he would not be able to persuade Stalin. Govorov of course objected, but Zhukov told him the order had been given by Stalin himself, thus ending the discussion. The 9th Guards Rifle Division was to conduct the counterattack. Its commander, Beloborodov, thought it was tactically unsound, but he could not ignore Zhukov's direct order. A rifle company, supported by two tanks, retook the few houses that made up the small village of Dedovo.[20]

NINE

VYAZMA-BRYANSK

O n October 10, Major Shabulin, the NKVD officer, woke up in a car. It was not yet 7:00 a.m., the weather was cold and miserable, and large snowflakes were slowly falling. Despite the inhospitable weather, he was soon ready to have breakfast. Surplus from old stores was available and Shabulin washed it down with hot water, which brought him and his comrades pleasant warmth. At about 11:00 a.m., he set out on the road. He quickly realized that they were almost impassable, as rain had turned them to mud, vast quantites of sticky sludge. After much effort, he finally reached the village of Sloboda. There he met an old friend from the 217th Rifle Division, who told Shabulin that the division had suffered 75% casualties.[1]

On the following day, German indirect fire hit the area where the army staff was located. Shabulin also met colleagues who told him that a good friend of his had been killed and buried. The Fiftieth Army, in which Shabulin served, was being squeezed ever tighter. It was trapped in the pocket north of Bryansk, and the various units had become more confused with every passing hour. Vehicles and carts from baggage trains were intermingled with combat units on the muddy roads. Much equipment had already been abandoned, and had fallen into German hands. The Luftwaffe attacked the surrounded Soviet units from above.[2]

On October 12 the situation deteriorated even further. Shabulin had some vodka at breakfast and fell asleep afterwards, waking again at 10:00 a.m.. He had been sleeping so deep that he had not even stirred when German aircraft bombed and machine-gunned the village where he slept. In

The German High Command discusses the situation on the Eastern Front. From left to right, Hermann Göring, commander of the Luftwaffe, Adolf Hitler, and Wilhelm Keitel, head of Armed Forces Supreme Command (Oberkommando der Wehrmacht, OKW).

his fragmented diary, he complained that the local population was hostile towards him and the Red Army soldiers.[3]

Chaos continued to reign in the afternoon. The staff panicked and fled when fired upon by the enemy. The army commander drove past in his car, giving instructions by gesticulating. Shabulin's interpretation was that they should go to a forest a few kilometers away. They had hardly reached the forest before three men appeared, riding their horses hard, and reported that German soldiers were closing in. Their report was soon confirmed by incoming shells and bullets. Wild shooting began, as Soviet soldiers returned fire without much coordination. Shabulin pulled back, losing most of his documents, equipment and other valuable items in the process. He had to assume that it all fell into German hands, as they squeezed the encirclement tighter around the Fiftieth Army.[4]

∎ ∎ ∎

Shabulin's impressions were typical of how the situation in the Vyazma and Bryansk pockets developed. To many Soviet soldiers, it seemed futile to continue fighting. On October 13, a German armed forces high command communiqué announced that more than 350,000 prisoners had been captured. As the operation had been launched only about two weeks earlier, this was a very impressive number.[5]

The figure given by the German high command was of course only approximate, as the number of prisoners rose hour by hour, and the situation remained confused. Units would report the number of prisoners captured at irregular intervals rather than simultaneously. Some reports were belated, others were just estimates. Such problems were endemic and not unique to the German armed forces. The counting of prisoners required time, and for the moment, only a rough estimate was needed. That the number was not exact does not negate the fact that it was an extremely large figure. The logical conclusion was that the Soviet units were quickly succumbing, and this meant that German units would be free for other tasks in the near future.

It was clear to von Bock that the surrounded Soviet units would soon cease to fight. On October 13 he wrote in his diary that the fighting in the Vyazma area would end very soon, and the Soviet forces in the Bryansk pockets would only hold out a few more days. A few days may not seem very much, but von Bock observed that the surrounded Soviet forces had nevertheless delayed the Germans, meaning their resistance had not been altogether in vain.[6]

Field Marshal von Bock's comment is unsurprising. Autumn weather imposed serious restrictions on efforts to continue further east, and every day lost could prove invaluable. On the other hand it can be argued that the Germans attained a success of such magnitude that it was unrealistic to hope for more. They had attacked with about 1.2 million men against an equal-sized Soviet force. Holes had been immediately torn in the Soviet defenses and within a few days huge Red Army formations were surrounded. Within two weeks the encircled forces had either already surrendered or were on the verge of doing so. This was an exceptional success considering the circumstances.

With this background in mind, the surprise was not that the Germans were delayed at Vyazma and Bryansk, it was that they had managed to break through, encircle and capture such large forces in such a short time. This issue is very relevant, as it is difficult to see how the Germans could have defeated an enemy force of this size any faster.

The even force ratio should have meant that the Soviet defenders could hold their own. Of course the Germans, holding the initiative, could concentrate forces in certain sectors and create local superiority, but only at the expense of other sectors of their front. Undoubtedly, this was a risk a commander could accept, and an experienced officer like von Bock did not hesitate. German doctrine and training had also inculcated in him the importance of concentrating resources at critical points, even if this resulted in danger at other sectors. Of course, the Red Army, and the western Allies also concentrated their resources at points where they hoped to break through, but since they possessed overall numerical superiority they did not have to accept grave risks in order to follow such a strategy. That was an advantage the Germans lacked, they were fortunate enough that force ratios were fairly even on the Eastern Front in autumn 1941, including in Army Group Center's sector.[7]

The Germans' trump card was not the size of their forces, but the combat power of the individual units. High training standards, appropriate leadership and the military philosophy shaping how combat units acted enabled the German formations to wield great combat power, allowing them to break through Soviet defenses far quicker than the force ratios would indicate. As we have seen, the German panzer divisions punched through and penetrated about 30–40 kilometers (20–25 miles) behind the Soviet defenses on the first day. This was a remarkable feat, far exceeding the outcome that the force ratios suggested.

Without paying undue concern to dangers on their flanks, the German panzers continued to drive deep on the days following the breakthrough. Most Soviet units were unable to retreat fast enough, even if they had been granted permission to pull back. Unfortunately, Soviet communications were not up to the strains imposed by the swift German operations. Too few radios, combined with centralized command and control, made it difficult to adjust to such a rapidly changing situation. This was a serious handicap, and made it easier for the Germans to encircle very large Soviet forces.

Once the Soviet units had been encircled, the Germans managed to quickly quench the opposition in the pockets, even in comparison to previous encirclements on the Eastern Front. More than 300,000 Soviet soldiers were surrounded at Smolensk in mid-July, but it took three weeks of pressure from the Germans before all of them surrendered. During the large Kiev encirclement, about two weeks elapsed between the meeting of the German pincers and the Soviet forces surrendering. Furthermore, the Germans had taken far longer to close the encirclement at Kiev, compared to Operation *Taifun*.

By any reasonable standards, the initial phase of Operation *Taifun*—which was known also as the "double battle at Vyazma and Bryansk"—was a remarkable success. It is doubtful if any force of similar magnitude has so rapidly been dealt such a devastating blow. As the Germans did not enjoy numerical superiority, it is even more remarkable.

Red Army shortcomings contributed to the swift German success. The horrendous losses suffered before Operation *Taifun* was launched had forced the Soviet armed forces to commit many poorly trained units to replace the lost formations. For example, many of the militia divisions were not adequately trained. They had been hastily assembled and could not be compared to regular, well-trained units.

One common result of inadequate training is poor morale, which may have contributed to the rapidly increasing number of Soviet soldiers who surrendered during the operation. Limited supplies may also have contributed. Many of the soldiers who fell into German hands had not received enough rations, and lack of food cannot have boosted morale.[9]

The German success did not come without cost. Army Group Center reported 57,363 killed, wounded and missing between October 1 and October 20.[10] Considering the size of the forces involved and the enormous Soviet losses, the German casualties must be considered remarkably small. Not only did the Germans quickly inflict a resounding defeat on an army of one million, they also achieved their success at an unusually small price, by World War II standards.

RIFLE DIVISIONS IN FRONT OF MOSCOW, SEPTEMBER 30, 1941[8]						
NUMBER OF DIVISIONS	PREWAR DIVISIONS	PREWAR DIVISIONS*	FROM NKVD#	MILITIA	NEW DIV.	EX. MECH. DIV.
82	35	5	9	12	18	3
100%	42.5%	6%	11%	15%	22%	3.5%

*Prewar divisions that had not completed their training on June 22, 1941.
The NKVD supplied approximately 1,500 officers and soldiers for each division.

Even after the battle, the senior Soviet commanders were unaware of how low German casualty figures were. A man in Shabulin's position seldom had a clear understanding of the losses suffered by his own side, but he appears to have known perhaps a little more than others, and what he knew was disheartening. Had he known that the German losses were very small, he would have been even more depressed.

Shabulin did not sleep during the night of October 12–13. He lost two cars. It was very cold. He lacked gloves and he did not have warm water to wash himself. The vehicles could, at best, move slowly. About 1,000 of them were stuck in marshland, which was the reason he had to work hard during the night. Some vehicles were still stuck when the area came under German fire at dawn.[11]

Shabulin moved on during the day until he reached a stream. Something strange appeared. It turned out to be a German armored car, and the crew saw the Soviet soldiers and promptly opened fire on them. As darkness fell, fighting petered out. It was clear to Shabulin that the German grip had tightened. As the area held by the Fiftieth Army shrank, the Germans could more easily cover it with artillery fire, making it difficult to sleep. On October 14, Shabulin noted that he had not slept for 48 hours. It also crossed his mind that he had not read a newspaper since October 2, the day the German offensive began.[12]

The Soviet situation deteriorated rapidly. The words Shabulin scribbled in his diary on October 15 are illuminating:

> Everything is terrible. I'm reeling. Corpses, the horrors of war, uninterrupted shelling. Again, I am hungry and have not slept in a long time. I have confiscated a bottle of liquor. I went to a forest and reconnoitred. The disaster is complete. The army is defeated, the baggage train destroyed. I sit by a camp fire and write. In the morning I lost all my NKVD men, was alone and then got mixed up with unfamiliar people. The army has been turned into shambles.[13]

On the following day Shabulin complained that he had not received any bread for the past three days, but there would be a few moments of joy during the day. During a brief pause he managed to wash, and at noon he and a few comrades found some food and made lunch. They ate as much as possible, well aware that days could pass before they had another meal. The lunch was a really enjoyable occasion, but there were now many things to dishearten the men. Shabulin saw many fallen Soviet soldiers and much abandoned equipment. It rained before noon, and in the afternoon the rain was mixed with snow. Shabulin and his comrades were soaking wet, but they could not quench their thirst. However, in the evening they could at least dry their clothes over a fire. They could also put up tents and get some sleep during the night.[14]

After an uneasy night, Shabulin woke up hungry on October 17. He soon realized that some soldiers had already began to make breakfast. No bread was available, but they had found other things to eat. After breakfast, the group got moving, but without any clear idea of where to go. Shabulin managed to evade the Germans a few more days. By staying in wooded and marshy areas, he tried to avoid being found by the enemy. He met Major General Petrov, the Fiftieth Army commander, but then ran out of luck. On October 20, Shabulin was killed in action together with Petrov.[15]

■ ■ ■

Shabulin evaded the Germans for much longer then many of his comrades, so that by the time he was killed, the Germans regarded the pockets as essentially cleared up, although isolated groups of Red Army soldiers continued to fight. On October 19, Army Group Center reported that 673,098 prisoners had been taken since Operation *Taifun* was launched. Also, the booty was huge: 1,277 tanks, 4,378 field guns, 1,009 antiaircraft and antitank guns, 87 aircraft, and vast amounts of other equipment.[16]

In addition to the vast number of prisoners, a large number of Soviet soldiers must have been killed. Some wounded must have been evacuated before the German pincers met, although the swift pace of the German advance prevented many from being evacuated and the majority of the wounded Soviet soldiers must have fallen into German captivity.

It is impossible to establish the exact Soviet casualties. When military forces suffer defeats of the kind inflicted upon the Soviet defenders west of Moscow, the reporting system breaks down and documents disappear. This was indeed the case in October 1941. Russian historians have not found reliable figures, despite considerable efforts in the archives. Reports providing comprehensive and accurate information on casualties are not extant.[17]

One alternative approach is to compare the strength of the Soviet forces at the end of September with the strength after the encirclement battle, and compensate for reinforcements and replacements. This approach results in a reasonably accurate estimate, but it is not without its problems. For example, different reports on manpower strength need not include identical personnel categories. Some reports only deal with front-line personnel, while others include—which is more relevant in this case—those serving in supply units, supporting units and the like. The command and control structure may impose further difficulties. Local garrisons or units still training need not be placed under an army commander or similar, even if they are located within the area he is responsible for. Thus their manpower need not be included in army reports. This can apply to other types of units too. It should be noted that these complications could occur in any army. However, the difficulties are not insurmountable and the information available suggests that the German figure given for prisoners taken in the Vyazma–Bryansk pocket is reasonable (see Appendice 3 for further discussion). The total number of Soviet casualties may have been as high as 850,000, which of course is outrageous for a battle lasting less than three weeks. Undoubtedly, the Soviet forces west of Moscow had been dealt an annihilating blow.[18]

TEN

ONE HUNDRED KILOMETERS TO MOSCOW

While the Germans closed the ring around the Soviet forces at Vyazma and Bryansk, they also advanced east. Hoepner had initially kept the LVII Panzer Corps in reserve, but had committed it to advance in the Moscow direction, while the XL and XLVI corps completed the Vyazma encirclement. Even sending forward just one panzer corps—a small part of Hoepner's forces—would suffice to cause the enemy much concern.[1]

Soon after the 10th Panzer Division reached Vyazma and established contact with the 7th Panzer Division approaching from the north, parts of the 10th Panzer could be sent east, along the main road from Vyazma to Moscow. The major roads were especially important when the autumn rains made minor roads almost impassable. Also, the road used by the 10th Panzer Division ran along the railroad from Smolensk to Moscow, which was one of the more important railroads. As the mud got deeper, the importance of the railroads increased exponentially, particularly for moving supplies forward.[2]

Major General Rendulic, who commanded the 52nd Infantry Division, commented on the mud and its effects. Under normal conditions, it would have taken the division three days to march to its destination, but with the ground a veritable quagmire, the staff did not even dare to make a timetable. Double the number of horses were required for towing carts and howitzers. Only the light artillery batteries were brought, and only two of the four pieces in each battery. The remaining howitzers, especially the heavy 15cm ones, had to wait for better weather.[3]

■ ■ ■

The Germans struggled with the mud, but the Soviet leaders faced a far more ominous situation. The Kiev disaster had ruined all chances of halting the Germans in the Ukraine. Now, most of the forces defending Moscow had been either lost or were on the verge of surrendering. Only weak forces remained to cover the roads to the capital. Somehow, the Germans had to be stopped, but whether this could be accomplished west or east of Moscow remained uncertain.

Undoubtedly, massive reinforcements were needed to stop the Germans, irrespective of where they were to be halted. Clearly 1.2 million men had not sufficed. As most of them were already lost, vast reinforcements were needed. Close to a million men was probably be a bare minimum, but such forces could not immediately be brought to the front.

The vast country had to be combed for military units, and the great distances meant that the movements mostly had to be on railroads. As Moscow was a hub in the Soviet rail network, movements to the front west of Moscow were facilitated by the railroads that extended out from the capital like spokes in a wheel.

The railroads were one of the reasons it was thought imperative that an attempt should still be made to halt the Germans west of Moscow. It was, however, unclear how fast reinforcements could be thrown in and how much time there would be to prepare defenses. As the Germans and the weather dictated how much time the Soviet commanders would get, they could not know in advance how quickly they had to act in order to succeed.

■ ■ ■

Mud and slush seriously impeded the German operations, but nevertheless, preparations were made for the thrust to Kalinin, as ordered by the German high command. The mission was given to a rather small force, a battle group formed from 1st Panzer Division. Colonel Hans-Christoph von Heydebrand was entrusted with command of the battle group. His usual position was commander of one of the division's Panzergrenadier Regiments, and in addition to this unit, tanks and artillery were attached to his force.[4]

The battle group launched its attack on the morning on October 12, with an infantry company and a tank company in the lead. Thus far,

Kalinin had not been mentioned as an objective, but after two hours of fighting, when a breakthrough had been achieved, von Heydebrand could inform his forces that they would capture Kalinin.[5]

Staritsa, located northeast of Rzhev, was the first intermediate objective. The battle group staged its attack from the Subtsov area, east of Rzhev and southeast of Staritsa. It initially advanced in a northerly direction, which would allow von Heydebrand to reach the main road between Rzhev and Kalinin and advance more rapidly.

Staritsa itself was valuable, as it was located on the Volga and several bridges spanned the river. However, von Heydebrand's battle group was already on the eastern side of Volga, and captured Staritsa from that direction, even though all bridges had been blown up. It was still advantageous to have captured the destroyed bridges, as it was usually easier to create a new bridge when the abutments could be used.[6]

Unaware of the German 1st Panzer Division's plans, the 242nd Soviet Rifle Division tried to reach the same area. The Soviet unit did not head directly for Rzhev. Instead it passed east of the city and finally reached other Soviet forces west of Staritsa. They belonged to the 220th Rifle Division, commanded by Major General Khouzhenko. The 242nd Division became part of the 220th and Lieutenant Colonel Glebov became chief of staff, while Captain Dragunsky was given responsibility for the 220th Rifle Division's reconnaissance. On the evening of October 12, the Soviet general staff reported that the 242nd Rifle Division had again established contact with other Soviet units, and that 1,410 soldiers from the division had escaped encirclement.[7]

Dragunsky remained with the infantry for a while, until an order arrived instructing him to leave. He did not like to leave his post, which again irritated Glebov: first Dragunsky had protested at becoming an infantry soldier, now he protested at leaving that arm. As he had done previously, Glebov emphasized that it was an order and the recently promoted Major Dragunsky left the front for further training at Ufa.

■ ■ ■

Let us return to the 1st Panzer Division, which was unusual in one important respect. When Operation *Barbarossa* began, two of its four infantry battalions were equipped with armored half-tracks, which made it unique in the German army of 1941. Such vehicles were very desirable, but

German industry did not manage to keep up with demand. One infantry battalion in the 10th Panzer Division was also equipped with armored half-tracks, but the rest of the panzer divisions' infantry had at most one company equipped with such vehicles. Instead, the infantry was carried by unarmored lorries, which were more vulnerable and also much less capable of negotiating terrain. During the muddy season, the lorries were even more hampered. The generous allotment of half-tracks would be an advantage in the task given to von Heydebrand.[8]

The half-tracks were valuable, but they could not compensate for the supply difficulties. Lack of fuel made it impossible to use all the available tanks. By redistributing fuel between vehicles, two panzer companies could accompany the attack. The remaining tanks had to wait until more fuel became available.[9]

An armored infantry battalion, commanded by the Austrian Major Doctor Josef-Franz Eckinger, was reinforced with tanks and motorcycle infantry when it began to advance along the Staritsa–Kalinin road in the evening of October 12. There were several Soviet units on the road, but they were retreating. Several of them fled in panic when Eckinger's vehicles closed in. The Germans drove over or pushed aside abandoned vehicles and equipment, and spread terror and confusion among the fleeing Soviet soldiers.[10]

As darkness fell, Eckinger's force continued in a northeasterly direction. Before it was too late for aerial reconnaissance, a Fieseler Storch appeared over the German battle group. General von Richthofen himself was flying in the aircraft to reconnoitre the road to Kalinin. He shared his observations with Major Eckinger by throwing down a small container with a written report. It told Eckinger that the road ahead was crammed with fleeing Soviet vehicle columns, which could hardly mount any organized opposition.[11]

Eckinger took the report as his starting point and drove on. A platoon from the 113th Mechanized Infantry Regiment, reinforced with two Panzer IV tanks and an engineer platoon, formed the spearhead. Second Lieutenant Otto commanded this lead element of Eckinger's force. Without pausing, the German armored vehicles drove past or over retreating enemy units. Staffs, field kitchens, antiaircraft units, baggage trains and various other Soviet units were overtaken by Otto's men, who left it to following German units to mop up the road and keep communications open.[12]

German encirclements cost the Red Army huge losses both in manpower and equipment. Abandoned Soviet artillery, including a 152mm howitzer M1910/37.

A hilarious conversation took place over the German radio. The chief of staff of the 1st Panzer Division, Walther Wenck, had received reports from Eckinger's battle group and so knew that it was overtaking retreating Soviet units. Just for the fun of it, he sent the following request to the XLI Panzer Corps, to which the 1st Panzer Division was attached:

> The Division advances rapidly towards Kalinin. Russian units continuously intermingle with our columns and claim that they have priority on the road. Request decision to clarify who is to have priority on the road.[13]

The German army high command monitored the radio traffic and did not miss the humor in Wenck's request. Promptly, the following answer was sent: "The 1st Panzer Division has, as always, priority."[14]

Eckinger's battle group continued its swift advance in the darkness. It passed several villages. The German soldiers were tense, but tried to keep up high spirits with gallows humor. The Soviet units had so far been unable to offer organized resistance, but the German dash was still a gamble. Little could be seen in the dark and the Germans could drive into an ambush at any moment. The advance was based upon the assumption that the Soviet forces were too disorganized to offer anything resembling a coherent defense. However, had this assumption been proven wrong, Eckinger and his men would have paid a high price.[15]

At last the Germans saw lights gleaming ahead. They realized the light originated from a Soviet searchlight unit, defense against a German air attack. Eckinger realised that he was close to Kalinin and soon his men drove into Danilovskoe, a village about 10 kilometers from the center of the city. Soon Major Eckinger joined Otto's lead force. It was a critical moment, but the major remained calm and composed. His posture proved justified, as combat activity diminished and the night turned out to be almost tranquil.[16]

Early on October 13, the 1st Panzer Division's panzer regiment, except the two companies which had almost reached Kalinin, remained stranded at Staritsa due to lack of fuel. As the Germans had captured the small airfield outside Staritsa, they could air-transport fuel when the field had been cleared. Soon thereafter Junkers 52 aircraft brought fuel and ammunition for the tanks and the motorcycle battalion in the area.[17]

Although 75 kilometers (47 miles) separated Staritsa and Kalinin, it was a major advantage for Eckinger to know that a battle group with sufficient fuel and ammunition was on its way to him. It meant that he dared commit his force to capture a bridgehead across the Volga. Eckinger ordered two of his infantry companies to attack on foot, while the combat vehicles engaged in a firefight with Soviet defenders along a railroad embankment. This allowed the infantry to avoid detection and reach the railroad bridge in the western parts of Kalinin unmolested. As was expected, the bridge had been prepared for demolition, but the German soldiers quickly silenced the bunkers at each end of the bridge and cut the wires to the charges that had been placed.[18]

Eckinger's men had attained a great success, but their rapid advance and small numbers left them exposed. Furious Soviet counterattacks tested

Eckinger's men, but they held their positions until other German units were ready to attack into Kalinin. Further elements of 1st Panzer Division arrived during the evening and night of October 13–14, and at dawn of October 14 they began to attack the city.[19]

The Soviet soldiers defended stubbornly. Hard fighting raged on the streets and in the blocks, but the Germans were aided by flamethrower tanks and engineers equipped with flamethrowers. The battle lasted most of the day, but in the evening the Germans captured the large road bridge over the Volga. They could thus consolidate their bridgehead and take control of Kalinin.[20]

■ ■ ■

The German capture of Kalinin was a move in the wrong direction. But this fact should not be exaggerated, as some kind of defense line along the northern flank of Army Group Center had to be established, and it didn't matter much whether it was located at Kalinin or further south. Also, if all of Panzer Groups 3 and 4 had been used in a narrow thrust towards Moscow it might have proven very difficult to keep them supplied on the muddy roads. The supply problems that 1st Panzer Division experienced in its attack on Kalinin prevented it from using more than a fraction of its strength. The same problems would afflict units attacking straight east. Against this background it is doubtful that the capture of Kalinin resulted in a diversion of resources that seriously impaired German chances of taking Moscow.

The German capture of Kalinin of course caused problems on the Soviet side. The German northeasterly thrust made it difficult for Zhukov to control all his armies, especially those on the northern wing. When Zhukov assumed command, Konev was appointed deputy, with particular responsibility for a sector of the front. The coordination problems were aggravated when Kalinin fell, as the German move split Zhukov's front in two parts. A new front had to be created to control the northern armies.[21]

■ ■ ■

Colonel General Ivan Konev was the obvious choice as commander of the new Kalinin Front. A Stavka directive to effect this was signed by Stalin and Vasilyevsky on October 17. The Kalinin Front initially consisted of three armies, plus some units from the Northwest Front. The latter elements would soon be combined into a fourth army. The front staff was formed from the staff of the Tenth Reserve Army. This army was thus disbanded and a new Tenth Army was created. At the same time, Lieutenant General Mikhail Efremov, who had been intended to command the original Tenth Army, became available for another assignment. Unfortunately the staff of the original Tenth Army, including its equipment, did not arrive until October 26. Another problem was the new front's lack of a supply organization. It had to rely on the Northwest and West fronts in such matters.[22]

Konev did not possess much offensive power. His armor was limited to two tank brigades and his rifle divisions were below strength. All of them had been in action since October 2. Neither could Konev expect substantial reinforcements, as his front would not receive top priority. Most reinforcements would be sent to Zhukov's front. Unfortunately, the Stavka decided to place the boundary between the West and Kalinin fronts along the line Berendeevo–Verbilki–Reshetnikovo–Knyazhi Gory–Sychevka, instead of along the Moscow reservoirs, which were a more natural boundary.[23]

The distance from Kalinin to Moscow was approximately 160 kilometers (100 miles), so the 1st Panzer Division was not the German unit closest to the capital on October 13. That distinction was shared between elements of the 258th Infantry Division, 3rd Motorized Infantry Division and 20th Panzer Division. They were in the area north of Maloyaroslavets, about 100 kilometers (62 miles) from the Soviet capital.[24]

One of these units was the 479th Infantry Regiment, which belonged to the 258th Infantry Division. It had participated in the initial attack across the Desna on October 2 and had subsequently exploited the hole punched by Panzer Group 4. The regiment had advanced approximately 230 kilometers (140 miles) during the following ten days, an impressive feat for a non-motorized unit. Increasingly muddy roads hampered further efforts to advance east. The horses were straining to pull field kitchens, carts, ambulances, howitzers and other heavy equipment forward. Supply problems afflicted the regular infantry divisions just as much as the panzer divisions, as they needed ammunition, food, and also large quantities of fodder.[25]

Despite increasing difficulties, morale remained high in the 479th Infantry Regiment. The soldiers' goal was not far away and they were well aware of this in the morning on October 13. They were not allowed much time for their morning duties, but the veterans knew their business and were soon ready for march and combat.[26]

Most of the regiment had to cross the river Protva. The Germans had found fords, but the crossing was still time-consuming. Also, a troublesome situation developed on the right wing. The 1st Battalion had been detailed to attack and capture Borovsk from the north. The soldiers had just cocked their weapons when a counterattack was launched by a Soviet force which the Germans believed comprised the equivalent of one battalion.[27] A gap between the 479th Infantry Regiment and its neighbor to the right—the 8th Motorized Infantry Regiment from the 3rd Motorized Division—gave the Soviet force space to maneuver,

About 1,500 meters separated the German and the Soviet forces. The Germans concluded that they had not yet been observed by the advancing Soviets. Taking great care to avoid being detected, the Germans made ready their heavy weapons. They were even able to bring forward a 10.5cm howitzer and now they prepared to open direct fire on the unsuspecting enemy.[28]

The Soviet soldiers were surprised when the Germans opened fire with all the battalion's heavy weapons, and sustained heavy losses. The Soviets who did not fall fled in the direction of Borovsk. The fighting was intense, but lasted only 20 minutes.[29]

The regiment's commander immediately ordered 1st Battalion to attack Borovsk. The lead companies reached Borovsk at dusk and penetrated into the outskirts. Bridges across the Protva that were believed to exist in the northern part of Borovsk proved fictional. However, in the twilight was discerned the silhouette of a major road bridge. Before reaching it, they encountered an enemy force which appeared to be a motorcycle company. The Germans promptly opened fire and inflicted casualties, causing the enemy to disperse.[30]

The German success did not last long. Several Soviet units appeared and offered strong resistance. Lieutenant Albrecht, who commanded the two lead companies, decided to take up suitable positions just north of the bridge. From there, his men could rake it with fire, allowing them to repel several attacks during the night and prevent the enemy from blowing up the bridge. Their position was precarious and at dawn on October 14, Albrecht could not communicate with other elements of the regiment.

Orderlies could not get through and it was impossible to evacuate the wounded.[31]

Lieutenant Albrecht had only a vague idea about the whereabouts of the rest of the 479th Regiment, but more information would hardly have eased his mood. The bulk of the regiment did attack early on October 14, but made only slow progress. The muddy terrain was very troublesome, although the Germans nurtured hopes that it would also hamper the Red Army and perhaps allow the Germans to achieve surprise.[32]

Neither side managed to surprise the other, but the 479th Regiment plodded forward in the mud and did reach the exposed companies late on October 14. From their positions, Albrecht's men managed to prevent the bridge from being destroyed. At 6:30 p.m. the 479th Regiment reported that the bridge had been captured intact and large parts of Borovsk were in German hands. Soviet defenders clung to the southern parts of the town. The Germans established communications with the neighboring units on their right.[33]

■ ■ ■

Actions of the kind fought by the 258th Infantry Division lacked the depth of the advances of the first week of the offensive. The Germans still cleared the cauldrons at Vyazma and Bryansk, but the worst problem was the mud, which made it extremely difficult to bring supplies forward. The 20th Panzer Division, committed south of the 258th Infantry Division, was fighting battles very similar to those of the 258th Infantry Division.[34]

Most of 20th Panzer Division's vehicles trailed behind on roads running southwest from Borovsk. They were caught in the mud together with elements of the 19th Panzer Division, which was attempting to reach Maloyaroslavets. Panzer Regiment 21 was the tank component of 20th Panzer Division and it was, like the rest of the division, scattered over a large area. Sergeant Bahls commanded a Panzer IV in the 12th Company of the 21st Panzer Regiment. He remembered October 13 as a sunny but chilly day. The low temperature made the ground firm so he could drive his tank more easily than on preceding days.[35]

The Germans' heaviest tank was the Panzer IV, and many of the tanks were light types, such as the Panzer II or the Czech Panzer 38(t). Their combat value was low and on this occasion, Bahls had been detailed to support a light company. The latter had been given a reconnaissance mission, advancing along the main road that the division planned to follow. Bahls noted that the light company was accompanied by the regiment commander and the battalion commander.[36]

The surrounding area was forested, but there were patches of open terrain on both sides of the road. The tankers could thus drive their vehicles alongside the road, which meant that a damaged tank did not block all vehicles behind it. Also, the Germans could choose to advance with more tanks abreast, enabling them to bring more gun barrels to bear on the enemy. Bahls advanced along the edge of the forest on the right side of the road.[37]

Initially, nothing remarkable happened. The German force reached a bend, from which they could see the village of Butovka, about a kilometer away. The tank commanders ordered their drivers to stop so careful observation could be carried out. The Germans did not know whether there were enemy forces in Butovka or not and the commanders scrutinized the terrain and the village, looking through their binoculars. The gunners used their magnifying sights to search for enemies. Their efforts were rewarded as two Soviet light tanks were observed at a distance of 800 meters. No time was wasted. The German gunners opened fired, but soon more Soviet tanks appeared. Three heavy tanks, identified as T-34s by the Germans, attacked from Butovka. They drove straight towards the German tanks.[38]

Bahls and the other Germans knew the T-34 had superior armament and protection. However, few options remained but to fight. The German gunners opened fire on the approaching enemy. Experienced and well trained, they quickly found their mark. The commanders remained in their cupolas to observe, but the sight must have been distressing. Despite being aware of the T-34's excellent armor protection, the German tankers were still astonished to see how their shells simply bounced off the front glacis of the Soviet tanks.[39]

The shortcomings of the German guns were serious. Not only did they fail to knock out the Soviet tanks, they even failed to intimidate the Soviet tank crews, who pressed home the attack. At a speed that Bahls regarded as insane, the T-34 tanks stormed towards the German company. The Soviet tankers did not even appear to be bothered by the German force. They simply drove past. Bahls turned around and caught a last glimpse of the enemy tanks before they disappeared.[40]

The Soviet behavior puzzled the Germans. Could their daring be explained by further battle-ready forces in Butovka? The Germans abandon all plans to attack the village. After some deliberation, they decided to pull back on a small road in the forest. After driving for some time, they found one T-34 stuck in a swamp. A German soldier had seized the opportunity to throw a hand grenade into the tank and knocked it out. Further forward, the German tankers found a second T-34, which had been hit in the tracks and immobilized.[41]

The sight of two knocked-out T-34s was heartening to the returning German tankers. They were soon informed that the third one had been knocked out by German artillery. The daring Soviet dash had thus not resulted in anything to boast of. The German lead company had been forced to turn back, but the price appears inordinate for such a small success.[42]

Several German tank crews had never seen a T-34 and they climbed out from their vehicles to have a look. No order to renew the attack was given. Instead, the German tankers chatted and studied the vehicle. The tranquil scene was suddenly shattered by two more T-34s. The surprised Germans did not have time to remount their tanks. Bahls thought that it perhaps did not matter much, as the German guns were virtually useless.[43]

Bahls and the other Germans remained frozen to the ground for a moment, unable even to throw themselves to the ground. Not until the Soviet tankers let their machine guns talk did the Germans react. However, they hardly accomplished anything before the Soviet tanks disappeared into the distance. These two T-34s also met their fate further along the road. A German second lieutenant was killed in a bizarre twist of fate when he was hit by a German antitank shell that simply bounced off a T-34.[44]

The German tankers were of course impressed by the qualities of the T-34. However, the Soviet tank crews lacked the training to make good use of their vehicles. Bahls described the enemy as a pack of charging boars and indeed this description has some merit. From a tactical point of view, the Soviet use of their tanks in this action was deplorable.

This was far from the first occasion on which the Germans encountered heavy Soviet tanks. The first week of the war had seen clashes between German tanks and heavy KV tanks, whose armor was as impenetrable as that of the T-34. The Germans had also met the T-34 on many occasions before and actions of the kind experienced by Bahls had been fought earlier. Despite their technical superiority, the Soviet tank units equipped with the T-34 and KV rarely achieved much success. Poor leadership and inadequate training were the culprits, both resulting at least partly from the fact that many Soviet units were formed at speed due to the immense losses suffered by the Red Army. It is, however, not the only explanation, as prewar units also performed poorly. The tank officer Lt Aleksandr Bodnar remembered how little time even officers were given to train during the war:

> In October, after 18 months at the academy instead of the prescribed 24 months, I was appointed lieutenant. I was sent to Vladimir and the forming 20th Armor Brigade. We were given a week to complete the process of forming the brigade, a process that was begun on October 1, and already on October 9 did we entrain. We were sent to the Moscow area.[45]

The brigade received its tanks and it arrived at Borodino on October 11. Initially kept in reserve, it was soon committed to fighting. Bodnar experienced hard fighting during a period of six weeks, during which the unit suffered heavy casualties. His rapid assignment was no exception. Before the war, a tank officer was supposed to receive 24 months' training, before being appointed lieutenant. During the war, the course was reduced to 18 months, which was too little time to master all the tasks related to fighting in a tank, including maintenance.

A driver was allowed three months' training at the factory training camp, while a loader or a radio operator received one month of training. Before being sent to the front, the crew conducted a 50-kilometer march exercise, a few rather simple tactical exercises, and some live firing exercises. Crews arriving with a replacement tank could be parted upon arrival at the front. Experienced soldiers could take over the new tank and in those cases, the green commander and driver were often sent back to the factory to collect another tank.[46]

In other cases, as Bodnar experienced, the green crew could be assigned to a completely new unit. At this stage, many tank brigades were raised by using cadres from disbanded mechanized corps, for example, Colonel Mikhail Katukov's 4th Tank Brigade, which fought at Mtsensk. He had commanded the 20th Tank Division during its battles in western Ukraine. At that time it was part of Rokossovsky's mechanized corps. At the end of August Katukov, who would soon turn 41, was summoned to the main office of the armor troops for a new assignment. There he was met by Lieutenant General Fedorenko. The two men had known each other since they had served together in the Kiev military district in the late 1930s. Katukov could not avoid noting that the months of war had left Fedorenko looking older and thinner.

"To keep it brief Katukov," Fedorenko said after a short greeting, "you will assume command of the 4th Tank Brigade."

"The brigade?"

"Yes, a brigade. Mechanized corps and tank divisions will be disbanded as tank production is dwindling while factories are moved east. We don't have enough tanks to sustain larger units and have decided that brigades will be formed."[47]

Katukov's new brigade did not yet exist and Fedorenko instructed him to raise one and prepare it for hard fighting. This process would take place at Stalingrad because a large tank production plant was situated there.[48] Katukov departed for Stalingrad, where the sky vibrated from the heat. The parks allowed some shade though. Steam whistles were heard from ships navigating on the Volga. Except for the painted windows on the hospital, very little suggested that a war raged. Katukov calmly began the arduous task of creating a battleworthy tank brigade.

■ ■ ■

The battles fought by the German 258th Infantry Division and 20th Panzer Division on October 13–14 were much more local in character that the wide-ranging operations that had taken place during the first week of *Taifun*. These two divisions were in the area where the Germans were closest to Moscow. They attacked from the southwest and could thus be regarded as the right prong in an attack against the Soviet capital.

It was less clear which German units that would make up the left prong. The most realistic candidates were the 10th Panzer Division and the Waffen-SS division "Das Reich," which advanced along the main road from Vyazma to Moscow. The two divisions cooperated at all command echelons. Infantry from the Das Reich rode on 10th Panzer Division tanks when they attacked east on October 13.[49]

The Waffen-SS and the regular army have often been described as rivals. This may have been true to some extent, but it seems that the rivalry mainly took place at the top command level. Soldiers on the battlefield often co-operated; in fact, on the very first day of the war the 7th Panzer Regiment, which was the armor component of 10th Panzer Division, had cooperated with units that would eventually become part of the Waffen-SS.[50]

At 7:45 a.m. on October 14, 2nd Battalion of 7th Panzer Regiment set out with infantry from Das Reich riding on top of the tanks. The German force encountered only weak opposition as it advanced towards Koloskoe, where a pause was ordered. A platoon was sent to reconnoitre along the main road to Golovini, where German air reconnaissance had identified a Soviet defensive position. Aided by the information provided by the ground reconnaissance, the German tanks and infantry captured the Soviet position.[51]

After the brief but demanding fight, the regiment commander ordered the commander of the panzer battalion to send reconnaissance to an area 25 kilometers (15 miles) north. The mission was completed without much difficulty, but at 4:00 p.m. the battalion was ordered to rejoin the regiment. Thereafter the force marched west to receive a new mission.[52]

■ ■ ■

The Soviet commanders worked hard to establish the Mozhaisk defense line, but in the short time available they could not rectify the most important shortcoming: the poor training received by Soviet units. This severely reduced their chances of holding the Mozhaisk Line, should the Germans launch a determined attack.

No German units were better positioned to attack the Mozhaisk Line than the Fourth Army and Panzer Group 4. The efforts by 258th Infantry Division, 20th Panzer Division, SS-Das Reich and the 10th Panzer Division were part of the German design to crack the Mozhaisk Line, although it was not yet apparent to the Germans that such a line existed. They simply aimed for the Soviet capital—if there were Soviet defense lines blocking the way, they had to be cracked.

On October 13, Panzer Group 4 had reported that most of its units were available for new missions. In particular, this included the 2nd, 5th, 10th and 11th panzer divisions. As we have seen, the 10th Panzer Division did attack towards Moscow on October 13. The muddy roads, a very well-known problem at this stage, did, however, prevent the units from immediately attacking towards Moscow through the Mozhaisk Line.[53]

Night frost caused the roads to harden, but during the day they thawed back into a morass. The Panzer Group 4 staff experienced the effects of the mud when they moved 75 kilometers (47 miles) to Gzhatsk on October 13. No more than a few hours would be required in normal circumstances, but the muddy roads caused such delays that the staff needed 12 hours to complete the march to its new location.[54]

The mud didn't just slow down individual vehicles. As vehicles moved slower, they spent more time on any given stretch of road, and it was much more difficult to predict how long it would take for units to complete their movements. All of this made traffic control much more difficult, which in turn caused movement to require even more time. Local commanders were often close to desperation and tempted to use other roads than those allotted. Panzer Group 4 complained that Ninth Army units used important roads in the area for which the panzer group was responsible. It should, however, be noted that Panzer Group 4 instructed its own units to ignore boundaries when necessary.[55]

The fact that the Germans had units available to advance towards Moscow mattered little as they could not immediately be committed to that task. Most units were not significantly battleworn, except possibly the 11th Panzer Division, but not even this unit was in particularly bad shape. Clearly, Panzer Group 4 had resources on hand to attack, but the poor roads prevented it from striking east.[56]

Despite the adverse conditions, the Germans attacked in the third week of October, using both the Fourth Army and Panzer Group 4. Efforts were local, but the Fourth Army attacks were of particular importance. At this stage, the LVII Panzer Corps had been transferred to Fourth Army from Panzer Group 4. It gave the Fourth Army more striking power and mobility, but of course the mud remained as sticky as it had been during the past week.[57]

The temperature was notably lower at night, leaving the Germans cold, as noted in a letter written by Cpl. Josef Schmidt. He did not post it before it was captured by Soviet soldiers. It read:

The cold has already arrived, such cold as we don't experience before January at home. It is still mid-October. What temperature will it be when the winter comes? I don't believe we can endure the winter in Russia . . .[58]

From October 13 to October 19, the Fourth Army, and in particular the LVII Panzer Corps, launched successful attacks against the central parts of the Mozhaisk Line, including the towns of Maloyaroslavets and Mozhaisk. Supplies of artillery ammunition were scarce, as the bad weather had thwarted efforts to bring significant amounts to the forward units. The muddy terrain of course also hampered the attacking units' mobility. Despite these limitations, the Germans punched a large hole in the Mozhaisk Line in the Maloyaroslavets area. Further north, in Panzer Group 4's area, the Germans also penetrated the Mozhaisk Line, along the main road from Vyazma to Moscow. Fighting was hard and lasted several days in the latter sector, as Soviet reinforcements arrived in the area.

On the evening of October 11, Major General Dmitri Lelyushenko, with accompanying officers from the 1st Guards Rifle Corps, arrived at Mozhaisk to assume command over the Fifth Army. He was greeted by Col. Semen Bogdanov, the outgoing commander. Like Lelyushenko, Bogdanov was a tank officer. At the outbreak of the war, Bogdanov had commanded the 30th Tank Division and found himself facing Guderian's panzer group. Bogdanov's division had 211 tanks, but they were all light T-26s, no match for the Germans. The division was disbanded in July. Bogdanov had then been responsible for the armored units of the Moscow Military District before being sent to Mozhaisk.

Lelyushenko's main defense lines comprised the 32nd Rifle Division, which had arrived in the Mozhaisk area after travelling from the Far East, Its traditions dated back to 1922 and it had retained the prewar organization that included 15,000 officers and men. Most importantly, it was made up of veterans who had fought the Japanese in the Far East. About 1,700 men from the division had been decorated for deeds in battle.[59]

During the battles near Mozhaisk, the Fifth Army possessed four tank brigades. Altogether, these brigades brought 244 tanks into action, almost half of which were T-34s. Thus, in this area alone, far more T-34s were available than had been on Konev's entire West Front on October 2. Two of the brigades, the 18th and 19th, arrived on October 9–10 to block the German advance from Gzhatsk to Mozhaisk. On October 14 they made up the first defense line at Mozhaisk. It was hoped they would slow down the German XL Panzer Corps before it reached Lelyushenko's main defense line at Borodino, where the 32nd Rifle Division had dug in. Flank cover was provided by a motorcycle regiment and some militia units. There were also four antitank gun regiments in the area. Three of them were attached to the division, while the fourth was part of the defense of Mozhaisk. The 20th Tank Brigade, with 61 tanks and an antitank gun regiment, formed the reserve.[60]

Bitter fighting ensued. The Germans gradually pushed towards Mozhaisk, but October 14 was an unhappy day for the SS-Division Das Reich. Its commander, SS-General Paul Hausser, followed the progress of the attack from the forward positions. Shells from Soviet tanks were detonating all around. SS-Captain Erich Windish was near the general when he was hit: "Suddenly he covered his right eye with his palm. We were terrified. We immediately rushed to help him." The general was badly wounded on the right side of his face and after receiving first aid, he was evacuated by a Fieseler Storch aircraft.[61]

The fighting continued and German tanks attacked the Fifth Army staff on October 16, forcing the staff officers into close combat. At the same time Lelyushenko's reserve tank brigade was committed. Lelyushenko himself was badly wounded and lost consciousness. He later wrote in his memoirs that when he woke up, he was informed that the defenses still held and he "had never been as happy as at that moment."[62]

Lelyushenko was evacuated during the evening of October 18 and taken to a hospital in Gorky, 400 kilometers (250 miles) east of Moscow. The 44-year-old Lt. General Leonid Govorov assumed command of the Fifth Army. He had made his career in the artillery and had commanded the artillery in the Reserve Front from August until it was disbanded in October. On the same day, October 18, Mozhaisk fell to a combined force from the SS-Das Reich Division and the 10th Panzer Division. The Fifth Army launched counterattacks—involving tanks, artillery and rocket artillery—to recapture Mozhaisk. The XL Panzer Corps commander, General Georg Stumme, reported to Panzer Group 4 that further attacks were not feasible unless the corps was reinforced by the 5th Panzer Division.[63]

At first, Panzer Group 4 hesitated to send 5th Panzer Division to Stumme's corps. It intended to place the center of gravity at the XLVI Panzer Corps, further north. However, the 5th Panzer Division was engaged on Stumme's front sector in the evening on October 19, when Govorov's attack was repelled. The battles were costly to both sides. The SS-Infantry Regiment "Deutschland" had been reduced to such an extent that the rifle companies mustered between 30 and 100 men, although it must be remembered that they had already been depleted before the fighting at Mozhaisk. In five of the rifle companies, not a single officer remained in command.[64]

The Soviet generals had hoped to halt the Germans along the Mozhaisk Line, but their hopes had been thwarted. Indeed, it began to seem as if Moscow could not be saved, and it would only become clear later that the Germans would have to halt where they had broken through. Not even where they made their most determined efforts could they overcome their supply problems. Field Marshal von Bock grudgingly had to accept that the fears he had expressed before the operation had come true. After an immensely successful beginning, the offensive was stuck in the autumn mud.[65]

It was clear to German soldiers and officers at the front that the chance to capture Moscow might have been lost. Possibly they would get another opportunity when the ground had frozen hard enough to allow the vehicles to move, but nobody knew when frost would come.

The Soviet decision-makers were not aware of the extent of the supply issues that the Germans were struggling to overcome. Of course, generals like Zhukov, who was fairly well informed, suspected that the mud was seriously impairing the German efforts to keep the offensive going, but he could not presuppose that the danger was temporarily over. To the contrary, he had to continue his frantic work to patch up the defenses west of Moscow.

Except for the Stavka, few were as well informed about the situation at the front as Zhukov—even the senior representatives of state agencies knew less. The citizens in Moscow were also badly informed about what transpired at the front. Gradually, information about the collapse in early October leaked out. All kinds of rumors were mixed up with correct information. In this particular case the correct information boded very ill. As a result, remarkable scenes took place in Moscow while the Germans punched through the Mozhaisk Line.

Zhukov's reports on the available forces at the front, combined with the fact that the Mozhaisk Line had been broken in several places and Kaluga had fallen on October 13, led to discussion of evacuating Moscow. The defense might not hold. All Soviet leaders knew their history. In 1812, Napoleon and Kutuzov had fought near Borodino. One week after the battle, on September 7, Napoleon's troops had marched into Moscow. The

Soviet authorities ordered preparations for evacuation and the destruction of important objects. This, however, was not something entirely new. People had in fact been evacuated from Moscow since the beginning of the war, but as the front came ever-closer to the capital, the evacuation was intensified. Not only women and children, but also factories and their workers were moved to the Urals. There were many complexities and difficulties involved in transportation on such a vast scale. While trains brought soldiers and equipment to the front, other trains carried important cargo east. When evacuated men, women and children arrived, lodgings and factories were not always ready. The famous composer, Dmitri Shostakovich, was evacuated from Leningrad to Moscow on October 1. On October 16 he had to travel again, this time to Kuybyshev. He and his family had to sleep on the floor in a classroom with 14 other people. After a while, Shostakovich and his family were given a room, which included a grand piano.[66]

Foreign diplomats were sent to Kuybyshev, as was Molotov as representative of the Soviet government. The central administration of the NKVD left for Kuybyshev, but Beria remained in the capital. On October 16, Nina Uborevich and Nina Tukhachevskaya were executed. Their husbands, General Yeromin Uborevich and Marshal Mikhail Tukhachevskiy, had been executed in June 1937 when the Red Army was purged. Beria continued to order more executions. He allowed some prominent prisoners to be evacuated to Kuybyshev, but then had second thoughts. An executioner was sent and several of the prisoners were executed before the end of October.[67]

Chief of staff Shaposhnikov, with parts of the general staff, had been ordered to leave Moscow on October 16 should the city, like Leningrad, be surrounded. Vasilyevsky assumed command of the part that remained in Moscow. Not knowing what the future held, Vasilyevsky rang Stalin to ask for permission to go to the station and bid farewell to his mentor. Stalin did not give permission, as he needed Vasilyevsky at headquarters.[68]

Unrest spread in Moscow. The newspaper *Pravda* announced on October 13 that Vyazma had fallen. Two days later it reported that the Germans threatened Moscow, which caused further unrest. Those who could began to flee east. New forms of crime appeared, for example violent robbery against motor vehicles heading east. Many took the chance to appropriate money and valuables. Brawls occurred in queues for shops. Everybody realized that food and other items would become scarce. The police did not intervene, finding an excuse in the fact that no instructions had been given.[69]

Did Stalin consider leaving Moscow? According to one of the men closest to the dictator, Anastas Mikoyan, Stalin said on October 15 that the Politburo should leave Moscow on that day and he would himself leave next day. Probably this was simply idle talk. Stalin knew history. Leningrad had been the tsar's capital, but soon after the Bolsheviks seized power they made Moscow the hub of their realm. Should he, the great leader, abandon the Bolsheviks' capital?[70]

He had endured chaos and hardship before, when the entire world seemed to have united against the Bolsheviks. This time, they had strong allies, and "lend-lease" deliveries of weapons, munitions, and equipment had begun to arrive. New Soviet armies were forming.

As long as Stalin did not clearly state his intention, many of his henchmen pursued preparations for evacuation. Their faith in victory began to waver as the Germans moved closer to Moscow, but when Stalin publicly announced on October 16 that he would remain in Moscow, attitudes changed. Aleksandr Shcherbakov made a speech on the radio on October 17, with the intention of restoring law and order, but disturbances still occurred. A state of siege was declared on October 20 and after that there was no question about Stalin's intentions—he would remain in Moscow, and the city would be defended to the last bullet.[71]

STALIN'S HUB OF POWER—THE CITY OF MOSCOW

Moscow was not just a political center in the Soviet Union; it had many other important roles. It was a hub of the communications network, as well as for many railroads. The Volga Canal gave it an important position in inland water transport, which was important in the Soviet Union as it had many navigable rivers. Moscow was also home to important industries. In 1940, about 50% of all cars manufactured in the Soviet Union were assembled in Moscow, and its share of the production of machine tools for the manufacturing industry was similar. About 40% of all electrical equipment was produced in Moscow. There were 475 major enterprises in the capital; some of them were evacuated east in July, but it was not until October that the process of moving industry gathered momentum. Approximately 210,000 workers and their enterprises were moved east in October and November.[72]

Moscow had a population of only 2 million in 1927. It expanded rapidly during the 1930s, and the population numbered 4.1 million at the end of 1940. The first subway line had opened in 1935.[73]

Evacuation of Moscow's inhabitants began when Germany's military might was unleashed against the Soviet Union. More than 1.3 million people were evacuated before July 26 and the process continued at the same rate. By September 10, 2.2 million had been evacuated. Not all the evacuated were the pre-war population of the city, as refugees from the western parts of the country had gathered in the capital. So despite the evacuations, the population of Moscow stood at 4.2 million in September. This increase in population was partly offset by the fact that almost 800,000 Moscow citizens were sent to the front during 1941. In October, evacuations began to outpace the influx of people, and by the end of 1941, Moscow's population numbered 2.1 million.[74]

Moscow was home to an object of great symbolic value for the Soviet Union: the Lenin Mausoleum, which contained the embalmed remains of the founder of the Soviet state. It could not be allowed to fall into German hands or be destroyed. If the government failed to protect Lenin's dead body, its legitimacy would inevitably suffer. The decision to evacuate it was taken at the end of June and in July the body was moved to Chumen in Siberia, 2,144 kilometers (1,332 miles) away from Moscow. This move did not become public knowledge. Several factories were also evacuated to Chumen, an important junction for railroads, roads and telephone lines..[75]

The number of physicians in the city shrank during 1941 from almost 16,000 to 5,000. Many were probably called up for military service. On July 17, it was decided to introduce ration cards in the city. They were handed out at places of work, but children and others in need received cards from house administrators. Clothes were also rationed, leading many to use their best clothes carefully.[76]

Moscow's fire-fighting service was improved early on. There were many wooden buildings in the city and German bombing could have grave consequences. Air defenses had been strengthened before the war, with antiaircraft guns as well as fighters, but after the war broke out, the protection of the population received more attention. More shelters were prepared and training programmes for the civilian population were initiated: civilians were taught how to take care of incendiary bombs, and movie theaters showed instruction films alongside the main feature. In mid-July, British air-defense experts arrived from London to share the knowledge they had gained during the German "Blitz."[77]

Moscow was known for its thriving cultural life, but this would change. Stalin ordered the four most prominent theaters to evacuate on October 13. They were sent to Kuybyshev, Saratov, Gorki and Omsk. No fewer than 43 passenger cars and 35 freight cars were required for the evacuation of the theaters.[78]

The leading architects in Moscow drew up plans to conceal the central squares, roads, and buildings to make it more difficult for German aircrews to find their targets. Dummy factories were created in uninhabited areas at some distance from the center. Moscow had a hectic nightlife before the war, when bars and clubs stayed open until two hours after midnight, but the threat from German bombers caused all this to change as blackouts were enforced.[79]

The German infantry had fought constantly for months, with attendant losses and wear and tear. There was no time for rest and recuperation when battles were fought day after day, week after week, and month after month.

ELEVEN

ON TO TULA

Panzer Group 4 and Fourth Army posed an immediate threat to Moscow, as they were only 60 kilometers (37 miles) away. Further south, Guderian's Second Panzer Army had more than 200 kilometers (125 miles) to cover before it reached Moscow's suburbs.

The half-hearted German attempt to advance from Orel to Tula on October 6–7 had been followed by a period when Guderian focused his efforts on closing the pockets in the Bryansk area. The miserable weather did not allow other options. Guderian let the 4th Panzer Division remain in the Orel-Mtsensk area where it would soon be joined by the 3rd Panzer Division.[1]

Paul-Heinz Flemming served in the 11th Company of the 3rd Motorized Infantry Regiment, which was part of the 3rd Panzer Division. The regiment's heavy company, it was equipped with 15cm infantry howitzers. These weapons lacked the range of ordinary howitzers, but were considerably lighter. This was a significant advantage in bad weather, but it would be a gross exaggeration to say that they were easy to move in the mud.

On October 6, the company was ordered to leave the area south of Kromy. As the company prepared to march, rain began to fall. Nobody knew how long the rain would continue, but in any case the company set out. The roads turned out to be in better condition than expected. A strong easterly wind swept away the rainclouds to shed their contents elsewhere. But the wind brought an unpleasant companion: cold. The motorcyclists were the first to suffer from the temperature. Later, the roads became icy and slippery. Flemming's unit was unable to ascend an uphill slope about 100 meters long because it was so slippery. Instead they had to drive their vehicles over the fields, which were not as slick. In this way they coaxed their vehicles forward, slowly and arduously.[2]

When this difficult obstacle had been negotiated, the men of the 11th Company experienced yet another weather change. Heavy snowfall made it difficult to move even on flat ground. Often the vehicles did not get further than 25 meters before getting stuck in snow. The company continued laboriously and it did not reach Kromy until 9:00 p.m. As this town is situated well south of Orel, a considerable distance still remained to cover.[3]

The soldiers were given very little time to sleep that night. They were roused at 4:00 a.m. and the march resumed soon after. The roads had not improved and the large number of units that crowded the road to Orel exacerbated the problems. Some of the vehicles ran out of fuel, but nobody knew when more might arrive. Only 40 kilometers (25 miles) separated Orel and Kromy, and in fair conditions a motorized company like Flemming's should have been able to cover that distance in under two hours. However, on October 7 the conditions were very bad. The men in 11th Company, covered head to toe with mud and dirt, had to work hard all day to reach Orel in the evening.[4]

When they reached Orel, the soldiers were able to eat, wash and enjoy the comforts of being billeted indoors—a joy for soldiers who had fought the elements for many days. Flemming and his comrades were allowed to stay in Orel a few days, to rest and perform maintenance. Flemming was happy to do most of his tasks indoors. As usual, most days, including Saturdays, were workdays, but on October 12, a Sunday, a day of rest was allowed, to Flemming's surprise.[5]

Flemming was served yet another surprise on October 12. The company commander, Lieutenant Comberg, called for Flemming to tell him that he would be transferred to the 2nd Platoon, where he would assume an NCO position. Comberg also told Flemming that he would become gun commander after gaining experience in his new position.[6] Personnel matters like this were not unusual during operations. To the contrary, they became even more important as casualties had to be replaced. A company commander had to ensure that suitable candidates were available when commanders were killed or wounded.

The 11th Company left Orel on October 13 and drove north toward Bolkhov, on the left flank of the 4th Panzer Division. The road was relatively firm, which made it passable, but it was very bumpy. Just north of

Bolkhov, Soviet defenders halted the company. The Germans initiated an outflanking move, which again took Flemming and his comrades into the fields. The ground had frozen during the night, but rising temperatures during the day turned them into a sea of mud. Flemming was travelling on a motorcycle and got very dirty. He soon changed to travelling in a car, but that turned out to be a bad decision as it got stuck in a water-filled pit. Flemming and the others gathered straw, which they tried to get under the wheels. Then they pushed as hard as they could, but the mud refused to release its grip on the car.[7]

Many cars suffered the same fate. The soldiers had to give up their efforts and instead began to look for shelter for the night. At 6:00 p.m., they went to the small village of Karandakov. The place did not make a good impression on Flemming, but the houses were warm and that was what mattered as the soldiers slept well, despite the cold outside. In the morning, Flemming noted that the ground had frozen during the night. He heard distant artillery fire, which he believed originated from the area where the 4th Panzer Division was fighting. He later saw Soviet aircraft above the village, but the aviators did not appear to have seen the Germans. Nothing notable took place during the following days. The platoon was stuck at Karandakov, and Flemming used the time to cook potatoes in several different ways.[8]

Flemming's hiatus in Karandakov during the advance makes sense in the context of the German army's movements. The 3rd Panzer Division had initially advanced on 4th Panzer Division's southern flank, but the success enjoyed by the latter unit prompted the Germans to shift 3rd Panzer north. Its components of course had to be shifted, but events taking place further west also had consequences for the 3rd Panzer Division. On October 7, Army Group Center had designated Tula as the next goal for Second Panzer Army. Guderian had objected, as the poor roads and lack of fuel ruled out a thrust to Tula. Instead he would have to focus on less far-reaching missions, such as completing the encirclement of the Bryansk Front. The 3rd and 4th Panzer Divisions, located quite far to the east of the area where the Soviet forces would be surrounded, found themselves in a kind of backwater, despite being the furthest advanced units of Second Panzer Army. These circumstances allowed Flemming and his comrades their few calm days.[9]

Lack of fuel, muddy roads, and the need to finish the encirclement battles at Bryansk suffice to explain why the Germans did not advance to Tula, but there were other factors too. On October 8, Guderian flew to Orel and met commanders from the XXIV Panzer Corps, including the commander of 4th Panzer Division. During the meeting, much attention was given to the heavy Soviet tanks which had been encountered, for example at Mtsensk. As the German tank guns—and antitank guns—were marginally effective against these tanks at best, the Germans had to rely on 8.8cm and 10cm guns to knock them out. These two types of guns fired shells at such high muzzle-velocity that they could destroy the T-34 even at long range, but few of them were available. Armor-piercing rounds for these guns were also in short supply. Guderian and the corps' officers agreed that it would be possible to resume the advance when sufficient guns with ample supply of ammunition were available to them. However, given the condition of the roads, this would not occur in the near future.[10]

The 4th Panzer Division resumed its attack toward Mtsensk on October 9, but it was not a determined effort. The spearheads came within about 10 kilometers of the town before being halted by Soviet tanks. On the same day the 3rd Panzer Division received orders to advance on Mtsensk from the west. Fuel was finally brought to the forward elements of the 4th Panzer Division northeast of Orel, and the division captured Mtsensk on October 10.[11]

Despite the arrival of some fuel, the supply situation remained precarious. It was hoped that the Second Panzer Army could rely on the Bryansk–Orel railroad to transport ammunition, fuel, food, winter equipment and all other supplies, but it was not expected to be ready until October 20. Meanwhile fighting in the Mtsensk area continued. The 4th Panzer Division only had a weak grip on the town and Soviet forces counterattacked. Fighting raged in the northern outskirts of Mtsensk, while the roads deteriorated even further. The ground had not yet frozen, so the snow melted as it landed, making the roads virtually impassable. Nevertheless, the 4th Panzer Division finally managed to secure Mtsensk on October 12.[12]

It was clear that the fighting in the Mtsensk area had come to an end. Colonel Katukov, the commander of the Soviet 4th Tank Brigade, wrote in his memoirs that it was hard to form an accurate impression of the fighting during these days. Senior staff often failed to coordinate units. Sometimes he did not know the units on his flanks. When Katukov's forces were withdrawn across the Susha River on October 10, he was surprised to find other Soviet units moving in the area. It soon transpired that they were men of the Thirteenth Army who had managed to escape the encirclement further south.[13]

Another sign that the fighting in the Mtsensk area was abating was the fact that Major General Lelyushenko, commander of the 1st Guards Rifle Corps, was called back to Moscow. Major General Aleksey Kurkin assumed command over the Twenty-Sixth Army, which was formed from the 1st Guards Rifle Corps on October 10. Back in Moscow, Lelyushenko met Stalin, with Shaposhnikov and Molotov also present. Molotov stared at Lelyushenko and asked, "Why did you not throw the enemy out of Orel?" Lelyushenko responded bitterly, but Stalin interrupted and dismissed Molotov with a wave of his hand. Stalin thanked Lelyushenko for his work at Mtsensk and gave him a new mission. As usual, Shaposhnikov gave Lelyushenko the details. He would be assuming command of the new Fifth Army, and he departed for the Mozhaisk Line soon after.[14]

■ ■ ■

Army Group Center issued a new directive to Second Panzer Army on October 12. Both Second Army and Second Panzer Army were assigned new missions, which meant that they would have to cross each other's lines of communications. From its staging area on the southern wing of Army Group Center, Guderian's forces advanced northeast. Simultaneously, Col. General Maximilian von Weichs' Second Army advanced straight east. This maneuver would require time. Not only were the two armies engaged in fighting with the surrounded Soviet forces, the Second Army was also on the "wrong" side of the cauldrons. Army Group Center's directive would have to be regarded as a long-term goal under the prevailing conditions.[15]

On October 13 it was noted in the Second Panzer Army war diary that the roads were so muddy that they were unusable. No operation stood any chance of success until frost made the ground hard. Virtually nothing happened in the 4th Panzer Division sector at Mtsensk. The intention to attack Tula, expressed by the army group on October 7, remained a mere pipe dream as long as the mud reigned. In addition, the 3rd Panzer Division had been committed to action further west, but this was just a nuisance compared to the state of the roads. It was utterly impossible to bring forward the supplies needed for the continuation of the offensive.[16]

A teleprinter message from Army Group Center sent to Second Panzer Army on October 15 outlined a situation assessment and provided guidance for future operations. The Soviet units confronting the army group were regarded as thoroughly beaten and the remnants were trying to escape east. At most, enemy counterattacks were taking place locally. Accordingly, the Second Panzer Army was given the mission to cut off Moscow from south and east. The industrial cities of Tula and Kashira should also be captured.[17]

These instructions prompted Second Panzer Army to designate the thrust from Mtsensk to Tula as its main mission. When this goal had been attained, Guderian's units should establish bridgeheads across the Oka, a tributary of the Volga. It was aimed that they would capture river crossings in the sector between Ryazan and Serpukhov. As so often before, the XXIV Panzer Corps would spearhead the attack, and its tanks would be concentrated into Kampfgruppe Eberbach. Wear and tear had rendered many of the tanks inoperable. The attack should be launched on October 20, unless some unexpected development motivated an earlier start.[18]

There was one suitable supply road from Bryansk to Orel, and from Orel a major road led to Tula. The Second Panzer Army would therefore haul most of its supplies along a single road. Furthermore, the spearheads as well as follow-up forces would use the same road. In the mud, congestion was unavoidable and this came as no surprise to Guderian and his staff. As they could not change the conditions, the road was divided into sections and commandants controlled each section. The commandants were responsible for maintaining an uninterrupted flow of traffic and ensuring that high-priority movements were given precedence.[19]

It was easier for the Luftwaffe to move supplies forward, as the distance between its bases and the railheads was usually shorter. Airpower was probably of greater importance during the "mud" period than it had been earlier in Operation Barbarossa. Field Marshal Kesselring, the commander of Luftflotte 2, arrived at Second Panzer Army on October 17 to discuss air support. He intended to commit two Stuka-Gruppen, which had recently received replacements and new aircraft, and two Zerstörer-gruppen, which were equipped with twin-engined Messerschmitt Bf-110 fighters, to support Second Panzer Army. As Second Panzer Army's stocks of fuel and ammunition were dwindling, despite the fact they had not fought any significant battles, the air support was indeed welcome.[20]

On October 18, Guderian met General Leo Geyr von Schweppenburg, commander of XXIV Panzer Corps. They discussed the imminent
attack and paid particular attention to the assessment of enemy forces and
intentions. Air reconnaissance had reported numerous wheel tracks on
either side of the Mtsensk–Tula road. This suggested that substantial
Soviet reinforcements might have arrived and taken up defensive positions
along the road. Stronger opposition could thus be expected, which probably would require faster consumption of their precious ammunition.[21]

Guderian had problems, but the Soviet commanders were struggling
with even greater difficulties. The Bryansk Front had been ruptured by
the German attack and the northern part (Fiftieth Army) had retreated
towards Tula, the middle part (mostly the Third Army) tried to escape in
the Elets direction, and the southern part (Thirteenth Army and Group
Ermakov) folded back towards Kursk. The weather prevented the Germans from advancing faster than the Soviet soldiers retreated, as the latter
did not concern themselves unduly with horse-drawn carriages, vehicles
and howitzers. Anything that could not be moved quickly enough was left
behind. Furthermore, the Soviet forces were retreating towards their rail
heads and supply lines, while the Germans became more and more separated from theirs. Most rifle divisions in the Bryansk Front managed to
escape, although badly mauled. Only eight of 25 were fully destroyed or
disbanded. The remaining divisions continued to fight as well as they could
in their depleted state. Almost all of them had lost their heavy artillery,
which consisted of 122mm howitzers.[22]

The chaotic situation became even more difficult on October 13 when
Eremenko was wounded and flown to Moscow. He had been visiting units
at the front and was in a forester's hut, where the staff of the 269th Rifle
Division was located, when German dive-bombers attacked. A bomb fell
not far from Eremenko, and he was wounded. Major General Georgiy
Zakharov, the chief of staff, assumed command of the Bryansk Front.[23]

It was difficult to create a coherent defense line from the shattered
remnants. The units in the south tried to escape east while delaying the
enemy. In the north, the Bryansk Front had to defend Tula. Anything that
could be raked together was sent to defend the approaches. Major General
Aleksey Kurkin's Twenty-Sixth Army defended the sector southwest of
Tula. Various NKVD units were positioned on the western side of the
town, to slow down enemy forces approaching from Kaluga and Kozelsk.

Simultaneously, the Fiftieth Army tried desperately to withdraw to Tula, but the Bryansk Front staff could not get a clear picture of what was going on at the Fiftieth Army. Radio communications were poor, and on October 17 the Bryansk Front also temporarily lacked any communications with Third and Thirteenth armies.[24]

The Stavka regarded the threat against Tula, along the Kaluga–Tula road, as serious. Hence, the full-strength 238th Rifle Division, which had recently arrived from Alma-Ata in Central Asia, was directed to Aleksin to defend the threatened area. The Forty-Ninth Army, which was part of Zhukov's West Front, was responsible for that part of the front line.[25]

■ ■ ■

When it was decided to launch the attack towards Tula on October 20, Guderian made the observation that he could start earlier if Soviet resistance slackened. Instead, he was forced to postpone, as the supply roads were so miserable that the attacking units had not received sufficient ammunition and fuel. A few days passed during which Guderian suffered agonies, but in the evening on October 22, both the 3rd and 4th Panzer Divisions stood in the designated jump-off area.[26]

Soldiers serving in the lowest echelons of the military structure rarely received more than sporadic information about the overall situation. Flemming did not know what mission the 3rd Panzer would receive, but on October 15 he was at least informed of the overall situation on the army group sector. He also learned that the 2nd and 5th Panzer Divisions had arrived from France and had participated in the attack on October 2. Otherwise he was left with no alternative but to guess and listen to rumors. This lead to mundane matters being more often included in the diary. For example, he found, for the first time, a louse that had attacked him and already laid several eggs.[27]

The almost incessant rain and the boggy roads suggested to Flemming that an offensive was unlikely to be launched soon. However on October 21 his unit was ordered to move into positions from which the attack on Tula would be launched. Flemming caught a glimpse of the sun on this day, a pleasant break in the dull weather. The unit did not begin to move until October 22.[28]

Flemming's task before the attack was to bring ammunition forward using a horse-drawn cart. The process was very slow. Not until 10:00 p.m.

did he reach the designated place, from where the platoon's infantry how-itzers would provide fire support on the following day. It was of course desirable to move into the jump-off positions under cover of darkness, but Flemming's late arrival was solely attributable to the muddy ground.[29]

As the attack was to be launched in the early morning, the men hurried to get everything ready. The horses were exhausted and had hardly got any fodder in the past days. The soldiers had to do the hard work themselves. At last they managed to get the infantry howitzers in firing positions, but Flemming could not allow himself any rest. He went to the fire directors' observation post while the men carried shells to the firing position. Not until 11:00 p.m. had all preparations been completed. Only a few hours remained. Flemming went to a small, heated hut for some rest. It was crammed but he found a corner where he could rest an hour or two.[30]

■ ■ ■

The attack started at dawn on October 23. Flemming's platoon would attack a farmstead where Soviet defenders had entrenched themselves. It proved to be a difficult task, as the short range of the infantry howitzers meant they could barely reach the enemy. The crews could not tell how effective the fire was, but they ceased firing at the designated moment and began to observe the advancing German infantry.[31]

When Flemming and the fire directors had completed their mission, they moved to another position, from which they could identify new tar-gets. Owing to the limited number of horses, only one of the howitzers could be moved at a time. The second had to wait. Flemming accompanied the howitzer, which need to be moved across a stream. The Soviet artillery took advantage of the opportunity and opened fire, but this did not ham-per Flemming and the men significantly. The emaciated condition of the horses was a greater problem, as the poor beasts were hardly capable of pulling the gun. However, when it was needed most, a vehicle appeared and helped pulled the piece.[32]

After laboriously moving ahead on muddy roads, Flemming reached the stream, where a ferry constructed from inflatable rafts waited. It took the infantry howitzer across, but once the Germans had reached the bank on the other side, they had to throw themselves down, as shells from Soviet artillery began to explode around them. One of Flemming's comrades was wounded, although not seriously.[33]

After the curt greeting from the Soviet artillery, Flemming and his comrades resumed the hard work of bringing infantry howitzers forward. It was so time-consuming that they did not have time to do anything else before the sun set. At the end of the day, Flemming witnessed a tank battle from a distance. He tried to follow the action, but found it hard to get an overview. Tracers darted back and forth between the duelling tanks. When the spectacle was over, Flemming found the house where he was supposed to sleep during the night. All windows had been destroyed so the cold night air invaded the house, making it difficult to sleep.[34]

What Flemming had experienced on October 23 was quite characteristic of the efforts of XXIV Panzer Corps on this day. Only the 3rd Panzer Division, supported by Stukas, attacked initially, and it was severely hampered by the conditions under foot. It did gain ground, but it took longer than expected to prepare a bridge across the Susha River. The Germans had decided to let the 4th Panzer Division wait until a firm bridgehead had been established. Thus the delays affected Major General Willibald von Langermann und Erlencamp's 4th Panzer too, despite the fact that it would attack further south.[35]

The mud delayed the 3rd Panzer Division, and at noon the designated objectives had not been attained. Lt. General von Schweppenburg decided that the 4th Panzer Division could no longer be held back. Instead of waiting for its neighbor, the 4th Panzer was ordered to attack, and its artillery opened fire at 12:45 p.m. The shells hit the hills northeast of Mtsensk during 30 minutes of artillery preparation. When the guns fell quiet, Stukas entered the scene and dived towards the ground; at the last moment the pilots released their bombs and began to pull up. The critical hour had arrived for the riflemen and the tankers of the Soviet Twenty-Sixth Army.[36]

It would be Twenth-Sixth Army's last fight, as Stalin had decided to disband the army and incorporate its units into the Fiftieth Army for the defense of Tula, though he had not yet sent the order.[37]

The terrain did not offer the advancing soldiers of 4th Panzer Division much cover, but the riflemen found some consolation in the 18 tanks that spearheaded the attack. Still, the task proved difficult. Some of the tanks got stuck in a minefield, where they were exposed to Soviet antitank weapons. Engineers began to lift the mines, but by 3:00 p.m. the attack had become bogged down, despite German efforts. Casualties mounted and would have been heavier had not Soviet artillery fire been so weak, a fact the Germans attributed to the effectiveness of their artillery barrage and the air attacks.[38]

Fighting still raged in the 4th Panzer Division sector in the evening of October 23, for example at the heights three kilometers northeast of Mtsensk, where Soviet tanks had dug in. The 3rd Panzer Division enjoyed greater success. It established a bridgehead across the Susha and expanded it to a depth of six kilometers. An entry in the Second Panzer Army war diary says that the ground was so muddy that tanks could only get forward by using first gear. The supply vehicles of course suffered even more.[39]

It was not only the lack of major success that was worrying Guderian. Since the start of Operation *Barbarossa*, the 1st Cavalry Division had been attached to 2nd Panzer Group most of the time. At this moment, the division was recalled from the Eastern Front. The only German cavalry division would be converted into the 24th Panzer Division and it would not return to the East until the early summer of 1942.[40]

In response to the German attack, the Soviet 290th Rifle Division was ordered to take up defensive positions at Shchenko, to cover Tula from the south. The division was badly depleted, mustering only about 2,100 men on October 23. However, it was reinforced by the 58th Reserve Rifle Regiment, and the 447th Corps Artillery Regiment provided fire support from its 152mm howitzers.[41]

The limited progress on October 23 disappointed Guderian and led to an argument with von Schweppenburg. According to Guderian, the 4th Panzer Division had not attacked according to the Second Panzer Army's intentions. Von Schweppenburg argued that the marginal success could be attributed to well-concealed Soviet defense positions. This made the task of German fire directors very difficult, while the tankers and riflemen found it hard to spot the Soviet positions, which included fieldworks such as bunkers.[42]

Undoubtedly, von Schweppenburg's explanations, combined with very limited mobility due to the weather, were plausible. Reinforcements were on their way, as the elite Grossdeutschland Regiment would join the XXIV Panzer Corps. The regiment would subsequently be expanded first into a division and later a corps. At this time it was a reinforced regiment. The bad roads would prevent it from participating in the attack until later on October 24. The roads were described as bottomless canals of mud and it was even difficult to walk on the slippery ground.[43]

Despite the welcome reinforcement, XXIV Panzer Corps did not enjoy much greater success on October 24. Partly, this could be attributed to the delays suffered by the Grossdeutschland Regiment on the muddy roads. The attack could not be launched until noon, when the artillery fired a strong barrage. Infantry from the 4th Panzer Division and the Grossdeutschland Regiment surged forward, but to little avail as they were met by intensive fire from the Soviet defenders.[44]

At 4:00 p.m. the Germans renewed their efforts. The artillery, including rocket artillery, again opened fire. Observing German soldiers thought that a hailstorm had hit the Soviet positions. Blossoming black clouds rose from the target area before the German soldiers again moved forward. Despite an even heavier barrage, the 4th Panzer Division made little headway. The Grossdeutschland Regiment enjoyed somewhat greater success, denting the Soviet defenses, but still not achieving a decisive result.[45]

The 3rd Panzer Division managed to push the Soviet defenders back three kilometers in the northern part of its sector on October 24. German lead elements engaged Soviet tanks in the evening. The southern wing had advanced almost as far, and the 3rd Panzer Division captured many prisoners.[46]

In the evening, another order from Army Group Center was received by the Second Panzer Army teleprinters. According to the situation assessment, Soviet forces were expected to offer stronger resistance in the area west of Voronezh than had previously been assumed. The army group believed the Red Army would hang on to this area, in order to protect the railroad that connected Moscow and Rostov. Also, Soviet forces could use the region as a staging area for mounting threats to the flanks of army groups Center and South.[47]

Accordingly, the Second Army's mission appeared more important and also more demanding. To manage its more challenging task, the Second Army would receive XLVIII Panzer Corps from Second Panzer Army. This did not have much impact on Guderian's operations, as the XLVIII Panzer Corps, consisting of 9th Panzer Division, and 16th and 25th Motorized Infantry Divisions, had already attacked in the direction of Voronezh. The decision did not reshuffle units as much as it meant a change of responsibilities for the two armies. Guderian would focus on the Tula area and Second Army on the Kursk-Voronezh area.[48]

Guderian's attack on Tula had only resulted in small gains during the first two days, and in the evening he and his staff were seriously concerned about the supply situation. Ammunition was so scarce that it might be impossible to continue the attack. Even more alarming, Eberbach's tanks had no gas. If they could not refuel, they would lay stranded on the following day.[49]

During the night of October 24–25, forward German units noted that Soviet fire slackened. It was hard to form a correct picture in the darkness, and when the sun rose, fog limited visibility. Nevertheless, after a while the Germans concluded that the Soviet forces were pulling out. Such an opportunity ought to be exploited, but lack of fuel stopped the Germans from taking advantage of the situation. Fortunately for the German ground troops, the Luftwaffe offered help. Only 12 cubic meters (2,640 gallons) could be flown to the spearheads, but the quantity allowed at least some of the tanks to advance.[50]

Wheeled vehicles could hardly move at all in the mud, but Eberbach sent a tank battalion to haul fuel to the other tanks. The tanks moved slower in the mud, but they could at least move, and there was fuel to pick up at Orel. This allowed Kampfgruppe Eberbach to capture Chern, almost 30 kilometers (19 miles) northeast of Mtsensk, and seize two intact bridges across the river in the town.[51]

It became clear on October 25 that the German advance on Tula was gaining momentum after two days of hard fighting. Guderian rejoiced, but he realized that the strained supply lines were becoming even longer. The situation was so bad that even units further back were receiving food by airdrop. The many destroyed bridges between Chern and Mtsensk further hampered vehicle movement. The Soviet defenders had also created minefields in many areas.[52]

The Soviet withdrawal allowed the Germans to advance to Tula, but the state of the roads and the associated supply problems precluded any rapid movements of the kind seen during the first week of *Taifun*. Engineers worked hard during the night of October 25–26 to improve the road between Mtsensk and Chern, and before noon on October 26 their efforts had paid off. However, the roads remained almost impassable north of Chern, not least because of the destroyed bridges. The wheeled vehicles could not negotiate such obstacles, as they were unable to drive off-road to find fords when the ground was muddy.[53]

Since launching the attack on October 23, XXIV Panzer Corps had captured 2,481 prisoners, according to a report dated October 26. Almost all of the prisoners were from the 6th Guards Rifle Division. The German losses were far smaller. The 4th Panzer Division, which had met the strongest opposition, recorded 27 killed in action and 135 wounded in the period October 23–25. Altogether, the XXIV Panzer Corps lost 136 killed in action, 580 wounded, and three missing in the period October 21–31.[54]

When the engineers had cleared minefields, repaired demolished bridges, and removed obstacles on the road from Mtsensk and Chern, the vehicles could be allowed to use the road. However, the macadam surface did not stand up to the heavy volume of traffic. It deteriorated so quickly that it was all but useless by October 27. The Germans resorted to stealing macadam from the nearby railroad to render the road passable again, but it only provided temporary help. Furthermore, Guderian and his staff had to realize that what appeared as good roads on their 1:300,000 maps were not much more than paths.[55]

It seemed to the Second Panzer Army that there was not a single met-alled road in the area. The chief of staff cautioned against conducting operations east of Tula when the roads were so poor. Guderian agreed and was of the opinion that the area south of the Oka River had to be cleared before an offensive east of Tula could be considered.[56]

While Guderian and his staff pondered on the future offensive, the lead elements of XXIV Panzer Corps battled on towards Tula. Somewhat ironically, the corps staff noted that its vehicles got stuck on the so-called road to Tula while regrouping. The tanks in the lead received fuel from Luftwaffe transport aircraft, which enabled them to continue northeast. However, the advancing Germans could not accomplish anything more than following on the heels of the retreating foe.[57]

The scenario pretty much repeated itself on October 28 and 29. Early on October 29 Guderian flew from Chern to Orel, where the Second Panzer Army staff was located. In Orel he met General Gotthard Heinrici, the XLIII Corps commander. The latter reported on the supply situation and his message was disheartening, but hardly surprising.[58]

Heinrici's corps had not received any bread or decent rations since October 20. His soldiers were surviving on anything they could find in the corps area. Fuel reserves were exhausted. There was still some fodder on hand, but the horses would soon devour the little that remained. As the Red Army had already consumed most of the local fodder, there was little prospect of finding much for the German horses. Guderian promised to help, but there was little he could do about the long distance to the rail-heads, or the muddy roads.[59]

Guderian received more encouraging information in the evening. By 3:00 p.m., the 3rd Panzer Division spearhead, which included the 6th Panzer Regiment, had reached within five kilometers of Tula. German aerial reconnaissance had indicated that there was hardly any defense before the city. Tula remained the primary objective and the Germans hoped to seize it by a coup-de-main, but they also knew that defenders in the built-up area could easily conceal themselves from the Luftwaffe. Also, some Soviet units still offered resistance behind the lead elements of 3rd Panzer Division.[60]

Later in the evening, Guderian was visited by two representatives from the Heereswaffenamt, the agency responsible for development and procurement of munitions and equipment for the army. They wanted to discuss future tanks following the experience the Germans had gained from fighting the heavy Soviet tanks. Guderian focused on four main areas. The first was improving the armament of the Panzer III and Panzer IV. He wanted longer barrels, larger propellant charges and improved ammunition, in order to increase the armor-piercing capabilities of the tanks' 5cm and 7.5cm guns. This would allow them to remain in production for a while.[61]

The second point was to develop a new medium tank, quite similar to the T-34. The Germans were well aware that the Soviet tanks suffered from poor internal layout, limited means of observation and were usually hard to command. The first of Guderian's wishes would be fulfilled in about six months. The second would result in two different tank prototypes. One of them, conceived by Daimler-Benz, was almost a carbon copy of the T-34. The other, designed by MAN, was larger and more powerful. After testing and evaluation, the Germans selected MAN's design for mass-production and it would receive its baptism of fire at Kursk in 1943, when it was known as the "Panther."

The two remaining points Guderian emphasized did not deal with tanks directly, but were nevertheless important for the panzer divisions. He wanted the antitank battalions to be equipped with 8.8cm and 10.5cm antiaircraft guns, to defeat heavy enemy tanks. Guderian had found the existing ammunition of the 8.8cm gun inadequate against the heaviest Soviet tanks.[62]

The latter demand would not be met, but the German panzer divisions were allowed to retain the antiaircraft battalion that had been temporarily included in their TO&E. Finally Guderian wanted to upgrade the artillery, by replacing the towed howitzers with self-propelled howitzers. Eventually, part of the panzer divisions' artillery would be self-propelled.[63]

Late in the evening, the Second Panzer Army staff received an assessment of the enemy compiled by Fremde Heere Ost, the department of the army high command responsible for intelligence in the east. The report, dated October 22, was very optimistic, as it concluded that the Red Army lacked substantial reserves.[64]

As we have seen, Stalin had already ordered the formation of ten reserve armies, which were scheduled to be committed from early December onwards. In November these included 59 rifle divisions, 13 cavalry divisions, 75 rifle brigades and 20 tank brigades. They were positioned along the line Vytegra–Rybinsk–Gorki–Saratov–Stalingrad–Astrakhan, but were not yet ready for action. Also during October, 12 fresh rifle divisions arrived to bolster the defenses west of Moscow and at the same time two motorized rifle divisions, three cavalry divisions, 20 artillery regiments and 28 antitank regiments arrived.

Finally, 17 tank brigades arrived, a number that surpassed the number of tank brigades facing Army Group Center when the Germans began their offensive on October 1. The brigades mustered approximately as many tanks per unit as had been the case on October 1, but there was a significant difference. There was a much larger proportion of T-34s in the recently arrived units. Training standards appear to have been similar. Despite bringing all these reinforcements forward, Stalin still had not exhausted his reserves, as we have seen. The Germans began to think that they were fighting a hydra, and they would never get rid of that feeling. Despite immense losses, Stalin continued to put new units in front of the Germans.[65]

■ ■ ■

The German 3rd Panzer Division attacked Tula on October 30, but only two infantry battalions and two tank battalions were available. Such a small force might have sufficed, had the city been weakly defended, but that was no longer the case. Several units, including the 156th NKVD Regiment with three battalions, the Tula workers' regiment's four battalions, the

732nd AA Regiment with 40 85mm antiaircraft guns, and elements from the 32nd Tank Brigade defended Tula. The defenders could expect additional fire support from the 152mm howitzers of the 447th Corps Artillery Regiment.[66]

A few hours later, Hitler sent an order that the Second Panzer Army should capture bridges across the Oka River at Serpukhov and cut the railroads south of Moscow. The order was fanciful. It did not take into account the fact that the Orel–Tula road was a ditch of knee-deep mud. The German spearhead was receiving all its supplies by air. Hitler claimed that a small detachment could accomplish the task, but that was utterly unrealistic. In fact, the Second Panzer Army had reached as far as could reasonably be expected. Attempts to capture Tula were repeated on October 30 and 31. More Soviet units arrived to take part in the fighting. Clearly, the Germans would need a larger force to seize Tula.[67]

Another Siberian division, the 413th Rifle Division with 12,000 men, had arrived and taken up positions east of Tula, in the Stalinogorsk area. It could threaten Guderian's right flank and at the same time block German attempts to get around Tula. The division had been raised in the Far East in August 1941, largely from manpower available in the area, for example officers and men from various military schools. It was deemed ready for action on October 1 and sent west.[68]

The defense of Tula grew even stronger. Retreating Soviet units arrived almost simultaneously with the German spearhead. Major General Popov was appointed city commandant on October 30. The defense of Aleksin-Aleshnaya, northwest of Tula, was entrusted to the Forty-Ninth Army, which was part of the West Front. Major General Arkadiy Ermakov, who had assumed command of the Fiftieth Army upon Petrov's death, had overall responsibility for the defense of Tula. Ermakov's army had ten divisions, to which various supporting units could be added, as well as air support. Almost all his units were depleted, but their main task was still to keep Tula and its communications to the east and northeast open, and to prevent the city from being surrounded. It would require large resources to capture Tula by direct assault. It is notable that Ermakov and his staff relocated from Tula to a place situated eight kilometers northeast of the city on October 30, without asking for permission from either the Bryansk Front or the Stavka. However, Ermakov seems to have escaped reprimands.[69]

Despite the immense difficulties, Guderian's forces had actually made the greatest progress of all Army Group Center forces in the ten final days of October, when the rest of the army group made almost no progress at all. A glance at the situation maps from the final days of October reveals most of Guderian's panzer army scattered along the Kromy–Orel–Tula road, or rather the mud-filled grove that was indicated as a road on the maps. Like a string of pearls, vehicles and soldiers from various divisions lay stranded along the route. Not until the ground froze could the Germans expect to regain momentum.[70]

THE SOVIET GUARDS AT MOSCOW

The guards designation was a honorific given to units that had proved themselves in battle. Guards had since long implied an elite unit, and the first guards units were supposed to be powerful tools for front comanders facing a crisis situation. They should be dependable units.

The first four guards divisions were created from four rifle divisions on September 18, 1941, and another three followed eight days later. On the same day, the 1st Motorized Rifle Division "Moscow" also received its guards designation. Two of the eight guards divisions were found in the fronts defending Moscow on October 1, but three more would soon arrive.[71]

After October 1, 6th and 7th Guards Rifle Divisions arrived, as well as the 1st Guards Motorized Rifle Division. The latter fought at Mtsensk, while the 7th Guards Rifle Division was used as a fire brigade. It was first sent to the Kursk area, then to Serpukhov and finally, after the fall of Solnechnogorsk on November 25, to Rokossovsky's Sixteenth Army. The 7th Guards Rifle Division had an unusually long history for a Soviet unit, having been been raised as the 64th Rifle Division during the Civil War. The motorized division mainly fought with the Thirty-Third Army.

Heavy casualties were incurred by the guards divisions. The 2nd Guards Rifle Division, for example, reported that only 3,189 men remained of its original strength on November 7. On the same day, the 6th Guards Rifle Division reported 5,130 men. The 5th Guards Rifle Division, which was initially with the West Front but was soon sent south and fought at Kaluga, lost 50% of its strength before October 15.[72]

Only two divisions were appointed guards during the defense of Moscow: the 78th and 316th rifle divisions. They received this honor in November, when they were renamed the 9th and 8th Guards Rifle Divisions respectively. Both had been sent to Rokossovsky's Sixteenth Army from Siberia. The soldiers in the 316th Division rejoiced when they heard that the division had been chosen to become a guards division, but this was clouded by the death of their popular commander, Lt. General Ivan Panfilov, on November 18.[73]

Not only rifle divisions were appointed guards. For example, Belov's and Dovator's cavalry corps and their divisions received guards designations on November 26, 1941. Also, the 4th Tank Brigade, commanded by Colonel Katukov, was appointed the 1st Guards Tank Brigade on November 11, 1941 after its battles at Mtsensk.[74]

When Katukov's brigade recieved its new designation, an order was sent to all fronts, armies, tank divisions, and brigades. The battles at Mtsensk, October 4–11, were emphasized and the order included formulations that reveal the state of affairs in the Red Army. For example, it was said that:

The brigade owed its exceptional actions and results to:
- Continous reconnaisance.
- Coordination between tanks, motorized infantry and artillery.
- Tanks were used in ambush positions.
- The brigade's soldiers fought bravely.
- The brigade's actions should be a good example for all units in the Red Army, fighting to liberate our country from the fascist invaders.[75]

Actually, points 1 to 3 should be regarded as standard procedures rather than something extraordinary. However, the Red Army considered it important to emphasise them. Hence, the order can be seen as indicating significant short-comings in prewar Soviet officer training.

TWELVE

THE END OF OCTOBER—HALFTIME FOR OPERATION TAIFUN

Guderian's tanks had reached the outskirts of Tula, but they were only the lead elements of his panzer army. On the army group's left flank, the Ninth Army straightened the front line, from the arch held on October 19 to a more or less straight line from Peno to Kalinin on November 2. Konev's Kalinin Front fell back but lost no positions of great value. It remained in the vicinity of Kalinin and halted the German efforts to capture Torzhok, as well as conducting local counterattacks. More reinforcements and weakened German defenses might allow Konev to recapture the city from which his front had received its name.[1]

Zhukov's new West Front was mainly attacked by forces from Panzer Group 4 and Fourth Army. The Volokolamsk–Mozhaisk–Malojaroslavets–Kaluga defense line had been broken in many places. The Germans had captured all these towns except Volokolamsk, but it too would soon fall.

The 2nd Panzer Division battle group, consisting of mechanized units such as tanks, armored personal carriers and other tracked vehicles, attacked towards Volokolamsk. The division had 16 infantry companies, but only one of them had armored half-tracks, a ratio not uncommon in contemporary German panzer divisions. The 35th Infantry Division also attacked directly towards Volokolamsk. Slightly to the south, the 11th Panzer Division attacked.[2]

Responsibility for the defense of Volokolamsk fell on the 316th Rifle Division, commanded by Major General Panfilov of Rokossovsky's Sixteenth Army. It was lavishly furnished with antitank guns. The crews manning these guns suffered severe losses during the battle, which turned into something akin to a defense to the last man. Militia battalions and companies from Moscow arrived during the battle and were used as replacements.[3]

During the battle for Volokolamsk, General Boldin arrived with a group of soldiers after escaping the Vyazma encirclement. He had yet again broken out from a German cauldron, although his latest feat was not as epic as the previous occasion. Boldin was wounded and immediately transferred to a hospital in Moscow.

Panfilov and his division acquired hero status from their conduct during the battle of Volokolamsk, even though they were unable to hold the Germans back. The Volokolamsk rail station was located south of the town and it was captured by tanks from the 2nd Panzer Division on October 25. Two days later, the 35th Infantry Division captured Volokolamsk. Istra was also threatened from the south by the 10th Panzer Division, but it would hold out another month. Panzer Group 4 discontinued its attacks, as it needed 1,000–1,500 tons of supply each day. As only 200 tons were arriving daily, this was utterly insufficient to maintain the offensive.[4]

Zhukov had to create new defenses along the line Klin–Istra–Dorochovo–Vorovsk–Serpuchov, but the German Fourth Army had already broken through at Dorochovo and Vorovsk in October. Von Kluge and his army had already reached the next Soviet defense line, Naro–Fominsk. However, poor weather, lack of supplies and stiffening opposition compelled von Kluge to cancel further attacks.

During the second half of October, more and more German units were reporting that the enemy seemed to be growing stronger. Battles were more bitterly fought and the enemy appeared to be fighting to the last man and bullet. As Zhukov received militia units from Moscow, the Germans concluded that the Soviet manpower reserves were dwindling. They believed that few regular soldiers remained, and instead workers from the factories were being sent to the front. The Germans were unaware that Stalin had held back several new formations, awaiting the proper moment to release them.[5]

Zhukov decided to use the Thirty-Third Army headquarters, which had been kept in reserve, in the front line between the Fifth and Forty-Third armies. Thus, each army would defend a specific major road leading to Moscow. He settled for a defense in depth and deemed it suitable to make one commander responsible for each major attack route. Lieutenant General Mikhail Efremov was appointed commander of the Thirty-Third

Army. He had previously served as commander of a reserve army, namely the Tenth Army, whose staff had been used to form the Kalinin Front staff. The 44-year-old Efremov was an experienced commander who had led the Twenty-First Army during the summer battles. Before the war he had been inspector general of the Red Army infantry. Zhukov's center in front of Moscow thus consisted of three armies, Fifth, Thirty-Third and Forty-Third, while his flanks were defended by the Sixteenth Army in the north and Forty-Ninth Army in the south.[6]

The German army supreme command, OKH, believed victory was imminent. After the conclusion of the Vyazma-Bryansk battle, it ordered one corps headquarters, four infantry divisions and the cavalry division to be pulled out and sent west. Obviously this weakened von Bock's forces. Also, due to orders from above, his remaining forces were diluted, as the Ninth and Second armies were sent on missions on the flanks. The former was ordered, together with Panzer Group 3, to conduct a joint operation with Army Group North, but von Bock at least managed to keep Panzer Group 3 out of the scheme. The Second Army was directed towards Voronezh, as already mentioned.[7]

The bad weather robbed the Germans of one of their most highly prized assets: their mobility, which had previously allowed them to concentrate their forces rapidly and beat the enemy by utilizing speed of movement. Their mobility and speed was in no small part due to their command process, which moved significantly faster than the Red Army's. The Germans dominated in maneuver warfare, but the mud slowed everything down, and the once-fluid operations were turning into something resembling the stalemate of World War I. Hence, the German speed of action ceased to be an advantage. Also, swift operations demanded supply and the Germans no longer had a smoothly running supply system. General Gotthard Heinrici, who commanded the XLIII Army Corps, noted on October 23 that it had taken 36 hours to drive 35 kilometers (22 miles)! On the same day, the 137th Infantry Division reported that it had taken 53 hours for three trucks to drive 40 kilometers (25 miles). Most Soviet roads were no better than gravel tracks, which became canals of mud after heavy rains. Vehicles and horses simply sank in the mud. Furthermore, there were fewer roads per square kilometer than in Western Europe. Fewer alternative roads existed, and the distances involved were larger. According to Carl Wagener of the Panzer Group 3 staff, Moscow would have lost its best protection against a modern conqueror had the roads in the country been better.[8]

The mud was at least 50 to 75 centimeters deep on the roads. German motor vehicles, designed for metalled roads, constantly got stuck. To make matters worse, the heavy going caused fuel consumption to soar, which precluded major offensive operations. For example, the vehicles of 6th Panzer Division were spread out along a 150-kilometer (93-mile) stretch of road between Kalinin and Gzhatsk without fuel on October 17. There could no longer be any talk of major German offensive operations.[9]

General Hermann Geyer, commander of IX Corps, gives another example of the difficulties moving. He frequently had to walk, as his personal vehicle, a Kübelwagen car, could not negotiate the muddy roads. He finally got hold of a heavy half-track, but it only took him halfway to his destination before running out of fuel. Generally, the heavy half-tracks really proved their worth as they could tow other vehicles through the mud.[10]

The Germans resorted to drastic measures to solve the traffic chaos. One of the divisions slated to pull out and march west, the 5th Infantry Division, committed the division staff as well as the engineer and the anti-tank battalions to overcome the chaos on the road between Yarzevo and Vyazma. They began to improve the roads and direct the traffic. The division commander, Major General Karl Allmendinger, was called "Autobahn dictator." All other components of the division had to march to the station at Smolensk to entrain. Most of the division reached Smolensk within 11 days, but some elements of the supply services needed even more time. The first train departed for France on November 6 and it was unloaded on November 14. During the journey, the trains occasionally had to stop and unload the carcasses of horses that had died during the transport. The poor beasts had simply been overexerted during their service at the front. The artillery regiment left its howitzers and horses to be distributed to other units.[11]

■ ■ ■

What fate befell the top Soviet commanders after the disaster at Vyazma-Bryansk? Two of the three front commanders were fired, and the third was wounded. Budjonny never again received a front command. Konev was given another chance, but he was sent to a front sector of secondary importance, where he remained until spring 1943, when he was given a

The rain made the roads wet, and if bad weather continued, they would deteriorate rapidly.
Von Bock's offensive ground to a halt when roads became a quagmire of mud.

more prominent position. He participated in the battle of Kursk in 1943.

Eremenko recovered from his wounds and was appointed commander of the Fourth Shock Army in December 1941. Later he became front commander on the southern sector and participated in the battle at Stalingrad. Mixed fates befell the 15 Soviet army commanders. Two were killed in action and three were captured, while three were fired in October and one was fired in November. The remaining six stayed in their positions.[12]

Three of the four fired army commanders had a background in the NKVD, and the fourth was Maj. General Piotr Sobennikov, commander of the Forty-Third Army. He had commanded the Eighth Army in the Baltic Military District on June 22, 1941, but was appointed commander of the Northwest Front on July 4. He held that position until August 23, when he was relieved, and on September 8, he was given command of the Forty-Third Army. An investigation of Sobenniko's conduct as commander was opened on October 16 and he was sentenced to five years in labor camps. He was stripped of his rank and all his honors were recalled. The verdict was appealed, but his career as a field commander was over, although he would get positions as deputy army commander from 1942 onwards.[13]

It seems unlikely that any other commander would have done significantly better than Sobennikov. He had 83,000 men to defend against Hoepner's panzer group. The heavy equipment available included 476 guns and mortars, 70 antitank guns and 88 tanks, of which very few were T-34s. This force covered a front sector of 60 kilometers (37 miles) and faced four German panzer divisions, two motorized divisions, and four infantry divisions. If the superior German training and junior leadership is added to this equation, then we can conclude that Sobennikov could not have stopped Hoepner. Any blame for his failure must be directed at his superiors.[14]

Deputy chief of general staff Vasilevsky admitted in his memoirs that the general staff, as well as headquarters, had failed to correctly assess the enemy's intentions. This caused the three fronts to position their forces incorrectly, particularly the West Front and the Reserve Front. According to Vasilevsky, this rendered command difficult and also hampered cooperation between the fronts.[15]

Lieutenant General Stepan Akimov replaced Sobennikov as commander of the Forty-Third Army, but he died in an aircraft accident on October 29. Major General Konstantin Golubev assumed command after Akimov's death and retained his position until May 1944. Brigade Commissar Dmitry Onuprienko, the commander of the Thirty-Third Army, received further training and was given command of the 6th Guards Rifle Division in the summer 1943. He was later given the distinction "Hero of the Soviet Union." When the Red Army attacked Berlin in 1945, Onuprienko commanded the 24th Rifle Corps. Major General Vasiliy Dolmatov was—with his chief-of-staff and commissar—court-martialled for the loss of Rzhev. Maslennikov, the Twenty-Ninth Army commander, had realized that Rzhev would fall and made Dolmatov and his staff scapegoats. The court did not find evidence for this, but it found flaws in Dolmatov's command. He would later become commander of the 134th Rifle Division.[16]

Major General Vasiliy Khomenko, who had commanded the Thirtieth Army, was relieved in November 1941, but returned as an army commander in the Caucasus in August 1942. He was killed in action during the Melitopol operation late in 1943.[17]

As the Red Army was not far from the western edges of Moscow, there was little room for retreat. Every meter counted, and Zhukov resorted to drastic measures to impress the gravity of the situation on his forces. For example, on at least two occasions he ordered the execution of commanders who had retreated without permission. On October 22, Colonel P.S. Kozlov, who commanded the 17th Rifle Division, was executed with his commissar. The deputy commander of the 133rd Rifle Division, Lt. Colonel A.G. Gerasimov, led a battle group of the division and he was executed with commissar G.F. Shabalov on November 3. Clearly, Zhukov blamed the political leadership as well as the military commanders.[18]

■ ■ ■

The end of October can be regarded as "halftime" for Operation *Taifun*. The Germans had been immensely successful in defeating the Soviet forces along the front line facing Army Group Center, which reported that it had taken 673,098 prisoners of war. Most of the prisoners had belonged to the three Soviet fronts, but men from other units in the area, such as local garrisons, air defense units and NKVD, also ended up as prisoners in German captivity.

The Vyazma-Bryansk encirclement was the largest on the Eastern Front and cost the Red Army dearly. No fewer than 36 rifle divisions and seven tank brigades were removed from its order of battle. Those that remained were often only shadows of their former selves, numbering 1,500–3,000 men and missing heavy equipment such as 122mm howitzers. Under Zhukov's command, reserves and replacements were rushed forward, gradually strengthening the defenses again.

The Germans had captured the entire Volokolamsk–Mozhaisk–Maloyaroslavets–Kaluga defense line by October 27. However, the weather and German supply problems did combine to give the Red Army time to create another defense line, which was in place by the beginning of November. Zhukov had the resources he needed to hold the line in the current weather, and further units were on their way.[19]

Interestingly, when the Germans attacked at the end of September, there were 13 tank brigades and one tank division on the three Soviet fronts, but no fewer than 17 tank brigades were brought forward during

October. At the end of October, there were two tank divisions and 23 tank brigades at the front west of Moscow. A few of the arriving brigades were already in battle on October 9–10, and casualties suffered in these engagements have to be included in von Bock's figures on the Vyazma-Bryansk battle. The new brigades were not necessarily less well trained or equipped than other older units. In fact, modern tanks like the T-34 were more common in the new brigades. A fully equipped brigade mustered 61 tanks and some had as many as 29 T-34s. None of the brigades present on October 2 had more than 22 T-34s and usually had around ten. As the German antitank guns were only marginally effective against the T-34, a larger proportion of this model significantly boosted the combat power of the Soviet tank brigades.[20]

Lieutenant Erich Bunke served in the antitank battalion of the 31st Infantry Division and he commented:

An antitank gun capable of penetrating the thick skin of the T-34 must be delivered immediately. We cannot count on 8.8cm anti-aircraft guns being available. Besides, they are as difficult to hide as a barn door in this terrain.[21]

Another example was a Soviet tank attack on an infantry battalion in the German 6th Infantry Division. The Germans quickly got two 3.7cm antitank guns in position and they quickly scored a succession of hits on a T-34 of the 8th Tank Brigade. Shot after shot was fired without any noticeable effect. The Soviet tanks drove straight towards the German guns and crushed them.[22]

The increasing number of T-34s is illustrated by the many reports from German units on their first encounters with the powerful Soviet tank. The Germans were forced to organize small teams to destroy enemy tanks in close combat using explosive charges. Clearly, the 3.7cm antitank gun was utterly insufficient, and the 5cm antitank gun was at best marginally effective. The 8.8cm antiaircraft guns and 10cm field guns were too few to rely upon except in rare cases.[23]

Another notable difference with earlier in the campaign was the increasingly active Soviet air force. The number of Soviet combat aircraft had increased, while German airpower in the east had been weakened when units such as Kampfgeschwader 2 (bombers) and Jagdgeschwader

*– See note # 20 pg 305

27 (fighters) were pulled out. Also, as the Germans drove deeper into the Soviet Union, the problem of supplying the airfields became ever greater. Lack of spare parts kept many German aircraft on the ground, and the weather hampered air missions. The Soviet air force could, in contrast, operate from good bases in the Moscow area. It was only 80 kilometers (50 miles) from the center of Moscow to Mozhaisk, 100 kilometers (60 miles) to Serpukhov, and 110 (68 miles) to Volokolamsk—distances quickly covered by aircraft.[24]

The Germans had suffered losses, but on a different scale to the immense Soviet casualties. However, the virtually uninterrupted fighting since June 22 had resulted in considerable strain and wear on men, animals and equipment. Neither replacements nor new equipment had arrived in quantities sufficient to cover the accumulated losses. After many months, the effects began to tell. For example, the 98th Infantry Division had a ration strength of 15,000 when the campaign started. It was in action from July 31, and by October 31 it suffered 5,881 casualties, of which 1,388 were killed in action and 209 missing. An infantry regiment at full strength numbered about 3,000 men; by October 31, the 282nd Infantry Regiment in the 98th Infantry division lost 1,723 officers and men, of which 432 were killed in action and 61 missing. In fact, all the infantry regiments in the division had been reduced to the equivalent of reinforced battalions. On the other hand, there were infantry divisions that were better off, such as the 6th Infantry Division, which had suffered fewer casualties.[25]

The infantry in the SS-Division Das Reich was reduced to such an extent that the division decided to disband SS-Regiment 11 and distribute its manpower to the regiments "Der Führer" and "Deutschland." The staffs of the disbanded regiment were not retained. Instead, the officers and NCOs were assigned to vacant positions in the other two regiments.[26]

The 6th Panzer Division's panzer regiment, which was mainly equipped with Czech tanks, had operational vehicles for one battalion only. This made the regiment staff superfluous and it was used for special purposes. On October 24, the regiment commander, Colonel Richard Koll, was appointed city commandant of Kalinin. Tank crews without tanks were sent to Vyazma, where they formed company Glässgen.[27]

Major General Walter Nehring, the commander of the 18th Panzer Division, reported on October 31 that the combat power of his division was approximately half that of a full-strength division. Another German report from November 6 showed the diminishing combat power of the units on the Eastern Front. The 17 present panzer divisions were assessed to be the equivalent of 6 full-strength panzer divisions, while the 136 infantry divisions had about as much combat power as 83 fresh divisions.[28]

As October ended, von Bock, his generals and Hitler were waiting for the weather to improve. The German supply system supporting the operations in the east lacked a margin for error, and the autumn weather dashed all hopes of sustaining major offensive operations. Lack of ammunition and fuel ruled out large-scale attacks. A pause was clearly needed, while both sides discussed future actions. The Stavka as well as Zhukov believed the German offensive had not yet culminated. Hence, they still favored a defensive posture. The Germans, on the other hand, believed Stalin had exhausted his reserves and wanted to attack as soon as the weather permitted.

The German machine gun MG-34 could be used either as a light machine gun for the rifle squad or in a heavier role. In the heavier role, it is mounted on a large tripod instead of a bipod. It could be placed to allow the gun to be fired "remotely" while it swept an arc in front of the mounting with fire.

WE NEED OATS

So much has been written about the German armored troops that it has almost been forgotten how many horses the German army fielded during World War II. Every German infantry division had up to 5,400 horses. There were 47 infantry divisions in Army Group Center on October 1, which meant that there should have been almost 250,000 horses in these units. Altogether, the German army had approximately one million horses. The Red Army also had many horses, not least because of its many cavalry divisions. A Soviet rifle division was supposed to field 2,500 horses and the three fronts that defended Moscow when Operation *Taifun* was launched had 226,000 horses.[29]

The grave supply problems in October affected horse fodder as well as ammunition and fuel, and deliveries plummeted. Without horses, the infantry divisions' howitzers could not be moved. Daily rations for horses were 5 kg of oats, 5 kg of hay. and 5 kg of straw, which meant that a full-strength infantry division required 80 metric tons each day. On October 19, the German VIII Army Corps reported that it had oat rations for only one more day. A day later, Panzer Group 4 reported to Army Group Center that it was suffering from severe shortages of fuel, oats and rations.[30]

The German 98th Infantry Division provides another interesting example. At the end of November it organized a team of 50 men to search the area 130 kilometers (80 miles) behind the division for rations and fodder. The work was dangerous, as the area was infested by Soviet partisans. The German 6th Infantry Division provides another example, as it reported that "oat teams" from the artillery were constantly moving, as they could not cope without their animals. Despite such special teams, the front units had to cope the best they could. However, the fodder shortage was difficult to alleviate, and there was no light at the end of the tunnel. Every straw and each hay bale in the surrounding area were ferreted out. More and more Russian panje horses—small hardy horses used in Soviet agriculture—were commandeered by the German army, as they could eat birch bark and roof straw. However these horses were smaller, and could not pull as heavy loads.[31]

The horses in the German 137th Infantry Division fared no better, as the supply of fodder had broken down. With all the problems afflicting the railroads, bulky horse fodder was pushed down on the list of priorities. Straw roofs and unoccupied wooden buildings could be used to feed horses. Deliveries of drugs and items needed by blacksmiths also dwindled. This did not cause grave problems immediately, but in the long run such difficulties, together with lack of fodder, reduced the animals' life expectancy. March 1942 saw the highest number of equine deaths in the division, when no fewer than 650 horses died: half of them from exhaustion and starvation, 40% were killed by partisans and 10% died from injuries and diseases.[32]

Infantry battalions were occasionally pulled out of the front line to give the soldiers rest and recuperation. Usually this took place rather close to the front, but it was still far preferable to the misery in the foxholes. The same procedure had to be used for horses. As the fighting turned into static warfare, the German 6th Infantry Division created a rest camp some 60 kilometers (37 miles) behind the front for horses that were not urgently needed.[33]

The Red Army also found it difficult to nourish its horses, but as the Soviet units had retreated towards their supply lines, they were not as badly afflicted by supply problems as the Germans. However, the snow forced the Red Army to rely more on horse-drawn sledges. Its horses were also fed from straw roofs and great efforts were made to find hay. In the Soviet Forty-Ninth Army, it was learnt during the autumn that hay bales from the summer could be found in the Oka valley, further east. Nikolay Antipenko, head of the supply section on the Forty-Ninth Army staff, sent an expedition to the area, and in December and January, approximately 5,000 tons of hay was able to be distributed to the units in the army. Despite such efforts the horses suffered dearly. There were 21 million horses working in Soviet agriculture in 1940, but only 10.7 million remained in 1945.[34]

There were other problems associated with horses in the theater. In November, Lieutenant General Rokossovsky, commander of Sixteenth Army, received four cavalry divisions, which all came from the Caucasus. So arriving into a theater with snow on the ground and ice already covering the streams came four divisions of horses with horseshoes unsuitable for winter use.[35]

THIRTEEN

THE NOVEMBER 7 PARADE

C olonel Andrei Kravchenko received an unusual order on November 4. He was told to prepare his tank brigade for parade, instead of going straight to the front. For this purpose, his tanks should assemble at Krasnoy Polyani.

Kravchenko, formerly chief of staff of the 18th Mechanized Corps, had been appointed commander of the brand-new 31st Tank Brigade in September 1941. The formation was created at the Southwest Front before being transferred to Vladimir northeast of Moscow. Now, it was suddenly being given the honor of participating in the great celebration of the Revolution.[1]

Each year, on November 7, a great military parade was held at the Red Square in Moscow to commemorate the revolution when the Bolsheviks had seized power. A party meeting was usually held on the evening of November 6. Stalin realized the importance of holding the parade even when the Germans were not far from the capital. However, it was by no means certain that it was feasible, as the Germans might try to interfere. Despite such concerns, Stalin had decided in October to continue with existing plans for the celebrations, but he also wanted to discuss it with Artemev and Zhukov. Stalin met Zhukov on November 1, and heard that at the moment, the Germans could not launch any major operations posing an immediate threat to Moscow. The weather remained poor and Zhukov had recently received reinforcements from Siberia. He did, however, point out that the Luftwaffe could be active. He recommended that the Moscow air defense be reinforced with fighters from adjacent fronts. Stalin informed Zhukov that he had decided to make Lt. General Pavel

Artemev, the commander of the Moscow Military District, responsible for the parade.[2]

Traditionally, the parade began at 10:00 a.m., but Stalin permitted Artemev to choose the most suitable time, and to not tell anyone of his decision until the last moment. Stalin himself wanted to be informed after his speech at the party meeting on the evening of Thursday, November 6. Stalin decided to hold the party meeting at the Mayakovskiy subway station on Gorkiy Street, in central Moscow. It was inspected by Stalin with his entourage on the day before the meeting.

Army Commissar Nikolay Biryukov at the main office of tank troops (GABTU) wrote in his notes from November 4 that in addition to the 31st Tank Brigade, the 1st Tank Brigade would also participate in the parade. During the review the tanks would be ordered according to type. First, 69 T-60s, arranged three abreast, followed by BT-7s in the same formation. The T-34s travelling behind the lighter tanks would be echeloned with two tanks in each column. Last but not least, thirty armored cars and 300 motor vehicles of various types would also appear.[3]

The parade was not just for tanks and various motor vehicles, so several other units were ordered to prepare. Kuzma Sinilov, the commander of Moscow's garrison, tried to conceal the real purpose of the extensive drills. He told the troops that they were preparing for a major inspection in mid-November, before they would be sent to the front. Nevertheless, many soldiers probably guessed the true purpose of the exercises as the annual celebrations on November 7 were of course well-known. Infantry from the 332nd Rifle Division were among the troops preparing for the parade. Also, students from various military schools and from the navy were prepared for their participation. Antiaircraft units from the Air Defense (PVO) would also take part in the parade. Finally, units from the NKVD and the so-called OMSBON would participate. The latter were special units that could perhaps be regarded as the Spetsnaz of the 1940s. Two OMSBON battalions, as well as NKVD artillery and cavalry, would participate.[4]

Stalin's Red Square speech on November 7 was considerably shorter and more rhetorical than that given at the party meeting less than 24 hours earlier. However, in both speeches, he claimed that German casualties since they attacked the Soviet Union had amounted to 4.5 million men, while Soviet losses at 1.7 million men were far lower. This would appear implausible to any insightful observer, as few attackers—and certainly not the Germans—would be able to sustain an advance while suffering so many casualties, and therefore such a disadvantageous casualty exchange ratio.

In both his speeches, Stalin emphasized that his country was not fighting alone against Germany, as Britain and the United States were on their side. He also underscored the fact that the Red Army was fighting a just war, aiming to liberate their countrymen. His speech of November 7 referred to old military heroes of Russia, such as Aleksandr Nevskiy, Dmitriy Donskoy, Kuzma Minin, Dmitriy Pozharskiy, Aleksandr Suvorov and Mikhail Kutuzov.

Ovations from the listeners before Stalin echoed around the Red Square when the speech ended. The troops gave a salute, whereupon the orchestra began to play *The Internationale*. When it had faded, the troops began to march and the drums began to play martial music. Military songs from the Civil War followed. Altogether, the parade lasted approximately one hour according to Artemev.[5]

All radio stations broadcasted Stalin's speech and the parade. The famous announcer Yuri Levitan described the spectacle. Overall, the 24th anniversary of the revolution received a positive reception, including Stalin's speeches on November 6 and 7. Vasiliy Pronin, one of the most influential persons in Moscow, wrote on November 6 that a concert was held after Stalin's speech, in which popular artists performed works related to great moments in the history of Russia.[6]

The strict secrecy surrounding the preparations for the parade meant that the film of Stalin's speech was silent. The military parade was filmed by cameras positioned to be ready for the traditional parade. Although the film company Moskinochronika was not informed in advance, it had employees in place anyway to record the event. However, it was not the staff who usually taped Stalin's speech. The problem was solved by repeating the speech in the large Saint Georg's hall in the Kremlin. Stalin reproduced his speech before some architecture that resembled the podium at the mausoleum. It was far less than perfect, as it was obvious that Stalin was not on the podium in cold, snowy weather. A rumor spread that Stalin had not been present at the Red Square on November 7, something which has also been repeated by historians.[7]

It has been claimed that after the parade the combat units drove straight to the front, but this is not entirely correct. The 332nd Rifle Division remained part of the Moscow garrison. When it was committed to battle, it was attached to the Fourth Shock Army not far from Leningrad in January 1942. Kravchenko's 31st Tank Brigade was, however, sent to the front south of Moscow, to the Forty-Ninth Army where it was attached to the 2nd Cavalry Corps, which was led by Belov.[8]

Parades were also held in Kuybyshev and Voronezh. Various government agencies and foreign embassies had been evacuated to the former city and they could witness the parade. Lieutenant General Frank Noel Mason-MacFarlane, head of the British mission in the Soviet Union, reported to London on the November 7 parade in Kuybyshev. He was impressed and called it a first-rate parade in every respect.

According to MacFarlane, over 15,000 infantry participated and the soldiers were well equipped and clothed. Several heavy weapons, including almost 100 tanks, took part. He also reported that 20 armored cars, 70 artillery pieces, and 36 antitank guns had been shown in the parade. The weather at Kuybyshev was clear, unlike in Moscow, allowing the Soviet air force to appear.[9]

One Soviet marshal participated at each parade and all three had fought alongside Stalin in the 1st Cavalry Army during the Civil War.[10] Marshal Budjonny was in Moscow and Marshal Voroshilov was present at Kuybyshev, while Marshal Timoshenko attended the relatively small parade at Voronezh.

From a military point of view, these parades were inconsequential, but they seem to have bolstered resolve among Soviet leaders. Stalin took great care to emphasize that the Soviet Union had powerful allies such as the United States of America and Great Britain. The Soviet leaders had faced very difficult situations before, for example during the Civil War, but then they had fought alone. From a propaganda perspective, the November 7 anniversary was a great success for Stalin.

On the following day, Saturday, November 8, Pravda covered the parade generously. A large photo on the front page showed the assembled leaders on the Lenin mausoleum. Stalin stood in the center, flanked by men like Budjonny, Molotov, Beria, Shcherbatov, Malenkov, Mikoyan and Kaganovich. The article mentioned that the first snow had fallen over the capital that day, and the blizzard had prevented the intended fly-by of 300 aircraft. According to the general staff's 8:00 a.m. report, no air missions had been conducted on November 7 due to weather conditions, which is in stark contrast to the 1,300 missions flown the day before. Standing on the mausoleum, Stalin had pointed at the sky and said: "The Bolsheviks are lucky. God is on their side." The weather had supported the Soviet cause by preventing the Luftwaffe from interfering with the parade.[11]

THE RED CAVALRY ATTACKS

On June 22, 1941, the German army had only a single cavalry division, showing that the Germans did not put as much emphasis on the cavalry as the Red Army. Admittedly, the number of Soviet cavalry divisions had shrunk to 13 from 32 in 1937, but this still vastly exceeded the number of horsemen fielded by the Germans. The reduction of the number of cavalry divisions in the Red Army reflected a trend of creating major mechanized units that would take on many of the tasks traditionally given to the cavalry.

The prewar TO&E called for a cavalry division to comprise almost 9,000 men, as well as 64 tanks, 32 artillery pieces, 20 antiaircraft guns and 16 antitank guns. It was an impressive force but one that required considerable resources. When new cavalry divisions were raised during the summer and autumn of 1941, they were given a leaner structure of 3,500 men, 20 artillery pieces, eight heavy mortars, six antitank guns, and 31 light tanks. However, few cavalry divisions actually received the tanks, as the tank requirements of armored troops were given priority.

The Red Army found that cavalry divisions in open terrain were very vulnerable to air attack and needed fighter cover as well as antiaircraft guns, especially as the division no longer had organic antiaircraft artillery. No fewer than 82 new cavalry divisions were formed during the final six months of 1941, and 20 would fight in the battle for Moscow before December 6. Two cavalry commanders would become legends: Maj. General Pavel Belov and Maj. General Lev Dovator. Stalin was keen to initiate offensive operations, and when the German army stood almost idle in November while the Soviet build-up proceeded, the Soviet dictator wanted to attack in hopes of thwarting or delaying German advances.

Stalin called Zhukov: "Shaposhnikov and I want to forestall the enemy by counterattacking." One attack would be launched in the Volokolamsk area, where the Sixteenth Army faced German Panzer Group 4. The other would be conducted by the Soviet Forty-Ninth Army against the southern flank of the German Fourth Army in the Serpukhov area. Zhukov was sceptical and asked which troops he should use for the attacks, as he had nothing to spare. Stalin suggested Dovator's cavalry corps and the 58th Tank Division in the north and Belov's cavalry corps and the 112th Tank Division in the south. Zhukov again objected, but Stalin was not swayed by Zhukov's arguments and regarded the matter as settled. Zhukov should present a plan that evening. Stalin had served with the famous First

Cavalry Army during the Russian Civil War and the war against Poland in 1919–21, and he still had warm feelings towards the cavalry arm.[12]

Both tank divisions had recently arrived from Siberia and each had about 6,200 men and 210 tanks, but no T-34s or KVs. Two other cavalry divisions, the 17th and 24th from the Caucasus, would conduct the northern attack instead of Dovator's corps, which had been in action since July. Also, the very weak 126th Rifle Division would cover the flank.

The attack in the north, launched on November 16, turned out to be a fiasco, as it ran straight into a combat-ready German panzer group that started its own attack in response. The commander of 58th Tank Division, Maj. General Aleksander Kotlyarov, shot himself after losing 129 of 198 tanks in two days of fighting. The 17th Cavalry Division fought heroically, according to Soviet sources. It suffered 75% losses as it was subjected to a German tank attack.[13]

A few days later, on November 21, Zhukov issued an order that the commanders and commissars of the 17th and 24th Cavalry Divisions would be arrested and put on trial for unauthorized retreats, a misdemeanor for which one could be shot on the spot. Lists of commanders show that both divisions received new commanders and commissars, but does not reveal the fate of the men who had previously held the positions.[14]

The southern attack, in the Serpukhov area, was directed against German infantry in Fourth Army, among them the 34th Infantry Division, and was conducted not only by Belov's 2nd Cavalry Corps and the 112th Tank Division, but also the 415th Rifle Division, which had recently arrived from Siberia, as well as veterans from the 5th Guards Rifle Division. According to Shaposhnikov, it soon became evident during the advance that coordination between the cavalry corps and the tank division was poor. The tank division lost one third of its tanks in two days and the results were meagre. German defenders held firm and made it impossible for the cavalry to advance. The Soviet forces shifted to defense on November 20.[15]

The Soviet medium tank T-34 had superior armament and protection compared to German tanks. Their numbers grew as the Germans advanced toward Moscow. The German tankers were of course impressed by the qualities of the T-34. However, many Soviet tank crews lacked the training to make good use of their vehicles.

FOURTEEN

THE ORSHA MEETING, NOVEMBER 13

F ranz Halder's horse had thrown him during a recreational ride on October 10, resulting in serious injuries. His right arm had to be temporarily fixed to facilitate healing. The chief of general staff did continue to take part in much of the work at the general staff, but he was not fully recovered until November.

On November 3, Halder assessed the situation on the Eastern Front, noting good progress on the flanks. The Eleventh Army in the south had taken control of most of the Krim peninsula, while German forces east of Leningrad advanced towards Tikhvin. However, these sectors were not the most important according to Halder. A decisive success could only be attained at Moscow and the mud had slowed the German advance to a crawl. The German advance had lost pace in Ukraine too.[1]

On the south flank of Army Group Center, the Second Army advanced towards Kursk and was instructed to continue towards Voronezh, which meant crossing the Don River. Crossing the Don was a sheer fantasy according to Halder. It was difficult enough to get food to the soldiers while the mud restricted movement. It would require a miracle to reach Voronezh.[2]

The supply situation for Fourth Army and Panzer Group 4 was slightly better, but still precarious. North of the main Smolensk–Moscow road, the transport situation was disastrous. In these conditions, it was little consolation that Fourth Army and Panzer Group 4 had broken through the Soviet defenses between Kaluga and Mozhaisk.[3]

Of course any alternatives available to the Germans were also limited by the Soviet defenses. Halder believed that Soviet resources did not suffice to warrant more than an effort to hold the Moscow area, in which he included the sector from Vologda to Tambov, and farther south the approaches to the Caucasus area. Halder believed the area between Tambov and the northern parts of Caucasus were weakly defended by the Red Army. Similarly, he did not expect much opposition between the Leningrad and Moscow areas. Halder assumed that Stalin would husband his forces so they could adopt an offensive stance in 1942, using formations brought forward from the Urals. He thought the Caucasus would be defended by the units presently in the region, as the terrain favored defensive rather than offensive action. Halder also expected British and American units to be sent to the Caucasus to support the Soviet forces.[4]

With hindsight it is possible to see how Halder's assessment of the enemy was remote from reality. He correctly assumed that most of the Soviet reinforcements would be sent to the Moscow area, but he apparently underestimated the reserves available to Stalin. Such underestimation would be a recurring theme in Halder's assessments of the Soviet war potential, just as it was for that of other German decision-makers. Clearly Moscow received top priority, but the weakening of the sectors south and north of the capital that Halder expected did not take place.

Halder realized the immense impact that supplies had on future operations. In particular, railroads were of crucial importance. The chief of the general staff found it pointless to launch a major offensive before the supply situation had improved considerably. So Halder concluded that there was time to evaluate options while the ground remained so muddy and difficult, and neither did his assessment of the enemy imply urgency.[5]

The forthcoming week would allow plenty of time to discuss with those commanders involved in the decision-making—and many regarded themselves as highly involved. In particular, Field Marshal von Bock was involved, as his army group would have to do the job, but he was not alone. The army general staff and the chief of the army, Field Marshal von Brauchitsch, were obviously deeply interested in the matter, as was Hitler. Two other commanders with a vested interest were Field Marshals von Leeb and von Rundstedt, the commanders, respectively, of Army Groups North and South. They were well aware that von Bock would play the lead role, which might affect their chances of receiving reinforcements and supply. Indeed, they might be ordered to send significant forces to Army Group Center.

Those responsible for war production were also interested. When the Germans planned Operation *Barbarossa*, they had assumed Stalin would be defeated before the end of 1941. The victory would improve the German raw materials situation and also allow the German armament industry to focus on producing equipment and weapons for the air force and the navy, when no major opposing land power remained. In October, it became more and more doubtful that the campaign in the east would soon be concluded, which was very serious, as German industry had already begun to reduce production of ammunition and weapons for the army.[6]

There were therefore many with opinions on what should happen outside Moscow. In such cases, it is often difficult to reach a decision, but in this case, the Germans were all convinced that the risks involved were insignificant. As German intelligence assured them that Soviet reserves were virtually exhausted, major operational setbacks were unlikely. Therefore the discussion focused mainly on how ambitious the objectives should be, and how best to achieve them. The second point was mainly a matter for von Bock, but Halder was also deeply concerned.

Early in November, the majority of von Bock's force was at a standstill. Admittedly, the Second Army captured Kursk on November 2, but that success was an exception. More typical was the conversation that von Bock had with von Kluge, the Fourth Army commander. They agreed that the Fourth Army could advance, but they also regarded it a futile effort. The units would have to halt after a few kilometers, as artillery pieces, ammunition and other kinds of supply could not be brought forward. They regarded it wiser to remain in their current positions and prepare to advance when the weather was more suitable.[7]

It might be expected that the commander in chief of the army would have significant influence on such an important operation, but von Brauchitsch was troubled by poor health, and had suffered a heart attack on October 9. Halder visited von Brauchitsch in the evening on November 11 and discussed the military situation. Early on the following day, Halder boarded a train to the Eastern Front.[8]

The journey took time, partly because Halder made a stop at Minsk. He made a tour through the city and saw how badly damaged it was. Nevertheless, about half the population remained, surviving by living in ruins and those buildings still standing. Halder then proceeded by train to Orsha, where he would conduct a conference on November 13.[9]

Chiefs of staff of the three army groups, and of the armies and panzer groups in Army Group Center had been summoned to the conference to discuss the forthcoming operations. The German army chief of general staff traditionally had much influence on overall planning, and the field commanders worked closely with their chiefs of staff. A meeting of this kind would have been preceded by much discussion, involving commanders and chiefs of staff. On November 11, von Bock and Halder had discussed matters by telephone. Von Bock raised the fact that only 23 trains per day were arriving at Army Group Center, which he felt was a major problem. This rate barely sufficed to keep his units supplied and did not allow any stockpiling.[10]

The objectives Halder advocated coincided with the line Ryazan–Vladimir–Kalyazin, about 250 kilometers (155 miles) east of the present German positions. Field Marshal von Bock felt these objectives were worth targeting, but were unattainable for his battleworn and badly supplied units. Instead von Bock proposed that the army group should strive for less ambitious goals, but still aim to surround the Soviet capital according to the instructions issued by Hitler a month previously. This more modest ambition was feasible, according to von Bock, provided that the railroads functioned reasonably well.[11]

Von Bock proposed the Moscow-Volga canal as the first objective, where the Germans would secure bridgeheads. This canal connected the Moscow River with the Volga and ran north from the capital to Dubna, approximately 70 kilometers (45 miles) east of Kalinin. The armies affected had reported that they would soon be ready to conduct such an operation. According to von Bock, this might be as far as the Germans would get as long as the supply situation remained precarious.[12]

The Army Group Center commander believed the situation precluded any "strategic masterpiece." Mobility had been very restricted in the wet conditions and it would be rash to assume that it would improve when the snow came, as deep snow would also curtail mobility severely. Thus, there might only be a brief interval suitable for offensive operations.[13]

Halder considered von Bock's points of view, asking about the Second Panzer Army situation, as Soviet counterattacks had hit Guderian's forces. Halder wondered if they were a menace to von Bock's right flank. The field marshal, however, was not particularly concerned. He was of the opinion that Guderian would in any case comprise flank protection for von Kluge's Fourth Army and would also be able to attack, if the weather and supply situation permitted.[14]

Von Bock's chief of staff, Major General Hans von Greiffenberg, had participated in many of these discussions and so was well informed when the conference began at 10:00 a.m. on November 13. During the first two hours, the situation was discussed thoroughly. Eberhard Kinzel, from the intelligence service Fremde Heere Ost, gave his estimate of the enemy.[15] After discussing the situation, the assembled officers turned to the tactical problems and the supply situation. Winter equipment was also discussed before the lunch break at 2:00 p.m.

An hour later, Halder began individual discussions with the representatives from the army groups and armies, until 7:00 p.m. when supper was served. When the officers had had their meal, Halder concluded the conference, before embarking on a train that would bring him back to Germany.[16]

As none of the commanders had participated in the conference, no binding decisions were made, but von Greiffenberg soon reported to von Bock. The situation was grave, but von Greiffenberg's report still gave von Bock some relief. Much of what had been said at the conference was in line with von Bock's thoughts. The more far-reaching ambitions had been shelved.[17]

At this time, the temperature fell in the Moscow area. On November 13, temperatures of between -15°C and -20°C were recorded and in many cases, German tank engines failed to start. Trucks stuck in the mud now froze fast in. Worst of all, the German soldiers suffered in their thin and worn clothes.[18]

It was not only German soldiers who suffered in the cold. When travelling back from Orsha, Halder paused at Molodechno, where several prisoner-of-war camps had been established. In one of them typhoid fever was rife. Almost 20,000 former Red Army soldiers were effectively condemned to death. Some German doctors had also been infected and were dying. In other camps, inmates were starving to death. Halder found the scenes ghastly, but could not find any remedy.[19]

Decisions made by commanders are sometimes discussed on the basis of the assumption, conscious or otherwise, that the commander had several different options to choose from. For Army Group Center in November 1941, few options remained. One option, which was rejected, was to halt for the winter. This would have allowed the units to occupy good defensive positions, while the limited railroad capacity was dedicated to bringing forward winter equipment and other items needed for the harsh winter months ahead.

The other option, which was selected, was that Army Group Center would try to advance as far as possible when conditions allowed. The Germans hoped this would suffice to encircle Moscow. Any more ambitious objectives were unrealistic, so these two alternatives were the only options.

Why then did the Germans settle for an advance, rather than halting for the winter? It seems that their underestimation of the Soviet reserves had much to do with the choice. Since they did not believe the Red Army would be able to bring substantial reinforcements into action soon, the option to advance appeared not to involve any significant risks. Should the weather deteriorate, the Germans would then simply halt and assume a defensive posture. There were few realistic options, and the one chosen by the Germans appeared very reasonable, given their intelligence. Unfavorable outcomes were rather the result of faulty intelligence than of the decision itself.

FIFTEEN

THE FINAL ATTEMPT

While the senior commanders discussed forthcoming operations, Lt. Georg Hoffmann and his soldiers in the 14th Company remained at the front. As part of the 34th Infantry Division's 80th Infantry Regiment, they had held positions east-northeast of Maloyaroslavets since mid-October. Two replacement NCOs arrived on November 4. On that day Hoffmann dragged himself to the dressing station and stayed there for two days to recover from exhaustion and malnutrition.[1]

Not much happened to Hoffmann on November 5, but he successfully chased lice. On the following day he was instructed to remain at the dressing station for three days while following a suitable diet. The very day Hoffmann was about to leave the station, his friend Second Lieutenant Hetterich was brought in. He had been shot in the leg and would be sent to Germany for treatment.[2] Hoffmann was saddened to lose one of his most trusted men.

A few uneventful days followed after Hoffmann returned to the front, but on November 13, all hell broke loose. In the morning, Soviet artillery poured shells onto 14th Company's positions. Soon Soviet tanks and infantry attacked, the beginning of a battle which would last days. Not until November 16 did the fighting abate. Hoffmann had to conceive a new plan for the antitank defense and at the same time he ensured that a stove was installed in his bunker. This acquisition did not warm Hoffmann for long, however, as his company was transferred to another sector on November 19.[3]

His company did not move far. When they reached their new area the soldiers immediately began to prepare defenses. A new bunker was created

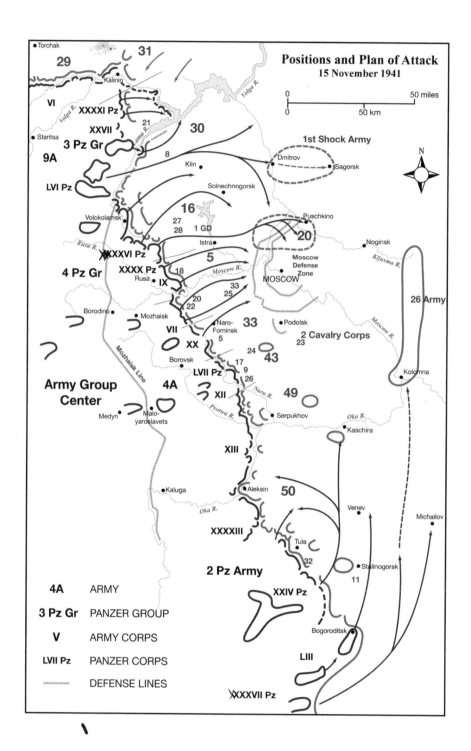

Positions and Plan of Attack
15 November 1941

0   50 miles
0   50 km

4A   ARMY

3 Pz Gr   PANZER GROUP

V   ARMY CORPS

LVII Pz   PANZER CORPS

•••••••••• DEFENSE LINES

on November 20 while Hoffmann reconnoitred the terrain before making plans for the defense. As commander of an antitank company, he had to ensure his unit were prepared for future challenges; as he could not know how long they would remain in their present position, he and his men had to avoid temporary measures if possible.[4]

Nothing in his diary suggests that Hoffmann had heard anything about an impending offensive. To the contrary, he only made notes regarding defensive preparations. He also wrote that winter equipment had been promised. No comments on fighting can be found in the entries for the final ten days of November, nor did Hoffmann see any action during the first days of December.[5] His unit was part of von Kluge's Fourth Army, positioned southwest of Moscow. The 34th Infantry Division was located south of the road connecting Maloyaroslavets and Podolsk. It would turn out that von Kluge had no intention of attacking.[6]

■ ■ ■

There were three armies, two panzer groups and one panzer army in Army Group Center. Two of the armies, Second and Ninth, were on the flanks, too far from Moscow to have any significant impact on events in the near future. The Fourth Army was closer to the capital than any other German formation, but von Kluge had no intention of attacking and von Bock did not give him an order. Instead, the army group commander let his subordinate judge when his army was ready to attack. This left the encirclement of Moscow to the Second Panzer Army and Panzer Group 3 and 4.

During the days after the Orsha meeting, Guderian's Second Panzer Army moved its right wing forward, to improve the prospects of an attack east of Tula. It appeared to the Germans that the Soviet defenses were stronger around and north of Tula, than south and east of the city. When Guderian attacked on November 18, this German assessment proved to be correct.[7]

On November 17, Paul-Heinz Flemming heard rumors about an imminent attack, in which the 3rd Panzer Division was said to be involved. He noted that the talk about being relieved—which the soldiers had been eagerly anticipating—had ceased and all focus seemed to be on the presumed attack that apparently aimed to encircle Tula and cut the railroads running east from Moscow. Furthermore, engineers created a bridge across the Upa River that evening, ready for the 7th Company to use the next day.[8]

Flemming and his comrades began to move their infantry howitzers into new firing positions in the evening, but secrecy still shrouded the purpose of the offensive. Nevertheless, the rumors were fairly accurate. Tanks and other combat vehicles had been positioned far forward and concealed. To Flemming, they bore testimony of an imminent attack.[9]

Flemming was aroused at 4:00 a.m. when the riflemen had already left. He went to his firing position an hour later, but it turned out that he would not have much to do during the morning. Dense fog prevented any of the company's infantry howitzers from opening fire. At last, they fired a few shells while the infantry and the tanks attacked.[10]

The tanks of the 3rd Panzer Division belonged to the 6th Panzer Regiment. On November 18 it had 52 combat-ready tanks, of which the majority—37—were Panzer IIIs.

The tank crews had started to drive their tanks forward to the jump-off positions at 3:00 a.m. The roads turned out to be very icy, preventing the tracks from gripping the surface beneath them. Not until 6:15 a.m. did the 3rd Company, which was in the lead, reach its staging area. The other companies followed slowly behind. One of the companies had been detached to support an infantry battalion that was to attack Trushkino.[11]

Most of Panzer Regiment 6 reached Upa and captured a bridgehead, but the attack on Trushkino failed to attain its objective. The regiment commander sent two companies on an outflanking move to attack Trushkino from the north and this brought the desired success by noon. The panzer regiment pushed on during the afternoon and captured a number of villages before halting for the night.[12]

The 3rd Panzer Division attacked southeast of Tula, but it was closer to the city than any other panzer division. As such it could expect to meet stronger resistance, and indeed, the 6th Panzer Regiment encountered heavy Soviet tanks on November 19. Although no German tank was knocked out, they made little progress.[13]

Further south, the 4th and 17th Panzer Divisions advanced to the railroad running east from Tula. The 17th Panzer continued north on the following days and reached Venev, located about 50 kilometers (30 miles) northeast of Tula, on November 23. This success gave Guderian reason to hope that he could encircle Tula.[14]

The Germans also launched attacks on the northern part of the Army Group Center sector on November 18. The LVI Panzer Corps attacked south of Kalinin. It captured a bridgehead across the Lama River and according to the LVI Panzer Corps situation assessment, the conditions were very favorable. It suggested that infantry follow immediately. On its southern flank, the V Corps also attacked, but it only gained ground slowly, as it faced stiff Soviet opposition. The XLI Panzer Corps made an attack in the Kalinin area, but it only had limited aims, as the corps would be pulled out and sent to attack alongside the LVI Panzer Corps.[15]

With so many corps involved in the attack, von Bock had clearly made his last bid for Moscow. The Soviet capital was most seriously threatened from the north, where Panzer Group 3 and Panzer Group 4 attacked towards the Moscow canal. These German forces were far closer to Moscow than Guderian's men, making the threat from the north more palpable to Stalin and other influential Soviet leaders. To make matters worse for the Russians, the German attack was widened on November 20, when six panzer divisions and two motorized divisions pushed forward in the Klin area.[16]

There were still three Soviet fronts covering the approaches to Moscow, but most of the responsibility for the defense of the capital rested upon Zhukov's West Front. German attacks against the other fronts were too far from the capital to be of immediate concern. The Soviet Thirtieth Army was however somewhat of an exception. It was subordinated to the Kalinin front, but positioned south of the Moscow reservoirs and was thus protecting Zhukov's right flank. Given the operational circumstances, it would have been more logical to include it in Zhukov's West Front. Eventually, the Stavka realized this and transferred the Thirtieth Army to Zhukov on November 17. At the same time, Lelyushenko replaced the NKVD general Khomenko as commander of the Thirtieth Army.

Lelyushenko, who was an old tank officer, had been in Gorkiy to inspect British lend-lease tanks when he was ordered to Moscow. Stalin received him on November 17 and asked: "Which army would you like to command?" Lelyushenko tried to avoid a direct answer, but Stalin did not relent. Finally, Lelyushenko asked for the Fifth Army, which he had commanded before being wounded. Stalin bluntly replied: "We intended to send you to the Thirtieth Army, where the situation is complicated." There was nothing for Lelyushenko to do but yield. He left Moscow and travelled to the front sector where he could find the Thirtieth Army. Stalin sometimes asked questions despite having already made up his mind. He probably realized Lelyushenko would ask for the Fifth Army. This was a way to demonstrate his power; Zhukov had been subjected to the same experience as Lelyushenko.[17]

Bearing in mind what had taken place in October, it is tempting to conclude that the Soviet situation was desperate. However, unlike the Germans, Zhukov had received substantial reinforcements. Field Marshal von Bock had the same divisions as he had had on September 30, except those which had been withdrawn. Zhukov, on the other hand, had built up a new force. A more accurate comparison of the Russian and German forces would include the Thirtieth Army in Zhukov's forces against Army Group Center. The Thirtieth Army covered a relevant part of the front line and would soon be transferred from Konev to Zhukov, who would thus command seven armies during the final German assault. Another important addition was the Fiftieth Army, which defended Tula. It was subordinated to Zhukov on November 10. The front from Tula to the Moscow reservoirs was approximately 400 kilometers (250 miles) long, while only 75 kilometers (47 miles) separated the Germans from Moscow.[18]

Zhukov had about 940 tanks on November 15. This was fewer than the three fronts had possessed on October 1, but then Zhukov's front line was little more than half the length of the original 760-kilometer (470-mile) front line of the three fronts. Furthermore, Zhukov had about 200 of the powerful T-34 and KV tanks in his forces, a much higher proportion than there had been in early October. This boosted the combat power of the Soviet tank units, as these vehicles could cause the Germans much trouble if employed properly.[19]

On average, Zhukov's rifle divisions had fewer soldiers than those divisions on the front line on September 30, but that was balanced by the fact that the average front sector defended by each division was one third shorter. The number of soldiers per kilometer of front line was almost identical. Several cavalry divisions from the Stavka reserve had been sent to Zhukov during November. Their combat power was limited, but they possessed significantly better mobility than the rifle divisions.[20]

In addition to complete formations, Zhukov also received substantial numbers of replacements, allowing him to reconstitute many battleworn units. In some cases he received completely new rifle regiments, but otherwise the new soldiers arrived in unspecified groups. The Forty-Ninth Army supply commander, Antipenko, visited wounded soldiers in the army rear area and talked to them. He noticed that many soldiers did not know which unit they had belonged to when they were wounded. There were no cards to fill in for wounded at the front. Not until the soldiers had already been evacuated were they registered.

Antipenko soon realized that these soldiers did not know their unit because they had been sent to the front as replacements and almost immediately had been wounded. For example, the Forty-Ninth Army had received one or two platoons each day. During the night they were transported to the forward defense line by truck. When they entered battle on the following day, they may not even have known the name of their squad leader. They knew only that they had been wounded when fighting outside Moscow.[21] Thousands of soldiers shared this fate.

■ ■ ■

With every day that passed, the hours of daylight shortened. The Luftwaffe had fewer aircraft available for the Moscow sector in November 1941. At the same time, the Red air force had improved, and Zhukov possessed twice the number of antiaircraft guns per kilometer of the front compared to September 30. Further behind the lines was positioned the 1st Air Defense Corps (PVO).

There were, however, cracks in Zhukov's defenses. His forces possessed fewer artillery pieces, mortars and antitank guns, in absolute numbers as well as per kilometer of front, compared to September 30. But the greater number of heavy tanks compensated for the shortage of antitank guns, and the large number of heavy antiaircraft guns also partly made up for the shrinking number of antitank guns. Like the German army, the Red Army occasionally employed heavy antiaircraft guns to engage enemy tanks.

Friction sometimes prevented, or made difficult the use of antiaircraft guns in other roles. For example, Lieutenant General Ivan Boldin, who assumed command of the Fiftieth Army on November 22, believed that 85mm antiaircraft guns were effective against German tanks and wanted to use them in this role, but the commander of the antiaircraft division, Major General Ovchinnikov, argued that the guns should only be used in their intended role. The discussion became heated and Boldin finally felt forced to remind Ovchinnikov that he was in command. Ovchinnikov was not satisfied and Boldin told him to complain to the West Front staff, but

Ovchennikov replied that he was not subordinated to the West Front. Boldin brusquely retorted: "Complain wherever you want, even Moscow."

Soon after, Boldin received a phone call from the Stavka. Shaposhnikov was at the other end of the line. Boldin received a rebuke, but it was not about the use of antiaircraft guns. Instead Shaposhnikov said: "Please, take care of this matter yourself and solve all problems where they belong. You are responsible people. Do what the situation requires. You know the details." Boldin would employ the 85mm guns in the front line.[22]

Behind Zhukov's troops, the Moscow garrison with its 65,000 men (not including the NKVD) could be relied upon. Also, the previously mentioned 1st Air Defense Corps, with its 750 heavy and 350 light guns, bolstered his rear area. Further back, several reserve armies were forming. They comprised 59 rifle divisions, 13 cavalry divisions, 75 rifle brigades and 20 tank brigades in November. None of them were ready for immediate frontline deployment, but nevertheless Stalin had ensured that he would have ample reserves.[23]

The German 2nd Panzer Division, which was one of the two fresh panzer divisions brought to the Eastern Front for Operation *Taifun*, participated in the attack on Klin, northwest of Moscow. It was already cold when the division attacked on November 19 and the soldiers were frozen in their summer uniforms. Winter clothing actually arrived the following day, but the quantity was not sufficient for all the soldiers in the division. Gun and howitzer crews received coats, which were highly prized, but they did not offer any cover for the head, hands and feet.[24]

It was still not very cold, and the wet, muddy ground was not yet frozen solid. When the 2nd Panzer Division advanced towards Klin on November 20, its vehicles were forced to halt or make detours quite often when the thin sheet of ice on marshes proved too weak. On the following day, Soviet tanks, including T-34s, fought against the German 2nd Panzer Division. One T-34 was knocked out at point-blank range by a 3.7cm antitank gun. The gun had little chance of penetrating the T-34's armor, but the gunner, Sergeant Niese, was lucky. At 10 meters, he found a weak spot in the Soviet tank. The small shot hit the mantlet into which the machinegun was fitted and entered the otherwise impenetrable armor, setting the T-34 ablaze. The tank's momentum was sufficient to overrun the German gun and Sergeant Niese and his loader threw themselves out of danger at the last moment. The T-34 continued another 30 meters, before coasting to a halt.[25]

The 2nd Panzer Division advanced to Davydkovo, a village located along the main road between Klin and Solnechnogorsk, reaching it on November 23. This success brought the division further than any other German unit on the sector and only 50 kilometers (30 miles) remained to the outskirts of the Soviet capital. One day later, on November 24, the 2nd Panzer Division captured Solnechnogorsk, and on its northern flank, the 7th Panzer Division and the 14th Motorized Division advanced almost as far to the east.[26]

The German capture of Solnechnogorsk seriously worried Zhukov and many other Red Army commanders. The defense line was bent alarmingly and there were many weak spots, aggravating the risk of a German breakthrough. Zhukov threw everything he had on hand to the threatened area, including antiaircraft battalions from Moscow's air defense. The 7th Guards Rifle Division with supporting units was ordered north from Serpuchov and the Forty-Ninth Army. However, it could not reach the Solnechnogorsk area immediately and Stalin did not release formations from the Moscow garrison or the Stavka reserves, despite many units being available in the vicinity of the capital. Zhukov would have to make do with what he had on hand, while Stalin hoarded his trump cards.[27]

German pressure on the Soviet Sixteenth Army remained strong, and Rokossovsky wanted to pull back to a more suitable defense line at Istra, where he could more easily ward off tank attacks. Zhukov firmly rejected the proposal and made clear that not a single step backwards would be accepted. Everyone should fight to the last bullet. Rokossovsky was not daunted and saw it as his duty to bring the matter to the chief of the general staff, Shaposhnikov, who he had known since before the war.

Shaposhnikov listened to Rokossovsky and a few hours later he called back and gave him the desired answer. The latter rejoiced as did his staff, but the joy did not last long. Apparently, Shaposhnikov had not discussed the matter with Zhukov. The first line in the next order that arrived from Zhukov read: "I command the troops fighting on this front!" There would be no step back. Instead, the Germans would have to push the Sixteenth Army backwards.[28]

At the beginning of the last week of November, von Bock's attacks on the flanks had certainly got moving, but they were not the kind of lightning attacks that had been such an outstanding feature of the first phase of Operation *Taifun*. Von Bock was not surprised by the slow progress.

His units were worn, particularly the vehicles. Many of the vehicles could not be used, as they badly needed repairs, but there were few spare parts. And many of those vehicles in relatively good conidtion refused to start in the cold.

All this, combined with the poor supply situation, ruled out swift success, but the goal was tantalizingly close. Although the advance rate was slow compared to previous German offensives—the 2nd Panzer Division averaged approximately ten kilometers a day—Moscow was getting near.

■ ■ ■

In the evening of November 22, Guderian instructed the XXIV Panzer Corps to attack north to capture Kashira and Venev. Its units were located east of Tula, and if the attack succeeded there would be a good chance of cutting off the industrial city. It appeared to be a better choice than a frontal assault on Tula, but it would result in a very long eastern flank for Guderian's panzer army. That was a gamble for the tired units that would have to cover very long front sectors. It would also further extend the stretched supply lines: ammunition, fuel, food, winter clothing and spare parts would have to be brought around Tula by the badly worn trucks. Frustratingly, all the useful railroads ran through Tula.

When Eberbach's soldiers fired up their tank engines early on November 23, the thermometers registered temperatures between -6°C and -10°C. Nevertheless, the Germans started at 4:00 a.m. and by noon they had reached Terebush, about ten kilometers south of Venev. At this stage, Kampfgruppe Cuno from the 17th Panzer Division joined Eberbach, who continued during the afternoon without encountering stiff opposition.

It became clear in the evening that precious little fuel was available. German vehicles waited for fuel at a railroad station 75 kilometers (47 miles) southwest of Tula, but the quantity received was only sufficient for one rifle regiment and two artillery battalions. To make matters worse, some of the precious fuel would be consumed as the trucks drove 130 kilometers (80 miles) from the railroad station to the 4th and 17th Panzer Divisions' spearheads. In contrast, the defenders of Tula could rely upon a railroad bringing supplies from the north.[29]

Kampfgruppe Cuno continued attacking on November 24 and reached Kuchtinka, almost 20 kilometers north of Venev. This meant that Guderian's lead units had reached a point approximately 50 kilometers northeast of Tula. A powerful German attack against the Soviet defenses north of Tula could have resulted in the encirclement of the city, but nothing of the sort was attempted. Mainly, this was because of the German units' condition, their extended front lines and lack of supplies. Guderian had decided to attack south and east of Tula because he expected to meet weaker defenses in that area. His expectations proved correct on November 25, when the 17th Panzer Division almost reached Kashira, after advancing 40 kilometers (25 miles) in a single day.[30]

It was an impressive feat, but it also entailed risks. Guderian had visited von Bock on November 23 to discuss the situation on his sector. According to von Bock, Guderian had arrived in the afternoon and reported that he would attain his goals, but he also emphasized that his units were very worn. Worse, if they did not reach the Oka River, they would be left in an exposed position unless the enemy retreated on the Fourth Army's sector.[31]

Only small resources could be found to cover the Second Panzer Army's long and exposed eastern flank. Field Marshal von Bock realized that Guderian's lead units might have to pull back again, but that was a risk that had to be accepted. Halder agreed with von Bock's assessment. It is also evident that von Bock was mainly striving to inflict as much damage as possible on the enemy in what he called "the eleventh hour."[32]

Guderian's progress east of Tula led to Ermakov being dismissed. It has been said that Tula's political strongman, Vasiliy Zhavoronkov, was dissatisfied with Ermakov. General Ivan Boldin assumed command of the Fiftieth Army on November 22 and Zhavoronkov later became a member of the army's staff.

The West Front ruled out retreat. Instead, it was decided to reinforce the Kashira area and Zhukov emphasized that Kashira must not fall into German hands. Pavel Belov and his 2nd Cavalry Corps was made responsible for the defense of Kashira and placed immediately under Zhukov. Belov arrived in Kashira on November 25 and set up his headquarters at the local post office. Other elements of his corps followed in his wake. Zhukov and Stalin regularly spoke with Belov, who received reinforcements such as the 112th Tank Division, which had arrived from the east early in November. He also received the 173rd Rifle Division, which had been rebuilt since the Vyazma-Bryansk disaster. On November 26, Belov and his corps, which had just been redesignated the 1st Guards Cavalry Corps, had enough strength to secure the Kashira area.[33]

While Guderian's forces probed the weakly defended area east of Tula, Panzer Group 3 and Panzer Group 4 met determined opposition. The 10th Panzer Division attacked along the Volokolamsk–Moscow road. One of its tank battalions, commanded by Major Gerhardt, attacked at 1:00 a.m. on November 25, supported by a motorized infantry regiment and a motorcycle battalion. Within two hours, the village of Skleskova had been captured. A panzer company was detached on a reconnaissance mission to investigate whether a farm located to the north was undefended. The commander of the company, Captain Hudel, soon reported that the farm was defended by Soviet armor, including T-34 tanks, as well as infantry.[34]

The knowledge that there was Soviet armor in the vicinity did not deter the Germans from attacking east. The force from the 10th Panzer Division set out towards Busharevo at 6:30 a.m., to establish a bridgehead over the Istra River.

At first, the German attack proceeded smoothly, but when the tanks drove out from a forest west of Busharevo, they were fired upon by various types of weapons, including antitank guns and artillery. After a fierce fight, the Germans emerged victorious and entered Busharevo.[35]

Near the town was an important bridge spanning the Istra river and Lieutenant Lohaus and his platoon captured it undamaged. After this success, the reinforced battalion remained in Busharevo and waited for fuel, which arrived at 2:00 p.m., at the same time as the field kitchen and ammunition. After refuelling and eating, the attack was resumed at 4:00 p.m., but at that time, Captain Hudel and his company had already been on the move for a while and they had crossed the Istra river about a kilometer south of Busharevo.[36]

The German battalion pushed on into the dusk, but as it received bad advice from the infantry, it lost its way and only reached Stepanivka by midnight. There the Germans thoroughly surprised a Soviet antiaircraft unit. After some hesitation, the battalion proceeded along bad roads to Anninskoye, which was captured at 5:00 a.m on November 26. After the arduous night action, the battalion rested until noon.[37]

Gerhardt's men deserved their rest, as they had been fighting all night. Many German aircrews in the formations that supported Army Group Center also rested on November 26, not because of night activities but because the poor weather prevented most air missions, as had been the case on many previous days. Some bombing missions were conducted against targets further behind the front line. Such efforts did not provide tangible assistance to Gerhardt's battalion and other German frontline units. At best, these Luftwaffe strikes could delay the arrival of Soviet reinforcements and supply.[38]

Gerhardt and his men resumed attacking at 1:00 p.m. and they aimed for the town of Istra. They chose a northerly route, which brought them into contact with Soviet tanks, but after mopping up the Soviet position, the German tanks continued and entered Istra from the north. Simultaneously, elements of the SS-Das Reich Division penetrated Istra from the south. This joint effort brought Istra into German hands during the night.[39]

The capture of Istra was an important success for Panzer Group 4. Further north, particularly the 2nd and 7th Panzer Divisions were enjoying success. They were not advancing as rapidly as during prior German blitzkrieg operations, but their advance rate nevertheless compares favorably with almost all Soviet and Allied offensives later during the war. At this pace, the Germans would be in Moscow within a week.

The catchphrase among Red Army soldiers was: "Russia is huge, but there is no room for retreat when Moscow is right behind us." Everybody realized this and tension grew among senior Soviet commanders as the fighting raged around Istra. When the town had fallen to the Germans, Zhukov and Rokossovsky argued hotly about the location of the new defense line. It was vital to prevent the Germans from capturing the next important town on the route to Moscow, Dedovsk.

When Rokossovsky arrived at his headquarters, he was informed that Stalin wanted to speak with him. He feared the worst, but Stalin's voice was calm: he wanted an assessment of the situation at Istra. Rokossovsky began to give Stalin a very detailed view of the situation, but was soon interrupted by the dictator, who said that he didn't need a complete situation report. He said that his confidence in Rokossovsky was unwavering and continued to ask if the Sixteenth Army was hard-pressed. Rokossovsky concurred, but Stalin asked him to hang on a few days more while reinforcements moved up. Already on the following day, a rocket artillery regiment, two antitank regiments and three tank battalions arrived.[40]

Despite the fact that Moscow was within their reach, the German commanders were deeply concerned about the ability of their units to continue the offensive. However, while their units were weak, intelligence suggested that the enemy was even weaker. It was worth making one more push. It must be emphasized that the German losses were actually far from remarkable. In fact, the German casualty rate on the Eastern Front had diminished with every passing month since August, and in November it was lower than ever before.[41]

One reason for the decreasing casualty rate was that Army Group North and Army Group South saw less combat, but casualties per division were also lower for Army Group Center during October and November. The average losses per division during November was only around 500, which was low for World War II.[42]

Neither were losses of equipment significant. Panzer Regiment 7, which was the armor component of 10th Panzer Division, can serve as an example. It possessed 146 combat-ready tanks when Operation *Taifun* was launched: 85 Panzer IIIs, 19 Panzer IVs, and 42 light Panzer IIs. Complete write-offs during October included eight Panzer IIs, 15 Panzer IIIs, and two Panzer IVs. In November, losses were slightly higher, as six Panzer IIs, 27 Panzer IIIs, and one Panzer IV were written off. Such losses were of course far from irrelevant, but were not exceptional for a panzer regiment spearheading a major offensive during such a long period of time.[43]

Altogether, the German forces on the Eastern Front lost 349 tanks per month during the period when Operation *Taifun* was conducted. This was significantly less than in previous months, when they lost an average of 510. Also only 115 new tanks were dispatched to the units on the Eastern Front before October 1, 1941, but no fewer than 397 were dispatched during October and November. Thus, tank losses shrank during the autumn, while replacements soared.[44]

Clearly, the German forces were not seriously weakened by the losses suffered during Operation *Taifun*. However, they had gradually accumulated casualties during five months of almost uninterrupted fighting. The losses suffered during the offensive aiming at Moscow were unremarkable, but they were sustained by units already weakened before the offensive began. And casualties inflicted by the enemy were only part of the problem. The German soldiers had been fighting for so long, exposed to physical and psychological hardships, that they were at the end of their stamina and endurance. Their unsuitable clothing in a harsh climate and insufficient rations also made them more susceptible to disease, exhaustion and other problems. Consequently, fewer soldiers were available in the foxholes.

Equipment of all kinds was seriously worn after many months of action. The 4th Panzer Division reported the status of its motor vehicles on November 11. Very few new vehicles had been received since the division crossed the border to the Soviet Union on June 22. Only 61% of the vehicles were operational and only 51% of the prime movers for artillery were in running order. Hardly any spare parts had been received, which meant that more vehicles would soon be inoperable. The division's capacity to move fuel to the combat element was less than half of what it originally had been.[45]

Shortcomings were not confined to weapons and vehicles. For example, the 98th Infantry Division had reported in September that supplies of simple items like pins, darning cotton, shoe polish, razor blades, toothpaste and safety pins were almost exhausted. The small quantities kept in reserve were used up, and as the supply situation deteriorated, the consequences at the front became graver.[46]

All these German problems contrasted starkly with the Red Army's situation. The immense losses meant that most of the units defending Moscow in November were either new or reconstituted, so most of the soldiers had not been on the front line for very long. Obviously, they were far less experienced than their German counterparts and they were not nearly as well trained, but they were fresh compared to their opponents. Some of the recently raised Soviet units, for example the 271st Rifle Division, 379th Rifle Division and 82nd Cavalry Division, were inadequately equipped. They did not enter combat with the prescribed equipment but with equipment of various types and ages, but it was rarely badly worn.

Some of the reinforcements were, like the 78th Rifle Division, organized according to prewar tables. Fielding 14,000 men, it was said to be the last division to be organized according to the old model. Other units were composed in peculiar ways, like the 112th Tank Division. When it was sent to the Moscow area, it was organized according to the new structure for tank divisions, with 6,200 men and 210 T-26 tanks. But all the tanks were old models.

At this time, tanks from the Western powers had begun to arrive. British tanks had been shipped to Archangelsk and Murmansk and then quickly brought forward to tank formations. Crews were rapidly trained on the new vehicles and then sent into combat. The German units became aware of the British tanks when they encountered them on the battlefield.

A British tank was knocked out by the 2nd Panzer Division on November 23. When the fighting had ceased, German soldiers inspected the wreck and noted that according to the odometer the tank had only been driven 40 kilometers since it left the factory in Britain.[47]

LICE, LICE, AND MORE LICE

As the weather turned colder during the autumn, the Germans began to find new places to sleep at night, as General Hermann Geyer, commander of IX Army Corps, explained:

> In September and early October, the temperature fell. The staff and troops did not sleep in tents if possible. They preferred to move into farmhouses that turned out to be lice-infested, instead of sleeping outdoors. The more severe the winter got, the greater the emphasis on controlling villages.[48]

The well-known Soviet propagandist Ilya Ehrenburg observed this and utilized it, depicting the Germans engaged in a quest for buildings and warm rooms, and saying that the Germans had become more humble since the summer, when they had sought manors rather than farmer's huts.[49]

The disadvantage of staying indoors was the lice. The battalion doctor Heinrich Haape of 6th Infantry Division, found lice on a wounded soldier when the frosts had begun and the men in the battalion had begun to sleep in houses. Haape began to investigate the matter more thoroughly to see if it was just an isolated case. He inspected a random sample of men and found anything from a single louse to a hundred on individual soldiers. Haape was irritated that nobody had reported the problem to him, saying indignantly: "There are medical orderlies in every company, but they all appear to have been asleep!" A moment later he exclaimed, full of drama: "Do you believe it was the Russians who defeated Napoleon? The lice had much more to do with him being driven back to France than the Russians!"[50]

Haape believed several factors had combined during Operation *Taifun* to cause the lice problem. First, the soldiers began to sleep in warm houses. Second, they had less time to attend to personal hygiene. Third, clothes were not being changed or washed frequently enough. In the cold weather the soldiers often wore two or three shirts, as well as extra underwear, to protect against the cold. This left the soldiers with no change of underwear.[51]

Haape and his colleague returned to their quarters, when Haape suggested that they should see if they had any lice. The colleague objected, saying that they had changed clothes in the morning, but they did find a few lice and used some

"Russla powder "against the vermin. Later, when they had dinner with three members of the staff, one of them suddenly exclaimed: "Where is the terrible stench coming from?" Other staff members concurred and one of them, Lammerding, sniffed at Haape and cried out: "You stink! Why?" Haape firmly replied: "I don't stink, Lammerding! I am hygienic, progressive and modern. That's all."

Lammerding disagreed and thought that Haape smelled "like a sewer at a hospital." After further discussion, lice were found on two of the staff members and they were also treated with Russla powder. Afterwards, Lammerding thought he smelled like a wild donkey, but Haape corrected him: "You are wrong Lammerding, you smell like a sewer at a hospital."[52]

The lice problem become worse and the Wehrmacht established delousing stations for all soldiers leaving the Eastern Front. Delousing was also conducted at railroad stations when the soldiers left the front on leave.

General Gotthard Heinrici, commander of the XLIII Corps, described the difference between Germany and Moscow in a letter to his family on November 19, 1941:

> November in Moscow: lovely sun, snow, tranquil and cold. Skates and sledges very good. Good skiing. Not comfortable, but cheap. Saunas everywhere! Lice, mice and rats in every house! Bedbugs prefer people with blood group O.[53]

SIXTEEN

AT THE GATES OF MOSCOW

D espite his doubts, von Bock continued the offensive after capturing Istra. Panzer Group 3 had attacked towards the Moscow canal on November 26, but in the evening von Bock instructed Reinhardt to turn south when his units reached the canal. Reinhardt, however, believed he could reap advantages by establishing a bridgehead on the eastern bank of the canal. If his units could also advance on the eastern bank, he would gain space to maneuver, as his units and those of Panzer Group 4 were competing for space on the western bank.[1]

As so often before, the 7th Panzer Division took the lead when it attacked towards the Moscow canal. Icy roads made the advance difficult, as was the case for the 14th Motorized Division on the northern flank, but Soviet resistance was weak. The German divisions reported that the enemy was pulling back to the south, and the perceived weakness of the Soviet defense was corroborated by the fact that the LVI Panzer Corps, to which 7th Panzer Division and 14th Motorized Division were attached, reported that 700 prisoners had been captured during the past day.[2]

Weather over the Army Group Center area was more favorable on November 27, which allowed more efficient air support. However, clouds obstructed the visibility above Panzer Group 3, which consequently received no close Luftwaffe support. The war diary of Panzer Group 3 mentions three Soviet air strikes and no German missions. Nevertheless, the 7th Panzer Division made good progress and broke through the Soviet defenses. It appeared that the Red Army only fought a delaying action in the area west of the Moscow canal.[3]

The 7th Panzer Division continued attacking during the night, aiming for Yakhroma on the Moscow Canal. Panzer Group 3 had expected that this goal could be reached later during November 28, but the 7th Panzer Division drove into Yakhroma in darkness and could report at 6:00 a.m. that day that it had captured an intact bridge across the canal in the town. This was a significant success, and the value of the bridgehead appeared great to LVI Panzer Corps. It requested fighter cover to protect the lucrative target against Soviet air strikes.[4]

Swiftly, LVI Panzer Corps directed reinforcements to the Yakhroma bridgehead. It was prudent, as the area received determined incoming fire. A Soviet armored train joined the fighting, on the railroad from Dmitrov. The LVI Panzer Corps repeated its request for air support. The corps commander, Lt. General Ferdinand Schaal, regarded reinforcements indispensable to any meaningful use of the bridgehead. General Georg-Hans Reinhardt, the Panzer Group 3 commander, agreed but he had no reserves available. Nor did Field Marshal von Bock have any resources he could dispatch. The 23rd Infantry Division and a motorized brigade were considered as reinforcements, but they would not suffice for the envisaged thrust to Zagorsk.[5]

Within 24 hours of capturing the Yakhroma bridgehead, the Germans began to doubt the utility of it. If they did not advance and expand the bridgehead, they might be dragged into a battle of attrition in the Yakhroma area. The Red Army did not appear to be giving way on the eastern bank of the canal. As the canal was expected to freeze soon anyway, the bridgehead was not of as great an importance as it might have first appeared. Operations on the eastern bank of the canal would then be possible even without a bridgehead.

An order from Army Group Center arrived at Panzer Group 3 in the evening of November 28. It instructed the panzer group to focus its efforts on the western bank of the canal. The panzer group asked whether the bridgehead at Yakhroma should be held. They soon received their answer: the bridgehead could be given up if it could not be held without costly fighting.[6]

The German bridgehead might have appeared menacing, but Zhukov was not unduly concerned. He knew that elements of the First Shock Army, commanded by Lt. General Vasiliy Kuznetsov, were available close by. These included one rifle division and eight rifle brigades. The First

Shock Army was one of two reserve armies that the Stavka had began to release for the West Front.[7]

Panzer Group 4 attacked south of Panzer Group 3. The 2nd Panzer Division enjoyed the most success and captured a bridgehead over the Klyazma River on November 27. On the other sectors, Panzer Group 4 was slowed by stubborn Soviet resistance. Colonel General Hoepner wanted the Fourth Army to attack, but Field Marshal von Kluge was recalcitrant. At last, Hoepner was told that von Kluge would attack with his northern wing on November 28.[8]

Hoepner visited XL Panzer Corps early on November 28. He met men from the 10th Panzer Division and the SS-Das Reich Division. The sol-

As the German supply system was strained, it was necessary to make priorities. Unsurprisingly, the urgently needed items, such as ammunition, food and fuel, were sent first, while winter clothing and other things that would be needed later had to wait. By the time the winter equipment was critically needed, the cold had already paralyzed German railroad movement.

diers were exhausted but they had confidence in the attack on Moscow. However, soon afterwards, alarming information from von Kluge arrived. The field marshal wanted to postpone his attack with the Fourth Army until the afternoon.

This was disheartening news, and Panzer Group 4 did not record an impressive advance during the day. Hoepner's forces did push forward, but not as fast as he wished. Still, the German generals clung to the notion that the Soviet forces were worse off than their own and so it was worth trying one more time.

More disappointing news reached Hoepner and his staff that evening. Von Kluge had decided to postpone the Fourth Army attack for 48 hours. Lt. Hoffmann's company was among the units concerned, and this meant he could continue to improve his defensive positions calmly. He did what he could to make them suitable for winter warfare.[9]

While Panzer Groups 3 and 4 approached Moscow from the northwest, Guderian's Second Panzer Army battled on in the Tula–Kashira area. Supply problems still severely hampered his efforts, and during the night of November 25–26, Guderian was informed that air transport could only occasionally bring supplies to his units. This contributed to the lack of significant gains made by his panzer army on November 26. Also Soviet units had been surrounded at Stalinogorsk. The efforts to contain them as they tried to break out caused German casualties and forced them to expend some of their precious ammunition.[10]

The situation on Guderian's long eastern flank remained unclear. It was reported on November 26 that the Soviet 52nd Cavalry Division had arrived in the area, and motorized reinforcements appeared to be on their way. The XXIV Panzer Corps intercepted an order from the Soviet Third Army, which operated east of Epifan. The order instructed its formations to liberate surrounded units in the Epifan area.[11]

Generally, the actions on November 26 can be described as tentative. Guderian's forces were spread out widely and they had to guard very long front sectors. The well-known panzer general could not concentrate his resources in a chosen direction, and the supply situation exacerbated his difficulties. At the same time, the Soviet units were in a difficult position. Tula and the front north of the city were well defended, but the areas east of Tula, where Guderian's mechanized formations rampaged, were weakly held. Also, the areas closer to Moscow had priority when reinforcements were directed. However, as the Germans would soon realize, the Soviets were able to reinforce more than one sector at a time.[12]

The Germans had intended to cut the Moscow–Ryazan railroad. The 10th Motorized Infantry Division's reconnaissance battalion was directed towards Ryazan and a demolition team had been sent in advance to destroy parts of the railroad. However, on November 27 German air reconnaissance reported Soviet reinforcements, including tank units, travelling through Ryazan towards the southwest. Thus, the recon battalion could not be expected to reach Ryazan. No reports from the demolition team had been received.[13]

Many Soviet reinforcement movements were observed, while German efforts produced little. The 17th Panzer Division launched an attack, but there was only sufficient fuel for one of the two battle groups to move. Fighting also raged at Tula, but was inconclusive. The soldiers most certainly disagreed, but from the perspective of the generals, the area around Tula was uneventful. This was ominous to Guderian, but not to the Soviet generals. Guderian and his staff also lamented von Kluge's inactivity. Had he attacked, he might have attracted the attention of some of the Soviet reinforcements that were being sent to other sectors.[14] This is borne out by Zhukov's memoirs, where he wrote that the inactivity on the central part of his front allowed him to direct reinforcements to the flanks, where fighting was more fierce.[15]

A disheartening report reached the Second Panzer Army staff on November 28. Two soldiers of the 131st Infantry Division had frozen to death during the night, heralding new problems for the Second Panzer Army to address. Other reports were generally negative. The major exception was the situation at Stalinogorsk, where a surrounded Soviet force had been holding out. The fighting seemed to have reached its final stage. More than 1,000 prisoners had been captured during the last two days, as well as much equipment.[16]

The 17th Panzer Division was ordered to direct artillery fire at power stations and industrial plants in the Kashira area. It was an indication of how much German ambitions had been cut back. Had they expected to continue forwards, such a measure would have been a waste of very scarce artillery ammunition. Furthermore, the small amounts of ammunition available could cause little long-term damage.[17]

Field Marshal von Bock had been monitoring the events of the past days and was increasingly concerned. He painted a gloomy picture of the situation to Halder on November 29. The Army Group Center commander believed that unless the Soviet defenses northwest of Moscow collapsed within a few days, it would be prudent to halt the offensive. To prolong it would, according to von Bock, only lead to "a soulless head-on clash with an opponent who apparently commands very large reserves of men and material." Despite having raised his assessment of remaining Soviet potential, von Bock still underestimated it. He ended by saying that he did not want to provoke "a second Verdun."[18]

To officers who had, like von Bock and Halder, fought in World War I, Verdun was a symbol of prolonged, costly and pointless battles of attrition. The Germans had not envisaged anything like Verdun when they were planning for Operation *Barbarossa*. But despite the immense Soviet casualties—approximately seven times greater than German losses—Red Army reinforcements were so numerous that the force ratio had not shifted to the Germans' advantage during 1941. Nothing suggests that Halder or von Bock realized the magnitude of Soviet military capacity, and the intelligence they were receiving provided no clues.

It was not only problems at the front that diminished von Bock's optimism. For most of Operation *Barbarossa*, his army group had been supported by Luftflotte 2, led by Field Marshal Albert Kesselring. Now this major air unit was about to be transferred to the Mediterranean, although some important components, most notably VIII Air Corps, would remain. The effects of the withdrawal of Luftflotte 2 must not be exaggerated, as the impact of airpower had been marginal in the bad weather.[19] Also, General Wolfram von Richthofen's VIII Air Corps was one of the most skilled and experienced close air support units in the Luftwaffe.

Luftwaffe bombing of Moscow, which had concerned Soviet leadership, did not produce the effects hoped for by the Germans. Between July 1941 and January 1942, the Luftwaffe made 122 attacks on Moscow, comprising 8,000 indvidual missions. From the end of September until December 1941, the Soviet air force made 51,300 individual missions; 86% were combat support, and the remaining 14% were in air defense of Moscow. When the Luftwaffe "blitzed" London in 1940, it had made much greater efforts. Approximately 2,000 people were killed during bombings of Moscow, which can be compared to the attacks on London from September 7, 1940 to May 10, 1941, when almost 30,000 people died. Luftwaffe attacks on Moscow were a harassment, but very far from a war-winning strategy.[20]

Nothing happened on the front during the last day of November to liven up the atmosphere at the Army Group Center staff. To make matters worse, strange comments were received from Berlin. Hitler criticized the army group's conduct of the attack and argued that the purpose was to encircle the enemy. Somewhat later, Heusinger, the head of the army high command operations department, called and informed them that the ongoing Army Group Center attack should be regarded as the prelude to a general offensive directed at Yaroslav and Voronezh.[21] From such comments von Bock concluded that the men in Berlin did not understand the situation at Army Group Center, nor did they realize the expansion of the enemy's forces. To make his views clear, von Bock called von Brauchitsch, but he doubted that the army commander-in-chief had understood him correctly. Von Brauchitsch's ailing health may have rendered him unable to correctly appraise the situation.[22]

Field Marshal von Bock himself probably did not have an accurate picture of the Red Army's situation. Zhukov had already been informed that two reserve armies, the First Shock Army and the Tenth Army, were on their way to his front. He began to plan the employment of these two armies, which were to be directed to the northern sector of the West Front and Tula, respectively. After preparing plans, he was informed on November 29 that the Twentieth Army would also be subordinated to the West Front. It would be used to bolster the northern wing. Zhukov thus received three armies totalling over 165,000 men. Had a grave crisis occurred, Zhukov would most likely have received further reinforcements from the Stavka. There were more armies available, but they remained in reserve for some time.[23]

The movement of these armies to the front represented the first steps toward a Soviet counteroffensive. The First Shock Army would attack between Yakhroma and Dmitrov, while the Twentieth Army would attack from the Krasnaya Polyana area, together with its neighbors, the Sixteenth and Thirtieth armies. The first objective would be Klin. At the same time, the Tenth Army and the Fiftieth Army would attack toward Stalinogorsk and Bogoroditsk, and push back Guderian's Second Panzer Army. Zhukov believed the Germans had reached their culmination point and he began preparations for striking back.[24]

According to Vasilevsky, the Red Army had 4.2 million men, 22,000 guns and mortars, 1,730 tanks and 2,500 combat aircraft at the front early in December. These figures do not include Stavka reserves. These, positioned quite close to the front, amounted to more than 530,000 men with 4,100 guns and mortars. Evidently, the Soviet defenses were not on the brink of collapse.[25]

Compared to Soviet forces, German strength, which barely totaled 2.5 million men in November and December, including reserves in the East, did not look that impressive. The Soviet forces were almost twice as large and the contribution from Germany's allies did little to alter the scales.[26]

It is remarkable that the Red Army at this time, after suffering such horrendous casualties, actually held a significant numerical advantage. When the Germans attacked on June 22, 1941, the force ratio at the front was even. During the months that followed, the Soviet forces incurred casualties between five and ten times the German losses. Despite this, the Red Army was actually numerically superior after five months of gruesome war. This is ample testimony to the Soviet capacity to create new military resources, a capacity the Germans dramatically underestimated.[27]

The German army high command continued to push von Bock to attack in force during December. The Army Group Center commander was thus sandwiched between his superiors and his subordinates, as the latter regarded reinforcements necessary to continue the offensive. Undoubtedly, von Bock's situation assessment was closer to that of his subordinates. The Germans made no significant gains on December 1. They continued to search for tactically favorable situations that might allow local advances.[28]

Undoubtedly, von Bock realized that his army group would not attain the ambitious aims advocated by the men in Germany. At best, he reasoned, he could capture some ground and knock out a few Soviet units, but any strategic achievements were highly unlikely. The field marshal again emphasized the fact that the idea of an imminent Soviet collapse lacked any foundation in reality.[29]

If his units halted outside Moscow, they would be in very unfavorable positions, according to von Bock. The railroads and roads emanating from the city, resembling spokes from a wheel, made it easy for the Red Army to move reinforcements, while the Germans, who could count on few reinforcements, would have to reposition units laterally, which meant essen-

tially movement between, rather than along, the roads. At this time, von
Bock was responsible for a front stretching approximately 1,000 kilometers
(620 miles) and he only had one division in reserve. The soldiers were
exhausted after long campaigning. He believed they would be unable to
withstand a determined assault.[30]

These points, which von Bock pondered during the first days of
December, were not his only concerns. Following the onset of low temperatures in November, the railroads and trains had ceased to function
properly. This boded ill for an army so dependent on railroad transport.

Field Marshal von Bock doubted that it would be possible to prepare
suitable defenses and provide the units with adequate supplies while simultaneously conducting offensive operations, as long as the supply system
was in disarray. He firmly believed that the men in Berlin did not realize
the gravity of the situation, and again contacted Halder on December 1.
The chief of general staff accepted von Bock's description of the situation
and said that it was in accordance with reports that the general staff had
received from many of the units. However, in the circumstances, it was
difficult to convey objections that appeared too pessimistic.[31]

On this day, Hitler replaced Field Marshal von Rundstedt, who had
commanded Army Group South, with Field Marshal von Reichenau.[32] The
German corps that had captured Rostov had been attacked in the flank
and withdrawn, and the question about how far it should retreat had turned
into an argument leading to von Rundstedt's dismissal. The 65-year-old
field marshal retired, but not for long; he would be given another important command in 1942.

While von Bock worried about the overall situation, his soldiers did
what they could to manage. Life was hard at the front, not only for the
soldiers, but also for any civilians in the combat zone. A soldier serving in
the antitank battalion of the 131st Infantry Division described events taking place at Aleksin on December 1. The town, situated on the Oka River
east of Kaluga, had recently been abandoned by the Red Army after hard
fighting. The Soviet forces had carried out extensive demolitions while
retreating. Only a few buildings were still usable when the Germans
entered Aleksin, and broken windows let the cold wind and snow into
those that were still standing.[33]

Bridges across the Oka had been destroyed and the German engineers
had to work hard in the cold to create a pontoon bridge to connect the

old town with the more industrialized parts on the other side of the river. The thermometer showed -30°C. A dead horse lay in the river, where it attracted the attention of some of the Russian civilians enrolled to work for the Germans. One of them held the carcass in position with a stake, while another hacked chunks of meat off the animal's rump with an axe.[34]

A strong wind made the bitter cold even worse and caused the snow to drift. Those German soldiers who slept in buildings were lucky, despite the broken windows. It was, after all, better than spending the night in fox-holes outside the town. However, defense positions had to be manned. The fact that the Red Army had abandoned Aleksin did not mean that fighting had ceased.[35]

Effectively, the German offensive had run out of steam. As predicted by von Bock, all the army group could manage at this stage was tactical efforts without any overall coordination. The 19th Panzer Division had been employed at Maloyaroslavets since October, but had only fought local actions, despite the fact that only 60 kilometers (37 miles) separated them from Moscow, when the 1st Battalion of Panzer Regiment 27 initiated an attack.[36]

At 5:00 a.m. on December 1, German tanks had driven to the posi-tions from which they would launch the attack a few hours later. They had travelled along a road cluttered with carts, vehicles and other materiel belonging to a horse-drawn baggage unit. Despite these difficulties, the tanks had reached the designated positions in time. The crews calmly waited while the accompanying infantry climbed up on the steel monsters. The attack would be conducted in the 292nd Infantry Division's sector and one of the division's infantry regiments was responsible for the attack.[37]

The commander of the 1st Panzer Battalion kept an eye on his watch. At exactly 6:45 a.m. he saw the first shells from the artillery explode in front of him. This signalled the beginning of a ten-minute barrage. When the German howitzers went silent, the tanks began to advance. In addition to the mounted infantry, a mine-clearing troop and an antitank platoon accompanied the attack, which was initially directed toward an intact bridge over the river Nara.[38]

When the tanks closed in on the bridge, they saw German assault guns engaging an enemy they could not identify. Second Lieutenant Fröhlich led the forward platoon and he communicated with the assault-gun unit.

He was informed that minefields prevented the assault guns from advancing further, and Fröhlich immediately passed the information on.[39]

It proved fortuitous that the mine-clearing troop had accompanied the tanks, and it immediately set out to remove the mines. It was risky, but the soldiers did benefit from fire support provided by the tanks and assault guns. Before 10:00 a.m., enough mines had been cleared to allow the vehicles to proceed. They crossed the river Nara without any difficulties and then turned north to capture the village of Golovenkino, which turned out to be virtually undefended.[40]

A few prisoners were taken, and they informed the Germans that the asphalt road leading north to Akulova was free of mines, but there might be extensive minefields on either side of the road. At this moment, the regiment commander instructed that a tank company should be sent north for a surprise attack on Akulovo.[41]

The battalion commander set off north with the 2nd Company. The remaining elements of 1st Battalion were delayed at a narrow bridge where an assault gun had skidded half off the road and become stuck, blocking the entrance to the bridge. The 2nd Company dashing north was soon instructed to slow down, to avoid the alarming gap between the elements caused by the delay widening further.[42]

The 2nd Company continued north at a slightly slower pace, with the battalion commander Major Mecke's tank one of two in the lead. Suddenly a very powerful charge exploded and tore away a large part of the road and completely demolished the tank on it. A few seconds later, another charge detonated, again tearing apart the road and this time it was Mecke and his crew who met with misfortune. Their tank was completely destroyed and it was not even possible to identify the remains. However, Mecke's pay book was found, establishing beyond doubt that he had been in the tank.[43]

A moment later, yet another explosion broke the silence, but this time the Germans did not sustain any losses. The road had been rendered impassable by the exploding charges and the lead company turned back. Using alternate roads, the Germans finally reached Akulovo, which was surrounded by dense woods and bisected by a stream.[44]

The Germans advanced slowly, and their caution was soon justified as they found that minefields and remote-controlled charges had been placed in the area by the Soviet defenders. The mine-clearing troop was again very useful, clearing many of the dangerous fieldworks, while the tanks fired on bunkers. A platoon entered the village at the same time and reached the bridge across the stream. More tanks from the battalion gradually reached Akulovo, tipping the scales in the Germans' favor. The success did not come without cost, though, as two German company commanders and one doctor were killed.[45]

By the time the rest of the battalion, and supporting infantry, arrived, the Germans had already captured Akulovo. The infantry soldiers took up defensive positions during twilight. The tired German soldiers hoped to get a chance to sleep in a decent building for a few hours, but the night was still young when Soviet artillery fire hit the village. Harassing attacks were also made during the night by Soviet infantry.[46]

Early on the following day, Field Marshal von Kluge sent his greetings and expressed particular gratitude to the force that had fought in the Akulovo area. The fact that such a message was sent at this moment is illuminating. An attack of this scale had hardly been mentioned by an army commander during the first part of October. Circumstances had changed, and a regiment-sized attack now attracted attention out of proportion to its strategic significance. On the Soviet side, the raid was regarded as a desperate last attempt to reach Moscow.[47]

On December 2, the tank battalion and its supporting infantry and engineers remained at Akulovo. Fuel supply was uncertain, as the blown road could not be used by trucks. Further east, a small motorized German force drove on a minor road between the main Naro–Fominsk–Moscow road and the Mozhaisk–Moscow highway. It reached a point approximately 20 kilometers (12 miles) from the center of Moscow, but on the following day it had to turn back.

The tankers at Akulovo were also ordered to return. They received the order at 4:00 p.m. on December 3, but the retreat proved difficult. The blown roads made it almost impossible to recover damaged but repairable tanks. They were prepared for demolition before the withdrawal started at 3:00 a.m. on December 4. It was hoped that darkness would provide cover and this was correct to some extent, but the noise from the tank engines was loud and could be heard at least as well as during the day. The Soviet soldiers realized something was going on and called in artillery fire.[48]

The withdrawal turned into a confused episode, but those tanks not previously damaged made it to the positions from which they had set out on December 1. The damaged tanks were blown up. Thus, nothing of lasting importance had been achieved, neither by the tank battalion that captured Akulovo, nor by the motorized battalion that turned back after glimpsing the outskirts of Moscow.

During the first days of December, the Germans lacked the stamina to do any more than conduct minor raids of the kind undertaken northeast of Naro-Fominsk. Their units were badly worn, while further Soviet reinforcements continued to arrive. The gloomy picture painted by von Bock at the end of November had not been overly pessimistic. In fact, the situation was even worse than the Germans realized: Soviet reserves of which the Germans were completely unaware waited behind the front lines. They would soon open a new chapter in the struggle on the Eastern Front. Operation *Barbarossa* had finally got stuck.

Many German soldiers realized that the decisive success they had strived for had eluded them, as is evident in letters sent home. One example is a letter written by Corporal Hermann Matthias in the 18th Infantry Regiment, 6th Infantry Division. On November 20, he wrote:

> I can tell you that I have been informed that soldiers who have graduated from high school and served for three and a half years may continue studying at no cost after the war. However, we shall not rejoice prematurely, it will have to come after the war. Who knows when the war will end and how old I will be then. To study at the university as a grandfather does not appeal to me.[49]

Many generals shared these sentiments. General Gotthard Heinrici, the XLIII Corps commander, wrote to his wife on November 19 and told her she would have to celebrate Christmas without him: "The war will continue next year. Russia is badly beaten, but not dead."[50] Moscow would neither fall, nor be surrounded. Hitler had lost the baton and Stalin had picked it up. The Soviet ruler and the Red Army would make the next move.

THE EASTERN FRONT
5 December 1941

FRONTLINE ON 5 DEC. 1941

ARMY GROUP
HEADQUARTERS

ARMY
HEADQUARTERS

PANZER ARMY
HEADQUARTERS

SEVENTEEN

CAUSES AND CONSEQUENCES

ew offensive operations have been launched with forces as large as those involved in Operation *Taifun*; and seldom have defending forces been as large as the Soviet forces guarding the approaches to Moscow in late September 1941. The scope of the battle for Moscow was immense. Given these conditions, it may appear surprising that the Germans so swiftly inflicted an overwhelming defeat on the Soviet defenders. The general tendency is that it takes longer to defeat larger forces, particularly when the attacker—as in this case—lacks numerical superiority. There are many explanations for the Germans' initial success and only a few of them can be directly traced to the battle and its origins.

Unsuitable Soviet initial deployments contributed to German success. In particular, the Reserve Front was awkwardly deployed and this was exacerbated by Budjonny's decision to place some low-quality units where Panzer Group 4 would attack. This facilitated Hoepner's breakthrough, but as the Germans also broke through sectors defended by better Soviet units, it was probably not a decisive factor.

A fundamental problem for the defender on the Eastern Front was the sheer size of the theater. The length of front to defend was very great, and it was difficult to concentrate defensive artillery fire as the guns were spread too thinly. The attacker, who held the initiative, could more easily concentrate assets at the critical sectors. Good intelligence could enable the defender to strengthen threatened sectors in time, but this was seldom the case. An important exception is the battle at Kursk in 1943, when the Red Army received information on the forthcoming German attack

The German soldiers had not only the fighting to worry about, they also had to endure the hardships of a cold winter without proper winter gear.

months in advance, allowing it to deploy very strong forces where they were most required.[1]

Several circumstances made Kursk somewhat of an anomaly in this respect. First of all, information had to be obtained somehow, for example from spies, deserters or traitors. However, such sources seldom had insight into decision-making at the top level. They could therefore not often provide information on overall intentions. Monitoring of enemy radio traffic was another source of information. Deciphered messages could of course provide valuable information, and analysis of the radio traffic could give clues. However, it did usually not reveal decisions made by senior commanders. On the other hand, enemy radio traffic could disclose troop concentrations, which in turn might suggest where he intended to attack. Aerial reconnaissance and reports from partisans could provide similar information.

The basic problem was that each source of information seldom gave more than a fragmentary picture of the enemy and his intentions. Success of the kind the British enjoyed with the decryption of the German Enigma messages is unusual. Intelligence work is difficult, and it is further complicated by the enemy's efforts to conceal his whereabouts and his attempts to mislead.

Given the difficulties with which military intelligence struggles, it would be unreasonable to expect an accurate and reliable understanding of the enemy's intentions. Should this occur it would be a bonus, but usually officers had to contend with incomplete and unreliable information. They had to make an estimate of the options available to the enemy and try to conclude which he would choose. It was the Soviet commanders that had to face this task in 1941. They could not know what the Germans would do next. In fact, it was not evident that they would attack Moscow so late in the year.

A few ways to circumvent the genuine uncertainty existed. One of them was to take the initiative, thereby passing the burden of incomplete information to the opponent. This was, however, not a realistic option for the Red Army during the autumn of 1941. The string of defeats suffered by the Soviet forces meant that the Red Army was firmly on the defensive. It was unrealistic to wring the initiative from German hands in September 1941.

A second option would be to create such a dense defense that the enemy would hardly be able to penetrate it, but the length of the Eastern Front made this impossible, particularly following the outrageous losses suffered by the Red Army. This was especially clear at Eremenko's front.

From the summer of 1942, the Soviet forces along the Eastern Front would usually exceed six million men, enabling them to create denser defenses as well as reserves for offensive thrusts. In contrast, the Germans would only occasionally muster more than three million men on the Eastern Front.[2]

As it was difficult to foresee the enemy's next move in sufficient detail, and equally difficult to create a solid defense on every threatened sector, it is hardly surprising that the Soviet commanders could not concentrate their defenses in the areas where they were most needed. It would have been surprising if they had managed to do so. Despite this, Konev and Budjonny were replaced after the Vyazma disaster, but it is doubtful that other commanders would have been more successful. The root causes of the Soviet defeat were deeper than specific decisions made by a few commanders.

As the Germans planned and prepared Operation *Taifun* quickly, there was little time for the Soviet commanders to realize what was going to happen and take action accordingly. Guderian's panzer group had hardly concluded the Kiev operation before it began attacking towards Orel. When the Germans spent so little time on preparations, it was difficult to arrange to block their attacks in time.

Panzer Groups 3 and 4 also prepared very quickly. In fact, it could be argued that the Germans allotted too little time for preparations, as all units were not fully ready on October 2. However, the Germans had placed much emphasis on the time factor and so launched the offensive despite the fact that some units were not fully ready. The Soviet commanders would have needed a copy of the German plans to make the right decision, but even that advantage might not have been enough.

Aside from the swift German deployment, the German decision-making process made it hard to uncover their intentions. Had the Germans formulated a detailed plan well in advance and then proceeded to move the units to the jump-off areas, the Soviet commanders might have thwarted the German plans if they had received early notice. However, as the Germans planned their offensive while they moved the units to the staging areas, and also conducted the planning work in parallel on several command echelons, there was no single, detailed plan. Not until a few days before the offensive was to begin had the preparations reached a point after which only minor alterations would be made. Effectively, Soviet officers could only surmise German intentions from analyses of terrain, road network, supply lines and other factors. Unfortunately, such analysis could disclose more than one plausible alternative.

The Germans lacked significant numerical superiority, but they had many other advantages. As their units were better led, better trained and often better equipped, the German generals could act as if they had far more units than the Soviet commanders. Clearly, the German commanders possessed the initiative and they were not unduly concerned about possible Soviet actions.

One thing the German generals feared was that the Soviet commanders would refuse battle and retreat rapidly, thereby evading encirclement. Had the Soviet forces retreated, the German booty would have been smaller, but it seems unlikely that most of the Soviet forces could have escaped. After all, most of the units relied on men and beasts for their mobility. Coordination and traffic control would also have been very challenging. A Soviet retreat could definitely not have resulted in a German defeat.

The fact that German superiority came from fielding units with a greater level of skill rather than fielding a greater number of units brought advantages; for example, it was easier to move combat power around. This was particularly important in a theater where the capacity of the roads was limited, and facilitated deployment before the offensive as well as advances when the operation had started.

Another advantage the Germans enjoyed was their ability to launch an attack and then follow up with the same units in the lead. This made it possible to exploit a breakthrough more rapidly than if some units had created the breakthrough and others exploited it. The high standards of training also meant that commanders in higher echelons could focus on the overall planning, rather than details. Various unexpected difficulties— so common in war—could usually be dealt with by the local commanders and units. All of this allowed the Germans to break through quickly and encircle over 700,000 men.

Such an overwhelming victory is of course not common in the history of warfare. According to the Germans it ranked, together with the Kiev operation, as the greatest encirclement battle in history, with the number of prisoners exceeding those taken in all previous encirclements. There is only one real rival and that is the encirclement of the Allied forces in northern France and Belgium in 1940, but that German success was tarnished by the Dunkerque evacuation.[3]

Irrespective of how one ranks these encirclement operations, it is clear that the German victory in the initial part of Operation *Taifun* was exceptional, and that it can mainly be attributed to their advantage in training, tactics and leadership at the lower echelons. Still, despite the overwhelming success, the ultimate goal eluded the Germans and it is of course tempting to ask why.

Previous literature has provided many explanations. One is that the Germans were halted by the weather. Another is that the Red Army stopped them. These two can appear to be poles apart, but that would be an oversimplification. Those who stress the weather as the main cause can hardly have meant that the weather alone halted the Germans, after they closed the cauldrons at Vyazma and Bryansk. Had no Soviet forces been in position between the Germans and Moscow, the Soviet capital would have fallen, despite adverse weather. It is more relevant to discuss whether the Red Army could have halted the Germans if the weather had not changed from the fair days of early October. First, it must be emphasized that it was not the winter weather that was the most problematic type of weather for the Germans, but the muddy phase. The winter did not begin until a month and a half after the Germans launched Operation *Taifun*, and when it arrived, the Red Army had already been given a precious respite. When investigating the impact of weather, it is the period around October 10 that is most relevant.

At that point in October, Guderian's forces were still 280 kilometers (175 miles) away from Moscow. They had not yet sealed off the Bryansk pocket completely. Guderian had no forces available to send thrusting towards the Soviet capital. He could not have posed an immediate threat to Moscow even if the weather had been favorable. Furthermore, his forces had jumped off on September 30, a great distance from Moscow, and so had extended their supply lines significantly. The Second Panzer Army was thus not an immediate threat to Moscow, but if the weather had remained favorable and his supply lines shortened, Guderian could have attacked northeast after October 20.

If the German right wing was thus not in a position to conduct powerful attacks in the Moscow direction, then the German center and left wing posed the greatest threat. The most powerful component was Panzer Group 4 and the Fourth Army. Hoepner had initially kept one of his three panzer corps in reserve, but after four days he sent parts of it straight toward Moscow. He thus had a force available, which not only could but actually was directed toward the Soviet capital. Furthermore, the XL Panzer Corps, which had closed the Vyazma cauldron from the south, could disengage and attack east.[4]

Unlike Guderian, Hoepner had the units to attack Moscow, and they were much closer to the objective. As the Germans closed the ring around the encircled Soviet units very quickly, they could mop up the cauldron without undue delay, thus freeing units for other tasks. All this could have allowed Hoepner and von Kluge to advance east, but there were three factors that could slow them down: the weather, supply problems, and of course, the Red Army.

The Soviet defenders' chances of preventing the Germans from capturing Moscow can be judged by comparing with other situations. The initial phase of Operation *Taifun* offers a suitable comparison. The Germans easily broke through the Soviet defenses and immediately exploited their advantage in depth. The Soviet defense proved incapable of halting the offensive. It must thus be asked what advantages the Red Army enjoyed on and after October 10 that it had lacked at the beginning of October.

The Soviet efforts to man the Mozhaisk Line had not yet produced any tangible results. Some units were arriving without having received thorough training, and also lacked combat experience. Other units were defeated remnants, with all the morale problems that come with defeat. Few units had had much time to prepare their defenses, unlike those who had defended the front line at the end of September. Lack of time also meant that communications were not as extensive as before, as the Red Army depended on telephone lines to a great extent. The immense losses suffered at Vyazma-Bryansk meant that fewer soldiers were available to man the front line, which resulted in lower troop density, which tends to favor an attacker.

Given the ease with which the Germans broke through at the start of Operation *Taifun*, it seems unlikely that the Red Army would have coped better along the Mozhaisk Line without some new advantages. It is, however, difficult to see any improvement to the Soviet defense when comparing the situation in mid-October with the defenses at the end of September. To the contrary, the defenses were weaker and in many ways the conditions were worse. As the Germans easily broke through during the first week of October, it would have required considerably improved Soviet defenses to stop the Germans in mid-October, had the conditions remained unchanged.

Evidently, in mid-October the Germans must have suffered from one or more problems that had not affected them at the beginning of Operation *Taifun*. One of them was the surrounded Soviet forces, which tied up German units. This was mainly a problem in the Second Panzer Army and

Second Army sectors, on the southern flank, but as we have already seen, Panzer Group 4 and Fourth Army were best positioned to attack Moscow. Some of Fourth Army's units were still fighting at the Vyazma pocket, but it was rapidly collapsing. Field Marshal von Bock noted on October 10 that 200,000 prisoners had been captured at Vyazma. Although hard fighting remained, the German units would be free for other tasks soon. Three days later, he was of the opinion that the Vyazma fighting was petering out and would be over in a few days.[5]

Clearly the encircled units were causing delays for the Germans, but it was a matter of days, not weeks. In fact, the Soviet resistance ended quite rapidly and did not provide much time for the Soviet commanders to bring reinforcements to the area west of Moscow. Also, the Germans did not have to extinguish all resistance before attacking east. They could have attacked with the mechanized units and some of the infantry divisions and leave the mopping up to other units, well aware that the latter would soon follow. This did in fact take place.

It is of course conceivable that casualties in the first stage of the operation had drained the Germans of offensive power, but the facts do not support such a thesis. Casualties suffered by Army Group Center only constituted a tiny proportion of its overall strength. Losses of that extent were not difficult to absorb, and compare favorably with those of many other operations which did not run out of steam. A few examples of German units' losses have been cited in the literature, which could appear to support the notion that the German units suffered serious casualties. The most common example is probably the German 4th Panzer Division and its battles at Mtsensk. However, these descriptions are based on an erroneous interpretation of Guderian's memoirs and are contradicted by the archival records. The reports from the German panzer groups and their war diaries do not indicate that losses limited the German units' offensive power, although of course the cumulative effects of losses would be felt in prolonged operations.[6]

It is hard to accept any conclusion other than that the weather seriously impeded German efforts during the second half of October. Nothing suggests that the Soviet defenders were in a better position to repel a strong German attack than they had been on October 1, had the weather remained favorable to offensive operations.

The effects of the weather can be illustrated by fuel consumption. The

7th Panzer Division reported that 220 cubic meters (48,393 gallons) of fuel usually allowed the division to move 60 kilometers (37 miles). In the mud, however, it was barely sufficient to move the division 15 kilometers (9 miles). At the same time, it was of course more difficult to bring up fuel for the division.

The weather change was certainly not surprising. Field Marshal von Bock had expressed concerns about the weather, and he was not the only one to do so. Autumn precipitation usually turned the roads into a morass and this was very likely to occur in October.

During the summer, it had already become painfully clear to the Germans that even a short downpour could make the roads almost impassable. Weather was thus crucial and contributed significantly to the halting of the German offensive in mid-October, but that was hardly a surprise. When the Germans began Operation *Taifun*, they knew they were in a race against the clock, but they did not know when their time would run out.

Despite concerns about the weather, it can hardly be argued that the Germans made a mistake by launching Operation *Taifun*. It would of course have been better to launch it earlier, but Army Group Center did not cause the late start. The date was settled by decision-makers elsewhere and determined by operations conducted in other areas. Of course, Operation *Taifun* could have been cancelled, but that would appear to be a bad option. The massive losses inflicted upon the Red Army was an important result and had the Germans called off the offensive after mopping up the Vyazma and Bryansk cauldrons, they would not have been in an exposed position. They would have had ample time to establish suitable defenses for the winter and secure their supply lines. Such a scheme would have given the Germans a great victory at the end of the campaigning season and allowed them to repel a possible Soviet winter offensive.

Why then did the Germans not settle for such a solution? To answer this question, we have to look at the logic behind Operation *Barbarossa*. The rationale was the thirst of Hitler—and many other Germans—for "living space," but this did not in itself cause them to hurry. The German haste was caused by their awareness of their limited industrial capacity and access to raw materials. Hitler and his collaborators believed that the United States would eventually enter the war in 1942, but in 1941 they could still dictate events. Therefore, the German decision-makers believed they had the best chance to defeat the Soviet Union in the second half of

1941, when the United States had not yet entered the war and Britain alone was not regarded as a serious threat. When the enemy in the east had been slain, Germany would not have anything to fear from that direction, and also her precarious raw materials situation, not least her access to crude oil, would have benen considerably improved.[7]

The German belief that the United States would enter the war seems reasonable, even considering that the Japanese plans to attack Pearl Harbor were unknown to them at the time. We also know today that lend-lease agreements were signed before the United States became a belligerent. Furthermore, the Germans correctly believed they would be inferior in industrial capacity and raw materials. If the Germans made any incorrect assessment, it may have been their belief that they had any chance at all of winning. This is, however, another question which is outside the scope of Operation *Taifun*. The Germans had started Operation *Barbarossa* in the belief that circumstances were more propitious than they would later prove to be.

When the Germans surrounded Soviet forces in the Vyazma and Bryansk pockets, they could expect to soon capture vast booty and innumerable prisoners; but it was clear that the war in the east would continue into 1942 should the Germans halt in mid-October. That was an unappealing scenario to the German planners, which could potentially bring future misfortune—and if anything, the Germans underestimated these misfortunes.

Against this background, it is hardly surprising that the Germans decided to continue attacking as soon as the ground froze. It was a gamble, but there was no safe and secure alternative to choose. To remain idle would have provided the enemy time to recoup and brought no dividends for the Germans. Continuing the offensive at least appeared to have the potential to achieve something positive. Armed with hindsight, we can conclude that this was highly unlikely, but in retrospect we are much better informed on the Soviet reserves than the Germans were. They believed Stalin no longer possessed any major reserves, which meant that there were no significant risks involved in a continuation of the offensive. It therefore appeared sensible to make one more push and see what it yielded. However, the German decision rested upon false premises, and the consequences would only become apparent later.[8]

There were two fundamental problems that caused the German dilemma. Most fundamental was the fact that they were fighting enemies whose combined economic, industrial and manpower resources far exceeded German assets, and this was compounded by the Allies' much greater access to raw materials. In addition, the Germans underestimated the war-fighting capacity of their opponents, particularly the Soviet Union. The Germans had started a war they could not win, but they did not realise that they had done so.

General Ernst-August Köstring, German military attaché in Moscow for many years, told Wilhelm Canaris, head of the military intelligence service Abwehr, that it was "easier for an Arab in traditional dress to move unnoticed on the streets of Berlin, than for foreign agents to pass through Russia." Köstring's comparison illustrates how hard it was to get information on the Soviet armed forces.[9]

In all fairness, it must be said that even if the German perception of their enemies had been accurate, they would still have faced a monumental task. They fought a total war without any margin for error. It was almost inevitable that their actions would turn into a gamble.

One example of the small margins the Germans were operating with was their supply of winter equipment. As the German supply system was strained, it was necessary to prioritize. Unsurprisingly, items needed immediately—such as ammunition, food and fuel—were sent first, while winter clothing and other things that would be needed later had to wait. By the time that winter equipment was urgently needed on the Eastern Front, the cold had already paralyzed German railroad movement. Zhukov made an interesting comment on this in his memoirs: "Warm clothes and uniforms are also weapons. Our country provided its soldiers with adequate clothing."

■ ■ ■

The Soviets were in a very different situation than the Germans. While the latter had to strive for quick results, Stalin had time on his side. On the other hand, this advantage was not necessarily apparent to the Soviet leaders in October 1941, as Soviet intelligence was also imperfect. Soviet losses to this point had been nothing short of disastrous. Unless the rate of losses slowed, it would be impossible in the long run to replace the vast number of casualties and the huge losses in equipment. The Vyazma-Bryansk disaster was the worst calamity suffered yet by Russia in World War II, and it was impossible to tell what the future might bring.

When the roads to Moscow were open to the Germans, the Soviet situation was indeed desperate, and there was little the Red Army could do except play for time in which to recover from the punishing blows it had sustained. The mud was therefore extremely welcome to Stalin, Zhukov and the other Soviet commanders. Admittedly, the mud made it harder for them, too, to move units and supplies, but as the distance from the railheads to the front was shorter for the Red Army, this was a far less serious problem than for the Germans.

During the desperate days in the first two weeks of October, Soviet units had had to be rushed forward to the front line no matter what their state of readiness. When the German offensive got stuck in mud, Stalin had two options. Units could still be dispatched to the front immediately, without having completed training, but it now suddenly became possible to wait and send units forward later, when they had become more prepared. These two options were, of course, not sharply separated, rather representing two endpoints on a gradual scale, but they elucidate the decisions Stalin and his entourage faced.

When the Germans resumed their advance during the second half of November, the matter again took on crucial importance. Should units within reach be sent to the front, or should they remain in training for a while and be sent to the front when their combat power had been increased? As the Soviet units generally had to make do with short periods of training, a few extra weeks could make a significant difference.

At the end of November, many Soviet units in the Moscow region were about to complete their training. Stalin decided to keep them in reserve, despite being urged by front commanders to release them. Hindsight supports Stalin's decision. The resources committed to the front sufficed to keep the tired German units at arm's length, while those kept back could be better prepared for the forthcoming counteroffensive.

Siberian divisions have often been described as playing a very important role in the battle for Moscow. Information from the spy Richard Sorge told the Soviet leaders that Japan did not intend to attack eastern Siberia, meaning that Soviet forces in the Far East could be sent west. A significant portion of the units in the area were indeed moved to the Moscow area.

Nevertheless, the role of the Siberian divisions may have been exaggerated. These divisions only made up a minor share of all reinforcements sent to the Moscow sector during the final three months of 1941. Admittedly, they were often better equipped and trained, but not radically so. Mostly, the defense of Moscow rested upon the shoulders of soldiers serving in other units.

The period after the Germans closed the Vyazma and Bryansk pockets was vital, as the Germans needed a decisive victory, while Stalin could for the moment be content with staying in the war. This also illustrates that even a disaster of the magnitude inflicted upon the Red Army at Vyazma-Bryansk was insufficient for the Germans to win the war. Perhaps a sequence of such immense defeats would have toppled the Soviet Union, but the Germans could not cause enough of them in a short enough period. Effectively, the Germans could probably not have won the war before the autumn rains, and in the long run, their prospects were even dimmer.

It is conceivable that the Germans could have encircled Moscow and doomed its citizens to starvation—as envisaged by Hitler—had the offensive started earlier. However it does not follow that the Germans would have won the war in the east if they had managed to turn Hitler's scheme into reality. The loss of Moscow would have been a serious blow to the Soviet Union—the city was important in many ways—but Stalin could have battled on even without the capital. German generals may have believed otherwise, but there are no strong arguments suggesting that the Soviet Union would have collapsed had the Germans captured Moscow. With hindsight, we may even doubt that the Germans could have held it for longer than a few months had they even captured the city.

■ ■ ■

Hardly anything suggests that Germany could have won World War II. Hence, it seems doubtful to call any single battle decisive. What happened at the fronts could at most hasten or delay the inevitable outcome.

German armaments production and manpower resources were so inferior that the outcome could hardly be doubted, but this is a conclusion that may not have been as obvious at the time as it is now. We have more information than those assessing the situation and making decisions in 1941. To some of them, the events outside Moscow were profoundly shocking. Walter Borbet was deeply involved in the German war economy and planning. He knew what was at stake and realised what the events in November and December 1941 meant. He found the situation so disastrous that he committed suicide.[10]

Among the many important positions held by Walter Borbet was chairman of the committee responsible for ammunition production, which conferred insight as well as responsibility. He knew that many of the plans for the future rested upon the explicit assumption that the Soviet Union would be defeated in 1941. When the enemy in the east had been eliminated, the army—except the mechanized units—could be reduced, as could the production of ammunition. Instead, German industry would focus on the production of equipment for the air force and navy. These plans had already been put into effect—some industries had already shifted production, and investments had for many months been directed accordingly.

Not only had the Germans begun to shift production, they also lacked sufficient quantities of crude oil. They had hoped to capture enough oil fields in the Soviet Union, particularly in the Caucasus area, to meet their demands. Should the Germans need to wage a war dominated by airpower and naval forces, as was inevitable in the west, consumption of petrol and

As the weather became harsher, resupply became more difficult for the German forces.

fuel oil would soar. Such forces required far greater quantities of fuel than the Germans possessed, and they could not have used them effectively without access to more crude oil. Hence, the Germans' long-term strategy was undermined by the failure to knock the Soviet Union out of the war in 1941.

Borbet and many others could read the signs. They realized Germany no longer had a reasonable chance of winning the war. In addition, considering the brutality of the German occupation of many European countries, they could hardly expect a conciliatory peace. With the launch of Operation *Barbarossa* came an intensification of the Holocaust, after which there was no way back—there could be no negotiated peace with the Nazi regime once the world had seen the full extent of its crimes. Despite the fact that the failure to capture Moscow had completely undermined Hitler's strategy, he had no option but to continue a war that was futile.

In a way, the battle for Moscow can be seen as a turning point in the war. It was Hitler's first major failure, which indicated that the initial German strategy had come to its end and the war would in the future have a different character. The German war effort had already made heavy demands on the economy. Now it would be necessary to increase production even further. This would require additional labor, but simultaneously more soldiers would be needed. The armed forces would have to compete with industry for manpower.

It has been said that women were not mobilized to a significant extent in Nazi Germany, but recent research challenges this view. To the contrary, a large number of women were inducted into the labor force. When more men were needed at the front, there were few alternatives for German industry. To alleviate the labor shortages, the German regime cast its eyes on the occupied countries, where workers were recruited using all conceivable means, from voluntary enlistment to force. The economy would thus be strengthened to meet future demands, but it must have been clear to the German regime that the war, which had truly become global, had entered a phase in which the Germans were grasping at straws to survive.

■ ■ ■

Stalin had seen his armed forces suffer one disaster after another. Losses that would have ruined any other army had already been endured many times. Whenever the Germans had made a determined attack, the Soviet dictator's armies had been defeated. Although the Soviet reserves were huge—far larger than the Germans imagined—losses of the magnitude suffered would be unsustainable in the future.

When the German offensive bogged down outside Moscow, Stalin and his generals could begin to hope. The events outside Moscow were not the first success;—the important city of Rostov, on the Don River, had been recaptured on November 28—but that was almost a skirmish compared to the battle for Moscow. The Germans had only sent a corps to Rostov, a force far smaller than Army Group Center.

The Soviet leadership saw clearly that the Germans made their most important effort in the Moscow sector in October and November 1941. When the offensive in this area bogged down, the German war machine as a whole lost momentum. Suddenly, Stalin was presented with the opportunity to make decisions without being under pressure from the enemy's actions. He could choose where and how reinforcements would be deployed, according to his long-term ambitions. Stalin did still have to consider the enemy, particularly the condition that German units were in. How depleted were the German divisions at the beginning of December? Precise information could not be provided by Soviet intelligence, but any decision would have to consider German combat power, operational mobility and their supply situation.

If the Germans were only temporarily and moderately weakened, Stalin might be prudent to set less ambitious goals. On the other hand, had the Germans spent themselves, Stalin would do better to make the most of the present opportunity, as the Germans might recover if given the chance. Furthermore, there were strong reasons to believe that the winter would not favor the Germans. If so, it was even more important to make the most of the opportunity.

As always, it was difficult to get an accurate picture of the opponent, and the grossly exaggerated reports on enemy casualties did nothing to further accurate understanding of the enemy's capabilities. Nevertheless, decisions had to be made. Stalin had not yet made a clear choice at the beginning of December, and he could still have put off the decision a while longer. But in fact he would make his decision soon, shaping the operations during the winter, and subsequent operations during 1942. His decision would ultimately result in what was perceived as the turning point of the war.

APPENDICES

1. GERMAN TANK LOSSES ON THE EASTERN FRONT OCTOBER 1–DECEMBER 10, 1941

	PANZER I	PANZER II	PANZER III	PANZER IV	PANZER 38 (T)	StuG
OCT 1–10	7	13	28	5	2	2
OCT 11–20	10	15	37	17	4	15
OCT 21–31	1	37	38	33	52	6
NOV 1–10	17	20	93	19	51	3
NOV 11–20	4	3	10	9	26	5
NOV 21–30	12	7	13	10	72	2
DEC 1–10	2	32	66	25	48	9

- During October, one Panzer II, 187 Panzer IIIs, 72 Panzer 38(t)s, 56 Panzer IVs, and 7 StuGs were dispatched to the Eastern Front.
- During November, 12 Panzer Is, 16 Panzer IIs, 39 Panzer IIIs, no Panzer 38(t)s, 7 Panzer IVs, and no StuGs were dispatched to the Eastern Front.
- The figures apply to the entire Eastern Front, not just the Moscow sector. Losses refer to complete write-offs.
- The model Panzer 35(t) is not included explicitly in the data, but we have seen many examples of it being explicitly included in Panzer 38(t).

Sources: BA-MA RW 19/1390 & RW19/1391.

2. ARMY GROUP CENTER CASUALTIES

Note that some panzer groups were occasionally attached to armies, which may possibly have caused losses to be recorded for the army rather than the panzer group. Also, reporting may have lagged behind slightly, causing losses to be recorded in a subsequent period. The latter problem seems mainly have occurred during defensive fighting and is unlikely to be much of a problem during this battle. Casualties include killed, wounded, and missing, but not non-combat losses.

	OCT 1–6	OCT 7–13	OCT 14–20	OCT 21–26	OCT 27–31
NINTH ARMY	17,988	3,789	516	3,773	1,691
PANZER GROUP 3	939	1,782	2,734	969	838
FOURTH ARMY	10,525	756	4,347	2,715	2,734
PANZER GROUP 4	772	3,059	3,434	1,243	17
SECOND ARMY	2,537	616	143	19	11
PANZER GROUP 2	966	1,600	860	1,283	214
TOTAL	**33,727**	**11,602**	**12,034**	**10,002**	**5,505**

	NOV 1–6	NOV 7–13	NOV 14–20	NOV 21–26	NOV 27–DEC 3
NINTH ARMY	3,011	1,105	941	756	1,159
PANZER GROUP 3	406	343	589	487	1,001
FOURTH ARMY	3,182	1,604	4,315	2,556	1,959
PANZER GROUP 4	3,883	1,573	4,658	5,233	3,989
SECOND ARMY	311	40	46	283	638
PANZER GROUP 2	426	947	1,165	2,370	1,559
TOTAL	**11,219**	**5,612**	**11,714**	**11,685**	**5,505**

Source: BA-MA RW 6/v.556.

3. SOVIET LOSSES DURING THE VYAZMA-BRYANSK BATTLE, 1941

Russian authors and experts on the battle at Moscow in 1941, B. I. Nevzorov and M. Chodarenok, have concluded that the Red Army suffered 959,200 casualties during October 1941, which is a staggering number. They have, among others, studied reports on the forces that managed to escape German encirclement. Irrevocable casualties—killed and missing—amounted to 855,100, while the Germans captured 673,098 men in the Vyazma-Bryansk battle. The balance was made up by 104,100 wounded. Nezorov and Chodarenok also conclude that approximately 6,000 guns and mortars, as well as 830 tanks were lost in the encirclement battle.[1]

If we compare these figures with the oft-quoted casualties given by G. F. Krivosheev in his work, *Grif Sekrenosti Sniat*, a different picture emerges. According to Krivosheev, irrevocable losses from September 30 to December 5 amounted to 514,338 and to this can be added 143,941 wounded, for a total of 658,279 casualties, from an initial strength of 1,250,000 men. Not that Krivosheev's figures refer to the entire period from the beginning of Operation *Taifun* to December 5, which make them appear implausible.[2]

Another approach is to compare the size of the Soviet force on October 1 with the strength on hand in front of Moscow on November 15. From October 1 to November 15, Soviet strength shrank from 1,250,000 men to 785,281. Thus there was a deficit of 463,719 men. However, losses must have been much greater, as substantial reinforcements arrived during the period.[3]

MAJOR COMBAT UNITS THAT ARRIVED OCTOBER 1—NOVEMBER 15[4]	
12 RIFLE DIVISIONS, 10,000 MEN EACH	120,000
2 MOTORIZED RIFLE DIVISIONS, 9,000 MEN EACH	18,000
2 TANK DIVISIONS, 6,000 MEN EACH	12,000
1 AIRBORNE CORPS	5,000
10 CAVALRY DIVISIONS, 3,000 MEN EACH	30,000
18 TANK BRIGADES, 1,500 MEN EACH	27,000
2 MOTORIZED RIFLE BRIGADES, 2,500 MEN EACH	5,000
TOTAL	**217,000**

This has to be added, indicating overall casualties amounting to 680,719 men. However, various supporting units also arrived and if these are added, the total will increase by 55,500.

NON-DIVISIONAL COMBAT UNITS ARRIVING OCTOBER 1–NOVEMBER 1[5]	
5 MOTORCYCLE REGIMENTS, 800 MEN EACH	4,000
3 NKVD REGIMENTS, 1,500 MEN EACH	4,500
20 ARTILLERY REGIMENTS, 1,300 MEN EACH	26,000
28 ANTITANK REGIMENTS, 500 MEN EACH	14,000
4 ROCKET ARTILLERY REGIMENTS, 700 MEN EACH	2,800
8 ENGINEER BATTALIONS, 350 MEN EACH	2,800
7 AA BATTALIONS, 200 MEN EACH	1,400
TOTAL	55,500

This increases losses to 736,219 men, which clearly exceeds the figure give by Krivosheev. However, there are also the reinforcements sent up until November 15 and any replacements sent to the units at the front. Finally, the ad-hoc units formed are not included, such as the 2nd Training Brigade, the student regiments from the RSFSR military academy, and from the Moscow military-political school. The machinegun battalions that took up positions on the Volokolamsk–Mozhaisk–Malojaroslavets–Kaluga Line are not included. Finally a number of reserve rifle regiments should also be included.

How many replacements were sent? We have not found exact figures, but the 2nd Guards Division, for example, received over 5,000 replacements in October. Another example is the 144th Rifle Division, which was rebuilt using two reserve rifle regiments. Nezorov's and Chodarenok's numbers appear very plausible. It should be remembered that in addition to the 1,250,000 men included in the three fronts, there were other uniformed personnel in the area that were not attached to the fronts, such as air defense units, local garrisons, NKVD forces and personnel working in the supply system. The NKVD had 13,190 men in the area, while in the Bryansk Front area there were at least 85,000 men constructing fieldworks and doing other kinds of work to enhance defenses.[6]

Vyazma-Bryansk was an immense disaster for the Red Army. Close to one million men were lost, but despite this, no fewer than 785,000 men were available on November 15, with further reserves behind. This was indeed an accomplishment.

NOTES

1. Lev Lopukhovskii, *Vyazemskaya Katastrofa 41-go goda* (Moscow: Eksmo, 2007) pp. 550–551. See also Nevzorovs text on Mosow 1941 in *Velikaya Otechestvennaya Voyna 1941–1945, Kniga 1 Surovye Ispytaniya* (Moscow: Nauka, 1998) p. 226.
2. Krivosheyev, G. F., *Grif Sekrenosti Sniat* (Moscow: Voenizdat, 1993) pp. 171–172.
3. Based on information in Voenno-Istoricheskii Zhurnal 1967 no 3: Dokumenty i Materialy: *Moskovskaya bitva v tsifrach,* pp. 69–79.
4. See appendix 19. Note that strength figures are approximate and in some cases units were most likely stronger than we indicate.
5. Based on a comparison of the order of battle 1 October and 1 November 1941, see *Boevoy Sostav Sovetskoy Armii, khast I* (East View Publications).
6. Lev Lopukhovskii, *Vyazemskaya Katastrofa 41-go goda* (Moscow: Eksmo, 2007) p. 538. Charles C. Sharp, *Soviet Order of Battle World War II, Volume IV "Red Guards"* (West Chester: George F. Nafzinger, 1995) p. 42. Charles C. Sharp, *Soviet Order of Battle World War II, Volume VIII "Red Legions"* (West Chester: George F. Nafzinger, 1996), p. 72.

---

4. THE STRENGTH OF GERMAN ARMIES ON THE EASTERN FRONT, OCTOBER–DECEMBER 1941

In his book *Die Wende vor Moskau* (1972), Klaus Reinhardt claimed that Army Group Center numbered 1,929,406 men at the beginning of October 1941.[1] The figure has been iterated by many other authors and is clearly higher than the Soviet strength, which is usually stated as approximately 1.2 million men. If this were correct, the Germans would have enjoyed numerical superiority at the beginning of Operation *Taifun.* This is not the case and Reinhardt's figure is very problematic.

Reinhardt's source is an Army Group Center report,[2] but this particular report is very problematic. It could be assumed that number of soldiers is easy to establish, but unfortunately this is not the case. When reporting manpower strength, the Germans (as well as the other belligerents) used various categories.

Several terms were in use and each had its own advantages and disadvantages, depending on what kind of question was to be answered. Two of them were "Iststärke" and "Verpflegungsstärke."[3]

Verpflegungsstärke simply referred to the number of people a formation was supposed to provide with rations. For smaller units, like battalions and regiments, this figure usually shows the strength of the unit reasonably accurately. However, as we move upwards in the military hierarchy, problems multiply. This results from the fact that larger formations, e.g. armies, can be responsible for feeding many people who have little or no impact on its combat power, it may indeed be tasked with the provision of thousands of non-military personnel. Even prisoners of war are included in "Verpflegungsstärke."[4]

The figure given by Reinhardt is something called "Kopfstärke" in the document. It is not a word defined in the German military terminology and we have almost never seen it, despite studying an immense number of documents from various units, command echelons, and operations. It seems likely though that "Kopfstärke" is close to "Verpflegungsstärke," a conclusion supported by information in the annex to the document.

For higher-command echelons, i.e. corps and above, "Iststärke" is usually more relevant, but this category is also not unproblematic. It includes, for example, personnel absent at various schools, personnel temporarily attached to other units, men on leave and men hospitalized for shorter periods (usually eight weeks or less). "Iststärke" may thus also give an inflated impression of strength, but it is the best figure in the extant documents.

The table below gives the "Iststärke" for the German armies on the Eastern Front. Thus, units not attached to armies are excluded, but this has little impact, as there were very few German units relevant to the strength comparison that were not attached to armies. The Germans had no equivalent to the Soviet reserves positioned relatively close behind the fronts, but controlled by the Stavka. The figures in the table are averages for the respective months.

Unfortunately, not even these figures are completely unproblematic. Some of the reports are preliminary and might thus underestimate Iststärke. On the other hand, as Iststärke included many men not present, it may inflate German strength. We believe that Army Group Center had a manpower strength at the beginning of October that was very close to the sum of the armies, as given in the table. Hence, the opposing forces should have been of equal size when Operation *Taifun* was launched.

	OCTOBER	NOVEMBER	DECEMBER
SECOND ARMY (AGC)	117,914	124,520	121,796
FOURTH ARMY (AGC)	313,548	287,732	187,533
SIXTH ARMY	195,787	215,568	169,432
NINTH ARMY (AGC)	246,782	213,608	180,137
ELEVENTH ARMY	146,067	141,134	138,406
SIXTEENTH ARMY	310,433	286,559	220,909
SEVENTEENTH ARMY	182,338	174,851	166,685
EIGHTEENTH ARMY	213,831	232,467	274,028
PANZER GROUP 1	149,172	156,683	179,560
PANZER GROUP 2 (AGC)	202,446	182,321	174,550
PANZER GROUP 3 (AGC)	113,005	91,726	98,980
PANZER GROUP 4 (AGC)	189,998	249,294	199,986
TOTAL ON EASTERN FRONT	**2,381,321**	**2,356,463**	**2,112,002**

Sources: The basis for this table is a compilation from files BA-MA RW6/553, RW6/535, RH 20-9/357 and RH 20-9/358 made by Kjetil Aasland. We are indebted to him for this information.

NOTES
1. Klaus Reinhardt, *Die Wende vor Moskau* (Stuttgart: Deutsche Verlags-Anstalt, 1972), p. 51.
2. See BA-MA RH 19 II/123, Bl. 48
3. We have discussed this in more detail in N. Zetterling and A. Frankson, "Analyzing World War II Eastern Front Battles," *Journal of Slavic Military Studies*, vol 11, No 1 (March 1998).
4. Ibid.

5. ORDER OF BATTLE PANZER GROUP 2, SEPTEMBER 27, 1941

XXIV Panzer Corps

3rd Panzer Division, 4th Panzer Division, 10th Motorized Infantry Division
Artillery Commander 143, Artillery Regiment Staff 623, Artillery Battalion
II./69 (10cm gun), Field Howitzer Battalion II./62 (heavy), Artillery Battalion
604 (21cm howitzer), Engineer Regiment Staff 515, Engineer Battalion 45,
Antitank Battalion 521, Reconnaissance aviation squadron 9./LG2 (with 3rd
Pz.Div.), Bridge Column B10, Bridge Column B39, Bridge Column B79,
Bridge Column B 2./403, Reconnaissance aviation squadron 6./H (Pz) 41
(with 4th Pz.Div.), Antiaircraft Battalion I./11, Antiaircraft Battalion II./11,
Antiaircraft Battalion 91

XLVII Panzer Corps

17th Panzer Division, 18th Panzer Division, 29th Motorized Infantry Division
Artillery Commander 146, Artillery Regiment Staff 792, Artillery Battalion
631 (10cm gun), Field Howitzer Battalion 422 (heavy), Artillery Battalion 817
(21cm howitzer), Observation Battalion 1, Engineer Regiment Staff 413,
Engineer Battalion 42, Antitank Battalion 529, Flame Thrower Tank Battalion
100, Reconnaissance aviation squadron 9./LG2 (with 3rd Pz.Div.), Bridge
Column B10, Bridge Column B39, Bridge Column B79, Bridge Column B
2./403, Reconnaissance aviation squadron 6./H (Pz) 32 (with 17th Pz.Div.),
Reconnaissance aviation squadron 6./H (Pz) 13 (with 18th Pz.Div.), Antiaircraft Battalion I./12, Antiaircraft Battalion I./22, Antiaircraft Battalion 77

XLVIII Panzer Corps

9th Panzer Division, 16th Motorized Infantry Division,
25th Motorized Infantry Division
Artillery Commander 108, Artillery Regiment Staff 697, Artillery Battalion
616 (21cm howitzer), Engineer Regiment Staff 520, Engineer Battalion 651,
Reconnaissance aviation squadron 9./LG2 (with 9th Pz.Div.), Bridge Column
B25, Bridge Column B660, Bridge Column B672, Bridge Column B675,
Reconnaissance aviation squadron 5./H 32, Reconnaissance aviation
squadron 5./H 31, Antiaircraft Battalion I./66, Antiaircraft Battalion IV./66,
Antiaircraft Battalion II./43

XXXIV Army Corps

45th Infantry Division, 134th Infantry Division

XXXV Army Corps

1st Cavalry Division, 95th Infantry Division, 262nd Infantry Division, 293rd Infantry Division, 296th Infantry Division.

Artillery Battalion 635 (21cm howitzer), Engineer Battalion 41, Armored Reconnaissance Battalion Lehr (with 1st Cavalry Division), Bridge Column B 1./41, Bridge Column B 2./41, Bridge Column B 2./422, Antiaircraft Battalion 602, Antiaircraft Battalion 94

Directly attached to Pz.Gr. 2

Artillery Regiment Staff 53, Nebelwerfer Regiment 53 (three battalions), Engineer Battalion, 635, Bridge Construction Battalion 159, Bridge Column B. 635, Bridge Column B 1./402, Bridge Column B 22, Road Construction Battalion 504, Machine Gun Battalion 5, Reconnaissance aviation squadron 6 (F)/31, Liaison aviation squadron 63

Source: Kriegsgliederung der Panzergruppe 2, Stand 27.9.41, in Anlagen zum KTB AOK 2 Ia, NARA T312, R1654, F000658.

6. ORDER OF BATTLE PANZER GROUP 3, OCTOBER 2, 1941

VI Army Corps

110th Infantry Division, 26th Infantry Division

Artillery Commander 126, Artillery Regiment Staff 677, Artillery Battalion IV./109 (mixed), Field Howitzer Battalion 848 (heavy), Observation Battalion 6, Balloon Battery 4./6, Engineer Regiment Staff Bollman, Engineer Battalion 743, Engineer Battalion 632, Construction Battalion 135, Construction Battalion 320, Bridge Column B2./404, Antiaircraft Company 1./46, Antiaircraft Company 6./47, Reconnaissance aviation squadron 2./H 12, Antiaircraft Battalion II./4

XLI Panzer Corps

14th Motorized Infantry Division, 6th Infantry Division, 36th Motorized Infantry Division, 1st Panzer Division

Artillery Commander 30, Artillery Regiment Staff 803, Artillery Battalion 803 (10cm gun), Artillery Battalion 620 (15cm gun), Field Howitzer Battalion II./59 (heavy), Assault Gun Battalion 600 with Assault Gun Batteries 660 and 665, Nebelwerfer Battalion III./51, Engineer Regiment Staff 628, Engineer Battalion 52 (motorized) with Bridge Column 52, Road Construction

Battalion 506, Flamethrower Tank Battalion 101 (with 36th Inf. Div.), Anti-aircraft Battalion 605 (with 36th Inf. Div.), 1. Coy from Antitank Battalion 8 (8.8cm SP), Antiaircraft Battalion I./29, Antiaircraft Battalion 83 (with 1st Pz.Div.), Reconnaissance aviation squadron 4./H 31, Reconnaissance aviation squadron 2./H (Pz) 23 (with 1st Pz.Div.)

LVI Panzer Corps

129th Infantry Division, 7th Panzer Division,

6th Panzer Division, 900th Brigade (Army Group Reserve)

> Artillery Commander 125, Artillery Regiment Staff 783, Artillery Battalion 151 (10cm gun), Field Howitzer Battalion II./38 (heavy), Artillery Battalion 733 (21cm howitzer), Assault Gun Battalion 210, Nebelwerfer Battalion I./51, Nebelwerfer Battalion II./51, Engineer Regiment Staff 678, Engineer Battalion 630 (motorized), Construction Battalion 218, Antitank Battalion 643 (4.7cm SP), Antiaircraft Battalion II./411 (with 6th Pz.Div.), Reconnaissance Aviation Squadron 1./H (Pz) 11 (with 7th Pz.Div.)

V Army Corps

5th Infantry Division, 35th Infantry Division, 106th Infantry Division

> Artillery Commander 22, Artillery Commander 136, Artillery Regiment Staff 627, Artillery Battalion 842 (10cm gun), Artillery Battalion II./51 (mixed), Artillery Battalion II./44, Field Howitzer Battalion 848 (heavy), Observation Battalion 15, Nebelwerfer Battalion 3, Nebelwerfer Battalion 5, Detoxication Battalion 103, Engineer Regiment Staff Behrisch, Engineer Battalion 745, Engineer Battalion 754, Construction Battalion 154, Construction Battalion 214, Bridge Column B35, Bridge Column B 1./403, Reconnaissance Aviation Squadron 4./H 10, Antiaircraft Battalion I./52

Directly attached to Pz.Gr. 3

> Construction Battalion 80, Bridge Construction Battalion (motorized) 548, Assault Boat Commando 905, Reconnaissance Aviation Squadron 2 (F)/33, Liaison Aviation Squadron 58,

Source: Pz.Gr. 3 Ia 1270/41, Kriegsgliederung Stand 2.10.41, BA-MA RH 21-3/v. 77.

7. ORDER OF BATTLE PANZER GROUP 4, OCTOBER 2, 1941

LVII Panzer Corps

19th Panzer Division, 20th Panzer Division, 3rd Motorized Infantry Division, Division SS-Reich, Infantry Regiment Grossdeutschland, 900th Brigade
  Artillery Commander 121, Engineer Regiment Staff 504, Engineer Battalion (motorized) 47, Bridge Column B3, 19, 92, Reconnaissance Aviation Squadron 7./H 13, Antiaircraft Battalion 74 (with 20th Pz.Div.), Antiaircraft Battalion 85 (with 19th Pz.Div.)

XLVI Panzer Corps

5th Panzer Division, 11th Panzer Division, 252nd Infantry Division
  Artillery Commander 101, Artillery Commander 139, Artillery Regiment Staff 606, Artillery Regiment Staff 801, Artillery Battalion 427 (10cm gun), Field Howitzer Battalion 646 (heavy), Field Howitzer Battalion 843 (heavy), Artillery Battalion 800 (15cm gun), Artillery Battalion 637 (21cm howitzer), Nebelwerfer Regiment 52, Observation Battalion 19, Engineer Regiment Staff 513, Engineer Battalion 85 (motorized), Bridge Column B. 85, Bridge Column B. 89, Bridge Column B. 209, Bridge Column K. 209, Bridge Column K. 643, Antiaircraft Battalion 601, Antiaircraft Battalion 71 (with 11th Pz.Div.), Antiaircraft Battalion I./3, Antiaircraft Battalion II./23, Reconnaissance Aviation Squadron 3./H 12 (with 5th Pz.Div.), Reconnaissance Aviation Squadron 3./H (Pz) 21 (with 11th Pz.Div.)

XL Panzer Corps

258th Infantry Division, 2nd Panzer Division, 10th Panzer Division
  Artillery Commander 128, Artillery Regiment Staff 618, Artillery Battalion II./41 (10cm gun), Artillery Battalion II./72 (10cm gun), Artillery Battalion II./61 (mixed), Field Howitzer Battalion II./67 (heavy), Nebelwerfer Regiment 54, Engineer Regiment Staff 614, Engineer Battalion 48 (motorized), Bridge Column B. 48, Bridge Column B. 49, Bridge Column B. 646, Bridge Column K. 38, Bridge Column K. 49, Antiaircraft Battalion 3 (with 10th Pz.Div.), Antiaircraft Battalion 76 (with 2nd Pz.Div.), Antiaircraft Regiment 6 (two battalions), Reconnaissance Aviation Squadron 1./H 14 (with 2nd Pz.Div.), Reconnaissance Aviation Squadron 3./H 14 (with 10th Pz.Div.)

XII Army Corps

98th Infantry Division, 34th Infantry Division

Artillery Commander 112, Artillery Commander 127, Artillery Regiment Staff 41, Artillery Battalion 858 (21cm howitzer), Field Howitzer Battalion 506 (heavy), Assault Gun Battalion 177, Observation Battalion 2, Observation Battalion 40, Detoxication Battalion 105, Engineer Battalion 745, Engineer Battalion 751, Bridge Column B 134, Bridge Column B 2./409, Reconnaissance Aviation Squadron 1./H 21, Antiaircraft Battalion I./26

Directly attached to Pz.Gr. 4

Antitank Battalion 611, Engineer Battalion (motorized) 62, Bridge Column B. 1./62, Bridge Column B. 2./62, Bridge Column B. 3./62, Bridge Column K. 62, Bridge Construction Battalion 42, Road Construction Battalion 507, Road Construction Battalion 508, Construction Battalion 24, Construction Battalion 125, Construction Battalion 213, Liaison Aviation Squadron 60

Source: Pz.Gr. 4 Ia Anlagen zum Kriegstagebuch, Kriegsgliederung Stand 2.10.41, NARA T313, R340, F86229756.

8. ORDER OF BATTLE 4TH ARMY, OCTOBER 2, 1941

IX Army Corps

292nd Infantry Division, 263rd Infantry Division,
137th Infantry Division, 183rd Infantry Division

Artillery Commander 44, Artillery Commander 147, Artillery Regiment Staff 622, Assault Gun Battalion 202, Field Howitzer Battalion II./213 (light), Artillery Battalion I./109 (10cm gun), Artillery Battalion II./71 (mixed), Field Howitzer Battalion 101 (heavy), Artillery Battalion 853 (21cm howitzer), Observation Battalion 7, Observation Battalion 17, Engineer Regiment Staff 516, Engineer Battalion 752, Bridge Column B 2./202, Bridge Column B 2./407, Road Construction Battalion 571, Construction Battalion 410, Antiaircraft Battalion I./24, Reconnaissance Aviation Squadron 2./H 4

XX Army Corps

268th Infantry Division, 15th Infantry Division, 78th Infantry Division

Artillery Commander 107, Artillery Commander 149, Artillery Regiment Staff 614, Artillery Battalion II./68 (10cm gun), Field Howitzer Battalion II./43 (heavy), Observation Battalion 20, Engineer Regiment Staff 512, Engineer Battalion 753, Bridge Column B. 48, Bridge Column B. 1./62, Construction Battalion 129, Construction Battalion 217, Antiaircraft Battalion I./701, Reconnaissance Aviation Squadron 1./H 12

VII Army Corps

267th Infantry Division, 7th Infantry Division, 23rd Infantry Division, 197th Infantry Division

Artillery Commander 7, Artillery Commander 11, Artillery Regiment Staff 788, Assault Gun Battalion 191, Assault Gun Battalion 203, Field Howitzer Battalion I./221 (light), Artillery Battalion 719 (10cm gun), Field Howitzer Battalion 845 (heavy), Artillery Battalion 735 (21cm howitzer), Artillery Battalion 857 (21cm howitzer), Artillery Battalion 740 (15cm gun), Observation Battalion 36, Balloon Battery 102, Detoxication Battalion 104, Antitank Battalion 519, Antitank Battalion 616, Engineer Regiment Staff 674, Engineer Battalion (motorized) 51, Engineer Battalion 221, Bridge Column B. 7, Bridge Column B. 15, Bridge Column B. 1./404, Bridge Column B. 1./178, Construction Battalion 17, Construction Battalion 136, Antiaircraft Battalion II./14, Reconnaissance Aviation Squadron 7./H12

Directly attached to Fourth Army

Higher Artillery Commander 302, Bridge Construction Battalion 21, Bridge Construction Battalion 593, Construction Battalion 46, Construction Battalion 97, Road Construction Battalion 580, Road Construction Battalion 544, Antiaircraft Battalion 276, Antiaircraft Battalion 611

Source: Pz.Gr. 4 Ia Anlagen zum Kriegstagebuch, Kriegsgliederung Stand 2.10.41, NARA T313, R340, F86229756.

9. SOVIET ORDER OF BATTLE OCTOBER 1, 1941

West Front—commander: Col Gen Ivan Konev

Sixteenth Army—commander: Lt Gen Konstantin Rokossovsky
    38th, 108th, 112th, and 214th Rifle Divisions
    127th Tank Brigade
Nineteenth Army—commander: Lt Gen Mikhail Lukin
    50th, 89th, 91st, 166th, and 244th Rifle Divisions

Twentieth Army—commander: Lt Gen Filipp Ershakov

73rd, 129th, 144th, and 229th Rifle Divisions

Twenty-Second Army—commander: Maj Gen Vasiliy Yushkevich
126th, 133rd, 174th, 179th, 186th, and 256th Rifle Divisions

Twenty-Ninth Army—commander: Lt Gen Ivan Maslennikov
178th, 243rd, 246th, and 252nd Rifle Divisions
Independent Motorized Brigade (unnumbered)

Thirtieth Army—commander: Maj Gen Vasiliy Khomenko
162nd, 242nd, 250th, and 251th Rifle Divisions

Directly under front control:
5th Guards Rifle Division
134th and 152nd Rifle Divisions
Cavalry Group (45th, 50th, and 53rd Cavalry Divisions)
101st and 107th Motorized Rifle Divisions
126th, 128th, and 143rd Tank Brigades
8th and 9th Motorcycle Regiments
62nd and 68th Fortified Regions

Reserve Front—commander: Marshal Semyon Budyonniy

Twenty-Fourth Army—commander: Maj Gen Konstantin Rakutin
19th, 103rd, 106th, 139th, 170th, and 309th Rifle Divisions
144th and 146th Tank Brigades

Thirty-First Army—commander: Maj Gen Vasiliy Dolmatov
5th, 110th, 119th, 247th, and 249th Rifle Divisions
296th and 297th Independent Machine Gun Battalions

Thirty-Second Army—commander: Maj Gen Sergey Vishnevskiy
2nd, 8th, 29th, and 140th Rifle Divisions

Thirty-Third Army—commander: Brigade Commissar Dmitri Onuprienko
17th, 18th, 60th, 113th, and 173rd Rifle Divisions

Forty-Third Army—commander: Maj Gen Piotr Sobennikov
53rd, 149th, 211th, and 222nd Rifle Divisions
145th and 148th Tank Brigades

Forty-Ninth Army—commander: Lt Gen Ivan Zakharkin
194th, 220th, 248th, and 303rd Rifle Divisions
29th and 31st Cavalry Divisions

Directly under front control:
147th Tank Brigade

Bryansk Front—commander: Lt Gen Andrei Eremenko

Third Army—commander: Maj Gen Yakov Krejzer
137th, 148th, 269th, 280th, and 282nd Rifle Divisions
4th Cavalry Division
855th Rifle Regiment (278th Rifle Division)

Thirteenth Army—commander: Maj Gen Avksentiy Gorodnyanskii
6th, 121st, 132nd, 143rd, 155th, 298th, and 307th Rifle Divisions
55th Cavalry Division
141st Tank Brigade
43rd Independent Tank Battalion

Fiftieth Army—commander: Maj Gen Mikhail Petrov
217th, 258th, 260th, 278th (-), 279th, 290th, and 299th Rifle Divisions

Ermakov's Group—Maj Gen Arkadiy Ermakov
2nd Guards Rifle Division
160th and 283rd Rifle Divisions
121st and 150th Tank Brigades
21st Mountain Cavalry Division
52nd Cavalry Division

Directly under front control:
154th and 287th Rifle Divisions
108th Tank Division
42nd Tank Brigade
114th and 115th Tank Battalions

Sources:
Gareev, M.M. & V.F.Simonov: *Pobediteli 1941–1945* (Moscow: Ekzamen, 2005).
Kolomiets, Maksim; *Bitva Za Moskvu, 30 sentyabrya–5 dekabrya 1941.* (Moscow: Strategiya KM, 2002).
Samsonov, A.M., *Moskva, 1941 god: ot tragedii porazhenii k velikoy pobede.* (Moscow: Moskovskii Rabochii, 1991).

10. ARMY GROUP CENTER, OCTOBER 2, 1941—COMMANDERS

Commander: Field Marshal Fedor von Bock

Second Army—commander: Col Gen Maximilian von Weichs

LIII Army Corps—commander: Gen Karl Weisenberger
    31st, 56th, and 167th Infantry Divisions

XLIII Army Corps—commander: Gen Gotthard Heinrici
    52nd and 131st Infantry Divisions

XIII Army Corps—commander: Gen Hans-Gustav Felber
    17th and 260th Infantry Divisions

Reserve:
    112th Infantry Division

Second Panzer Army—commander: Col Gen Heinz Guderian

XXXIV Army Corps—commander: Gen Hermann Metz
    45th and 134th Infantry Divisions

XXXV Army Corps—commander: Lt Gen Rudolf Kaempfe
    95th, 262nd, 293rd, and 296th Infantry Divisions

XLVIII Panzer Corps—commander: Lt Gen Werner Kempf
    9th Panzer Division
    16th and 25th Motorized Divisions

✓XXIV Panzer Corps—commander: Gen Leo Geyr von Schweppenburg
    3rd and 4th Panzer Divisions
    10th Motorized Division

✓XLVII Panzer Corps—commander: Gen Joachim Lemelsen
    17th and 18th Panzer Divisions
    29th Motorized Division

Fourth Army—commander: Field Marshal Günther von Kluge

VII Army Corps—commander: Gen Wilhelm Fahrmbacher
    7th, 23rd, 197th, and 267th Infantry Divisions

XX Army Corps—commander: Gen Friedrich Materna
    15th, 78th, and 268th Infantry Divisions

IX Corps—commander: Gen Hermann Geyer
    137th, 183rd, 263rd, and 292nd Infantry Divisions

Panzer Group 4—commander: Col Gen Erich Hoepner

XII Corps—commander: Gen Walter Schroth
    34th and 98th Infantry Division

XL Panzer Corps—commander: Gen Georg Stumme
    2nd and 10th Panzer Divisions
    258th Infantry Division

XLVI Panzer Corps—commander:
GEN HEINRICH VON VIETINGHOFF
    5th and 11th Panzer Divisions
    252nd Infantry Division

LVII Panzer Corps—commander: Gen Adolf-Friedrich Kuntzen
    20th Panzer Division
    3rd Motorized Division
    SS-Reich Motorized Division

9th Army—commander: Col Gen Adolf Strauß

XXVII Army Corps—commander: Gen Alfred Wäger
    86th, 162nd, and 255th Infantry Divisions

V Army Corps—commander: Gen Richard Ruoff
    5th, 35th, 106th, and 129th Infantry Divisions

VIII Army Corps—commander: Gen Walter Heitz
    8th, 28th, and 87th Infantry Divisions

XXIII Army Corps—commander: Gen Albrecht Schubert
    102nd, 206th, 251st, and 256th Infantry Divisions

Reserve:
    161st Infantry Division

Panzer Group 3—commander: Col Gen Hermann Hoth

LVI Panzer Corps—commander: Gen Ferdinand Schaal
    6th and 7th Panzer Divisions
    14th Motorized Division

XLI Panzer Corps—commander: Gen Georg-Hans Reinhardt
    1st Panzer Division
    36th Motorized Division

VI Army Corps—commander: Gen Otto-Wilhelm Förster
    6th, 26th, and 110th Infantry Divisions

Army Group Reserve
   1st Cavalry Division
   19th Panzer Division
   Großdeutschland Motorized Infantry Regiment
   900th Motorized Brigade

Commander of Rear Area—commander: Gen Max von Schenckendorff
   221st Security Division
   286th Security Division
   339th Security Division
   403rd Security Division
   454th Security Division
   707th ~~Infantry Division~~ *security DIv*
   SS-Cavalry Brigade

Sources: Klaus Reinhardt, Klaus, *Die Wende vor Moskau* (Stuttgart: Deutsche Verlags-Anstalt, 1972), appendix 9.

G. Heuer, *Die deutschen Generalfeldmarschälle und Grossadmirale 1933–1945* (VPM Verlagsunion Pabel Mowig KG, n.d).

11. STALIN'S RESERVES

The Germans fatally misjudged Stalin's reserves. On October 1 there were 213 rifle divisions along the front facing the Germans, and another 123 in other parts of the Soviet Union. Of them, 25 were in the Far East and 33 in the Caucasus. Except four rifle divisions formally belonging to the Stavka reserve, the remaining 72 rifle divisions were distributed in various military districts. Many of them were in the later stages of forming and can be regarded as part of Stalin's reserve which had not yet been transferred to the Stavka.

The Moscow and Orel Military districts had seven and five divisions respectively. There were also 21 artillery regiments, two antitank gun regiments and five artillery battalions in the Moscow District, while the Orel Military District had five antitank gun regiments.

The Vyazma-Bryansk disaster resulted in a reduction in the number of front-line rifle divisions, which had shrunk to 198, while 118 were in other parts of the Soviet Union, on November 1. Thus, the number of rifle divisions had decreased by 20. However, the Stavka reserve had increased by 22 rifle divisions. Twenty-six rifle divisions remained in the Far East and 24 in the Caucasus. Only one remained in the Moscow Military District and none in Orel Military District. Also, the Moscow defense zone had been created, with one rifle division and five militia divisions.

The number of divisions at the front grew to 230 by December 1, leaving only 84 in the other parts of the Soviet Union. Of the latter, no less than 44 were Stavka reserves. The number of rifle divisions in the Far East had shrunk marginally, to 25. Far more significant was the change in the Caucasus, where only nine divisions remained. Another important difference was the formation of rifle brigades, which largely superseded the formation of new divisions. The brigades were easier to raise and the number of brigades in the Red Army soared, from 25 on October 1 to 103 on December 1. There were 38 rifle brigades at the front on December 1, seven in Stavka reserves and 49 in military districts.

NUMBER OF UNITS IN THE RED ARMY DURING THE AUTUMN OF 1941			
	OCTOBER 1, 1941	NOVEMBER 1, 1941	DECEMBER 1, 1941
ARMY HEADQUARTERS	49	49	57
RIFLE DIVISIONS	336	316	314
RIFLE BRIGADES	25	92	103
CAVALRY DIVISIONS	68	67	84
TANK DIVISIONS	12	11	9
TANK BRIGADES #	59	70	68
ARTILLERY REGIMENTS*	210	213	212

NOTES:: # includes mechanized brigades, * also includes antitank gun regiments, as they were part of the artillery, according to Soviet definitions.

The trend to increase the number of brigades had already been seen in the Armored forces, where the number of brigades had increased from 22 to 59 during September 1941. The increase slowed down subsequently, but the number of tank brigades still reached 70 on November 1. Unlike the infantry, the number of divisions in the tank forces shrunk, as many were used as cadres for brigades. On September 1, there were 31 tank divisions and only 12 remained on October 1. On that day, 37 of 59 tank brigades were at the front and on November 1, 44 of 70 had reached the front.

Stalin had to keep forces in the Far East and the Caucasus, but there were still large forces in the interior parts of the Soviet Union, far larger than the Germans imagined.

Source: Boevoy Sostav Sovetskoy Armii, chast I.

12. ORGANIZATION OF KAMPFGRUPPE EBERBACH, SEPTEMBER 30, 1941

Battle groups were common in the German army. Battle group Eberbach was
part of the 4th Panzer Division and spearheaded the offensive from Gluchov to
Orel. It was mainly composed of elements from the 4th Panzer Division, but
there were a few other units as well. Eberbach decided to deploy his forces in
two groups, one on the northern wing and one on the southern, when attacking
early on September 30:

> *Southern group:* I. Battalion from Panzer Regiment 35, II. Battalion from
> Panzer Regiment 35 (minus one company), half of II. Battalion from
> AA Regiment 11, Motorcycle Battalion 34, Motorcycle Battalion 3
> (minus one company), elements from Armored Engineer Battalion 79,
> 3rd Company (minus two platoons) from Panzer Jäger Battalion 49, Staff
> from Panzer Regiment 35, 5th Panzer Brigade staff (Eberbach's own
> staff), II. Battalion Artillery Regiment 103, one battery from II. Battalion
> Artillery Regiment 69, I. Battalion Nebelwerfer Regiment 53.

> *Northern group:* II. Battalion from Panzer Regiment 6, half of II. Battalion
> from AA Regiment 11, one company from Motorcycle Battalion 3, 3rd
> Company from Armored Engineer Battalion 39

Evidently, Colonel Eberbach divided his battle group in two parts and he
himself commanded the southern (larger) group, while Lieutenant Colonel Mun-
zel led the northern group. The latter was given an independent mission. It could
thus be said that Eberbach created an tempoerary, independent battlegroup within
his own battle group.

Source: 5. Panzer-Brigade, O.U. 5.10.1941, "Gefechtsbericht für die Zeit vom 29.9–
   3.10.1941", BA-MA RH 39/373.

13. SIBERIAN TROOPS

Siberian units during the defensive phase of the battle at Moscow 1941
(i.e. units from the Ural, Central Asia, Trans-Baikal and Far East areas)

RIFLE DIVISIONS

32nd Rifle Division

Commander: Col V. I. Polosukhin

Arrived: October

Brief history: The division was raised in 1922, in the Volga Military District. It was stationed in the Far East on June 22, and had fought the Japanese at Lake Khasan in 1938. The 32nd Division was instructed to move west in September 1941 and arrived in the Moscow area in October. It had almost 15,000 men and was organized according to the prewar tables.

Attached: November 1, 1941—Fifth Army, December 1, 1941—Fifth Army

Guards status: yes, in May 1942—29th Guards Rifle Division

78th Rifle Division

Commander: Col A. P. Beloborodov (Maj Gen from November 27, 1941)

Arrived: October

Brief history: Formed at Tomsk in April 1932 and was in the Far East on June 22, 1941, near Vladivostok. It was not sent west until October 1941 and arrived in the Moscow area at the end of the month. It had about 14,000 men and retained the prewar organization. It seems to have been one of the last divisions to enter combat using the prewar organization.

Attached: November 1, 1941—front resource; December 1, 1941—Sixteenth Army

Guards status: yes, at the end of November 1941—9th Guards Rifle Division

93rd Rifle Division

Commander: Maj Gen K. M. Erastus

Arrived: October

Brief history: Raised at Chita in the Siberian Military District in 1936. It had moved to the Trans-Baikal District when the war broke out. The division received orders to move west on October 6. The 93rd Division was organized according to the prewar tables.

Attached: November 1, 1941—Forty-Third Army; December 1, 1941—Forty-Third Army

Guards status: yes, in April 1942—2nd Guards Rifle Division

238th Rifle Division

Commander: Col G. P. Korotkov

Arrived: October

Brief history: Raised in Alma-Ata in March 1941, it was the highest numbered prewar division. As it was not combat-ready on June 22, 1941, it was remained in Asia. In the autumn, the division was moved by rail to Leninsk, north of Tula, employed to defend the city's northwestern flank.

Attached: November 1, 1941—Forty-Ninth Army; December 1, 1941—Forty-Ninth Army

Guards status: yes, in May 1942—30th Guards Rifle Division

312th Rifle Division

Commander: Col A. F. Naumov

Arrived: October

Brief history: Began forming on July 10, 1941 at Akjubinsk in Central Asia Military District. Already sent to the Leningrad area a month later. However, the crisis at Moscow caused the division to be sent to Maloyaroslavets on October 6.

Attached: during October 1941—Forty-Third Army

Guards status: no—disbanded at the end of October 1941, after suffering very high casualties.

316th Rifle Division

Commander: Maj Gen I. V. Panfilov (KIA)

Maj Gen V. A. Revyakin (from November 20, 1941)

Arrived: October

Brief history: Raised at Alma-Ata on July 12, 1941 and sent to the Leningrad area, like the 312th Division. Sent to the Moscow area with 312th Rifle Division, but ended up at Volokolamsk, northwest of Moscow.

Attached: November 1, 1941—Sixteenth Army; December 1, 1941—Sixteenth Army

Guards status: yes, in mid-November 1941—8th Guards Rifle Division.

371st Rifle Division

Commander: Maj Gen F. V. Chernysyev

Arrived: November

Brief history: Began forming at Sverdlovsk in August 1941. Joined the West Front at the end of November.

Attached: December 1, 1941—Thirtieth Army

Guards status: no

379th Rifle Division

Commander: Col V. A. Chistov

Arrived: November

Brief history: Began forming in the Perm area, Ural Military District, in August 1941. Joined the West Front in November. The division was reported to have slightly more than 10,000, but there appears to have been shortcomings in equipment.

Attached: December 1, 1941—Thirtieth Army

Guards status: no—the division was dissolved in December 1944 and used to rebuild other units of the 2nd Baltic Front.

413th Rifle Division

Commander: Maj Gen A. D. Tereshkov

Arrived: October

Brief history: The division was set up in the Far East during August 1941, mainly from various resources available in the area, such as officers and men from different military schools. It was assessed to be combat ready on October 1 and arrived at Moscow at the end of October. It took up positions at Tula and was reported to have 12,000 men and to be well equipped.

Attached: November 1, 1941—Fiftieth Army; December 1, 1941—Fiftieth Army

Guards status: no

415th Rifle Division

Commander: Maj Gen P. A. Aleksandrovsk

Arrived: November

Brief history: Began forming on September 8, 1941. Sent west at the end of October, arrived in mid-November.

Attached: December 1, 1941—Forty-Ninth Army

Guards status: no

CAVALRY DIVISIONS

18th Cavalry Division

Commander: Maj Gen P. S. Ivanov

Arrived: November

Brief history: The 7th Tadzjik Cavalry Division was in 1936 converted to the 18th Mountain Cavalry Division. It remained in the Central Asia Military District and was not sent west until November 1941.

Attached: December 1, 1941—30th Army

Guards status: no—disbanded in July 1942.

20th Cavalry Division

Commander: Col A. V. Stavenkov

Lt Col M. P. Tavliev (from November 29, 1941)

Arrived: November

Brief history: Had been formed in 1936 in the Central Asia Military District from the 7th Turkestan Cavalry Brigade. It was sent west in October 1941.

Attached: December 1, 1941—Sixteenth Army

Guards status: yes, in September 1943—17th Guards Cavalry Division.

44th Cavalry Division

Commander: Col P. F. Kuklin

Arrived: November

Brief history: Set up in Tashkent during July 1941 and subsequently transferred to the 4th Cavalry Corps in Central Asia. Thereafter employed as garrison in northern Iran. The division returned to the Soviet Union and sent by rail to Moscow, where it arrived in November.

Attached: December 1, 1941—Sixteenth Army

Guards status: no—disbanded in April 1942 and amalgamated into the 17th Cavalry Division.

82nd Cavalry Division

Commander: Col V. K. Roshchinenko

Arrived: November

Brief history: Forming from August until October in the Sverdlovsk area. The division left the Urals in November and reinforced the Kalinin Front. It had almost 4,000 men on December 1, but appears to have suffered shortages of heavy weapons.

Attached: December 1, 1941—Thirtieth Army

Guards status: no—disbanded in August 1942 and remnants were incorporated in the 24th Cavalry Division

TANK/MOTORIZED DIVISIONS

58th Tank Division

Commander: Maj Gen A. A. Kotlyarov (committed suicide November 20, 1941)

Commissar P. D. Govorunenko (from November 21, 1941)

Arrived: November

Brief history: The division began forming in March–April 1941 in the Far East. Subsequently included in the 30th Mechanized Corps. The corps was soon disbanded and the 58th Tank Division was reorganized according to the new TO&E at the end of July. Sent west in October, It had 198 tanks, mainly older types like T-26 and BT.

Attached: November 1, 1941—Thirtieth Army; December 1, 1941—Thirtieth Army

Guards status: no—converted to 58th Tank Brigade at the end of December 1941.

82nd Motorized Rifle Division

Commander: Col G. P. Karamyshev

Arrived: October

Brief history. Initially formed as a motorized rifle division. It was converted to a
   mechanized division in 1940, bur was subsequently again converted to a
   motorized rifle division. It lost its tank regiment, but kept the 27th Tank Battalion with light tanks.

Attached: November 1, 1941—Fifth Army, December 1, 1941—Fifth Army

Guards status: yes, in March 1942—3rd Guards Motorized Division.

112th Tank Division

Commander: Col A. L. Getman

Arrived: November

Brief history: Formed in August 1941 from elements of the 239th Mechanized
   Division, which was converting to a rifle division. The 112th was organized
   along the new structure for tank divisions. When sent west during the battle
   at Moscow, the 112th Tank Division had approximately 6,200 men and 210
   T-26 tanks.

Attached: December 1, 1941—Forty-Ninth Army

Guards status: no—converted to 112th Tank Brigade in January 1942.

Sources:

Drig, Evgeniy, *Mechanizirovannye Korpusa RKKA v Boyu.* (Moscow: Tranzitkniga, 2005).

A. M. Samsonov, *Moskva, 1941 god: ot tragedii porazhenii k velikoy pobede* (Moscow: Moskovskiy
   Rabochii, 1991).

Charles C. Sharp, *Soviet Order of Battle World War II, Volume I "The Deadly Beginning"* (West
   Chester: George F. Nafzinger, 1995).

Charles C. Sharp, *Soviet Order of Battle World War II, Volume V "Red Sabres"* (West Chester:
   George F. Nafzinger, 1995).

Charles C. Sharp, *Soviet Order of Battle World War II, Volume VIII "Red Legions"* (West
   Chester: George F. Nafzinger, 1996).

Charles C. Sharp, *Soviet Order of Battle World War II, Volume IX "Red Tide"* (West Chester:
   George F. Nafzinger, 1996).

14. SOVIET GHQ UNITS

This appendix lists Soviet units that participated in the battle at Moscow, but were
not part of divisions or brigades. We have mainly included various types of combat units. First, the situation for October 1 is given and then the units that arrived
until November 1 are listed.

October 1

Motorcycle regiments: 8, 9

Artillery regiments: 17, 29, 43, 49, 50, 56, 57, 103, 104, 105, 109, 120, 126, 151, 207, 275, 301, 302, 305, 311, 320, 336, 360, 364, 375, 387, 390, 392, 396, 399, 420, 432, 445, 447, 455, 462, 467, 471, 472, 488, 542, 544, 545, 573, 587, 592, 596, 643, 644, 645, 646, 685

Artillery battalions: 42, 199, 200

Antitank regiments: 18, 58, 509, 533, 699, 700, 753, 761, 766, 871, 872, 873, 874, 875, 876, 877, 878, 879, 880

Antitank battalion: 213

Rocket artillery regiments: 1, 6, 9, 10, 11

Rocket artillery battalions: 42

Engineer battalions: 5, 6, 9, 22, 37, 39, 42, 50, 51, 56, 61, 62, 63, 64, 70, 71, 72, 78, 84, 88, 103, 111, 113, 114, 115, 122, 127, 129, 133, 226, 229, 238, 243, 246, 251, 263, 267, 273, 275, 288, 290, 312, 321, 498, 499, 512, 513, 537, 538

Antiaircraft battalions: 4, 7, 12, 16, 36, 46, 55, 64, 71, 86, 111, 112, 123, 164, 183, 185, 221, 230, 304, 311, 318, 386, 397

Mortar battalions:11, 12, 24

1 November—new units

Motorcycle regiments: 2, 11, 36, 38, 46

Artillery regiments: 138, 204, 403, 440, 486, 510, 517, 523, 538, 537, 557, 552, 554, 564, 570, 572, 590, 979, 995, 998

Artillery battalion: 275

Antitank regiments: 39, 121, 289, 296, 304, 316, 367, 395, 452, 455, 483, 525, 540, 551, 598, 600, 610, 641, 689, 694, 702, 703, 768, 863, 868, 869, 989, 992

Rocket artillery regimens: 5, 7, 12, 13, 14, 15

Rocket artillery battalions:1, 2, 4, 5

Engineer battalions: 27, 69, 136, 145, 291, 452, 467, 511

Antiaircraft battalions: 21, 61, 121, 152, 168, 244, 281

Source: Boevoy Sostav Sovetskoy Armii, chast I (East View Publications).

15. ORDER OF BATTLE FOR THE MOZHAISK LINE, OCTOBER 14

Commander Gen Georgiy Zhukov

Sixteenth Army—commander Lt Gen Konstantin Rokossovsky
   18th and 316th Rifle Divisions
   50th and 53rd Cavalry Divisions
   690th Rifle Regiment (126th Rifle Division)

Fifth Army—commander Maj Gen Dmitriy Lelyushenko
   from October 18 Lt Gen Leonid Govorov
   32nd Rifle Division
   330th Reserve Rifle Regiment
   18th, 19th, 20th, and 22nd Tank Brigades
   151st Motorized Rifle Brigade
   36th Motorcycle Regiment

Forty-Third Army—commander Lt Gen Stepan Akimov,
   from October 29 Maj Gen Konstantin Golubev
   53rd, 110th, 113th and 312th Rifle Divisions
   9th, 17th and 145th Tank Brigades

Forty-Ninth Army—commander Lt Gen Ivan Zakharkin
   5th Guards Rifle Division
   144th and 194th Rifle Divisions
   31st Cavalry Division

Later added:
Thirty-Third Army—commander Brigade Commissar Dmitri Onuprienko,
   from October 22 Lt Gen Michail Efremov
   110th and 113th Rifle Divisions (taken over from Forty-Third Army)
   1st Guards Motorized Rifle Division

retreating rifle units that attach themselves as they arrive:
   17th, 19th, 50th, 60th, 108th, 173rd, and 222nd Rifle Divisions

Further reinforcements in October:
   78th, 93rd and 238th Rifle Division
   7th Guards Rifle Division
   82nd Motorized Rifle Division
   152nd Motorized Rifle Brigade
   5th Airborne Corps
   4th, 5th, 23rd, 24th, 25th, 26th, 27th and 28th Tank Brigade.

Sources:

M. I. Khametov (ed), *Bitva pod Moskvoy* (Moscow: Voenizdat, 1989), p.59.

Maksim Kolomiets, *Bitva Za Moskvu, 30 sentyabrya–5 dekabrya 1941* (Moscow: Strategiya KM, 2002).

A. M. Samsonov, *Moskva, 1941 god: ot tragedii porazhenii k velikoy pobede* (Moscow: Moskovskii Rabochii, 1991).

Charles C. Sharp, *Soviet Order of Battle World War II, Volume VIII "Red Legions"* (West Chester: George F. Nafzinger, 1996).

Charles C. Sharp, *Soviet Order of Battle World War II, Volume IX "Red Tide"* (West Chester: George F. Nafzinger, 1996).

16. ORDER OF BATTLE, KALININ FRONT OCTOBER 17, 1941

Commander: Col Gen Ivan Konev

Twenty-Second Army—commander Maj Gen Vasiliy Yushkevich until October 19 Maj Gen Vladimir Vostrukhov from October 19.
178th, 179th, 186th, 220th, 249th, and 250th Rifle Divisions

Twenty-Ninth Army—commander Lt Gen Ivan Maslennikov
119th, 174th, 243rd, 246th, and 252nd Rifle Divisions

Thirtieth Army—commander: Maj Gen Vasiliy Khomenko
5th Rifle Division
21st Tank Brigade
20th Reserve Regiment

Group General Vatutin*
Commander: Lt Gen Nikolaj Vatutin
183rd and 185th Rifle Division
46th and 54th Cavalry Division
8th Tank Brigade
Independent motorized rifle brigade

NOTE: *Reorganized as Thirty-First Army on October 19—Commander: Maj Gen Vasiliy Yushkevich

Source:

Sbornik Voenno-Istoricheskikh Materialov Velikoy Otechestvennoy Voyny, Vypusk 7 (Moscow: Voenizdat, 1952).

M. M. Gareev and V. F. Simonov, *Pobediteli 1941–1945* (Moscow: Ekzamen, 2005).

17. ORDER OF BATTLE, WEST FRONT NOVEMBER 15

Commander Gen Georgiy Zhukov

Thirtieth Army (from 17 Nov)—commander Maj Gen Vasiliy Khomenko
Maj Gen Dmitrij Lelyushenko from November 17
5th and 185th Rifle Divisions
107th Motorized Rifle Division
46th Cavalry Division
8th and 21st Tank Brigades
46th Motorcycle Regiment
2nd Motorized Rifle Regiment
20th Reserve Rifle Regiment

Sixteenth Army—commander Lt Gen Konstantin Rokossovsky
18th, 78th, 126th, and 316th Rifle Divisions
58th Tank Division
17th, 20th, 24th, 44th, 50th, and 53rd Cavalry Divisions
1st Guards, 27th and 28th Tank Brigades
School Regiment

Fifth Army—commander Lt Gen Leonid Govorov
32nd, 50th, and 144th Rifle Divisions
82nd Motorized Rifle Division
18th, 20th, 22nd, 25th, and 33rd Tank Brigades
36th Motorcycle Regiment

Thirty-Third Army—commander Lt Gen Mikhail Efremov
108th, 110th, 113th, and 222nd Rifle Divisions
1st Guards Motorized Rifle Division

Forty-Third Army—commander Maj Gen Konstantin Golubev
17th, 19th, 53rd, and 93rd Rifle Divisions
10th and 202nd Airborne Brigades
9th, 24th, and 26th Tank Brigades

Forty-Ninth Army—commander Lt Gen Ivan Zakharkin
5th Guards, 7th Guards, 60th, 194th, and 415th Rifle Divisions
2nd Cavalry Corps with 5th and 9th Cavalry Divisions
112th Tank Division
31st and 145th Tank Brigades

Fiftieth Army—commander Maj Gen Arkadiy Ermakov
   154th, 217th, 258th, 260th, 290th, 299th, and 413th Rifle Divisions
   4th, and 31st Cavalry Divisions
   108th Tank Division
   156th NKVD Regiment
   Tula Independent Worker Regiment

Sources:
Khametov, M. I. (ed.), *Bitva pod Moskvoy* (Moscow: Voenizdat, 1989).
M. M. Gareev and V. F. Simonov, *Pobediteli 1941–1945* (Moscow: Ekzamen, 2005).
Maksim Kolomiets, *Bitva Za Moskvu, 30 sentyabrya–5 dekabrya 1941* (Moscow: Strategiya
   KM, 2002).
A. M. Samsonov, *Moskva, 1941 god: ot tragedii porazhenii k velikoy pobede* (Moscow: Moskovskii
   Rabochii, 1991).

18. OPOLCHENIE—THE SOVIET MILITIA DEFENDS MOSCOW

"They were beginners in the military craft, which they had to learn in battle."
—Gen Georgiy Zhukov

Historically, the Russian militia (Narodnoe Opolchenie) was called up when the homeland was seriously threatened. One example is Napoleon's invasion in 1812, when several militia units from Moscow fought in the battle at Borodino on September 7, 1812. However, before World War II, militia units were not widely discussed military matters within Russia. The Red Army's doctrine assumed that if an attacking enemy would be repelled and the war fought on enemy territory. Militia units did not fit into that concept and any suggestion of major operations being conducted deep within Soviet territory could be regarded as defeatist. Battles in the border region were conceivable, but not close to major cities like Leningrad, Moscow, or Kiev. Thus there was little or no need for militia units. Also, the task to raise militia units belonged to the NKVD, not the army.

On July 4, GKO (the state defense committee) decided that 25 militia divisions would be formed in the Moscow area by July 7. This ambitious goal had to be cut down to 12 divisions almost immediately, as there was insufficient equipment and manpower. As a consequence, the militia divisions were not sequentially numbered. According to the decision of July 4, each district of Moscow would raise one militia division and there were 25 districts in the capital.[1]

Most divisions were made up of volunteer workers from industry, but in two of the division, clerks, civil servants, and intelligentsia formed the majority of the manpower. Many of the volunteers lacked basic military training and were not part of the pool of military reserves. Their age ranged from 17 to 55. Compulsory military service had been established after the Revolution, but not all men served as there were various ways of being exempted from military service.[2]

The divisions soon left the capital to build new defense lines west of Moscow. One example was the Mozhaisk Line, ordered on July 18. Major General V. R. Vashkevich, who commanded the 2nd Militia Division, wrote:

> On July 12, the 2nd Militia Division sets out to the west for its military task. The division should build defenses in the form of a series of lines west of Moscow, to block the approaches from the west.[3]

All militia divisions suffered from shortages of manpower, weapons and ammunition. They were far from combat ready. Most of their time was spent constructing defense positions. Throughout July and August, the divisions were deployed to build fieldworks. In a report of August 8, Regiment Commissar F. S. Vishnevetski, at the 33rd Army staff, wrote on military training:

> In all units, incessant wishes to receive training on rifles, machine guns and guns are uttered. Mainly these come from the soldiers who lack training, who have not served in the Red Army and cannot make use of weapons. Most soldiers show a burning desire to learn how to handle technical equipment. Many are concerned that time for combat training is reduced due to frequent movements.

Vishnevetski also wrote:

> Upon arrival at the new location, units and sections were distributed to begin building fieldworks...[4]

At the end of August, the twelve militia divisions became part of the Red Army, received their banners and swore the military oath. They were renumbered on September 26 and received numbers from destroyed units. The militia divisions were reorganized in August–September, into a structure similar to the Red Army rifle divisions, but this was not easy to accomplish. The Thirty-Third Army can serve as an example. It had five militia divisions. Its manpower strength grew from 40,200 men on August 1 to 64,500 men on September 20, but there were still shortages in the divisions. Particularly scarce were 45mm AT guns, as well as 82- and 120mm mortars. On the other hand, most divisions had received their artillery regiment, which provided ample indirect fire capability, despite the lack of heavy mortars. The most serious shortcoming was the lack of antitank guns.[5]

Nine of twelve militia division were found in two armies: Thirty-Second and Thirty-Third, both belonged to the Reserve Front. The two armies were in reserve not very far from the front at the end of September. The Thirty-Third Army was positioned near Spas-Demensk, in the path of Hoepner's spearheads. The Thirty-Second Army was located near Izdeshkova, west of Vyazma, along the Smolensk–Moscow highway. Little did the soldiers of the Thirty-Second Army imagine that the German spearheads would meet behind them, at Vyazma, and encircle them. The remaining three divisions were not much more fortuitously located. Two were in the front line, of which one was in the Twenty-Fourth Army, in front of Hoepner's armor, while the other was attached to Group Ermakov, which would face Guderian's divisions. The Soviet militia, recruited from Moscow, was about to face its fate in the defense of their home city. Many of them would not see the capital again.

The militia divisions suffered differing fates during the battle at Moscow. Five militia divisions were destroyed, all of them belonging to the Twenty-Fourth and Thirty-Second Armies that were encircled west of Vyazma. All five militia divisions attached to Thirty-Third Army suffered severe losses. For example, the 173rd Rifle Division had only 1,400 riflemen in its three rifle regiments after the Vyazma-Bryansk battle. Its artillery regiment only mustered 119 men. In contrast, the 60th Rifle Division had suffered less. Almost 4,000 soldiers remained and its rifle regiments numbered more then 1,000 men each. The 17th Rifle Division also managed fairly well. It received several reserve companies with a combined strength of over 1,500 men on October 15–16. The two divisions on the flanks at Thirty-First Army and Group Ermakov escaped encirclement, but were badly mauled. For example, the 160th Rifle Division had only about 1,800 at the beginning of November.[6]

The surviving divisions would receive replacements and continue to fight, but the militia as such had perished in the Vyazma-Bryansk battle. Two of the former militia divisions would eventually become Guards Rifle divisions. One of them was the 18th Rifle Division, which avoided encirclement with Rokossovsky and later fought under him in the Sixteenth Army. In January 1942 it received the honor of becoming the 11th Guards Rifle Division. It was however no longer the same division, as none of the three rifle regiments present on October 1 remained. The second was the 110th Rifle Division, which became the 84th Guards Rifle Division in March 1943. It might be asked how many of the soldiers at that time, that remained from October 1, 1941. Probably preciously few.

FIRST BATCH OF MILITIA DIVISIONS RAISED IN MOSCOW				
MILITIA DIVISION	DISTRICT	RIFLE DIVISION	ARMY	STRENGTH SEPTEMBER 20, 1941
1st	LENINSK	60th	33rd	11,457
2nd	STALINSK	2nd	32nd	11,320
4th	KUYBYSHEVSK	110th	31st	11,755 (OCTOBER 1)
5th	FRUNZENSK	113th	33rd	11,501
6th	DZERZHINSK	160th	ERMAKOV	9,791 (AUGUST 31)
7th	BAUMANSK	29th	32nd	10,947
8th	KRASNOPRESNENSK	8th	32nd	10,513
9th	KIROVSK	139th	24th	11,543
13th	ROSTOKITSK	140th	32nd	11,490
17th	MOSKVORETS	17th	33rd	11,454
18th	LENINGRADSK	18th	33rd	10,668
21st	KIEVSK	173rd	33rd	10,608

Sources:
Lev Lopuchovski, *Vjazemskaja Katastrofa 41-go goda* (Moscow: Eksmo, 2007).
A. M. Samsonov, *Moskva, 1941 god: ot tragedii porazjenij k belikoj pobede* (Moscow: Moskovskij Rabotjij, 1991).

NOTES

1. A. M. Pegova (ed.), *Opolchenie na zashchite Moskvy (Moscow: Moskovskii Rabochii, 1978)* , p. 5.
2. The "white collar" and intelligensia militia dvisions were the 4th and 7th, which later became 110th and 29th Rifle Division. Another three divisions contained many soldiers from this category, but the number of workers were at least as large in these divisions. A. M. Samsonov, *Moskva, 1941god: ot tragedii porazhenij k velikoy pobede* (Moscow: Moskovskii Rabochii, 1991), pp. 54–61. Pegova, *Opoltjenie na zasjtjite Moskvy*, pp. 5–7. On conscription, see Roger R. Reese, *Stalin's Reluctant Soldiers* (Lawrence: University Press of Kansas, 1996), pp. 11–15.
3. On 2nd Division, see Lev Lopuchovski, *Vjazemskaja Katastrofa 41-go goda* (Moscow: Eksmo, 2007), p.124. For preparation of defenses, see Samsonov, *Moskva, 1941 god: ot tragedii porazjenij k velikoj pobede*, p. 57.
4. Pegova, *Opoltjenie na zasjtjite Moskvy*, pp. 9, 148–149.
5. Rodric Braithwaite, *Moscow 1941—A city and its people at War* (London: Profile Books, 2007), p. 123. Charles C. Sharp, *Soviet Order of Battle World War II, Volume IX "Red Tide,"* pp. 11, 24. For info on Thirty-Third Army, see Samsonov, *Moskva, 1941 god: ot tragedii porazjenij k velikoj pobede*, p. 60. Most divisions had their full complement of 5cm mortars, but they were far less powerful than the larger calibers which would be dropped from the TOE before the

end of the war. Pegova (ed.), *Opoltjenie na zasjtjite Moskvy*, pp. 173–175.

6. The following were deleted: 2nd, 8th, 29th, 139th, and 140th, see Sharp, *Soviet Order of Battle World War II, Volume IX "Red Tide."* For casualties suffered by 17th and 60th Rifle divisions, see Pegova (ed.), *Opoltjenie na zasjtjite Moskvy*, pp. 199–206. For losses incurred by 160th Rifle Division, see "Prilozjenie Boevoj i Tjislennyj sostav Brjanskogo Fronta na 7.11.41g," in *Sbornik Voevych Dokumentov Velikoj Otetjestvennoj Vojny, Vypusk 43* (Moscow: Voennoe Izdatelstvo Ministerstva Oborony Sojuza SSR, 1960).

19. MAJOR SOVIET UNITS ARRIVING AT THE FRONT WEST OF MOSCOW, SEPTEMBER 30, 1941–DECEMBER 4, 1941

(Location on June 22, 1941 in brackets.)

October 1
7th Guards Rifle Division (Western Military District, as 64th Rifle Division on June 22, 1941)

October 2
6th Guards Rifle Division (Orel Military District on June 22, 1941 as 120th Rifle Division)

5th Airborne Corps (Baltic Military District on June 22, 1941)

4th Tank Brigade (began forming in Stalingrad Military District in August 1941)

11th Tank Brigade (began forming in Moscow Military District in September 1941)

October 4
17th Tank Brigade (began forming in Moscow Military District in September 1941)

October 8
312th Rifle Division (began forming in Central Asia Military District on July 10, 1941)

18th Tank Brigade (began forming in Moscow Military District in September 1941)

19th Tank Brigade (began forming in Moscow Military District in September 1941)

October 10
1st Guards Motorized Rifle Division (including 5th Tank Brigade)

41st Cavalry Division (began forming at Northwest Front in July 1941)

32nd Rifle Division (Far East on June 22, 1941)

316th Rifle Division (began forming in Alma-Ata, Kazakhstan on July 12,1941)

9th Tank Brigade (formed in Moscow Military District in August 1941)

20th Tank Brigade (began forming in Moscow Military District in September 1941)

October 12

183rd Rifle Division (Baltic Military District on June 22, 1941)

185th Rifle Division (began forming at Northwest Front on August 25, 1941)

8th Tank Brigade (began forming in Ural Military District in August 1941)

October 13

21st Tank Brigade (began forming in Moscow Military District in September 1941)

151st Motorized Rifle Brigade (began forming in autumn 1941)

October 14

238th Rifle Division (Central Asia Military District on June 22, 1941)

22nd Tank Brigade (began forming in Moscow Military District in September 1941)

152nd Motorized Rifle Brigade (began forming in autumn 1941)

October 15

46th Cavalry Division (began forming in Volga Military District in July 1941)

54th Cavalry Division (began forming in Moscow Military District in July 1941)

October 22

82nd Motorized Rifle Division (Trans-Baikal Military District on June 22, 1941)

23rd Tank Brigade (began forming in Moscow Military District in September 1941)

24th Tank Brigade (began forming in Moscow Military District in September 1941)

25th Tank Brigade (began forming in Moscow Military District in September 1941)

October 23

93rd Rifle Division (Trans-Baikal Military District on June 22, 1941)

26th Tank Brigade (began forming in Ural Military District in September 1941)

October 24

27th Tank Brigade (began forming in Moscow Military District in September 1941)

28th Tank Brigade (began forming in Moscow Military District in September 1941)

October 28

32nd Tank Brigade (began forming in Moscow Military District in October 1941)

October 31

78th Rifle Division (Far East on June 22, 1941)

413th Rifle Division (began forming in Far East on August 6, 1941)

November 1

58th Tank Division (Far East on June 22, 1941)

November 5

112th Tank Division (began forming in Far East in August 1941)

33rd Tank Brigade (began forming in Moscow Military District in September 1941)

November 9

5th Cavalry Division (Odessa Military District on June 22, 1941)

9th Cavalry Division (Odessa Military District on June 22, 1941)

415th Rifle Division (began forming in Far East on September 8, 1941)

November 14

17th Mountain Cavalry Division (Caucasus on June 22, 1941)

18th Mountain Cavalry Division (Central Asia Military District on June 22, 1941)

20th Cavalry Division (Central Asia Military District on June 22, 1941)

24th Cavalry Division (Caucasus on June 22, 1941)

44th Cavalry Division (began forming in Central Asia Military District in July 1941)

November 19

145th Tank Brigade (rebuilt in Moscow Military District in October 1941)

November 20

31st Tank Brigade (began forming in Moscow Military District in October 1941)

146th Tank Brigade (rebuilt in Moscow Military District in October 1941)

November 29

331st Rifle Division (began forming on August 27, in Orel Military District)

354th Rifle Division (began forming on August 11, in Volga Military District)

379th Rifle Division (began forming in August in Ural Military District)

November 30

371st Rifle Division (began forming in August in Ural Military District)

82nd Cavalry Division (began forming in Ural Military District in August 1941)

December 1

212th Rifle Division (from Southwest Front, began forming on July 29, 1941)

262nd Rifle Division (from Northwest Front, began forming on June 26, 1941)

348th Rifle Division (began forming on August 15 in Volga Military District)

352nd Rifle Division (began forming August 1 in Volga Military District)

December 2

323rd Rifle Division (began forming on August 1 in Orel Military District)
324th Rifle Division (began forming in August in Moscow Military District)
325th Rifle Division (began forming on September 8 in Orel Military District)
326th Rifle Division (began forming in August in Moscow Military District)
328th Rifle Division (began forming on August 26 in Moscow Military District)
330th Rifle Division (began forming in August in Moscow Military District)
340th Rifle Division (began forming in August in Volga Military District)

COMMENTS:

The dates above are approximate. The arrival of a unit can be a process lasting several days. Furthermore, a unit may be positioned very close to the front, but remain in Stavka reserve, while other units went straight from the railhead to the battlefield. It must be emphasized that there were many important units smaller than brigades that arrived in the period. For example, between October 1 and November 1, the following arrived: five motorcycle regiments, two NKVD regiments, 20 artillery regiments, 28 antitank gun regiments, four rocket artillery regiments, eight engineer battalions, and seven antiaircraft battalions. Also, in November, fewer tank brigades arrived, but this was balanced by more tank battalions arriving. At least ten tank battalions arrived in November, but it is difficult to keep track of tank battalions, as some of them were used to strengthen existing tank brigades.

Sources:

Bitva pod Moskvoy, Khronika, Fakti, Ljudi. Kniga Pervaya (Moscow: Olma-Press, 2002).

Boevoy Sostav Sovetskoy Armii, khast I (East View Publications).

M. I. Chametov (ed.), *Bitva pod Moskvoj, Chronika, Fakti, Ljudi. Kniga Pervaja* (Moscow: Olma-Press, 2002).

Maksim Kolomiets, *Bitva Za Moskvu, 30 sentjabrja–5 dekabrja 1941* (Moscow: Strategija KM, 2002).

Ilja Mostjanskij, *Tanki T-34-76, T-34-57 v bojach za Moskvu* (Moscow: BTV-Kniga, 2008).

A. M. Samsonov, *Moskva, 1941 god: ot tragedii porazjenij k velikoj pobede* (Moscow: Moskovskij Rabotjij, 1991).

Charles C. Sharp, *Soviet Order of Battle World War II, Volume I "The Deadly Beginning"* (West Chester: George F. Nafzinger, 1995).

Charles C. Sharp, *Soviet Order of Battle World War II, Volume IV "Red Guards"* (West Chester: George F. Nafzinger, 1995).

Charles C. Sharp, *Soviet Order of Battle World War II, Volume V "Red Sabers"* (West Chester: George F. Nafzinger, 1995).

Charles C. Sharp, *Soviet Order of Battle World War II, Volume VIII "Red Legions"* (West Chester: George F. Nafzinger, 1996).

Charles C. Sharp, *Soviet Order of Battle World War II, Volume IX "Red Tide"* (West Chester: George F. Nafzinger, 1996).

20. SOVIET ROCKET ARTILLERY 1941

NUMBER OF UNITS AND PIECES						
	UNITS			TYPES OF PIECES		
	REGIMENTS	IND. BATTALIONS	IND. BATTERIES	BM-8	BM-13	**TOTAL**
JULY 1	0	0	1	0	7	**7**
AUGUST 1	0	0	3	0	17	**17**
SEPTEMBER 1	1	1	9	8	41	**49**
OCTOBER 1	9	8	4	160	246	**406**
NOVEMBER 1	11	20	2	192	325	**517**
DECEMBER 1	8	35	2	199	355	**554**

Source: ViZh 1976 no 12: Gurkin, V.: *Stanovlenie i razvitie reaktivnoy artillerii v pervom periode voiny.* p. 27.

DISTRIBUTION OF ROCKET ARTILLERY BATTALIONS AT THE WEST FRONT			
	OCTOBER 22	NOVEMBER 16	DECEMBER 3
FIFTH ARMY	5	4	4
SIXTEENTH ARMY	2	7	10
THIRTIETH ARMY	0	1	2
THIRTY-THIRD ARMY	3	3	3
FORTY-THIRD ARMY	2	3	2
FORTY-NINTH ARMY	1	4	5
FIFTIETH ARMY	0	3	1
2ND CAVALRY CORPS	0	3	3
FIRST SHOCK ARMY	0	0	3
TENTH ARMY	0	0	1
TWENTIETH ARMY	0	0	2
TOTAL	**13**	**28**	**36**

Source: ViZh 1976 no 12: Gurkin, V.: *Stanovlenie i razvitie reaktivnoy artillerii v pervom periode voiny*, p. 29.

NOTES

PROLOGUE

1. Hermann Türk's diary, BA-MA MSg 2/5354.
2. Ibid; Verlustmeldungen PzAOK 2 Ia, BA-MA RH 2-21/757.
3. Hermann Türk's diary, BA-MA MSg 2/5354.
4. Ibid.
5. Ibid.
6. For a more extensive discussion on the Soviet units and reserves, see *The Journal of Soviet Military Studies* (Vol.5, No.3, September 1992), David M. Glantz, *Soviet Mobilization in Peace and War 1924–1942: A Survey*, pp. 323–362, and (Vol.5, No.3, September 1992), James M. Goff, "Evolving Soviet Force Structure, 1941–1945: Process and Impact," *The Journal of Soviet/Slavic Military Studies* (Vol 5., No.3, September 1992), pp. 363–404.
7. Shabulin's diary, BA-MA RH 37/901.
8. Ibid.
9. Ibid.
10. Ibid.
11. Ibid.
12. Ibid.
13. Walter Görlitz (ed.), *Generalfeldmarschall Keitel Verbrecher oder Offizier?* (Göttingen: Musterschmidt-Verlag, 1961), p. 271.
14. Barry A. Leach, *German Strategy against Russia 1939–1941* (Oxford University Press, 1973), pp. 32–33. Georg Meyer (ed.), *Generalfeldmarschall Wilhelm Ritter von Leeb, Tagebuchaufzeichnungen und Lagebeurteilungen aus zwei Weltkriegen* (Stuttgart: Deutsche Verlags-Anstalt, 1976), p. 195.
15. Carl Wagener, *Moskau 1941—Der Angriff auf die russische Hauptstadt* (Bad Nauheim: Podzun Verlag, 1965), pp. 34, 189; Bernard Von Loßberg, *Im Wehrmachtführungsstab* (Hamburg: H. H. Nölke Verlag, 1950), p. 130; Görlitz, *Generalfeldmarschall Keitel Verbrecher oder Offizier?*, pp. 272–274.

16. Albert Seaton, *The Battle for Moscow 1941–1942* (London: Rupert Hart-Davis, 1971), p. 87.

17. G. K. Zhukov, *Vospominaniya i Razmyshleniya* (Volume II). (Moscow: Novosti, 1986), pp. 107–111. It has been argued that the number of Soviet soldiers in the Kiev area was lower than the German prisoner claim, hence the latter would be inflated. However, the German operation encompassed a far larger area and the Soviet forces facing it included armies and rear-area units that were located far from Kiev, such as the Twenty-First Army which was broken through when the Germans began their offensive. The Soviet Twenty-First Army was not even part of the Southwest Front, which was responsible for the defense of Kiev.

CHAPTER 1: THE SOVIET DEFENSE OF MOSCOW

1. Dokumenty i Materialy, "Moskovskaya bitva v tsifrakh," *Voenno-Istoricheskii Zhurnal* (1967, No.3), pp. 69–79. Lev Lopukhovskii, *Vyazemskaya Katastrofa 41-go goda* (Moscow: Eksmo, 2007), pp. 93–94.

2. The three armies were Third, Thirteenth, and Fiftieth. Also, Eremenko had the so-called Group Ermakov. The three reserve divisions were the 154th and 287th Rifle divisions, and the 108th Tank Division. The latter two were designated for the planned counterattack. See *Rysskii Arkhiv: Velikaya Otechestvennaya T. 15 (4-1), Bitva pod Moskoy, Spornik dokumentov* (Moscow: Terra, 1997), p. 75.

3. The 141st Tank Brigade was with the Thirteenth Army, while the 121st and 150th Tank brigades were attached to Ermakov, see A. M. Samsonov, *Moscow, 1941 god: ot tragedii porazhenii k velikoy pobede* (Moscow: Moskovskiy Rabochii, 1991), p. 236. See also *Rysskii Arkhiv: Velikaya Otechestvennaya T. 15 (4-1), Bitva pod Moskoy, Spornik dokumentov*, p. 75.

4. The ratio between available troops and the length of the front line was admittedly lower at Eremenko's front, but it was not in any way exceptionally low. Dokumenty i Materialy, "Moskovskaja bitva v tsifrach"; Maxim Kolomiets, *Bitva Za Moskvu, 30 sentyabrya–5 dekabrya 1941* (Moscow: Strategija KM, 2002), pp. 6–8; Lopukhovskii, *Vyazemskaya Katastrofa 41-go goda*, pp. 93–94; Samsonov, *Moscow, 1941 god: ot tragedii porazhenii k velikoy pobede*, pp. 235–236.

5. The Twenty-Fourth and Forty-Third armies were placed in the front line, while the Thirty-Third Army was positioned behind the other two, with five divisions. See Lopukhovskii, *Vyazemskaya Katastrofa 41-go goda*, p. 94 and Samsonov, *Moscow, 1941 god: ot tragedii porazhenij k velikoy pobede*, and Tsamo, *RF sostave armii sentyabr 1941*, fond 219, op. 679, delo 6, list 134–140, 159.

6. The second surviving marshal was Kliment Voroshilov, who had also served together with Stalin during the Civil War.

7. M. M. Gareev and V. F. Simonov, *Pobediteli 1941–1945* (Moscow: Ekzamen, 2005), pp. 114–117.

8. Samsonov, *Moscow, 1941 god: ot tragedii porazhenii k velikoy pobede*, p. 235.

9. The Dorogobyzh reserve consisted of the 134th and 152nd Rifle divisions, 101st Motorized Rifle Division, 45th Cavalry Division, the 126th, 128th, 143rd, and 147th

Tank brigades. The Belyy reserve comprised the 107th Motorized Rifle Division, 251st Rifle Division, 50th, and 53rd Cavalry divisions, see M. I. Chametov, (ed.), *Bitva pod Moskvoj* (Moscow: Voenizdat, 1989), p. 32 and *Sbornik Voenno-Istoritjeskich Materialov Velikoj Otetjestvennoj Vojny, Vypusk 7* (Moscow: Voenizdat, 1952), map 2 and Samsonov, *Moscow, 1941 god: ot tragedii porazjenij k velikoj pobede*, p. 235–236. For number of tanks, see Kolomiets, *Bitva Za Moskvu, 30 sentyabrya–5 dekabrya 1941*, p. 6, and Dokumenty i Materialy "Moskovskaja bitva v tsifrakh"; Lopukhovskii, *Vyazemskaya Katastrofa 41-go goda*, pp. 93–94.

10. K. K. Rokossovsky, *Soldatskij Dolg* (Moscow: Voenizdat, 1988), pp. 47–48.

11. A. G. Fedorov, *Aviatsiya v bitve pod Moskvoy* (Moscow: Nauka, 1975), pp. 59, 98; Dokumenty i Materialy, "Moskovskaya bitva v tsifrakh."

12. N. A. Antipenko, *In der Hauptrichtung* (Berlin [East], Militärverlag der DDR, 1982), pp. 63–66.

13. This difference would persist until the end of the war. We have discussed it previously, for example in N. Zetterling and A. Frankson, *Kursk 1943—A Statisical Analysis* (London: Frank Cass, 2000).

14. Charles C. Sharp, , *Soviet Order of Battle World War II, Volume IX "Red Tide"* (West Chester: George F. Nafzinger, 1996). p. 2.

15. D. A. Dragunsky, *Gody v brone* (Moscow, Voenizdat, 1973), p. 4.

16. Dragunsky, *Gody v brone*, pp. 6–7.

17. Dragunsky, *Gody v brone*, p. 7. On the Red Army's emphasis on offensive warfare, see N. E. Eliseeva, "Plans for the Development of the Workers' and Peasants' Red Army (RKKA), on the Eve of War," *Journal of Soviet/Slavic Military Studies* (Vol.8, No.2, June 1995), pp. 356–365.

18. Dragunsky, *Gody v brone*, p. 7. The 110th Tank Division was created from the 51st Tank Division of the 23rd Mechanized Corps. Evgenij Drig, *Mechanizirovannye Korpusa RKKA v Boyu* (Moscow: Tranzitkniga, 2005), pp. 543, 645.

19. Dragunsky, *Gody v brone*, p. 26.

20. The Smolensk battle lasted from July 10 to September 10, 1941, according to Soviet sources. See G. F. Krivosheev (ed.), *Grif sekretnosti Snyat* (Moscow: Voennoe Izdatelstvo, 1993), pp. 168–169. Kovalenko is mentioned as division commander in many works on the battle for Moscow, but in fact Glebov commanded the division until it was disbanded.

21. Dragunsky, *Gody v brone*, p. 51.

22. Charles C. Sharp, , *Soviet Order of Battle World War II, Volume VIII "Red Legions"* (West Chester: George F. Nafzinger, 1996), pp. 104–105.

23. If the division was equipped with 54 antitank guns, they were distributed as follows: two in each rifle battalion (9 bn x 2), another six in each rifle regiment (3 reg x 6), and one AT battalion with 18 guns. Divisions with 18 guns had no AT battalion and no AT guns in the rifle battalions.

24. Alex Buchner, *Das Handbuch der Deutschen Infanterie 1939–1945* (Friedberg/Hess: Podzun-Pallas, 1989), p. 9.

25. S. Zaloga and L. S. Ness, *Red Army Handbook 1939–1945* (Stroud: Sutton Publishing, 2003), p. 13.

26. The Soviet M-30 model 1938 122mm howitzer and the German 10.5cm leFH 18 and 15cm sFH 18 have been used for the comparison.

27. On front sectors, see Dragunsky, *Gody v brone*, p. 56. On Sixteenth Army, see Chametov, *Bitva pod Moskvoy*, p. 36.

28. Dragunsky, *Gody v brone*, p. 56.

29. Dokumenty i Materialy, "Moskovskaya bitva v tsifrakh"; Kolomiets, *Bitva Za Moskvu, 30 sentyabrya–5 dekabrya 1941*, pp. 6–8; Lopukhovskii, *Vyazemskaya Katastrofa 41-go goda*, pp. 93–94; Samsonov, *Moskva, 1941 god: ot tragedii porazhenii k velikoy pobede*, pp. 235–236.

30. Gareev and Simonov, *Pobediteli 1941–1945*, pp. 255, 351–355.

31. They were V. N. Dolmatov (Thirty-First Army), V. A. Chomenko (Thirtieth Army), I. I. Maslennikov (Twenty-Ninth Army), D. P. Onuprienko (Thirty-Third Army), and K. I. Rakutin (Twenty-Fourth Army).

32. Zhukov, *Vospominanija i Razmysjlenija (Volume II)*, p. 111.

33. Metz commanded the XXXIV Corps, which was temporarily attached to Guderian at the end of September and in the beginning of October. Model commanded the XLI Panzer Corps, which was part of Panzer Group 3 when Operation *Taifun* started.

34. More on mission-oriented command and control can be found in N. Zetterling, *Blixt-krig 1939–1941* (Stockholm: Prisma, 2008).

35. S. M. Shtemenko, *Generalnyj Shtab v gody Voyny* (Moscow: Voenizdat, 1968), p. 190.

36. Johannes Hürter, *Ein deutscher General an der Ostfront. Die Briefe und Tagebücher des Gotthard Heinrici 1941/42* (Erfurt: Alan Sutton, 2001), p. 95.

37. KTB Pz. Gruppe 3 Abt. Ia/Meß, 20. 10. 1941, NARA T313, R231, F7496656f; Anders Frankson, "Summer 1941," *Journal of Slavic Military Studies* (Vol.13, No.3, September 2000), p. 138.

38. Topographic support of troops see *Soviet Documents on the Use of War Experience Volume 2* (Frank Cass, London 1991), pp. 202–206.

CHAPTER 2: OPERATION *TAIFUN*—THE GERMAN PLANS

1. H. R. Trevor-Roper, *Hitler's War Directives 1939–45* (London: Pan, 1983), p. 152ff.

2. Ibid.

3. KTB Halder III, September 11, 1941.

4. Ibid.

5. Ibid; Horst Boog, Jürgen Förster, Joachim Hoffmann, Ernst Klink, Rolf-Dieter Müller, Gerd Ueberschär, *Das Deutsche Reich und der Zweite Weltkrieg, vol 4* (Stuttgart: Deutsche Verlags-Anstalt, 1983), p. 572.

6. Fedor von Bock, *The War Diary 1939–1945* (Atglen, PA: Schiffer, 1996), p. 313.

7. Von Bock, *The War Diary 1939–1945*, p. 313; Boog at al, *Das Deutsche Reich und der Zweite Weltkrieg, vol 4*, p. 572.

8. Ibid; Seaton, *The Battle for Moscow 1941–1942*, p. 101.

9. KTB Pz. Gruppe 4 Ia, 25 sept. 1941, NARA T313, R340, F8622651f; Kriegs-gliederung AOK 4 Stand 2.10.41, Anlage AOK 4 Ia Nr. 3434/41 g. Kdos, NARA T313, R340, F8622976.

10. KTB Pz. Gruppe 4 Ia, 13–16 sept. 1941, NARA T313, R340, F8622640ff

11. KTB Pz. Gruppe 4 Ia, 17 sept. 1941, NARA T313, R340, F8622642; von Bock, *The War Diary 1939–1945*, p. 314.

12. KTB Pz. Gruppe 4 Ia, 17–20 sept. 1941, NARA T313, R340, F8622642ff.

13. KTB Pz. Gruppe 4 Ia, 20–30 sept. 1941, NARA T313, R340, F8622644ff; von Bock, *The War Diary 1939–1945*, p. 315.

14. Lothar Rendulic, *Soldat in stürzenden Reichen* (Damm Verlag, München 1965), p. 250.

15. KTB Pz. Gruppe 4 Ia, 19–22 sept. 1941, NARA T313, R340, F8622643ff.

16. KTB Pz. Gruppe 4 Ia, 22 sept. 1941, NARA T313, R340, F8622645; Anlagen zum KTB Pz. Gruppe 4 Ia, NARA T313, R340, F8623220ff.

17. GHQ units denote those corps and army units called "Heerestruppen" by the Germans i.e. independent units, usually battalion-sized, subordinated to corps and armies according to the needs of the situation. It could be e. g. artillery, engineer, and assault gun units. See "Anlagen zum KTB Pz. Gruppe 4," "Eintreffübersicht, Stand 27.9.41 abends," NARA T313, R340, F8623216. On Hoepner's proposal, see Panzergruppe 4 Ia Nr. 2057/41 geh, 29.9.1941, NARA T313, R340, F8623217.

18. Anlage 4 zu AOK 4 Ia Nr. 3333/41 g. Kdos. v. 23.9.1941, "Anordnungen für die Nach-richtenverbindungen zum Armeebefehl für die Bereitstellung und den ersten Ansatz zum Angriff," NARA T313, R340, F8622944ff.

19. See Anlagen PzGruppe 4 Ia, NARA T313, R340, F8623571-3

20. Ibid. The reserve found by the Germans in the Spas-Demnskoe area was the Thirty-Third Army, which included five former militia divisions. The reserve found at Vyazma was in fact Konev's main reserve. See Chametov, *Bitva pod Moskvoy*, p. 32, and *Sbornik Voenno-Istoricheskikh Materialov Velikoy Otetjestvennoy Voiny, Vypusk 7* (Moscow: Voenizdat, 1952), map 2 and Samsonov, *Moscow, 1941 god: ot tragedii porazhenij k velikoy pobede*, pp. 235–236.

21. VIII. Fliegerkorps, Russland-Feldzug, Mittelabschnitt II. Teil, ab 28. 9. 1941, BA-MA RL 8/49.

22. Von Bock, *The War Diary 1939–1945*, p. 317.

23. It has often been purported that Army Group Center mustered 1,929,406 men, according to Reinhardt, but that figure includes many irrelevant personnel. See appendix 4 for more on this.

24. *Moskau im Krieg 1941–1945* (Berlin: Espresso Verlag, 2002), p. 19.

25. On Soviet papers, see Cathy Porter and Mark Jones, *Moscow in World War II* (London: Chatto & Windus, 1987), p. 92. Examples of Soviet leaflets can be found in Willi Kubik, *Erinnerung eines Panzerschützen 1941–1945* (Würzburg: Flechsig, 2004), pp. 160–163.

26. Andrew Nagorski, *The Greatest Battle* (New York: Simon & Schuster Paperbacks, 2008), p. 140.

27. Carl-Fredrik Geust and Gennadiy Petrov, *Red Stars Volume 4: Lend-lease aircraft in Russia* (Tampere: Apali Oy, 2002), p. 179

28. *Moskau im Krieg 1941–1945* (Berlin: Espresso Verlag, 2002), p. 19; Andrew Nagorski, *The Greatest Battle*, pp. 162–163; Porter and Jones, *Moscow in World War II*, pp. 100–101.

29. Maksim Kolomiets and I. Moshchanskii, *Tanki Lend-Liza 1941–1945* (Moscow: Eksprint, 2000), pp. 12, 39.

30. Carl-Fredrik Geust and Gennadiy Petrov, *Red Stars Volume 4: Lend-lease aircraft in Russia* (Tampere: Apali Oy, 2002), pp. 37, 182, 193.

31. Porter and Jones, *Moscow in World War II*, pp. 132, 141.

CHAPTER 3: GUDERIAN ATTACKS

1. KTB Pz. Gruppe 2 Ia, 29. 9. 1941, NARA T313, R86, F7326852-8.

2. Flemming's diary, BA-MA MSg 2/4304.

3. Ibid.

4. KTB Pz. Gruppe 2 Ia, 30. 9. 1941, NARA t313, R86, F7326861-7. See also Luftwaffe Tagesmeldung, 30. 9. 1941, BA-MA RL 2 II/262.

5. KTB 4. Pz. Div. Ia, 30. 9. 1941, NARA T315, R195, F000628f; 4. Pz. Div. Ia, "Gefechtsbericht der 4. Panzer-Division für die Zeit v. 30.9–6.10.41," BA-MA RH39/373; 5. Panzer-Brigade, "Gefechtsbericht für die Zeit vom 29.9–3.10.1941," U. O. 5. 10. 1941, BA-MA RH 39/373. See also Zetterling, *Blixtkrig 1939–41*, pp. 260f.

6. Ibid.

7. KTB Pz. Gruppe 2 Ia, 29.9.1941, NARA T313, R86, F7326852-8; 5. Panzer-Brigade, "Gefechtsbericht für die Zeit vom 29.9–3.10.1941," U.O. 5.10.1941, BA-MA RH 39/373.

8. KTB Pz. Gruppe 2 Ia, 30.9.1941, NARA T313, R86, F7326861-7.

9. KTB XLVII. Pz. Korps Ia, 30.9.1941, BA-MA RH 24-47/258.

10. Razgovor Stalina c Eremenko 2. 25 1. 10. 1941 see *Sbornik Voevykh Dokumentov Velikoy Otechestvennoj Voyny, Vypusk 43* (Moscow: Voenizdat, 1960). The three tank brigades were the 4nd, 121st and 150th.

11. L. M. Sandalov, *Na Moskovskom Napravlenii* (Moscow: Nauka, 1970), p. 204.

12. Direktiv Stavka no. 002488 01. 30 1 oktyabrya 1941, see *Rysskii Arkhiv: Velikaya Otechestvennaya T. 15 (4-1), Bitva pod Moskoy, Spornik dokumentov* (Moscow: Terra, 1997), p. 80.

13. Antipenko, *In der Hauptrichtung*, pp. 66–67.

14. KTB Pz. Gruppe 2 Ia, 30.9.1941, NARA T313, R86, F73268233-43.

15. 4. Pz. Div. Ia, "Gefechtsbericht der 4. Panzer-Division für die Zeit v. 30.9–6.10.41," BA-MA RH39/373.

16. 5. Panzer-Brigade, "Gefechtsbericht für die Zeit vom 29.9–3.10.1941," U. O. 5.10.1941, BA-MA RH 39/373; H. Guderian, *Panzer Leader* (London: Futura, 1982), pp. 228–30. See also Luftwaffe Tagesmeldung 1.10.41, BA-MA RL 2 II/262.

17. Ibid.

18. 5. Panzer-Brigade, "Gefechtsbericht für die Zeit vom 29.9–3.10.1941," U. O. 5.10.1941, BA-MA RH 39/373.
19. The losses suffered by Kampfgruppe Eberbach during the first four days of the operation amounted to six tanks, 34 killed and 121 wounded, see 5. Panzer-Brigade, "Gefechtsbericht für die Zeit vom 29.9–3.10.1941," U. O. 5.10.1941, BA-MA RH 39/373.
20. Luftwaffe Tagesmeldung 1.10.41, BA-MA RL 2 II/262.
21. Zapic Co Stalinym razgovor Zakharova 5. 20 2.10.1941, see *Sbornik Voevych Dokumentov Velikoy Otechestvennoy Voyny, Vypusk 43* (Moscow: Voennoe Izdatelstvo Ministerstva Oborony Soyuza SSR, 1960).

CHAPTER 4: THE MAIN GERMAN ATTACK BEGINS

1. KTB Pz. Gruppe 3 Ia, 2.10.1941, NARA T313, R231, F7496251ff.
2. Ibid.
3. Ibid; Luftwaffe Tagesmeldung 2.10.41, BA-MA RL 2 II/263.
4. KTB XLI. Pz. Korps Ia, 2.10.41, BA-MA RH 24-41/6.
5. Ibid.
6. KTB 7. Pz. Div. Ia, 2.10.41, BA-MA RH 27-7/46.
7. Hermann Hoth, *Panzer-Operationen* (Heidelberg, Kurt Vowinkel Verlag, 1956), p. 133f; KTB Pz. Gruppe 3 Ia, 2.10.1941, NARA T313, R231, F7496251ff.
8. KTB Pz. Gruppe 3 Ia, 2.10.1941, NARA T313, R231, F7496251ff.
9. Seaton, *The Battle for Moscow 1941–1942*, p. 100
10. KTB Pz. Gruppe 4 Ia, 1.10–2.10.1941, NARA T313, R340, F8622661ff; KTB XL. Pz. Korps Ia, 1–2.10.41, BA-MA RH 24-40/18; KTB XLVI. Pz. Korps Ia, 1–2. 10. 41, BA-MA RH 24-40/26.
11. KTB Pz. Gruppe 4 Ia, 1.10–2.10.1941, NARA T313, R340, F8622661ff.
12. KTB XL. Pz. Korps Ia, 1–2.10.41, BA-MA RH 24-40/18; KTB XLVI. Pz. Korps Ia, 1–2.10.41, BA-MA RH 24-40/26.
13. Ibid.
14. For a more detailed description of this action, see Zetterling, *Blixtkrig! 1939–1941*, pp. 265–8.
15. Ibid.
16. KTB Pz. Gruppe 4 Ia, 1.10–2.10.1941, NARA T313, R340, F8622661ff.; KTB XL. Pz. Korps Ia, 1–2.10.41, BA-MA RH 24-40/18; KTB XLVI. Pz. Korps Ia, 1–2.10.41, BA-MA RH 24-40/26; Klaus-Jürgen Thies, *Der Ostfeldzug, Heeresgruppe Mitte—Ein Lageatlas der Operationsabteilung des Generalstab des Heeres* (Bissendorf: Biblio Verlag, 2001), p. 95.
17. The three divisions from Thirty-Second Army were the 2nd, 8th, and 29th Rifle Divisions. Also, the 106th Rifle Division and the 144th Tank Brigade were to be sent from the Twenty-Fourth Army to the breakthrough sector. See *Rysskii Arkhiv: Velikaya Otechestvennaya T. 15 (4-1), Bitva pod Moskoy, Spornik dokumentov* (Moscow: Terra, 1997), p. 85.

18. Thies, *Der Ostfeldzug, Heeresgruppe Mitte–Ein Lageatlas der Operationsabteilung des Generalstab des Heeres*, p. 95.

19. Hoffmann's diary, BA-MA MSg 2/4539. Note that Hoffmann says that the offensive was launched on October 1, which is not supported by the war diaries and various reports. We have compared his statements with the war diaries and found that he is one day off.

20. Ibid.

21. Ibid.

22. Ibid; Thies, *Der Ostfeldzug, Heeresgruppe Mitte—Ein Lageatlas der Operationsabteilung des Generalstab des Heeres*, p. 95.

23. Von Bock, *The War Diary 1939–1945*, pp. 320f.

24. Ibid.

25. Luftwaffe Tagesmeldung 2.10.41, BA-MA RL 2 II/263.

26. *Bitva pod Moskvoy, Khronika, Fakti, Lyudi. Kniga Pervaya* (Moscow: Olma-Press, 2002), p. 212.

27. Shabulin's diary.

28. Ibid.

29. Gareev and Simonov, *Pobediteli 1941–1945*, pp. 224–225. See Kolomiets, *Bitva Za Moskvu, 30 sentyabrya–5 dekabrya 1941*, p. 6 for number of Soviet tanks.

30. *Bitva pod Moskvoy, Khronika, Fakti, Lyudi. Kniga Pervaya* (Moscow: Olma-Press, 2002), pp. 243–245.

CHAPTER 5: THE OFFENSIVE CONTINUES

1. KTB Pz. Gruppe 2 Ia, 2. 10. 1941, NARA T313, R86, F7326244ff; 4. Pz. Div. Ia, "Gefechtsbericht der 4. Panzer-Division für die Zeit v. 30.9–6.10.41," BA-MA RH39/373; 5. Panzer-Brigade, "Gefechtsbericht für die Zeit vom 29.9–3.10.1941," U. O. 5.10.1941, BA-MA RH 39/373.

2. 5. Panzer-Brigade, "Gefechtsbericht für die Zeit vom 29.9–3.10.1941," U. O. 5.10.1941, BA-MA RH 39/373.

3. Hermann Türk's diary, BA-MA MSg 2/5354.

4. Flemming's diary, BA-MA MSg 2/4304.

5. Chametov, *Bitva pod Moskvoy, Khronika, Fakti, Lyudi. Kniga Pervaya* (Olma-Press, Moscow 2002), pp. 218–219.

6. 5. Panzer-Brigade, "Gefechtsbericht für die Zeit vom 29. 9–3. 10. 1941," U. O. 5. 10. 1941, BA-MA RH 39/373; 4. Pz. Div. Ia, "Gefechtsbericht der 4. Panzer-Division für die Zeit v. 30. 9–6. 10. 41," BA-MA RH39/373.

7. Ibid.

8. Ibid; Seaton, p. 94.

9. M. E. Katukov, *Na Ostrie Glavnogo Udara* (Moscow: Voenizdat, 1974), pp. 27–29.

10. Sandalov, *Na Moskovskom Napravlenii*, p. 207.

11. 5. Panzer-Brigade, "Gefechtsbericht für die Zeit vom 29. 9–3. 10. 1941," U. O. 5. 10. 1941, BA-MA RH 39/373; 4. Pz. Div. Ia, "Gefechtsbericht der 4. Panzer-Division für

die Zeit v. 30. 9–6. 10. 41," BA-MA RH39/373. The reports show that almost all 4th Panzer Division casualties were incurred by Eberbach's battlegroup.

12. KTB Pz. Rgt. 6, BA-MA RH 39/707.

13. KTB 10. Pz. Div. Ia, 3. 10. 41, NARA T315, R561, F770ff.

14. Sandalov, *Na Moskovskom Napravlenii*, p. 207.

15. KTB Pz. Gruppe 4 Ia, 3. 10. 1941, NARA T313, R340, 8622666ff.

16. KTB Pz. Gruppe 4 Ia, 3. 10. 1941, NARA T313, R231, 7496260ff; KTB 6. Pz. Div. Ia, 3. 10. 41, BA-MA RH 27-6/19.

17. KTB 6. Pz. Div. Ia, 3. 10. 41, BA-MA RH 27-6/19.

18. Ibid.; Chametov, *Bitva pod Moskvoy, Khronika, Fakti, Lyudi. Kniga Pervaya* (Olma-Press, Moscow 2002), pp. 243–245.

19. KTB XLI. Pz. Korps Ia, 3. 10. 41, BA-MA 24-41/6.

20. Leach, *German Strategy against Russia 1939–1941*, pp. 91–92.

21. Dragunsky, *Gody v brone*, pp. 62–63.

22. Shabulin's diary.

23. Ibid.

24. KTB Pz. Gruppe 3 Ia, 4. 10. 41, NARA T313, R231, F7496264ff.

25. KTB 6. Pz. Div. Ia, 3. 10. 41, BA-MA RH 27-6/19.

26. Ibid.

27. Ibid; KTB 7. Pz. Div. Ia, 4. 10. 41, BA-MA RH 27-7/46.

28. KTB 6. Pz. Div. Ia, 3. 10. 41, BA-MA RH 27-6/19; *Bitva pod Moskvoy, Khronika, Fakti, Lyudi. Kniga Pervaya* (Moscow: Olma-Press, 2002), pp. 276–277, 302–303.

29. *Bitva pod Moskvoy, Khronika, Fakti, Lyudi. Kniga Pervaya* (Moscow: Olma-Press, 2002), pp. 276–277, 302–303.

30. KTB Pz. Gruppe 3 Ia, 4. 10. 41, NARA T313, R231, F7496264ff.

31. KTB Pz. Gruppe 4 Ia, 4. 10. 1941, NARA T313, R340, 8622670ff.

32. Ibid; KTB 10. Pz. Div. Ia, 4. 10. 41, NARA T315, R561, F770ff.

33. Thies, *Der Ostfeldzug, Heeresgruppe Mitte—Ein Lageatlas der Operationsabteilung des Generalstab des Heeres*, p. 96.

34. KTB Pz. Gruppe 2 Ia, 4. 10. 1941, NARA T313, R86, F7326264ff.

35. Thies, *Der Ostfeldzug, Heeresgruppe Mitte—Ein Lageatlas der Operationsabteilung des Generalstab des Heeres*, p. 96.

CHAPTER 6: ENCIRCLEMENT

1. See von Bock, *The War Diary 1939–1945*, and Halder's diaries for more on this.

2. Ibid.

3. A. M. Vasilevsky, *Delo Vsei Zhizni* (Moscow: Politizdat, 1976), p. 153.

4. Ibid, p. 159.

5. KTB 7. Pz. Div. Ia, 5. 10. 41, BA-MA RH 27-7/46.

6. Ibid.

7. KTB 6. Pz. Div. Ia, 5–6. 10. 41, BA-MA RH 27-6/19.

8. *Rysskii Arkhiv: Velikaya Otechestvennaya T. 16 (5-1), Stavka VGK Dokumenty i Materialy*

(Moscow: Terra, 1996), p. 220.

9. Rokossovsky, *Soldatskii Dolg*, pp. 49–50.

10. *Rysskii Arkhiv: Velikaya Otechestvennaya T. 16 (5-1), Stavka VGK Dokumenty i Materialy* (Moscow: Terra, 1996), pp. 221–222.

11. Dragunsky, *Gody v brone*, pp. 63–64.

12. KTB Pz. AOK 2 Ia, 5. 10. 1941, NARA T313, R86 F7326273ff.

13. Ibid; 4. Panzer-Division Ia, "Gefechtsbericht für die Zeit 30. 9–6. 10. 1941," BA-MA RH 39/373.

14. It was the 29th Cavalry Division and the 38th Motorcycle Regiment. On Shaposhni-kov's order of October 5, 1941, see *Bitva pod Moskvoy, Khronika, Fakti, Lyudi. Kniga Per-vaya* (Moscow: Olma-Press, 2002), p. 239.

15. KTB Pz. AOK 2 Ia, 5. 10. 1941, NARA T313, R86 F7326273ff.

16. Ibid.

17. Ibid.

18. Shabulin's diary.

19. Ibid.

20. KTB Pz. AOK 2 Ia, 4–6. 10. 1941, NARA T313, R86 F7326264ff.

21. Paul, Wolfgang, *Geschichte der 18. Panzer-Division 1940–1943 (mit Geschichte der 18. Artil-lerie-Division 1943–1944)* (Freiburg: Selbstverlag, 1975), pp. 92–93. *Rysskii Arkhiv: Veli-kaya Otechestvennaya T. 15 (4-1), Bitva pod Moskoy, Spornik dokumentov* (Moscow: Terra, 1997), pp. 128–129. Note that the 108th Tank Division was not at full strength. It only had 41 tanks, of which three were KV and 17 T-34. See Kolomiets, *Bitva Za Moskvu, 30 sentyabrya–5 dekabrya 1941*, p. 8.

22. Seaton, Albert, *The Battle for Moscow 1941–1942*, p. 94.

23. "Der handstreich auf Brjansk," BA-MA RH 37/901.

24. Ibid.

25. Ibid.

26. Ibid.

27. Ibid.

28. Ibid.

29. Ibid.

30. Erich Bunke, *Der Osten blieb unser Schicksal 1939–1944* (Wietze: Selbstverlag, 1991), p. 429.

31. Shabulin's diary.

32. KTB 10. Pz. Div. Ia, 5. 10. 41, NARA T315, R561, F799ff.

33. Ibid.

34. KTB 7. Pz. Div. Ia 5–6. 10. 41, BA-MA RH 27-7/46.

35. Ibid; KTB 6. Pz. Div. Ia 5–6. 10. 41, BA-MA RH 27-6/19.

36. Rokossovsky, *Soldatskii Dolg*, pp. 51–53.

37. The June 29, 1941 directive can be found in Rysskii Arkhiv: Velikaya Otechestvennaya T. 20 (9), *Partizanskoe Dvizhenie c gody Otechestvennoj Voiny 1941–1945 gg.* (Moscow: Terra, 1999), pp. 17–18.

38. Hamburger Institut für Sozialforshung (Hg.), *Verbrechen der Wehrmacht. Dimensionen des Vernichtungskrieges 1941–1944* (Hamburg: Hamburger Edition, 2002), p. 469. See also Peter Lieb, "Die Judenmorde der 707. Infanteriedivision 1941/42, *Vierteljahrhefte für Zeitgeschichte, oktober 2002.*

39. Johannes Hürter, *Ein deutscher General an der Ostfront. Die Briefe und Tagebücher des Gotthard Heinrici 1941/42* (Erfurt: Alan Sutton, 2001), p. 107.

40. Wilhelm Meyer-Detring, *Die 137. Infanterie-Division im Mittelabschnitt der Ostfront* (Eggolsheim: Dörfler Zeitgeschichte, n. d.), p. 86.

41. Klaus Reinhardt, *Die Wende vor Moskau* (Stuttgart: Deutsche Verlags-Anstalt, 1972), pp. 90–91.

42. Rendulic, *Soldat in stürzenden Reichen*, p. 272.

CHAPTER 7: CUT OFF

1. See *Rysskii Arkhiv: Velikaya Otechestvennaya T. 16 (5-1), Stavka VGK Dokumenty i Materialy* (Moscow: Terra, 1996), pp. 225–226 for the decision on the Mozhaisk Line, October 6. The complete 18 July order can be found on pp. 77–78. Artemev's three reserve armies were the Thirty-Second, Thirty-Third and Thirty-Fourth, see John Erickson, *The Road to Stalingrad* (London: Weidenfeld, 1993), p. 182.

2. V. A. Anfilov, *Krushenie Pochoda Gitlera na Moskvu 1941* (Moscow: Nauka, 1989), p. 277. Tsamo: fond 450, op. 11158, delo 75, list 3—*Moskvoy zona Oboroni MVO*.

3. Vasilevsky, *Delo Vsei Zhizni*, p. 153.

4. D. D. Lelyushenko, *Moscow—Stalingrad—Berlin—Praga* (Moscow: Nauka, 1987), pp. 21–24.

5. The written order on the formation of 1st Guards Rifle Corps was issued early on October 2, see *Rysskii Arkhiv: Velikaya Otechestvennaya T. 15 (4-1), Bitva pod Moskoy, Spornik dokumentov* (Moscow: Terra, 1997), pp. 82–83.

6. Lelyushenko, *Moscow—Stalingrad—Berlin—Praga*, pp. 24–25. On orders to the 17th Tank Brigade, see *Bitva pod Moskvoy, Khronika, Fakti, Lyudi. Kniga Pervaya* (Moscow: Olma-Press, 2002), pp. 229–230.

7. On orders concerning the 5th Guards Rifle Division, see *Rysskii Arkhiv: Velikaya Otechestvennaya T. 15 (4-1), Bitva pod Moskoy, Spornik dokumentov* (Moscow: Terra, 1997), p. 89.

8. Katukov, *Na Ostrie Glavnogo Udara*, pp. 41–42.

9. David Glantz, *A History of Soviet Airborne Forces* (London: Frank Cass, 1994), pp. 57–60.

10. 4. Panzer-Division Ia, "Gefechtsbericht der 4. Panzer-Division für die Zeit v. 30.9–6.10.41," Div. Gef. Stand, den 8.10.41, BA-MA RH 39/373; 5. Panzer-Brigade, "Gefechtsbericht vom 6. und 7.10.1941," O. U. 8.10.1941, BA-MA RH 39/373.

11. Ibid.

12. Ibid.

13. Ibid.

14. Ibid. During the period October 4–7 Eberbach's battle group (of which the forces

fighting in the Mtsensk area were part), lost 10 killed in action and 33 wounded. It is probable that most of these losses occurred on October 6.

15. Ibid.

16. See for example David M. Glantz and Jonathan M. House, *When Titans Clashed* (University Press of Kansas, 1995), p. 81. They refer to the English translation of Guderian's memoirs, but the translation is unfortunately bad on losses.

17. It is for example claimed in Glantz and House, *When Titans Clashed*, p. 81.

18. Franz Halder, *Kriegstagebuch, vol III* (Stuttgart: Kohlhammer, 1964); von Bock, *The War Diary 1939–1945*; KTB Pz. Gruppe 2 Ia, NARA T313, R86; KTB Pz. Gruppe 3 Ia, NARA T313, R231; KTB Pz. Gruppe 4 Ia, NARA T313, R340.

19. Ibid.

20. KTB Pz. Gruppe 2 Ia, 7.10.41, NARA T313, R86, F7326284.

21. Halder, *Kriegstagebuch, vol III*; von Bock, *The War Diary 1939–1945*; KTB Pz. Gruppe 2 Ia, NARA T313, R86; KTB Pz. Gruppe 3 Ia, NARA T313, R231; KTB Pz. Gruppe 4 Ia, NARA T313, R340.

22. KTB 2. Panzer-Armee Ia, 6–7.10.41, NARA T313, R86, F7326284ff.

23. KTB 2. Panzer-Armee Ia, 7.10.41, NARA T313, R86, F7326294ff.

24. KTB 2. Panzer-Armee Ia, 7–8.10.41, NARA T313, R86, F7326294ff; von Bock, *The War Diary 1939–1945*, pp. 325ff; Guderian, *Panzer Leader*, pp. 233ff.

25. Ibid; Thies, *Der Ostfeldzug, Heeresgruppe Mitte—Ein Lageatlas der Operationsabteilung des Generalstab des Heeres*, p. 96.

26. Shabulin's diary.

27. Ibid.

28. Ibid.

29. Thies, *Der Ostfeldzug, Heeresgruppe Mitte—Ein Lageatlas der Operationsabteilung des Generalstab des Heeres*, pp. 96f; von Bock, *The War Diary 1939–1945*, p. 327.

30. Von Bock, *The War Diary 1939–1945*, p. 327.

31. Ibid.

32. Ibid; Thies, *Der Ostfeldzug, Heeresgruppe Mitte—Ein Lageatlas der Operationsabteilung des Generalstab des Heeres*, p. 97

33. Dragunsky, *Gody v brone*, pp. 69–71.

34. *G. K. Zhukov v bitve pod Moskviy, Sbornik Dokumentov* (Moscow: Mosgorarkhiv, 1994), "Dokument no 1. Zapis peregovorov Verkhovnogo Glavnokomanduyushchego I. V. Stalina s komanduyushchim voyskami Leningradskogo fronta generalom armii G. K. Zhukovym 5 oktyabrya 1941 g."

35. On the meeting with Budjonny, see Zhukov, *Vospominaniya i Razmyshleniya (Volume II)*, pp. 193–196. *G. K. Zhukov v bitve pod Moskvoy, Sbornik Dokumentov* (Mosgorarkhiv, Moscow 1994), Dokument no 5. Direktiva Stavki VGK No. 002743 ot 8 oktyabrya 1941 g. o naznachenii generala armii G. K. Zhukova komanduyushchim voyskami Rezervnogo fronta. Dokument no 7. Direktiva Stavki VGK No. 002844 ot 10 oktyabrya 1941 g. ob obeninenii Zapadnogo i Rezervnogo frontov.

36. Rysskii Arkhiv: *Velikaya Otechestvennaya T. 15 (4-1), Bitva pod Moskoy, Sbornik dokumentov*

(Terra, Moscow 1997), pp. 99, 102.

37. *G. K. Zhukov v bitve pod Moskvoj, Sbornik Dokumentov* (Mosgorarkhiv, Moscow 1994), Dokument no 13 Prikaz Vojskam Zapadnogo Fronta No. 346 13 oktjabrja 1941.
38. Rokossovsky, *Soldatskij Dolg*, pp. 55–57.
39. Choroshilov, G., "Voopyzhenie Sovetskoi artillerii v gody Velikyj Otechestvennoj Voiny," *Voenno-Istoricheskii Zhurnal* (1971, No.7), pp. 83–85.
40. Fritz Hahn, *Waffen und Geheimwaffen des deutschen Heeres 1933–45, vol. 1–2* (Koblenz: Bernard & Graefe Verlag, 1998), vol.1, pp. 197–199.
41. Joachim Emde (ed.), *Die Nebelwerfer—Entwicklung und Einsatz der Werfertruppe im Zweiten Weltkrieg* (Friedberg: Podzun-Pallas Verlag, 1979), p. 17.
42. Wehrwissenschaftliche Rundschau 1968 Heft 9: I. Prochorkov and V. Trussov: *Die Raketenartillerie im Großen Vaterländischen Kriege* (introduction by W. Arenz [transl.]), p. 522.

CHAPTER 8: STRATEGIC DECISIONS

1. See Adam Tooze, *The Wages of Destruction* (London: Penguin, 2007), particularly chapters 12–15.
2. Ibid. See Dietrich Eicholtz, *Geschichte der Deutschen Kriegswirschaft 1939–1945, Band II 1941–1943* (Berlin: Akademie-Verlag, 1985), for production data.
3. Ibid.
4. Ibid.
5. Von Bock, *The War Diary 1939–1945*, p. 329.
6. Ibid, p. 330; Thies, *Der Ostfeldzug, Heeresgruppe Mitte—Ein Lageatlas der Operationsabteilung des Generalstab des Heeres*, pp. 96. ff.
7. Von Bock, *The War Diary 1939–1945*, p. 330; Thies, *Der Ostfeldzug, Heeresgruppe Mitte— Ein Lageatlas der Operationsabteilung des Generalstab des Heeres*, pp. 96. ff.
8. Von Bock, *The War Diary 1939–1945*, p. 329; Boog et. al., p. 579.
9. Von Bock, *The War Diary 1939–1945*, p. 331.
10. For more on this, see Tooze, *The Wages of Destruction*, particularly chapter 16.
11. Ibid.
12. The directive is reproduced in Piekalkiewicz, pp. 112 ff.
13. Piekalkiewicz, p. 112.
14. Rysskij Arkhiv: *Velikaja Otechestvennaya T. 15 (4-1), Bitva pod Moskoj, Spornik dokumentov* (Moscow: Terra, 1997), p. 102. *Tsamo: fond 450, op. 11158, delo 75, list 3, 11—Moskvoy zona Oboroni MVO*.
15. Rokossovsky, *Soldatskii Dolg*, pp. 60–64.
16. Antipenko, *In der Hauptrichtung*, p. 69.
17. Shtemenko, *Generalny Shtab v gody Voyny*, pp. 198–199.
18. Ibid., pp. 176, 180. Vasilevsky, *Delo Vsei Zhizni*, p. 158.
19. Shtemenko, *Generalny Shtab v gody Vojny*, p. 178. Vasilevsky, *Delo Vsei Zhizni*, pp. 517–518. Zhukov, *Vospominaniya i Razmyshleniya (Volume II)*, pp. 95–96.
20. Zhukov, *Vospominaniya i Razmyshleniya (Volume II)*, pp. 218–219.

CHAPTER 9: VYAZMA-BRYANSK

1. Shabulin's diary.
2. Ibid.
3. Ibid.
4. Ibid.
5. Piekalkiewicz, p. 115.
6. Von Bock, *The War Diary 1939–1945*, p. 331.
7. See Appendix 4.
8. Samsonov, *Moscow, 1941 god: ot tragedii porazhenii k velikoy pobede*. Charles C. Sharp, , *Soviet Order of Battle World War II, Volume VIII "Red Legions."* Sharp, *Soviet Order of Battle World War II, Volume IX "Red Tide."*
9. See Christian Hartmann, "Massensterben oder Massenvernichtung? Sowjetische Kriegsgefangene im Unternehmen *Barbarossa*," *Vierteljahrhefte für Zeitgeschichte 49 (2001)*, pp. 97–158.
10. See Appendix 2.
11. Shabulin's diary.
12. Ibid.
13. Ibid.
14. Ibid.
15. Ibid.
16. Befelshaber der Heeresgruppe Mitte, Tagesbefehl 19.10.1941, BA-MA RH 19 II/124.
17. See Appendix 3 for more on this.
18. We discuss the Soviet losses further in Appendix 3.

CHAPTER 10: ONE HUNDRED KILOMETERS TO MOSCOW

1. Thies, *Der Ostfeldzug, Heeresgruppe Mitte—Ein Lageatlas der Operationsabteilung des Generalstab des Heeres*, p. 96f.
2. Ibid.
3. Lothar Rendulic, *Soldat in stürzenden Reichen* (München: Damm Verlag, 1965), pp. 271–272.
4. Rolf Stoves, *1. Panzer-Division 1935–1945* (Bad Nauheim: Podzun, 1961), pp. 257ff.
5. Ibid.
6. Ibid.
7. Dragunsky, *Gody v brone*, pp. 74–76. On the strength of the 242th Division, see *Bitva pod Moskvoy, Khronika, Fakti, Ljudi. Kniga Pervaya* (Moscow: Olma-Press, 2002)), p. 302.
8. See Leo Niehorster, *German World War II Organizational Series, vol 3/1* (Hannover: Leo Niehorster, 1990), for information on the organization and equipent of the German panzer divisions.
9. Stoves, *1. Panzer-Division 1935–1945*, pp. 257ff.
10. Ibid.
11. Ibid.
12. Ibid.

13. Ibid.
14. Ibid.
15. Ibid.
16. Ibid.
17. Ibid.
18. Ibid.
19. Ibid.
20. Ibid.
21. Zhukov, *Vospominaniya i Razmyshleniya (Volume II)*, pp. 199–200, 206.
22. *Sbornik Voenno-Istoricheskikh Materialov Velikoy Otechestvennoy Voyny, Vypusk 7* (Moscow: Voenizdat, 1952), pp. 16–18. Gareev and Simonov: *Pobediteli 1941–1945*, pp. 260–261. Tsamo: fond 213, op. 2002, delo 31, list 1–3.—*Kalininskogo fronta oktyabr 1941*.
23. See appendice 16 for Kalinin Front order of battle October 17, 1941. Boundaries between the fronts found in *Rysskii Arkhiv: Velikaya Otechestvennaya T. 16 (5-1), Stavka VGK Dokumenty i Materialy* (Moscow: Terra, 1996), p. 248.
24. Thies, *Der Ostfeldzug, Heeresgruppe Mitte—Ein Lageatlas der Operationsabteilung des Generalstab des Heeres*, p. 96.
25. Ibid; *Geschichte der 258. Infanterie-Division, II. Teil* (Neckargemünd: Kurt Vowinckel Verlag, 1978), pp. 96–115.
26. *Geschichte der 258. Infanterie-Division, II. Teil*, p. 115.
27. Ibid.
28. Ibid.
29. Ibid.
30. Ibid.
31. Ibid.
32. Ibid.
33. Ibid.
34. Thies, *Der Ostfeldzug, Heeresgruppe Mitte—Ein Lageatlas der Operationsabteilung des Generalstab des Heeres*, p. 98.
35. Ibid; Das Panzer-Regiment 21 im Ostfeldzug 1941–1945, BA-MA RH 39/562.
36. Das Panzer-Regiment 21 im Ostfeldzug 1941–1945, BA-MA RH 39/562.
37. Ibid.
38. Ibid.
39. Ibid.
40. Ibid.
41. Ibid.
42. Ibid.
43. Ibid.
44. Ibid.
45. Artem Drabkin and Oleg Sheremet, *T-34 in Action* (Barnsley: Pen & Sword Military, 2006), pp. 45–47.
46. Drabkin and Sheremet, *T-34 in Action*, pp. 5–10.

47. Katukov, *Na Ostrie Glavnogo Udara*, pp. 17–18.

48. Ibid., pp. 19–20.

49. Thies, *Der Ostfeldzug, Heeresgruppe Mitte—Ein Lageatlas der Operationsabteilung des Generalstab des Heeres*, p. 98; KTB Pz. Rgt. 7, BA-MA RH 39/99.

50. The 7th Panzer Regiment had been part of the so-called "Panzerverband Kempf" during the campaign in Poland 1939. This temporary formation also included several SS units. See M. Smedberg and N. Zetterling, *Andra Världskrigets utbrott* (Stockholm: Norstedts, 2007), pp. 110ff and Zetterling, *Blixtkrig! 1939–1941*, pp. 50ff.

51. KTB Pz. Rgt. 7, BA-MA RH 39/99.

52. KTB Pz. Rgt. 7, BA-MA RH 39/99.

53. KTB Pz. Gruppe 4 Ia, 13.10.1941, NARA T313, R340, F8622700ff.

54. Ibid.

55. KTB Pz. Gruppe 4 Ia, 14.10.1941, NARA T313, R340, F8622706ff.

56 KTB Pz. Gruppe 4 Ia, 14–15.10.1941, NARA T313, R340, F8622706-10. Strength returns for the 11th Panzer Division can be found in BA-MA RH 27-11/24, Bl. 86ff.

57. KTB Pz. Gruppe 4 Ia, 14–15.10.1941, NARA T313, R340, F8622706-10; Die Kämpfe der 4. Armee im ersten Kriegsjahr gegen die Sowjets. 22.6.41–22.6.42, BA-MA RH 20-4/1158; Thies, *Der Ostfeldzug, Heeresgruppe Mitte—Ein Lageatlas der Operationsabteilung des Generalstab des Heeres*, p. 98.

58. *Bitva pod Moskvoy, Khronika, Fakti, Lyudi. Kniga Pervaya* (Moscow: Olma-Press, 2002), p. 333.

59. N. I. Krylov, N. I. Alekseev and I. G. Dragan, *Navstrechu Pobede. Voevoy Put 5-y Armii* (Moscow: Nauka, 1970), pp. 10–11. See Armstrong, Richard, *Red Army Tank Commanders, the Armored Guards* (Atglen: Schiffer, 1994), pp. 104–112 for details on Bogdanov.

60. Kolomiets, *Bitva Za Moskvu, 30 sentyabrya–5 dekabrya 1941*, pp. 20–25, 32. Krylov et al, *Navstrechu Pobede. Voevoy Put 5-y Armii*, pp. 10–11. Ilya Mostjansky, *Tanki T-34-76, T-34-57 v bojakh za Moskvu* (Moscow: BTV-Kniga, 2008), pp. 69–70.

61. Otto Weidinger, *Division Das Reich. Band III 1941–1943* (Munin Verlag, Osnabrück 1987), p. 136.

62. Lelyushenko, *Moscow—Stalingrad—Berlin—Praga*, pp. 37–39.

63. For XL Panzer Corps, see KTB Pz. Gruppe 4 Ia, 19.10.1941, NARA T313, R340, F8622719. On Govorov, see Gareev and Simonov: *Pobediteli 1941–1945*, pp. 83–86.

64. On 5th Panzer Division, see KTB Pz. Gruppe 4 Ia, 19.10.1941, NARA T313, R340, F8622719ff. On the SS Division, see Otto Weidinger, *Division Das Reich. Band III 1941–1943* (Osnabrück: Munin Verlag, 1987), pp. 164–165.

65. In his diary, von Bock wrote on October 21 that "the Russians are impeding us far less than the wet and the mud" (von Bock, *The War Diary 1939–1945*). The way he described the situation in his diary is in accordance with the war diaries of the units and the situation reports.

66. On Shostakovich, see Rodric Braithwaite, *Moscow 1941—A city and its people at War* (London: Profile Books, 2007), pp. 271–273.

67. For details on the evacuation of Moscow, see Samsonov, *Moscow, 1941 god: ot tragedii porazhenii k velikoy pobede*, p. 111–112. On Beria see Rodric Braithwaite, *Moscow 1941— A city and its people at War* (London: Profile Books, 2007), pp. 258–259.

68. Vasilevsky, *Delo Vsei Zhizni*, p. 156.

69. G. V. Andreevsky, *Povcednevnaya Zhizn Moskvy v Stalinskuyo Epochu 1930–1940 gody* (Moscow: Molodaya Gvardiya, 2003), pp. 142–145.

70. On Mikoyan, see Samsonov, *Moscow, 1941 god: ot tragedii porazhenii k velikoy pobede*, p. 109.

71. Simon Sebag Montefiore, *Stalin—Den röde tsarens hov* (Stockholm: Prisma, 2004), pp. 400–404; V. P. Pronin, *Gorod-voin* i *Bitva za Moskvu* (Moscow: Moskovskii Rabochii, 1966), p. 461. The complete directive can be found in Samsonov, *Moscow, 1941 god: ot tragedii porazhenii k velikoy pobede*, p. 115.

72. On industry, see Braithwaite, *Moscow 1941—A city and its people at War*, p. 22. For evacuations, see *Moskau im Krieg 1941–1945* (Berlin: Espresso Verlag, 2002), p. 10. See Samsonov, *Moskva, 1941 god: ot tragedii porazhenii k velikoy pobede*, p. 51 on aircraft production. The Volga canal is discussed in Seaton, *The Battle for Moscow 1941–1942*, p. 121.

73. Braithwaite, *Moscow 1941—A city and its people at War*, pp. 24, 29.

74. *Moskau im Krieg 1941–1945*, pp. 14–16; Andrew Nagorski, *The Greatest Battle* (New York: Simon & Schuster Paperbacks, 2008), p. 168.

75. Braithwaite, *Moscow 1941—A city and its people at War*, pp. 94–95.

76. *Moskau im Krieg 1941–1945*, p. 17.

77. Braithwaite, *Moscow 1941—A city and its people at War*, pp. 184–188; Porter and Jones, *Moscow in World War II*, pp. 54–56, 74–80.

78. Chris Bellamy, *Absolute War, Soviet Russia in the Second World War* (London: Pan Books, 2007), p. 288.

79. Porter and Jones, *Moscow in World War II*, pp. 56, 80.

CHAPTER 11: ON TO TULA

1. Thies, *Der Ostfeldzug, Heeresgruppe Mitte—Ein Lageatlas der Operationsabteilung des Generalstab des Heeres*, p. 98f.

2. Flemming's diary, BA-MA MSg 2/4304.

3. Ibid.

4. Ibid.

5. Ibid.

6. Ibid.

7. Ibid.

8. Ibid.

9. KTB 2. Pz. Armee Ia, 7.10.41, NARA T313, R86.

10. KTB 2. Pz. Armee Ia, 8.10.41, NARA T313, R86.

11. KTB 2. Pz. Armee Ia, 9.10.41, NARA T313, R86.

12. KTB 2. Pz. Armee Ia, 10.10.41–12.10.41, NARA T313, R86.

13. Katukov, *Na Ostrie Glavnogo Udara*, pp. 52–53.

14. Lelyushenko, *Moscow—Stalingrad—Berlin—Praga*, pp. 31–33.

15. Ibid.

16. KTB 2. Pz. Armee Ia, 13.10.41–19.10.41, NARA T313, R86.

17. KTB 2. Pz. Armee Ia, 15.10.41, NARA T313, R86.

18. Ibid.

19. Ibid.

20. KTB 2. Pz. Armee Ia, 17.10.41, NARA T313, R86.

21. KTB 2. Pz. Armee Ia, 18.10.41, NARA T313, R86.

22. Prilozhenie "*Voevoy i Chislenny sostav Bryanskogo Fronta Na 7. 11. 1941*" in *Sbornik Voevych Dokumentov Velikoy Otechestvennoy Voyny, Vypusk 43* (Moscow: Voennoe Izdatelstvo Ministerstva Oborony Soyuza SSR, 1960).

23. A. I. Eremenko, *V Nachale Voyny* (Moscow: Nauka, 1964), pp. 360–361; Sandalov, *Na Moskovskom Napravlenii*, p. 223.

24. Aleksey Safronov and Vladimir Kurnosov, *Srazhenie za Tulu* (Moscow: BTV-Kniga, 2008), pp. 15, 25. Sandalov, *Na Moskovskom Napravlenii*, p. 224.

25. Directive No. 003048, 2:20 p. m. on October 17, 1941, *Bitva pod Moskvoy, Khronika, Fakti, Lyudi. Kniga Pervaya* (Moscow: Olma-Press, 2002), p. 348.

26. KTB 2. Pz. Armee Ia, 18.10.41–22.10.41, NARA T313, R86.

27. Flemming's diary, BA-MA MSg 2/4304.

28. Ibid.

29. Ibid.

30. Ibid.

31. Ibid.

32. Ibid.

33. Ibid.

34. Ibid.

35. KTB 2. Pz. Armee Ia, 23.10.41, NARA T313, R86.

36. Joachim Neumann, *Die 4. Panzer-Division 1938–1943* (Bonn: Joachim Neumann, 1985), pp. 330f.

37. Directive No. 004037 to the Bryansk Front, 2:50 a. m. on October 22, 1941, *Bitva pod Moskvoy, Khronika, Fakti, Lyudi. Kniga Pervaya* (Moscow: Olma-Press, 2002), p. 388.

38. Ibid.

39. KTB 2. Pz. Armee Ia, 23.10.41, NARA T313, R86.

40. Ibid. For more on the 1st Cavalry Division/24th Panzer Division, see Ferdinand von Senger und Etterlin, *Die 24. Panzer-Division vormals 1. Kavallerie-Division 1939–1945* (Neckargemünd: Vowinckel, 1962).

41. Safronov and Kurnosov, *Srazhenie za Tulu*, pp. 22–23.

42. Neumann, *Die 4. Panzer-Division 1938–1943*, p. 331.

43. Ibid.

44. 4. Pz. Div. Ia, "Gefechtsbericht über die Kämpfe der 4. Pz. Div für die Zeit vom 8.10—25.10.41," BA-MA RH 39/373.

45. Ibid.
46. KTB 2. Pz. Armee Ia, 24.10.41, NARA T313, R86.
47. Ibid
48. Ibid
49. Ibid
50. KTB 2. Pz. Armee Ia, 25.10.41, NARA T313, R86.; 4. Pz. Div. Ia, "Gefechtsbericht über die Kämpfe der 4. Pz. Div für die Zeit vom 8.10–25.10.41," BA-MA RH 39/373.
51. Ibid.
52. Ibid.
53. KTB 2. Pz. Armee Ia, 26.10.41, NARA T313, R86.
54. Ibid; 4. Pz. Div. Ia, "Gefechtsbericht über die Kämpfe der 4. Pz. Div für die Zeit vom 8.10–25.10.41," BA-MA RH 39/373; PzAOK 2 IIa, Verlustmeldung vom 21–31.10.1941, NARA T313, R108, F7332784.
55. KTB 2. Pz. Armee Ia, 27.10.41, NARA T313, R86.
56. Ibid.
57. Ibid.
58. KTB 2. Pz. Armee Ia, 28–29.10.41, NARA T313, R86.
59. Ibid.
60. Ibid.
61. Ibid.
62. Ibid.
63. Ibid.
64. Ibid.
65. For the decision of October 5 on ten new armies, see Vasilevsky, *Delo Vsei Zjizni*, p. 159. Strength of reserves in early November, see *Velikaya Otechestvennaya Vojna 1941–1945, Kniga 1 Surovye Ispytaniya* (Moscow: Nauka, 1998). pp. 239–240. For number of T-34 in brigades, see Kolomiets, *Bitva Za Moskvu, 30 sentyabrya–5 dekabrya 1941*, sida 6–8, 40. The number of new regiments is based on the order of battles from October 1 and November 1, see *Boevoy Sostav Sovetskoy Armii, khast I* (East View Publications).
66. Safronov and Kurnosov, *Srazhenie za Tulu*, pp. 30–33.
67. KTB 2. Pz. Armee Ia, 30–31.10.41, NARA T313, R86.
68. For the general staff's report of 8:00 a. m. on October 31, 1941, see *Bitva pod Moskvoy, Khronika, Fakti, Lyudi. Kniga Pervaya* (Olma-Press, Moscow 2002), p. 453.
69. Ermakov's divisions were the 154th, 217th, 258th, 260th, 290th, 299th, and 413th Rifle Divisions, 31st and 41st Cavalry Divisions and the 108th Tank Division. Samsonov, *Moscow, 1941 god: ot tragedii porazhenii k velikoy pobede*, p. 238. For Ermakov's unauthorized movement, see Sandalov, *Na Moskovskom Napravlenii*, p. 231.
70. Thies, *Der Ostfeldzug, Heeresgruppe Mitte—Ein Lageatlas der Operationsabteilung des Generalstab des Heeres*, pp. 99f.
71. On September 18, the 100th, 127th, 153rd, and 161st Rifle Divisions were designated guards and on 26 September 64th, 107th och 120th rifle divisions. See V. A. Anfilov, *Krusjenie Pochoda Gitlera na Moskvu 1941* (Moscow: Nauka, 1989), p. 245. On

October 1, the 5th Guards Rifle division was at the West Front and the 2nd Rifle Division at the Bryansk Front. See Samsonov, *Moskva, 1941 god: ot tragedii porazhenii k belikoy pobede*, pp. 235–236.

72. On 2nd Guards and 6th Guards, see "Prilozhenie "Boevoi i chislennyy sostav Brjanskogo Fronta Na 7.11.1941," in *Sbornik Voevych Dokumentov Velikoy Otetjestvennoy Vojny, Vypusk 43* (Moscow: Voennoe Izdatelstvo Ministerstva Oborony Sojuza SSR, 1960). For 5th Guards losses, see *Bitva pod Moskvoy, Chronika, Fakti, Ljudi. Kniga Pervaya* (Moscow: Olma-Press, 2002), p. 334.

73. Charles C. Sharp, , *Soviet Order of Battle World War II, Volume IV "Red Guards"* (West Chester: George F. Nafzinger, 1995), p. 45. On Panfilov, see *Bitva pod Moskvoj, Chronika, Fakti, Ljudi. Kniga Pervaja* (Moscow: Olma-Press, 2002), pp. 120–121.

74. Charles C. Sharp, , *Soviet Order of Battle World War II, Volume V "Red Sabers"* (West Chester: George F. Nafzinger, 1995), pp. 74–79.

75. Katukov, *Na Ostrie Glavnogo Udara*, pp. 68–69.

CHAP 12: THE END OF OCTOBER—HALFTIME FOR OPERATION *TAIFUN*

1. Thies, *Der Ostfeldzug, Heeresgruppe Mitte—Ein Lageatlas der Operationsabteilung des Generalstab des Heeres*, p. 96–104.

2. Franz Josef Strauß, *Geschichte der 2. (Wiener), Panzer-Division* (Dörfler Zietgeschichte, Eggolsheim n. d). pp. 94–95.

3. Rokossovsky, *Soldatskii Dolg*, pp. 66–70.

4. KTB Pz. Gruppe 4 Ia, 23.10.1941, NARA T313, R340, F8622732.

5. Klaus Reinhardt, *Die Wende vor Moskau* (Deutsche Verlags-Anstalt, Stuttgart 1972), pp. 85–95.

6. Gareev and Simonov, *Pobediteli 1941–1945*, pp. 260–261. Zhukov, *Vospominaniya i Razmyshleniya (Volume II)*, pp. 210–211.

7. The units to be withdrawn were the VIII Corps, the 5th, 8th, 15th and 28th Infantry Divisions and the 1st Cavalry Division, see Klaus Reinhardt, *Die Wende vor Moskau* (Stuttgart: Deutsche Verlags-Anstalt, 1972), pp. 82–84.

8. Johannes Hürter, *Ein deutscher General an der Ostfront. Die Briefe und Tagebücher des Gotthard Heinrici 1941/42* (Erfurt: Alan Sutton, 2001), p. 96. Wilhelm Meyer-Detring, *Die 137. Infanterie-Division im Mittelabschnitt der Ostfront* (Eggolsheim: Dörfler Zeitgeschichte n. d.), p. 216. Carl Wagener, *Moskau 1941—Der Angriff auf die russische Hauptstadt* (Bad Nauheim: Podzun Verlag, 1965), p. 29. See also the war diary of Panzergruppe 4, which claimed that the roads were a greater problem than the enemy, KTB Pz. Gruppe 4 Ia, 23.10.1941, NARA T313, R340, F8622731.

9. For information on the depth of the mud, see Otto Weidinger, *Division Das Reich. Band III 1941–1943* (Osnabrück: Munin Verlag, 1987), p. 186. On the problems encountered by the 6th Panzer Division see Wolfgang Paul, *Brennpunkte. Die Geschichte der 6. Panzerdivision (1. leichte), 1937–1945* (Osnabrück: Biblio 1993), p. 154.

10. Geyer Hermann, *Das IX. Armeekorps im Ostfeldzug 1941* (Neckargemünd: Kurt Vowinckel Verlag, 1969), pp. 147–150.

11. Klaus Reinhardt, *Die Wende vor Moskau* (Stuttgart: Deutsche Verlags-Anstalt, 1972), p. 81. Adolf Reinicke, *Die 5. Jäger-Division* (Eggolsheim: Dörfler Zeitgeschichte n. d.), pp. 153–156.

12. Those killed in action were Maj Gen Mikhail Petrov, commander of the Fiftieth Army, and Maj Gen Konstantin Rakutin, commander of the Twenty-Fourth Army. Lt Gen Mikhail Lukin (Nineteenth Army), Lt Gen Philip Ershakov (Twentieth Army), and Maj Gen Sergey Vishnevsky (Second Army), were captured.

13. Gareev and Simonov, *Pobediteli 1941–1945,* pp. 403–404.

14. Chametov, (ed.), *Bitva pod Moskvoy*, pp. 34–35. Lopukhovskii, *Vyazemskaya Katastrofa 41-go goda*, pp. 93–95. Reinhardt, Klaus, *Die Wende vor Moskau* (Stuttgart: Deutsche Verlags-Anstalt, 1972), pp. 317–318.

15. Vasilevsky, *Delo Vsei Zhizni*, p. 151.

16. Rzhevskaya pravda 24 Oktober 2002, Gerasimova, S. : *Rzhev. Oktyabr 1941*.

17. Gareev and Simonov, *Pobediteli 1941–1945*, pp. 208–209, 243–244, 255–256, 351–352, 432–433.

18. See "Prikaz komanduyuschego voyskami Zapadnogo fronta 43–jarmiey ot 22 oktyabrya 1941 g." and "Prikaz komanduyuschego voyskami Zapadnogo fronta No. 054 ot 3 nojabrja 1941 g." in *G. K. Zhukov v bitve pod Moskvoy, Sbornik Dokumentov* (Moscow: Mosgorarkhiv, 1994). See also *Velikaya Otechestvennaya Voyna 1941–1945, Kniga 1 Surovye Ispytaniya* (Moscow: Nauka, 1998), p. 229.

19. Examples of the division's strength can be found in "Prilozjenie "Boevoj i tjislennyj sostav Brjanskogo Fronta Na 7.11.1941. i *Sbornik Voevych Dokumentov Velikoj Otetjestvennoj Vojny, Vypusk 43* (Moscow: Voennoe Izdatelstvo Ministerstva Oborony Sojuza SSR, 1960).

20. The new brigades were the 4th, 8th, 9th, 11th, 17th, 18th, 19th, 20th, 21st, 22nd, 23rd, 24th, 25th, 26th, 27th, 28th, and 32nd Tank Brigades. On the development of the Soviet tank forces, see Kolomiets, *Bitva Za Moskvu, 30 sentjabrja–5 dekabrja 1941*.

21. Erich Bunke, *Der Osten blieb unser Schicksal 1939–1944* (Wietze: Selbstverlag, 1991), p. 427.

22. Horst Grossmann, *Die Geschichte der rheinisch-westfälischen 6. Infanterie-Division 1939–1945* (Eggolsheim: Dörfler Zeitgeschichte, n. d.), pp. 81–82.

23. See for example Martin Gareis, *Kampf und Ende der Fränkisch-Sudetendeutschen 98. Infanterie-Division* (Eggolsheim: Dörfler Zeitgeschichte n. d.), p. 154. Ernst-Martin Rhein, *Das Rheinisch-Westfälische Infanterie-/Grenadier-Regiment 18 1921–1945* (Bergisch-Gladbach: Eigenverlag, 1993), pp. 104–105.

24. Williamson Murray, *The Luftwaffe 1933–45, Strategy for Defeat* (Brassey's Washington/London 1996), pp. 88–94. Klaus Reinhardt, *Die Wende vor Moskau* (Stuttgart: Deutsche Verlags-Anstalt, 1972), pp. 88–89. Hans Ring and Werner Girbig, *Jagdgeschwader 27* (Stuttgart: Motorbuch Verlag, 1994), p. 75; Dokumenty i Materialy, "Moskovskaya bitva v tsifrakh," pp. 72–73.

25. For general comments on losses in an infantry corps, see Hermann Geyer, *Das IX. Armeekorps im Ostfeldzug 1941* (Neckargemünd: Kurt Vowinckel Verlag, 1969), pp. 142–144. On the 98th Infantry Division, see Martin Gareis: *Kampf und Ende der Fränkisch-*

Sudetendeutschen 98. Infanterie-Division (Eggolsheim: Dörfler Zeitgeschichte n. d.), pp. 82, 153, 161. On the 6th Infantry Division, see Grossmann, *Die Geschichte der rheinisch-westfälischen 6. Infanterie-Division 1939–1945*, pp. 84–85.

26. Otto Weidinger, *Division Das Reich. Band III 1941–1943* (Osnabrück: Munin Verlag, 1987), p. 169.

27. Wolfgang Paul, *Brennpunkte. Die Geschichte der 6. Panzerdivision (1. leichte), 1937–1945* (Osnabrück: Biblio, 1993), pp. 154–155.

28. Wolfgang Paul, *Geschichte der 18. Panzer-Division 1940–1943 (mit Geschichte der 18. Artillerie-Division 1943–1944)* (Freiburg: Selbstverlag, 1975), p. 112. On the November 6 report see Seaton, *The Battle for Moscow 1941–1942*, pp. 128–129.

29. Alex Buchner, *Das Handbuch der Deutschen Infanterie 1939–1945* (Friedberg/Hess: Podzun-Pallas, 1989), pp. 8–9, 81–82. Sharp, *Soviet Order of Battle World War II, Volume IX "Red Tide,"* pp. 118–119. Voenno-Istoricheskij Zhurnal 1967 no 3: Dokumenty i Materialy: *Moskovskaya bitva v tsifrakh*, pp. 70–71.

30. Buchner, *Das Handbuch der Deutschen Infanterie 1939–1945*, p. 74; KTB Pz. Gruppe 4 Ia, 19. 10. 1941, NARA T313, R340, F8622721-22.

31. Martin Gareis, *Kampf und Ende der Fränkisch-Sudetendeutschen 98. Infanterie-Division* (Eggolsheim: Dörfler Zeitgeschichte n. d.), p. 167; Grossmann, *Die Geschichte der rheinisch-westfälischen 6. Infanterie-Division 1939–1945*, p. 86.

32. Wilhelm: Meyer-Detring, *Die 137. Infanterie-Division im Mittelabschnitt der Ostfront* (Eggolsheim: Dörfler Zeitgeschichte n. d.), p. 198.

33. Grossmann, *Die Geschichte der rheinisch-westfälischen 6. Infanterie-Division 1939–1945*, p. 87.

34. Antipenko, *In der Hauptrichtung*, pp. 78–79. Alec Nove, *An Economic History of the USSR* (London: Penguin Books, 1989), p. 269.

35. Rokossovsky, *Soldatskii Dolg*, p. 73.

CHAPTER 13: THE NOVEMBER 7 PARADE

1. Richard Armstrong, *Red Army Tank Commanders, the Armored Guards* (Atglen: Schiffer, 1994), p. 386.

2. Braithwaite: *Moscow 1941—A city and its people at War*, pp. 278–279. Zhukov, *Vospominaniya i Razmyshleniya (Volume II)*, p. 211.

3. His notes are somewhat unclear about the number of T-34 and KV per line. They can be interpreted as saying that there were either two or three per line. However, photos appear to show two per line. A. Zjerebilov (ed.), *N. I. Biryukov, Tanki—Fronty! Zapiski Sovetskogo generala* (Smolensk: Rusitj, 2005), p. 48.

4. Braithwaite, *Moscow 1941—A city and its people at War*, p. 282. *Moskovskaya bitva v khronike faktov i sobytii* (Moscow: Voenizdat, 2004), pp 202–203. Zhuk, *Neizvestnye stranitsy Bitvy za Moskvu*, p. 338.

5. V. A. Anfilov, *Krushenie Pokhoda Gitlera na Moskvu 1941* (Moscow: Nauka, 1989), pp. 295–296. P. A. Artemev, *Nepreodolimaya pregrada na podstupakh k stolitse* i *Bitva za Moskvu* (Moscow: Moskovskii Rabochii, 1966), pp. 117. *Bitva pod Moskvoy, Khronika, Fakti,*

Lyudi. Kniga Pervaya (Moscow: Olma-Press, 2002), pp. 528–532. Braithwaite, *Moscow 1941—A city and its people at War*, pp. 280–286.

6. V. P. Pronin, *Gorod-voin* i *Bitva za Moskvu* (Moscow: Moskovskii Rabochii, 1966), p. 456. Samsonov, *Moscow, 1941 god: ot tragedii porazjenij k velikoj pobede*, p. 153.

7. See Braithwaite, *Moscow 1941—A city and its people at War*, pp. 287–288, on details about Moskinokhronika. Zhuk, *Neizvestnye stranitsy Bitvy za Moskvu*, p. 338. Stalin's absence has been claimed by for example Richard Overy, *Russia's War* (New York: Penguin Books, 1998), p. 115.

8. P. A. Belov, *Za nami Moscow* (Moscow: Voenizdat, 1963), p. 47. Samsonov, *Moscow, 1941 god: ot tragedii porazjenij k velikoj pobede*, p. 253. Sharp, *Soviet Order of Battle World War II, Volume IX "Red Tide,"* p. 79.

9. National Archives, Kew Gardens. War Office WO 178/25—Cipher Message November 7 1941. Immediate D. M. I. from Macfarlane.

10. Anfilov, *Krushjenie Pochoda Gitlera na Moskvu 1941*, p. 296. Zhuk, *Neizvestnye stranitsy Bitvy za Moskvu*, p. 210.

11. *Bitva pod Moskvoy, Khronika, Fakti, Lyudi. Kniga Pervaya* (Moscow: Olma-Press, 2002), pp. 528–532. Braithwaite, *Moscow 1941—A city and its people at War* (London: Profile Books, 2007), p. 284. See *Moskau im Krieg 1941–1945* (Berlin: Espresso Verlag, 2002), p. 65 for the image on Pravda's first page.

12. Zhukov, *Vospominaniya i Razmyshleniya (Volumes I–III)*, pp. 211–213.

13. See Drig, *Mechanizirovannye Korpusa RKKA v Boju*, pp. 650–651 for info on the 58th Tank Division. *Moskovskaya bitva v khronike faktov i sobytij* (Moscow: Voenizdat, 2004), pp. 208–209.

14. Dokument No. 50 "Prikaz komanduyuschego voyskami Zapadnogo Fronta voennym sovetam armii ot 21 novjabrja 1941 g." in *G. K. Zhukov v bitve pod Moskvoy, Sbornik Dokumentov* (Moscow: Mosgorarchiv, 1994). For lists of commanders, see Samsonov, *Moskva, 1941 god: ot tragedii porazjenij k velikoy pobede*, pp. 232–233.

15. Shaposhnikov, *Bitva za Moskvu, Moskvovskaya operatsiya zapadnogo fronta, 16 noyabrya 1941 g—31 janvarja 1942 g.*, pp. 142–143.

CHAPTER 14: THE ORSHA MEETING, NOVEMBER 13

1. Halder's diary.
2. Halder's diary.
3. Halder's diary.
4. Halder's diary.
5. Halder's diary November 4 ,1941.
6. See Tooze, *The Wages of Destruction*, particularly chapters 12–15.
7. Von Bock, *The War Diary 1939–1945*, pp. 346–349.
8. Halder's diary, November 10–11, 1941.
9. Ibid., November 12, 1941.
10. Von Bock, *The War Diary 1939–1945*, pp. 354f.
11. Ibid.

12. Ibid.

13. Ibid.

14. Ibid; Halder's diary, November 11, 1941.

15. Ibid., November 13, 1941.

16. Ibid.

17. Von Bock, *The War Diary 1939–1945*, p. 358.

18. Ibid.

19. Halder's diary, November 14.

CHAPTER 15: THE FINAL ATTEMPT

1. Hoffmann's diary.

2. Ibid.

3. Ibid.

4. Ibid.

5. Ibid.

6. Thies, *Der Ostfeldzug, Heeresgruppe Mitte—Ein Lageatlas der Operationsabteilung des Generalstab des Heeres*, pp. 103–108.

7. Ibid; .

8. Flemming's diary, BA-MA MSg 2/4304.

9. Ibid.

10. Ibid.

11. KTB Pz. Rgt. 6, BA-MA RH 39/707.

12. Ibid.

13. Ibid.

14. Thies, *Der Ostfeldzug, Heeresgruppe Mitte—Ein Lageatlas der Operationsabteilung des Generalstab des Heeres*, p. 104.

15. Thies, *Der Ostfeldzug, Heeresgruppe Mitte—Ein Lageatlas der Operationsabteilung des Generalstab des Heeres*, p. 104f; von Bock, *The War Diary 1939–1945*, p. 362f.

16. Ibid.

17. Lelyushenko, *Moscow—Stalingrad—Berlin—Praga*, pp. 43–44. On Zhukov's meeting with Stalin 5 januari 1942, see Zhukov, *Vospominaniya i Razmyshleniya (Volume II)*, pp. 233–234.

18. Zhukov, *Vospominaniya i Razmyshleniya (Volume II)*, pp. 207–214. The November 9, 1941 Stavka order instructing Fiftieth Army to be transferred to the West Front can be found in Rysskii Arkhiv: *Velikaya Otechestvennaya T. 16 (5-1), Stavka VGK Dokumenty i Materialy* (Moscow: Terra, 1996), p. 280. Front-line length has been taken from Dokumenty i Materialy, "Moskovskaya bitva v tsifrakh," pp. 77–78.

19. Kolomiets, *Bitva Za Moskvu, 30 sentyabrya–5 dekabrya 1941*, pp. 45, 64. Safronov and Kurnosov, *Srazhenie za Tulu*, p. 41; Dokumenty i Materialy, "Moskovskaya bitva v tsifrakh," pp. 77–78.

20. Belov's 2nd Cavalry Corps (including 5th and 9th Cavalry Divisions), on November 9 and 17th, 18th, 20th, 24th, and 44th Cavalry Divisions on November 12. *Rysskii*

Arkhiv: Velikaya Otechestvennaya T. 16 (5-1), Stavka VGK Dokumenty i Materialy (Moscow: Terra, 1996), pp. 280, 286. On front line and divisions, see Dokumenty i Materialy, "Moskovskaya bitva v tsifrakh," pp. 77–78.

21. Antipenko, *In der Hauptrichtung*, pp. 73–74.
22. I. V. Boldin, *Stranitsy Zhizni* (Moscow: Voenzidat, 1961), pp. 175–177. Number of antiaircraft guns: Dokumenty i Materialy, "Moskovskaya bitva v tsifrakh," pp. 77–78.
23. In addition to the AA guns, there were 643 AA machine guns: Chametov, *Bitva pod Moskvoy*, p. 74. Strength of Moscow garrison and reserves: *Velikaya Otechestvennaya Voyna 1941–1945, Kniga 1 Surovye Ispytaniya* (Moscow: Nauka, 1998). pp. 239–240.
24. Strauß, *Die Geschichte der 2 (Wiener), Panzer-Division*, pp. 97ff.
25. Ibid.
26. Ibid; Thies, *Der Ostfeldzug, Heeresgruppe Mitte—Ein Lageatlas der Operationsabteilung des Generalstab des Heeres*, pp. 104f.
27. For Soviet strength in the Moscow area, see Shaposhnikov, *Bitva za Moskvu, Moskvovskaya operatsiya zapadnogo fronta, 16 noyabrya 1941 g.—31 janvarya 1942 g*, pp. 180–181.
28. Rokossovsky, *Soldatskii Dolg*, pp. 81–83.
29. Joachim Neumann, *Die 4. Panzer-Division 1938–1943*, p. 372.
30. Ibid; Thies, *Der Ostfeldzug, Heeresgruppe Mitte—Ein Lageatlas der Operationsabteilung des Generalstab des Heeres*, p. 104; Guderian, *Panzer Leader*, pp. 252–254.
31. Von Bock, *The War Diary 1939–1945*. Note that Guderian in his memoirs (Guderian, *Panzer Leader*, p. 252), provides a slightly different account of the meeting. As von Bock's diary was written during the war, and he died before the war ended, we have relied more on von Bock's account.
32. Ibid.
33. On Belov and Kashira see Belov, *Za nami Moscow*, pp. 70–80. Zhukov, *Vospominaniya i Razmyshleniya (Volume II)*, p. 216.
34. Ibid; Thies, *Der Ostfeldzug, Heeresgruppe Mitte—Ein Lageatlas der Operationsabteilung des Generalstab des Heeres*, p. 104; KTB Pz. Rgt. 7, 25.11.41, BA-MA RH 39/99. Bataljonen var I. bataljonen i Pansarregemente 7. The motorized regiment was the 86th Rifle Regiment.
35. KTB Pz. Rgt. 7, 25.11.41, BA-MA RH 39/99.
36. Ibid.
37. Ibid.
38. Gefechtsbericht über den Verlauf der Operationen und Einsatz des VIII. Fliegerkorps, 1. Teil (15–29.11.1941), BA-MA RL 8/280.
39. KTB Pz. Rgt. 7, 25.11.41, BA-MA RH 39/99.
40. Rokossovsky, *Soldatskii Dolg*, pp. 90–91.
41. German monthly casualties on the Eastern Front 1941 amounted to (according to BA-MA RW 6/v. 552):
    June: 41,084 (8 886 killed in action, 29,494 wounded and 2,704 missing).
    July: 172,217 (37,584 killed in action, 125,579 wounded and 9,054 missing).
    August: 196,663 (41,019 killed in action, 147,748 wounded and 7,896 missing).

September: 141,225 (29,422 killed in action, 106,826 wounded and 4,977 missing).

October: 114,865 (24,056 killed in action, 87,224 wounded and 3,585 missing).

November: 87,139 (17,806 killed in action, 66,211 wounded and 3,122 missing).

December: 77,857 (14,949 killed in action, 58,226 wounded and 4,682 missing).

42. Army Group Center casualties were (according to BA-MA RW 6/v. 556),

Jul 6–Aug 3: 69,546

Aug 4–Aug 31: 65,140

September: 30,518

October: 72,870

November: 40,580

At first glance, it would appear that casualties reached a peak in October, but per day and division, losses were actually lower in October than in July and August. When Operation *Barbarossa* was launched, Army Group Center possessed 51 divisions, but this was increased to 77 divisions for Operation *Taifun*.

43. Annex to KTB Pz. Rgt. 7, 25. 11. 41, BA-MA RH 39/99.

44. See appendix 1. See also file BA-MA RW 19/1390 for more information on losses of tanks and arrival of new tanks.

45. Neumann, *Die 4. Panzer-Division 1938–1943*, p. 345.

46. Martin Gareis, *Kampf und Ende der Fränkisch-Sudetendeutschen 98. Infanterie-Division* (Eggolsheim: Dörfler Zeitgeschichte n. d.), p. 127.

47. Strauß, *Die Geschichte der 2 (Wiener), Panzer-Division*, p. 98.

48. Geyer, *Das IX. Armeekorps im Ostfeldzug 1941*, p. 152.

49. Porter and Jones, *Moscow in World War II*, p. 126.

50. Heinrich Haape, *Endstation Moskau 1941–1942* (Stuttgart: Motorbuch Verlag, 1998), pp. 148–149.

51. Ibid.

52. Ibid.

53. Johannes Hürter, *Ein deutscher General an der Ostfront. Die Briefe und Tagebücher des Gotthard Heinrici 1941/42* (Erfurt: Alan Sutton, 2001), p. 110.

CHAPTER 16: AT THE GATES OF MOSCOW

1. Von Bock, *The War Diary 1939–1945*, p. 370; KTB Pz. Gr. 3 Ia, 27.11.41, NARA T313, R237, F8504189ff .

2. KTB Pz. Gr. 3 Ia, 27.11.41, NARA T313, R237, F8504189ff.

3. Ibid.; Gefechtsbericht über den Verlauf der Operationen und Einsatz des VIII. Fliegerkorps, 1. Teil (15. 11–29.11.1941), BA-MA RL 8/280.

4. KTB Pz. Gr. 3 Ia, 28.11.41, NARA T313, R237, F8504193ff.

5. Ibid.

6. KTB Pz. Gr. 3 Ia, 28.11.41, NARA T313, R237, F8504193ff.

7. Zhukov, *Vospominaniya i Razmyshleniya (Volume II)*, p. 217.

8. KTB Pz. Gr. 4 Ia, 27.11.41, NARA T313, R340, F8622809ff.

9. KTB Pz. Gr. 4 Ia, 28.11.41, NARA T313, R340, F8622811ff.

10. KTB 2. Panzerarmee Ia, 26.11.41, NARA T314, R93, F7335240ff.
11. Ibid.
12. Ibid.
13. KTB 2. Panzerarmee Ia, 27.11.41, NARA T314, R93, F7335245ff.
14. Ibid.
15. Zhukov, *Vospominaniya i Razmyshleniya (Volume II)*, p. 223.
16. KTB 2. Panzerarmee Ia, 28.11.41, NARA T314, R93, F7335252ff.
17. Ibid.
18. Von Bock, *The War Diary 1939–1945*, p. 373
19. Gefechtsbericht über den Verlauf der Operationen und Einsatz des VIII. Fliegerkorps, 1. Teil (15.11–29.11.1941), and 2. Teil (30.11.41–5.1.42), BA-MA RL 8/280.
20. Braithwaite, *Moscow 1941—A city and its people at War*, pp. 203–205; Olaf Groehler, *Geschichte des Luftkriegs 1910 bis 1980* (Berlin: Militärverlag der DDR, 1981) pp. 322–325; M. N. Kozhevnikov, *The Command and Staff of the Soviet Army Air Force in the Great Patriotic War 1941–1945* (Moscow 1977 [translated Washinton D. C.]) p. 60.
21. Von Bock, *The War Diary 1939–1945*, p. 374f.
22. Ibid.
23. On the strength of the First Shock, Tenth, and Twentieth armies, see Shaposhnikov, *Bitva za Moskvu, Moskvovskaya operatsiya zapadnogo fronta, 16noyabrya 1941 g–31 janvarya 1942 g.*, pp 40–44. For more information on armies, for example the Sixty-First, see *Rysskii Arkhiv: Velikaya Otechestvennaya T. 16 (5-1), Stavka VGK Dokumenty i Materialy* (Moscow: Terra, 1996), pp. 270–272.
24. Zhukov, *Vospominaniya i Razmyshleniya (Volume II)*, pp. 226–227.
25. Strength in early December from Vasilevsky, *Delo Vsei Zhizni*, p. 160. See V. Golubovich, "Sozdanie strategicheskikh rezervov," *Voenno-Istoricheskii Zhurnal* (1977, No.4), pp. 16–17 for information on reserves.
26. See Appendix 4 for more on German strength on the Eastern Front.
27. On force rations June 22, 1941, see A. Frankson, "Summer 1941," *Journal of Slavic Military Studies* (vol 13, No. 3, September 2000, London: Frank Cass). German losses up to November 30, 1941 amounted to 753,000 men (see BA-MA RW6/v. 552). Soviet losses for this period are harder to establish, but Krivosheev (*Grif Sekretnosti Sniat*, p. 146), gives almost 4. 5 million men during 1941. However, there are resons to suspect that this figure is too low (see Niklas Zetterling and Anders Frankson, "Analyzing World War II East Front Battles," *Journal of Slavic Military Studies* (vol 11, No.1, March 1998).
28. Von Bock, *The War Diary 1939–1945*, p. 375f.
29. Ibid.
30. Ibid.
31. Ibid.
32. Ibid; Halder's diary.
33. BA-MA MSg 2/3149, Bl. 36.
34. Ibid.
35. Ibid.

36. Gefechtsbericht vom 1–4. Dezember 41 (Vorstoss auf Akulowo), BA-MA RH 39/588, Bl. 185ff.

37. Ibid.

38. Ibid.

39. Ibid.

40. Ibid.

41. Ibid.

42. Ibid.

43. Ibid.

44. Ibid.

45. Ibid.

46. Ibid.

47. Ibid.

48. Ibid.

49. Ernst-Martin Rhein, *Das Rheinisch-Westfälische Infanterie-/Grenadier-Regiment 18 1921– 1945* (Bergisch-Gladbach: Eigenverlag, 1993), pp. 111–112.

50. Johannes Hürter, *Ein deutscher General an der Ostfront. Die Briefe und Tagebücher des Gotthard Heinrici 1941/42* (Erfurt: Alan Sutton, 2001), p. 113.

CHAPTER 17: CAUSES AND CONSEQUENCES

1. For more on the battle at Kursk, see Zetterling and Frankson, *Kursk 1943—A Statistical Analysis*, and A. Frankson and N. Zetterling, *Slaget om Kursk* (Stockholm: Norstedts, 2002).

2. Force ratios on the Eastern Front have been discussed frequently and many incorrect figures are in circulation. See N. Zetterling, "Loss Rates on the Eastern Front," *Journal of Slavic Military Studies* (Vol.9, No.4, Dec 1996).

3. Karl-Heinz Frieser, *Blitzkreig-Legende* (München: Oldenbourg Verlag, 1996), pp. 395– 400.

4. See Thies, and KTB, Pz. Gruppe 4 Ia, NARA T313, R340.

5. Von Bock, *The War Diary 1939–1945*, p. 329ff.

6. The poor English translation of Guderian's memoirs is the culprit. See also the 4th Pz. Div. reports in BA-MA RH 39/373. Another example can be found in Adam Tooze's otherwise excellent book *The Wages of Destruction*, p. 492. Tooze claims that the 10th Panzer Division lost 140 of its 200 tanks during the first two weeks of Operation *Taifun*. Both figures are wrong, as the division did not possess 200 tanks at the begining of *Taifun*. Losses are listed in an annex to the war diary of the panzer regiment, see KTB und Anlagen Pz. Rgt. 7, BA-MA RH 39/99. On October 1, the division had 36 Panzer IIs, 81 Panzer IIIs, and 19 Panzer IVs operational. Twenty days later, 22 Panzer IIs, 35 Panzer IIIs, and 12 Panzer IVs were operational. During all of October, thus not only the first two weeks, tank losses (complete write-offs), amounted to eight Panzer IIs, 15 Panzer IIIs, and two Panzer IVs, little more than one sixth of the number given by Tooze.

7. For more on this, see Tooze, *The Wages of Destruction*, and Leach, *German Strategy against Russia 1939–1941*, pp. 77–86.
8. The Germans had underestimated the Soviet reserves before Operation *Barbarossa* was launched and they would continute to do so even after the battle at Moscow. See Earl F. Ziemke and Magna E. Bauer, *Moscow to Stalingrad* (New York: Military Heritage Press, 1985), pp. 296ff.
9. Leach, *German Strategy against Russia 1939–1941*, p. 91.
10. Tooze, *The Wages of Destruction*, pp. 560f.

So much has been written about the German armored troops that it has almost been forgotten how many horses the German Army fielded during World War II. The horses were straining to pull field kitchens, carts, ambulances, howitzers and other heavy equipment forward. Supply problems afflicted the regular German infantry divisions just as much as the panzer divisions, as they needed ammunition, food, and also large quantities of fodder.

BIBLIOGRAPHY

ARCHIVAL RECORDS

We have used several archival documents which are mentioned in the endnotes for each chapter. These archival records are mainly from Bundesarchiv-Militärarchiv, Freiburg im Breisgau Tyskland (BA-MA), and National Archives, Washington DC, USA (NARA) We have also used archival records from The Central Archive of the Russian Ministry of Defense (Tsamo) in Podolsk. We would like to thank Kamen Nevenkin, who arranged the Russian archival records for us. Finally some documents from National Archives, Kew Gardens, London.

RUSSIAN ARCHIVAL DOCUMENT COLLECTIONS

Bitva pod Moskvoi, Khronika, Fakti, Lyudi. Kniga Pervaya (Moscow: Olma-Press, 2002)

Boevoi Sostav Sovetskoi Armii, Chast I(East View Publications)

G. K. Zhukov *v bitve pod Moskvoi, Sbornik Dokumentov* (Moscow: Mosgorarkhiv, 1994)

Pegova, A. M. (ed.), *Opolchenie na zashchite Moskvy* (Moscow: Moskovskii Rabochii, 1978)

Rossiya XX VEK, *1941 god, kniga Pervaja, Dokumenty* (Moscow: Mezhdunarodnii Fond Demokratiya, 1998)

Rossiya XX VEK, *1941 god, kniga Vtoraja, Dokumenty* (Moscow: Mezhdunarodnii Fond Demokratiya, 1998)

Rysskii Arkhiv, *Velikaya Otechestvennaya T.15 (4-1): Bitva pod Moskoi, Sbornik dokumentov* (Moscow: Terra, 1997)

Rysskii Arkhiv, *Velikaya Otechestvennaya T.16 (5-1): Stavka VGK Dokumenty i Materialy* (Moscow: Terra, 1996)

Rysskii Arkhiv, *Velikaya Otechestvennaya T.20 (9): Partizanskoe Dvizhenie c gody Ote-*

chestvennoy Voiny 1941–1945 gg. (Moscow: Terra, 1999)

Sbornik Voenno-Istoricheskikh Materialov Velikoy Otechestvennoy Voiny, Vypusk 7 (Moscow: Voenizdat, 1952)

Sbornik Voevych Dokumentov Velikoy Otechestvennoy Voiny, Vypusk 43 (Moscow: Voennoe Izdatelstvo Ministerstva Oborony Soyuza SSR, 1960)

Skrytaja pravda Voiny: 1941 god, Hezvestnye Dokumenty (Moscow: Rysskaja Kniga, 1992)

Soviet Documents on the Use of War Experience Volume 1 (London: Frank Cass, 1991)

Soviet Documents on the Use of War Experience Volume 2 (London: Frank Cass, 1991)

Zherebilov, A (ed.), *N. I. Biryukov, Tanki—Fronty! Zapiski Sovetskogo generala* (Smolensk: Rusich., 2005)

GERMAN ARCHIVAL AND DOCUMENT COLLECTIONS

Hamburger Institut für Sozialforshung (Hg.), *Verbrechen der Wehrmacht. Dimensionen des Vernichtungskrieges 1941–1944* (Hamburg: Hamburger Edition, 2002)

Thies, Jürgen, *Der Ostfeldzug, Heeresgruppe Mitte—Ein Lageatlas der Operationsabteilung des Generalstab des Heeres* (Bissendorf: Biblio Verlag, 2001)

BOOKS

Aders, Gebhard & Held, Werner, *Jagdgeschwader 51 Mölders* (Stuttgart: Motorbuch Verlag 1993)

Alman, K., *Mit Eichenlaub und Schwertern* (Rastatt: Manfred Pawlak 1986)

Alman, K., *Panzer Vor* (Rastatt: Erich Pabel 1966)

Andersson, Lennart, *Soviet Aircraft and Aviation 1917–1941* (London: Putnam Aeronautical Books, 1994)

Andreevskii, G. V., *Povcednevnaya Zhizn Moskvy v Stalinskuyo Epokhu 1930-1940 gody* (Moscow: Molodaya Gvardiya, 2003)

Anfilov, V. A., *Krushenie Pokhoda Gitlera na Moskvu 1941* (Moscow: Nauka, 1989)

Antipenko, N. A., *In der Hauptrichtung* (Berlin: Militärverlag der DDR, 1982)

Armstrong, Richard, *Red Army Tank Commanders, the Armored Guards* (Atglen, PA: Schiffer 1994)

Babadshanjan, A., *Hauptstosskraft* (Berlin: Militärverlag der DDR 1985)

Balke, Ulf, *Der Luftkrieg in Europa 1939–1941. Die Einsätze des Kampfgeschwaders 2 gegen Polen, Frankreich, England, auf dem Balkan und in Russland* (Augsburg: Bechtrermünz Verlag, 1997)

Barjatinskij, Michail, *T-34 v Boyu* (Moscow: Yauza [Eksmo], 2008)

Barnett, Correlli (ed.), *Hitlers generaler* (Stockholm: Prisma, 2004)

Bellamy, Chris, *Absolute War, Soviet Russia in the Second World War* (London: Pan Books, 2007)

Bellamy, Chris, *Red God of War, Soviet Artillery and Rocket Forces* (London: Brassey's 1986)

Belov, P. A., *Za nami Moscow* (Moscow: Voenizdat, 1963)

von Below, Nicolaus, *Als Hitlers Adjutant 1937–45* (Mainz: v.Hase & Koehler Verlag, 1980)

Bitva za Moskvu (Moscow: Moskovskii Rabochii, 1966)

von Bock, Fedor, *The War Diary 1939–1945* (Atglen, PA: Schiffer, 1996)

Boldin, I. V., *Stranitsy Zhizni* (Moscow: Voenzidat, 1961)

Boog Horst and Förster, Jürgen; Hoffmann, Joachim; Klink, Ernst; Müller, Rolf-Dieter; Ueberschär, Gerd, *Das Deutsche Reich und der Zweite Weltkrieg, vol 4* (Stuttgart: Deutsche Verlags-Anstalt, 1983)

Bradley, Dermot: *Walther Wenck, General der Panzertruppe* (Osnabrück: Biblio Verlag, 1985)

Braithwaite, Rodric: *Moscow 1941—A city and its people at War* (London: Profile Books, 2007)

Bunke, Erich, *Der Osten blieb unser Schicksal 1939–1944* (Wietze: Selbstverlag 1991)

Buchner, Alex, *Das Handbuch der Deutschen Infanterie 1939–1945* (Friedberg/Hess: Podzun-Pallas, 1989)

Chales de Beaulieu, Walter, *General Erich Hoepner* (Neckargemünd: Kurt Vowinckel Verlag, 1969)

Chamberlain, Peter & Doyle, Hilary & Jentz, Thomas, *Encyclopedia of German Tanks of World War Two* (London: Arms and Armour Press, 1978)

Drabkin, Artem & Sheremet, Oleg, *T-34 in Action* (Barnsley: Pen & Sword Military, 2006)

Dragunskii, D. A., *Gody v brone* (Voenizdat, Moscow: 1973)

Drig, Evgenii, *Mekhanizirovannye Korpusa RKKA v Boyu* (Moscow: Tranzitkniga, 2005)

Eicholtz, Dietrich, *Geschichte der Deutschen Kriegswirschaft 1939–1945, Band II 1941–1943* (Berlin: Akademie-Verlag, 1985)

Emde, Joachim (ed.), *Die Nebelwerfer—Entwicklung und Einsatz der Werfertruppe im Zweiten Weltkrieg* (Friedberg: Podzun-Pallas Verlag, 1979)

Erickson, John, *The Road to Stalingrad* (London: Weidenfeld, 1993)

Fedorov, A. G., *Aviatsiya v bitve pod Moskvoi* (Moscow: Nauka, 1975)

Foerster, Roland G. (ed.), *Unternehmen Barbarossa, zum historischen Ort der deutsch-sowjetischen Beziehungen von 1933 bis Herbst 1941* (München: R. Oldenbourg Verlag, 1993)

Frankson, Anders & Niklas Zetterling, *Slaget om Kursk* (Stockholm: Norstedts, 2002)

Fraschka, G., *Mit Schwertern und Brillanten* (München: Universitas Verlag, 2002)

Frieser, Karl-Heinz, *Blitzkrieg-Legende* (München: Oldenbourg Verlag, 1996)

Gareev, M. M. & Simonov, V. F., *Pobediteli 1941–1945* (Moscow: Ekzamen, 2005)

Gareis, Martin, *Kampf und Ende der Fränkisch-Sudetendeutschen 98.Infanterie-Division* (Eggolsheim: Dörfler Zeitgeschichte n.d.)

Geschichte der 258. Infanterie-Division, II. Teil (Neckargemünd: Kurt Vowinckel Verlag, 1978)

Getman, A. P., *Tanki idut na Berlini* (Moscow: Nauka, 1973)

Geust Carl-Fredrik & Petrov, Gennadiy, *Red Stars Volume 4: Lend-lease aircraft in Russia* (Tampere: Apali Oy, 2002)

Geyer, Hermann, *Das IX. Armeekorps im Ostfeldzug 1941* (Neckargemünd: Kurt Vowinckel Verlag, 1969)

Glantz, David, *A History of Soviet Airborne Forces* (London: Frank Cass, 1994)

Glantz, David, *Stumbling Colossus, the Red Army on the Eve of World War* (Lawrence, KA: University Press of Kansas, 1998)

Glantz, David & House, Jonathan M., *When Titans Clashed* (Lawrence, KS: University Press of Kansas, 1995)

Griehl, Manfred, *Junkers Ju 87 Stuka* (Shrewsbury: Airlife, 2001)

Groehler, Olaf, *Geschichte des Luftkriegs 1910 bis 1980* (Berlin: Militärverlag der DDR, 1981)

Grossmann, Horst, *Die Geschichte der rheinisch-westfälischen 6.Infanterie-Division 1939–1945* (Eggolsheim: Dörfler Zeitgeschichte n.d.)

Guderian, Heinz, *Erinnerungen eines Soldaten* (Stuttgart: Motorbuch Verlag, 1998)

Guderian, Heinz, *Panzerleader* (London: Futura, 1982)

Görlitz, Walter (ed.), *Generalfeldmarschall Keitel Verbrecher oder Offizier?* (Göttingen: Musterschmidt-Verlag, 1961)

Haape, Heinrich, *Endstation Moskau 1941–1942* (Stuttgart: Motorbuch Verlag, 1998)

Hahn, Fritz, *Waffen und Geheimwaffen des deutschen Heeres 1933–45, Band 1–2* (Koblenz: Bernard & Graefe Verlag 1998)

Halder, Franz, *Kriegstagebuch, vol III* (Stuttgart: Kohlhammer, 1964)

Haupt, Werner, *Die Schlachten der Heeersgruppe Mitte 1941–1944* (Friedberg: Podzun-Pallas Verlag, 1983)

Haupt, Werner: *Sturm auf Moskau 1941* (Friedberg: Podzun-Pallas Verlag, 1990)

Heuer, G., *Die deutschen Generalfeldmarschälle und Grossadmirale 1933–1945* (VPM Verlagsunion Pabel Mowig KG, n.d)

Hinze, Rolf, *Löwendivision, 31. Infanterie-und Grenadier-Division, 31. Volks-Grenadier-Division* (Meerbusch: Verlag Rolf Hinze, 1997)

Hogg, Ian, *German Artillery of World War Two* (London: Book Club Edition 1975)

Hoth, Hermann: *Panzer-Operationen. Die Panzergruppe 3 under der operative Gedanke der deuschen Führung Sommer 1941* (Heidelberg: Scharnhorst Buchkameradschaft, 1956)

Hürter, Johannes: *Ein deutscher General an der Ostfront. Die Briefe und Tagebücher des Gotthard Heinrici 1941/42* (Erfurt: Alan Sutton, 2001)

Isaev, Aleksei, V., *Kotly 41-go* (Moscow: Eksmo, 2005)

Jodl, Luise, *Jenseits des Endes, Der Weg des Generaloberst Alfred Jodl* (München–Wien: Langen Müller, 1987)

Kaltenegger, R., *Gefangenen im russischen winter* (Rosenheim: Rosenheimer Verlaghaus, 2007)

Katukov, M. E., *Na Ostrie Glavnogo Udara* (Moscow: Voenizdat 1974)

Kesselring, Albert, *The memoirs of Field-Marshal Kesselring* (London: Greenhill Books, 1988)

Khametov, M. I. (ed.), *Bitva pod Moskvoi* (Moscow: Voenizdat, 1989)

Knopp, Guido, *Hitlers krigare* (Lund: Historiska Media, 2001)

Knopp, Guido, *Hitlers krigsmakt—Die Wehrmacht 1935–1945* (Stockholm: Fischer & Co, 2009)

Kolomiets, Maksim, *Bitva Za Moskvu, 30 sentjabrja—5 dekabrja 1941* (Moscow: Strategija KM 2002)

Kolomiets, Maksim, *Istoriya Tanka KV (Chast 2, 1941–1944)* (Moscow: Strategiya KM, 2002)

Kolomiets, Maksim & Moshchanskii, I., *Tanki Lend-Liza 1941–1945* (Moscow: Eksprint, 2000)

Kondratchew, S. I., *Straßen des Krieges* (Berlin: Militärverlag der DDR, 1981)

Kozhevnikov, M. N, *The Command and Staff of the Soviet Army Air Force in the Great Patriotic War 1941–1945* (Moscow: 1977 [translated Washington D.C])

Krivosyeev, G. F. (ed.), *Grif sekretnosti Snyat* (Moscow: Voennoe Izdatelstvo, 1993)

Krylov, N. I, Alekseev, N. I. & Dragan, I. G., *Navstrechu Pobede. Voevoi Put 5-y Armii* (Moscow: Nauka, 1970)

Kubik, Willi, *Erinnerung eines Panzerschützen 1941–1945* (Würzburg: Flechsig, 2004)

Kurowski, Franz & Tornau, Gottfried, *Sturmartillerie, Die dramatische Geschichte einer Waffengattung 1939–1945* (Stuttgart: Motorbuch Verlag, 1978)

Leach, Barry A., *German Strategy against Russia 1939–1941* (London:Oxford University Press, 1973)

Lelyushenko, D. D., *Moscow—Stalingrad—Berlin—Praga* (Moscow: Nauka, 1987)

Lopukhovskii, Lev, *Vyazemskaja Katastrofa 41-go goda* (Moscow: Eksmo, 2007)

Losik, O. A., *Stroitelstvo i boevoe prichenenie Sovetskikh tankovykh voisk v gody Velikoy Otechestvennoy Voiny* (Moscow: Voenizdat, 1979)

von Loßberg, Bernard, *Im Wehrmachtführungsstab* (Hamburg: H. H. Nölke Verlag, 1950)

Mallman, Klaus-Michael (ed.), *Deutscher Osten 1939–1945* (Darmstadt: Wissenschaftliche Buchgesellschaft, 2003)

Megargee, Geoffrey, *Barbarossa 1941, Hitler's war of annihilation* (Stroud: Tempus Publishing, 2008)

Meier-Welcker, Hans, *Aufzeichnungen eines Generalstabsoffiziers 1939–1942* (Freiburg im Breisgau: Rombach + Co Gmbh, 1982)

von Mellenthin, F. W., *German Generals of World War II* (Norman: University of Oklahoma Press 1977)

Meyer, Georg (ed.), *Generalfeldmarschall Wilhelm Ritter von Leeb, Tagebuchaufzeichnungen und Lagebeurteilungen aus zwei Weltkriegen* (Stuttgart: Deutsche Verlags-Anstalt, 1976)

Meyer-Detring, Wilhelm, *Die 137.Infanterie-Division im Mittelabschnitt der Ostfront* (Eggolsheim: Dörfler Zeitgeschichte n.d.)

Montefiore, Simon Sebag, *Stalin—The Court of the Red Tsar* (London: Weidenfeld & Nicholson, 2003)

Moskau im Krieg 1941–1945 (Berlin: Espresso Verlag, 2002)

Moskovskaya bitva v khronike faktov i sobytii (Moscow: Voenizdat, 2004)

Moschanskii, Ilya, *Tanki T-34-76, T-34-57 v boyakh za Moskvu* (Moscow: BTV-Kniga, 2008)

Müller, R. & Ueberschär G., *Hitler's Krieg im Osten 1941–45, Ein Forschungsbericht* (Darmstadt: Wissenschaftliche Buchgesellschaft, 2000)

Murray, Williamson, *The Luftwaffe 1933–45, Strategy for Defeat* (Washington/London: Brassey's 1996)

Nagorski, Andrew, *The Greatest Battle* (New York: Simon & Schuster Paperbacks, 2008)

Nehring, Walther, *Die Geschichte der deutschen Panzerwaffe 1916 bis 1945* (Augsburg: Weltbild 1995)

Neulen, Hans Werner, *An deutscher Seite* (München: Universitas 1992)

Neumann, Joachim, *Die 4. Panzer-Division 1938–1943* (Bonn: Joachim Neumann, 1985)

Niehorster, Leo, *German World War II Organizational Series, vol 3/1* (Hannover: Leo Niehorster, 1990)

Nove, Alec, *An Economic History of the USSR* (London: Penguin Books, 1989)

Overy, Richard, *Russia's War* (New York: Penguin Books, 1998)

Paul, Wolfgang, *Brennpunkte. Die Geschichte der 6.Panzerdivision (1.leichte) 1937–1945* (Osnabrück: Biblio 1993)

Paul, Wolfgang, *Geschichte der 18.Panzer-Division 1940–1943 (mit Geschichte der 18.Artillerie-Division 1943–1944)* (Freiburg: Selbstverlag 1975)

Paul, Wolfgang, *Panzer-General Walther K.Nehring* (Stuttgart: Motorbuch 1986)

Piekalkiewicz, Janusz, *Die Schlacht um Moskau* (Herrsching: Manfred Pawlak Verlagsgesellschaft mbH, 1989)

Porter, Cathy and Mark Jones, *Moscow in World War II* (London: Chatto & Windus, 1987)

Price, Alfred, *Luftwaffe Handbook 1939–1945* (London: Ian Allan, 1986)

Reese, Roger R., *Stalin's Reluctant Soldiers* (Lawrence, KA: University Press of Kansas, 1996)

Rehfeldt, Hanz Heinz, *Mit dem Eliteverband des Heeres "Großdeutschland" tief in den Weiten Russlands* (Würzburg: Flechsig Verlag, 2008)

Reinhardt, Klaus, *Die Wende vor Moskau* (Stuttgart: Deutsche Verlags-Anstalt, 1972)

Reinicke, Adolf, *Die 5.Jäger-Division* (Eggolsheim: Dörfler Zeitgeschichte n.d.)

Rendulic, Lothar, *Soldat in stürzenden Reichen* (München: Damm Verlag, 1965)

Rhein, Ernst-Martin, *Das Rheinisch-Westfälische Infanterie-/Grenadier-Regiment 18 1921–1945* (Bergisch-Gladbach: Eigenverlag, 1993)

Ring, Hans & Girbig, Werner, *Jagdgeschwader 27* (Stuttgart: Motorbuch Verlag, 1994)

Rokossovskii, K. K., *Soldatskii Dolg* (Moscow: Voenizdat, 1988)

Rotmistrov, P. A., *Stalnaya Gvardiya* (Moscow: Voenizdat, 1984)

Safronov, Aleksei & Kurnosov, Vladimir, *Srazhenie za Tulu* (Moscow: BTV-Kniga, 2008)

Samsonov, A. M., *Moscow, 1941 god: ot tragedii porazhenii k Velikoy pobede* (Moscow: Moskovskii Rabochii, 1991)

Sandalov, L. M., *Na Moskovskom Napravlenii* (Moscow: Nauka, 1970)

Schäufler, Hans, *So lebten und starben sie, Das Buch von Panzer-Regiment 35* (Bamberg: Kameradschaft ehem.Pz Reg 35 n.d.)

Seaton, Albert, *The Battle for Moscow 1941–1942* (London: Rupert Hart-Davis, 1971)

von Senger und Etterlin, Ferdinand, *Die 24.Panzer-Division vormals 1. Kavallerie-Division 1939–1945* (Neckargemünd: Vowinckel, 1962)

Shaposhnikov, B. M., *Bitva za Moskvu, Moskvovskaya operatsiya zapadnogo fronta, 16noyabrya 1941 g. – 31 Yanvarya 1942 g* (Moscow: Transitkniga, 2006)

Sharp, Charles C., *Soviet Order of Battle World War II, Volume I "The Deadly Beginning"* (West Chester: George F. Nafzinger, 1995)

Sharp, Charles C., *Soviet Order of Battle World War II, Volume IV "Red Guards"* (West Chester: George F. Nafzinger, 1995)

Sharp, Charles C., *Soviet Order of Battle World War II, Volume V "Red Sabers"* (West Chester: George F. Nafzinger, 1995)

Sharp, Charles C., *Soviet Order of Battle World War II, Volume VI "Red Thunder"*

(West Chester: George F. Nafzinger, 1995)

Sharp, Charles C., *Soviet Order of Battle World War II, Volume VII "Red Death"* (West Chester: George F. Nafzinger, 1995)

Sharp, Charles C., *Soviet Order of Battle World War II, Volume VIII "Red Legions"* (West Chester: George F. Nafzinger, 1996)

Sharp, Charles C., *Soviet Order of Battle World War II, Volume IX "Red Tide"* (West Chester: George F. Nafzinger, 1996)

Shukman, Harold (ed) *Stalin's generals* (London: Weidenfeld & Nicolson, 1993)

Shtemenko, S. M., *Generalnyi Shtab v gody Voiny* (Moscow: Voenizdat, 1968)

Smedberg, Marco & Zetterling, Niklas, *Andra Världskrigets utbrott* (Stockholm: Norstedts, 2007)

Sperker, Karl Heinrich, *Generaloberst Erhard Raus, ein Truppenführer im Ostfeldzug* (Osnabrück: Biblio 1988)

Stapfer, Hans-Heiri, *LaGG Fighters in action* (Carrollton: Squadron/Signal Publications 1996)

Stoves, Rolf, *1. Panzer-Division 1935–1945* (Nauheim: Podzun Bad 1961)

Stoves, Rolf, *Die Gepanzerten und Motorisierten Deutschen Grossverbände 1935–1945* (Friedberg: Podzun Pallas, 1986)

Strauß, Franz Josef, *Geschichte der 2.(Wiener) Panzer-Division* (Eggolsheim: Dörfler Zietgeschichte, n.d.)

Tooze, Adam, *The Wages of Destruction* (London: Penguin, 2007)

Trevor-Roper, H. R., *Hitler's War Directives 1939–1945* (London: Pan, 1983)

Turney, Alfred.W., *Disaster at Moscow: von Bock`s Campaigns 1941–1942* (Albuquerque: University of New Mexico Press, 1970)

Ueberschär, G. (ed.), *Hitlers militärische Elite, Band 1* (Darmstadt: Primus Verlag 1998)

Ueberschär, G. (ed.), *Hitlers militärische Elite, Band 2 Vom Kriegsbeginn bis zum Weltkriegsende* (Darmstadt: Primus Verlag 1988)

Vasilevskii, A. M, *Delo Vsei Zhizni* (Moscow: Politizdat, 1976)

Velikaya Otechestvennaya Voina 1941–1945, Kniga 1 Surovye Ispytaniya (Moscow: Nauka, 1998)

Wagener, Carl, *Moskau 1941 – Der Angriff auf die russische Hauptstadt* (Bad Nauheim: Podzun Verlag, 1965)

Wagner, Erwin, *Tage wie Jahre. Vom Westwall bis Moskau 1939–1949* (München: Universitas, 2002)

Warlimont, Walter, *Im Hauptquartier der Wehrmacht 1939–1945* (Frankfurt am Main: Athenäum Verlag, 1964)

Weidinger, Otto, *Division Das Reich. Band III 1941–1943* (Osnabrück: Munin Verlag, 1987)

Woche, Klaus-R., *Zwischen Pflicht und Gewissen, Generaloberst Rudolf Schmidt 1886–1957* (Berlin-Potsdam 2002)

Wood, Tony & Gunston, Bill, *Hitler's Luftwaffe* (Leisure Books 1984)

Yeremenko, A. I., *V Nachale Voiny* (Moscow: Nauka, 1964)

Zaloga, Steven J. & James, Grandsen, *Soviet Tanks and Combat Vehicles of World War Two* (London: Arms and Armour 1984)

Zaloga, S., Kinnear, J., Aksenov, A. & Koschchavtsev, A., *Stalin's Heavy Tanks 1941–1945, The KV and IS Heavy Tanks* (Hong Kong: Concord Publications 1997)

Zaloga, S. & Ness, L. S., *Red Army Handbook 1939–1945* (Stroud: Sutton Publishing, 2003)

Zetterling, Niklas, *Blixtkrig 1939–1941* (Stockholm: Prisma, 2008)

Zetterling, Niklas, *Hitler mot Stalin* (Stockholm: Prisma, 2009)

Zetterling, Niklas & Frankson, Anders, *Kursk 1943—A Statistical Analysis* (London: Frank Cass, 2000)

Zhuk, Ju. A, *Neizvestnye stranitsy Bitvy za Moskvu* (Moscow: AST, 2008)

Zhukov, G. K., *Vospominanija i Razmysjlenija* (Volume I–III) (Moscow: Novosti 1986)

Ziemke, Earl F. & Bauer, Magna E., *Moscow to Stalingrad* (New York: Military Heritage Press, 1988)

ARTICLES

Dokumenty i Materialy, "Moskovskaya bitva v tsifrakh," *Voenno-Istoricheskii Zhurnal* (1967, No.3) pp. 69–79.

Ashcheulov, O. E., "Sovetskaya artilleriya v Moskovskoy Oboronitelnoy Operatsii 1941 goda," *Voenno-Istoricheskii Zhurnal* (2006, No.9), pp. 18–22.

Bacon, Edwin, "Soviet Military Losses in World War II," *The Journal of Soviet/Slavic Military Studies* (Vol.6., No.4, December 1993), pp. 613–633.

Bagrov, V., "Morskaya nekhota i morskie strekovye soedineniya v letne-osenney kampanii 1941 goda," *Voenno-Istoricheskii Zhurnal* (1973, No.7), pp. 97–101.

Bubur, V., "Razvitie protivotankovoy artillerii v gody Velikoy Otechestvennoy Voiny," *Voenno-Istoricheskii Zhurnal* (1973, No.6), pp. 79–84.

Eliseeva, N. E., "Plans for the Development of the Workers' and Peasants' Red Army (RKKA) on the Eve of War," *The Journal of Soviet/Slavic Military Studies* (Vol.8., No.2, June 1995), pp. 356–365.

Frankson, Anders, "Summer 1941," *The Journal of Soviet/Slavic Military Studies* (Vol.13., No.3, September 2000), pp. 131–144.

Frantsev, "O.,Nekotorye itogi boevogo primeneniya Voisk PVO strany v gody Velikoy Otechestvennoy Voiny," *Voenno-Istoricheskii Zhurnal* (1981, No.4), pp. 46–47.

Glantz, David M., "Soviet Mobilization in Peace and War 1924-1942: A Survey," *The Journal of Soviet/Slavic Military Studies* (Vol 5., No.3, September 1992), pp. 323–362.

Goff, James M., "Evolving Soviet Force Structure, 1941–1945: Process and Impact," *The Journal of Soviet/Slavic Military Studies* (Vol 5., No.3, September 1992), pp. 363–404.

Golubovich, V., "Sozdanie strategicheskikh rezervov," *Voenno-Istoricheskii Zhurnal* (1977, No.4), pp. 12–19.

Gurkin, V., "Stanovlenie i razvitie reaktivnoy artillerii v pervom periode Voiny," *Voenno-Istoricheskii Zhurnal* (1976, No.12), pp. 24–34.

Gurkin, V., "Strategicheskie i frontovye operatsii Krasnoi Armii," *Voenno-Istoricheskii Zhurnal* (1998, No.2), pp. 12–26.

Gurkin, V., "Lyudskie poteri Sovetskikh Vooruzhennykh Sil v 1941–1945 gg." *Voenno-Istoricheskii Zhurnal* (1999, No.2), pp. 2–13.

Hartmann, Christian, "Massensterben oder Massenvernichtung? Sowjetische Kriegsgefangene im Unternehmen Barbarossa," *Vierteljahrhefte für Zeitgeschichte* (2001, No.49), pp. 97–158.

Isaev, S., "Vklad voisk dalnego vostoka v razgrom nemetsko-fashistskikh zachvatchikov," *Voenno-Istoricheskii Zhurnal* (1979, No.8), pp. 73–77.

Kalutskii N., "Moskovskaya Bitva," *Voenno-Istoricheskii Zhurnal* (1990, No.4), pp. 19–28.

Karpov, N. & Frantsev, O., "Sovershenstvovanie vooruzheniya istrebitelnoy aviatsii i zenitoy artillerii voisk PVO strany," *Voenno-Istoricheskii Zhurnal* (1977, No.7), pp. 92–100.

Khoroshilov, G., "Voopyzhenie Sovetskoi artillerii v gody Velikoy Otechestvennoy Voiny," *Voenno-Istoricheskii Zhurnal* (1971, No.7), pp. 81–87.

Koldunov, A., "Organizatsiya i vedenie protivovozdushnoy oborony po opytu nachalnogo perioda Velikoy Otechestvennoy Voiny," *Voenno-Istoricheskii Zhurnal* (1984, No.4), pp. 12–19.

Krivosyeev, G. F., "Na podmoskovnykh rubezhach," *Voenno-Istoricheskii Zhurnal* (2006, No.12), pp. 3–7.

Nevzorov, B., "Poslednii rubezh," *Voenno-Istoricheskii Zhurnal* (1991, No.1), pp. 3–9.

Nevzorov, B., "Pylayustchee podmoskove," *Voenno-Istoricheskii Zhurnal* (1991, No.11), pp. 18–25.

Nevzorov, B. I., "O znachenii bitvy pod Moskvoi v khode Vtoroy Mirovoy Voiny," *Voenno-Istoricheskii Zhurnal* (2007, No.2), pp. 20–23.

Prochorkov, I. & Trussov, V., "Die Raketenartillerie im Großen Vaterländischen Kriege," *Wehrwissenschaftliche Rundschau* (1968 Heft 9), pp. 519–535.

Shlomik, B., "Dvadtsat pjat morskich strelkovych," *Voenno-Istoricheskii Zhurnal* (1970, No.7), pp. 96–99.

Smirnov, J. & Usjakov, V., "Moskovskie Chekisti v oborone stolitsi 1941–1942 gg," *Voenno-Istoricheskii Zhurnal* (1991, No.1), pp. 10–13.

Sokolov, Boris V., "The Role of Lend-Lease in Soviet Military Efforts, 1941–1945," *The Journal of Soviet/Slavic Military Studies* (Vol.7., No.3, September 1994), pp. 567–586.

Svetlishin, N., "Primenenie Voisk protivovozdushnoy oborony v letne-osenney kampanii 1941 goda," *Voenno-Istoricheskii Zhurnal* (1968, No.3), pp. 26–39.

Tsykin, A., "Taktika dalney bombardirovichnoy aviatsii v letne-osenney kampanii (1941 god)" *Voenno-Istoricheskii Zhurnal* (1971, No.12), pp. 64–69.

Van Dyke, Carl, "The Timoshenko Reforms: March–July 1940," *The Journal of Soviet/Slavic Military Studies* (Vol.9., No.1, March 1996), pp. 69–96.

Vilinov, M. A., "Tyl Zapadnogo Fronta v bitve pod Moskvoi," *Voenno-Istoricheskii Zhurnal* (2007, No.4), pp. 18–21.

Yashin, C. V., "Organy voennych soobshchenii v bitve nod Moskvoi," *Voenno-Istoricheskii Zhurnal* (2008, No.12), pp. 40–42.

Yumasheva, J., "Komandovali frontami," *Voenno-Istoricheskii Zhurnal* (1993, No.5), pp. 21–26.

Zetterling, Niklas, "Loss Rates on the Eastern Front," *The Journal of Soviet/Slavic Military Studies* (Vol 9, No.4, Dec 1996), pp. 895–906.

Zetterling, Niklas and Frankson, Anders, "Analyzing World War II East Front Battles," *The Journal of Soviet/Slavic Military Studies* (Vol 11, No.1, March 1998), pp. 176–203.

Here are soldiers from Hitler's elite regiment in the army, Grossdeutschland, preparing their position during the winter. The gun is the 3.7 cm Pak 36 anti-tank gun.

INDEX

Abwehr, 241
Aitken, William Maxwell (Lord
  Beaverbrook), 46
Akimov, Lt. Gen. Stepan, 178
Albrecht, Lt. (—), 137–138
Allmendinger, Maj. Gen. Karl, 176
Anisov, A. F., 106
Antipenko, Nicolai, 22–23, 52, 117, 184,
  204–205
Arnim, Lt. Gen. Hans-Jürgen von, 88
Artemev, Lt. Gen. Pavel, 96, 107, 185–187

Bahls, Sgt. (—), 138–140
Bechtolsheim, Maj. Gen. Baron von, 92
Belov, Maj. Gen. Pavel, 188, 190–191, 209
Beria, Lavrenti, 11, 148, 188
Beutelsbacher, Lt. (—), 92
Biryukov, Nikolay, 186
Blomberg, Field Marshal Werner von, 14
Bock, Field Marshal Fedor von, 79, 81, 100,
  124, 175, 177, 201, 209, 239, 262; age of,
  30; Bryansk pocket, 103–104, 123;
  casualties, 180; Commander Army
  Group Center, 15, 37; decline of overall
  situation, 225, 229; entries in his diary,
  63, 238; Hoepner's views, 40–41;
  interference from above, 112–114; Istra,
  217; lack of reserves, 218; last bid for
  Moscow, 203–204, 207, 221; no
  knowledge of Soviet capacity, 223–224;

prudent to halt the offensive, 222; supply
  issues, 147, 194–196; tight schedule for
  planning, 38; VIII Air Corps, 43; waiting
  for the weather to improve, 182, 197,
  226
Bodnar, Lt. Aleksandr, 141
Bogdanov, Col. Semen, 145
Boldin, Lt. Gen. Ivan, 65, 77, 174, 205–206,
  209
Borbet, Walter, 243–245
Brauchitsch, Field Marshal Walther von,
  194–195, 223; appointed by Hitler, 15,
  commander in chief of the army, 15,
  making plans for the offensive, 41, 43,
  79, 114
Brüll, Maj., 62
Bryansk, Russia, 11, 19–20, 45, 70, 78, 81,
  87–89, 95, 101–102, 129, 153, 158, 176
Bryansk, Russia, battle of, 52, 88–89, 102–
  103, 121–123, 125, 128, 138, 156, 175,
  179–180, 209, 236–237, 239–241, 243
Budjonny, Marshal Semen, 28–29, 231;
  commander of the Reserve Front, 20;
  German breakthrough at Desna, 61, 65,
  71; Moscow parade, 188; replaced by
  Timoshenko, 21; veteran of the Red
  Army, 20; Vyazma disaster, 176, 234;
  Zhukov assumes command of Reserve
  Front, 106
Bulganin, Nikolai, 83

327